MEDIA BIAS

MEDIA BIAS

Finding It, Fixing It

Edited by
Wm. David Sloan *and*
Jenn Burleson Mackay

McFarland & Company, Inc., Publishers
Jefferson, North Carolina, and London

By Wm. David Sloan and
Lisa Mullikin Parcell

American Journalism:
History, Principles, Practices (McFarland, 2002)

Library of Congress Cataloguing-in-Publication Data

Media bias : finding it, fixing it /
edited by Wm. David Sloan and Jenn Burleson Mackay.
p.   cm.
Includes bibliographical references and index.

ISBN-13: 978-0-7864-3042-0
(softcover : 50# alkaline paper) ∞

1. Journalism — Objectivity — United States.
I. Sloan, W. David), 1947–   II. Mackay, Jenn Burleson, 1975–
PN4888.O25M45   2007   302.23 — dc22   2006039471

British Library cataloguing data are available

Cover image ©2007 Digital Vision

Manufactured in the United States of America

McFarland & Company, Inc., Publishers
Box 611, Jefferson, North Carolina 28640
www.mcfarlandpub.com

Contents

Preface

Few issues can spark more debate than media bias. In the last few years, the issue has been the topic of hundreds of articles and several books, and innumerable Web sites are devoted to it. Whether the subject of debate is partisan bias, religious bias, conservative vs. liberal bias, or any other variety, scores of combatants have entered the fray.

With all that material having been produced, perhaps the first question readers might ask is "Why *another* book?"

Our answer is that *Media Bias* is different. Nearly all books dealing with the issue of media bias are written from the authors' own biased perspectives. The great majority — although quite stimulating — are polemical and are themselves biased. They are a good source of ammunition and may have encouraged the combatants; but if the media are critical to the functioning of our society, we need to do something to reduce the rancor and at the same time to eliminate, where it exists, media bias.

This book is not intended simply to add more fuel to the fire. Rather than arguing that the media are biased one way or the other, it attempts to put all the arguments into perspective and to answer the questions of how much bias really exists and what kind of bias it is.

The chapters, each written by a different author, cover seventeen different topics. With each chapter, we have tried to present the arguments about media bias in a way that is straightforward and fair. Here is the structure we have used:

• Each chapter is divided into sections presenting the differing views on the issue.

• After presenting the arguments, the authors analyze the evidence. How valid is the evidence that each side provides, and what are the strengths and weaknesses of the evidence? We've emphasized evidence in an attempt to assess the credibility of each argument.

1

• The authors then conclude with brief suggestions for what journalists should be doing to eliminate bias.

• Finally, each chapter provides a list of the most pointed works on the chapter's topic. The list is intended to help readers locate works that offer more information about particular arguments.

Our goal has been to be as fair as possible in dealing with all arguments. Our hope is that this book is at least a first step toward resolving the sometimes acrimonious disputes about media bias.

INTRODUCTION

The Bias Debate

Wm. David Sloan

"With the constant drum beat of radio show hosts, TV pundits, and book sales-men insisting there is a big liberal bias, it is quite an irony the exact opposite is true. That the media exhibits and conducts itself consistent with a right wing bias is readily apparent with even a cursory analysis of the facts and behavior shown by the mainstream media."— www.rushlimbaughonline.com (a Web site for criticizing Rush Limbaugh and conservative views)[1]

"Just don't ask a liberal if there is a liberal bias in the national news media. In answer to that question you'll continue to hear what conservatives have been hearing for decades. No matter how many times the obvious is proven, and no matter how many ways that evidence is documented, the response from the liberal elites is always the same. Noise."— Brent Bozell, Media Research Center[2]

"Those of us who pay close attention to the news media have known for years that the So-Called Liberal Media was a myth perpetrated by the GOP.... [T]he GOP has complained about an alleged liberal media bias for years as a tool for brow-beating the media towards favorable and sheepish coverage, while wanting voters to ignore that it is conservative Corporate America that actually owns the large majority of that same media and dictates its content."— Steve Soto, www.theleft coaster.com[3]

"Over 40-plus years, the only thing that's changed in the media's politics is that many national journalists have now cleverly decided to call themselves moderates. But their actual views haven't changed.... Their political beliefs are close to those of self-identified liberals and nowhere near those of conservatives. And the proportion of liberals to conservatives in the press, either 3-to-1 or 4-to-1, has stayed the same. That liberals are dominant is now beyond dispute. Does this affect coverage? Is there really liberal bias? The answers are, of course, yes and yes. It couldn't be any other way."—The Weekly Standard[4]

Whether you are a liberal or a conservative, a couple of the previous statements are bound to make you mad. The liberal critics are just as certain as the conservatives that the media are biased. It's an argument that has been going on for years — and no end seems in sight. The argument began decades ago. The difference today is that the argument has intensified. Books and magazine articles have increased in number, and a newcomer — the Internet — has made it easier and easier to get one's criticism of the opposition publicized.

These statements, made by writers who are convinced of their views, also indicate that people see media bias as it relates to their own beliefs. Conservatives think the media have a liberal bias, and liberals argue that the media are conservative. Everyone seems to be mad at the media.

Oddly, journalists take comfort in the conflicting views. They reason that if both liberals and conservatives think the media are biased, then the media must not be taking sides. The only reason liberals are mad at the media, journalists reassure themselves, is because the media are not liberal. The same is true for conservative arguments: the only reason that conservatives claim the media have a liberal bias, journalists reason, is because the media are not conservative.

To some extent, journalists are probably correct. Most of us do tend to evaluate media bias from our own perspective — our own biases. If a news report or editorial agrees with us, we tend to think, not that it is biased, but that it got things right. As a recent example, think of the so-called "Memogate" controversy during the 2004 presidential election. In that episode, CBS' program *60 Minutes Wednesday* ran a story based on photocopied memos claiming that President George W. Bush had performed improperly while serving in the Air National Guard in the 1970s. Immediately after the program aired, experts questioned the authenticity of the memos. It quickly was determined that *60 Minutes Wednesday* rushed the program onto the air without adequately checking out the suspicious documents and that the "memos" were forgeries. Republicans claimed that the episode proved that CBS and program host Dan Rather favored Democratic presidential candidate John Kerry. Democrats retorted that, even if the memos were fake, the charges still were true. CBS and Dan Rather, in Democrats' view, were simply providing a fair and necessary exposé.

Such reactions are natural for us humans. We tend to see bias in media content that disagrees with our views and fairness in content that supports them. And that is one of the reasons it is so difficult to determine whether the media are biased and, if they are, exactly in what direction. Many books, articles, Internet sites, and public opinion surveys reveal that at least one-half of the American public believes that the media are biased. That raises the question: Do audience perceptions accurately reflect the existence of real bias? A defender of the press could easily argue that claims of bias reflect only the fact that we tend to judge the media based on our own biases — and that bias does not exist in reality but only in the minds of the audience.

That is a comforting thought for journalists — but also a deceptive one. Just because differing sides perceive different bias doesn't mean there is no bias. Journalists who find satisfaction in the conflicting views about bias might as well hope that everyone would claim the media are doing a bad job, which would be a sure sign that the media are actually doing a good one. Criticism from all sides is not a sure sign that the media are performing well.

Journalists' arguments, in fact, represent one of the main positions in the debate about bias. For the most part, journalists claim that the media are generally unbiased. The question is: Can you believe their claims? Some journalists are, it appears, truly unbiased. Most stories that appear in newspapers and on television don't raise an eyebrow. Audience perception of bias exists, with rare exceptions, only with "hot button" topics. Stories about routine topics approached in routine ways hardly ever raise the hackles of readers. Even on controversial topics, many journalists report with apparent balance and fairness.

But in making claims about journalistic fairness, journalists may be the least qualified to comment. Because of the journalistic tradition of objectivity, balance, and fairness, many journalists — even those whom readers and viewers might identify as the most biased — have convinced themselves that they are truly objective. Ordinary people, who have not been trained in objective reporting, are usually open to the possibility that they may, indeed, be biased. "This is just my opinion," they will say, or "I could be wrong, but...." Journalists have been trained to deal with "facts" and to be "objective." Thus, they *know* that they are not biased. When any person *knows* he is fair, he is less likely to recognize his own bias. Journalists, unlike regular people, are convinced in their own minds that they are not biased. Whereas most of us may think we are right, journalists find it more than ordinarily difficult to admit that they may be biased. To do so takes a whole different mindset.

On the other extreme, there are critics who claim that everything about the media is biased. This claim comes most commonly from people with a "critical theory" perspective. They argue that, for example, the capitalistic structure of American media imparts to them an inherent bias. The problem with the argument, though, is that it also is made from its own bias. The discussion of media bias on the "Rhetorica" Web site (http://rhetorica.net/bias.htm) illustrates the problem. It attempts to explain the variety of reasons that the media are biased and declares that, in fact, all communication is biased. The author includes a list of many types of media bias and how we can judge that bias. While some readers might accept the analysis, just as many would probably conclude that it is itself biased.

The inherent logical error of the approach is that it is self-contradictory. "Simply communicating by written or spoken words," the analysis states, "introduces bias to the message. If, as asserted earlier [on this Web site], there is no such thing as an objective point of view, then there cannot be objective or transparent language...." The problem with the analysis is that, after stating that all communication is biased, it presents the author's own analysis as being correct — that is, unbiased or objective (which he has already said is impossible). "Everyone is biased," he is implying, "except me." We may accept the writer's analysis as being correct only if we exempt him from his principle of universal bias.

Saying that all communication is biased is taking the easy way out. We recognize, obviously, that people see things from their own perspective. They are influenced by their own backgrounds, their own views on politics and religion, and myriad other factors. Thus, we know that different individuals see things differently — that they have their own biases. We know, for example, that Muslims in Iran see things differently from Christians in the United States. We know that their different cultures influence the kind and degree of bias they see in the media.

Take, as an illustration, how Arabs and Americans feel about the reports from Al Jazeera, the Arab network in the Middle East. Al Jazeera was started in 1996 to serve mainly the Arab world and today has the largest audience in the Middle East. Unlike most other television and radio services in that region, it is not a government-run operation. That independence has helped establish its credibility among its Arab audiences, who are used to government censorship and biased coverage. Its benefactor is the emir of Qatar, whom it never criticizes. Instead, it reflects his views and, as one might expect, an Arabic perspective. It is stridently anti-Israeli and pro-Palestinian. It voices a positive view of the Arab world and Islam, and it is staunchly anti-West and particularly anti–America whenever it considers them in conflict with Arab interests. The emir himself has been accused of encouraging terrorism, and Westerners continually accuse Al Jazeera of inaccurate reporting and of inciting violence against Americans in Iraq. When criticized for encouraging such problems, the emir defended himself by declaring that he did not think Al Jazeera "was any more inflammatory than any other Arab media outlet."

Just as Americans think that Al Jazeera is biased toward Islam, most Muslims think that the American media are biased toward Western culture and values. They are probably right — but that does not mean that Al Jazeera and American media are equally biased. The reasons may be found in such factors as the Western and American traditions of press freedom, independence from government and other outside influences, the concept of emphasizing news over opinion, and the professional ideal of objectivity.

Of course, comparing Al Jazeera's and American media's degrees of bias raises the sticky question of how to define "bias." Just as people cannot agree on the type of bias that exists in the media — such as, for example, whether it is liberal or conservative — they don't agree on the definition of bias. For the purposes of this book, then, we have used no one strict meaning of the term but have defined it in ways that journalists and members of the public generally understand it. To us, "bias" involves some form of the following characteristics:

> Partiality
> One-sidedness
> Unbalanced selection or presentation
> Tendency or inclination that prevents a fair or balanced approach
> Temperamental or emotional leaning to one side
> Favoritism that distorts reality
> Personalized, unreasoned judgment
> Predisposition or preference

With those definitions in mind, here are some basic principles about media bias.

First, for this book, we consider the notion of "bias" within the American cultural context. To do otherwise would provide little frame of reference. Should we take, for example, an Arabic Islamic point of view, we probably would find just about everything that the American media publish or broadcast that touches on women's roles and rights, cultural customs, religion, entertainment, government, and any other meaningful topic to be biased. An analysis of bias for purposes of the American audience would be meaningless.

A discussion of bias necessarily involves values and judgments about those values. Although the debate about bias generally assumes that the media should be neutral, the expectation is based on our cultural norms. Most Americans would not expect the media — to use two simplistic examples — to treat democracy and fascism neutrally or to consider child abuse and benevolence toward the poor as equal. We as a people do not agree on everything, but there are certain broad values (such as democracy, benevolence, freedom, the supremacy of the Constitution, private property rights, and so forth) that nearly all of us accept. They comprise the mainstream. If the media frown on child abuse but look favorably on benevolence, we don't get upset about such "bias." Indeed, if the media did treat them equally, it is certain the media would be subject to wide censure. Criticism comes most often when the media are perceived as being neutral toward values on the extreme edges or as taking sides on values within the mainstream.

Members of the media — just like real people — have their own biases. The principle of objectivity is not revered as much as it was a few decades ago, but most journalists still accept the principle that journalism, at least news reporting, should be balanced and fair. Yet, even though journalists may be trained in such practices as objectivity, they have a human tendency to favor those views and principles that they consider to be "right." Thus, bias sometimes creeps into both news and opinion without the writer recognizing it.

Not all media content is biased — and obviously some content is liberal, and some is conservative. Every story may not be biased, and the degree of bias may not be the same on every issue. But the fact that so many readers and viewers perceive bias raises a red flag — a good indication that media bias really exists.

People tend to view the nature of media from the perspective of their own bias. That is, for example, conservatives think the media have a liberal bias, and liberals think they have a conservative bias. In the interest of fair disclosure, we will reveal that about two-thirds of the authors of the chapters in this book describe themselves as liberal, ranging from "slightly" to "very" liberal. The other third describe themselves as "slightly" to "moderately" conservative. All of the authors, furthermore, have backgrounds in journalism, and they tend to see issues from that perspective. It probably varies from the outlook of the general public. We hope, though, that each chapter is written in a balanced way so that you, the reader, cannot determine what the author's own bias is. Most of the authors researched their topic as part of the Graduate Project in Media Bias at the University of Alabama, with an emphasis on examining arguments fairly.

Even though our perception of bias is based on our own biases, the charges of media bias are more common from conservatives than from liberals. Why? Some liberal critics have claimed that conservatives simply are more predisposed to complain. Indeed, one of the arguments that liberals have developed is that conservatives complain mainly for the purpose of getting the media to give them favorable treatment. Most research indicates, however, that media content has a slightly liberal bias. Conservatives, therefore, complain more probably because they have more legitimate reasons for complaint.

Strongly ideological people tend to be the loudest in claiming media bias. People who don't feel passionately about an issue don't feel a passionate need to complain. Those who are most committed to a position predominate among critics of media bias. That is true whether the critic is a conservative or a liberal. Because such passion motivates criticism, one must take all such criticism with a grain of salt. That is not to say that all such criticism is misplaced, but neither does the mere fact of criticism make it true. Whenever we read criticism of media bias, we need to know something about the source of the criticism — for example: Is she liberal or conservative? Does he have a beginning point of view on the subject? What is the source's motivation? and so forth. That principle is true not just of transparent ideologues but even of apparently detached "scholars." Even "empirical data" can be interpreted to suit the writer's predisposition.

That is why it sometimes is difficult to sort through the various, conflicting criticisms about bias. Individuals from opposing sides can take the same episode and come to different conclusions. The best way to evaluate a charge of media bias is to evaluate the *evidence* the critic offers and to weigh it in relation to other evidence. Of course, when considering the evidence, we need to recognize our own biases and attempt to deal fairly with the evidence and the arguments. That is the approach we've tried to use in this book. First, the author of each chapter presents the various arguments in a balanced way; then he or she attempts to assess the evidence that each side offers.

Despite all the interest of late in the issue of media bias, one still may ask, Why is it important that the news media be fair, balanced, and unbiased? If we believe that the media are important to American democracy, then the answer is obvious. For the system to work, we must have a well-informed citizenry. The credibility of the news media, though, has been steadily declining for years. For the major news media, according to some surveys, fewer than one-third of the public believes the audience can "believe all or most" of the content. Some studies suggest that about 75 percent of the public believes the news media are biased. A recent Gallup poll found that a bare 3 percent of respondents believe that journalists have "high" or "very high" ethical standards. Other findings are similar. The news media are suffering a severe credibility crisis. And if the public doesn't believe journalists, then there is a wider problem for our society.

Why the decline in public trust? The answer is that, in the last few decades, journalism has seen a decline in the concept of "objectivity" and a corresponding increase in the partisanship and ideological and cultural bias of journalists. Certainly, many journalists still try to be objective, but a large portion of the public believes journalists cannot be trusted to be fair-minded and balanced.

Once the public trust has evaporated, the damage will have been done.

So, the purpose of this book is to examine two questions: To what degree does media bias exist? If it does exist, what is the nature of that bias? To address those questions, we have stayed away from making our own argument. We have, instead, presented the arguments on the different sides of various issues and then attempted to weigh the *evidence* that each side presents. We are not so naive as to think this approach will resolve all the disputes. It will not surprise us if our conservative readers think our analysis is too liberal, or if our liberal readers believe we're too conservative. But we do hope this book will appeal to fair-minded readers who — even though they may hold to one side or the other — are interested in a thoughtful discussion and not just an argument.

That said, our conclusion is that a large portion of the public believes that the media are indeed biased on most important issues. The nature of the bias they see depends on the issue. In politics, for example, the majority thinks the media are liberal, while on such issues as gender and race, most critics believe the media are biased against women and minorities. The total number of people who believe the media are biased in some way apparently is quite large. The strong views that some critics have expressed reinforce the survey figures. They reveal widespread suspicion of the media. It is not an exaggeration to say that the media are facing a crisis of confidence.

We don't wish to end this book concluding simply that people think the media are biased and can present a lot of arguments to make their case. If the media are important to a strong democracy, it is important that balance and fairness be restored to them. That may be difficult. In recent years, journalism has been moving away from the model of objectivity that held sway for much of the twentieth century. Journalists have felt freer to let their values and views influence their reporting. For much of their history, the American media were strongly partisan. There always was, though, an undercurrent in public thinking that journalism should be open equally to all sides. Because of the tradition of objectivity that became prominent in the twentieth century, the public has come to expect that the news media will present a picture of the day's events generally unclouded by the bias of the journalist. It is a goal still desired — and obtainable. "Few people today argue that perfect objectivity is possible," Steven Knowlton observed in his book *Fair & Balanced* (2005). "But then, few ever did. However, after attacks from left, right and the ivory tower, the fundamental principles have proved remarkably resilient. Changes in technology and in the behavior of the people and the institutions that journalists cover have argued for more analysis than was done in a more straightforward (and untelevised) age, but those are differences in degree, rather than in kind."[5]

Where bias exists, each chapter in this book suggests specific means of restoring balance. Whatever the prescription, each one rests in the attitudes of journalists. That means that much of the effort must begin in education, where attitudes are first introduced to many future journalists. College journalism education has grown increasingly ideological, as has the public culture — but that does not mean that the concept of fairness and balance can't be revived. Students can be imbued with the sense of a responsibility to report and editorialize fairly — but professors must decide that their commitment to the traditional values of journalistic fairness must trump their partisan fervor and their zeal for ideological causes. Journalists need to do the same. If there is one thing that may be learned from this book, it is that public perceptions of media bias are widespread. If those perceptions do not change, journalism as we have known it for several generations is in danger. Fair, unbiased news media have been critical to our culture and our democracy. Saving that tradition should be important to everyone.

Before analyzing the arguments over specific issues, we begin with a chapter written from the experience of Dr. Bruce Evensen, a journalism professor at DePaul University who worked as a network bureau chief in the Middle East. He points out the problems of reporting about the Israeli-Palestinian conflict in a manner that seems fair to both sides. His discussion re-emphasizes the difficulties of dealing with media bias.

NOTES

1. "Media Bias? BIG TIME!" Rush Limbaugh Online, http://www.rushlimbaughonline.com/articles/mediabias.htm.

2. "Are the Media Liberal? Yes — Brent Bozell," National Review Online, http://www.nationalreview.com/debates/debates020503.asp.

3. Steve Soto, "Democrats Show Signs of Realizing Conservative Bias In Media," http://www.theleftcoaster.com/archives/000993.php.

4. Fred Barnes, "Evidence of a Liberal Media," *The Weekly Standard*, 28 May 2004, http://www.weeklystandard.com/content/public/articles/000/000/004/143lkblo.asp.

5. Steven R. Knowlton and Karen L. Freeman, eds., *Fair & Balanced: A History of Journalistic Objectivity* (Northport, Ala.: Vision Press, 2005), 223.

1

Reporting the
Israeli-Palestinian Conflict:
A Personal View

Bruce J. Evensen

"Why is it that the media speaks of 'violence' and 'terrorism' when it informs us of Palestinian action but only of 'force' when concerning Israeli's attacks?"
—World Events Discussion Forum, http://moncom.net[1]

"Journalists are supposed to be objective and independent, delivering reporting that is as close to the 'real truth' as humanly possible. Journalists insist they belong to a profession that does just that. But, sadly, there often seems to be an unwarranted bias against Israel and in favor of Israel's opponents when covering events in the Middle East, a bias that ranges from blatant unfairness to much more subtle misrepresentation of Israel's situation."—www.palestinefacts.org[2]

The Israeli-Palestinian conflict is essentially rooted in a land dispute. Competing claims that the American media tilt toward Israel or have a bias in behalf of the Palestinians are often rooted in the critic's view of who has the right to live in a land the size of Connecticut that both sides claim to be their own. This is an ancient quarrel. The region has been occupied by Semitic tribes from the Early Bronze Age 5,000 years ago. Jews arrived in the "promised land" when Joshua and his army fought the battle of Jericho in the latter half of the thirteenth century B.C. Egyptian, Greek, Roman and Persian empires came and went before the beginning of Muslim rule in the middle of the seventh century. Many Arabs living in Palestine arrived after the Ottoman occupation of the sixteenth century. Europe's Zionist movement intensified Jewish settlement in the nineteenth century.

Western reporters arriving in the region can be forgiven for not knowing this long and complex history. Sometimes, however, their lack of historical understanding borders on the monumental. Shortly after arriving in Jerusalem in the spring of 1983 to report the ongoing Israeli-Palestinian conflict, I met with a young producer from one of the American television networks, who was equally new to the region. The reporter stood gazing at a map of the Eastern Mediterranean, where Israel sat surrounded by her Arab neighbors. "Hmmm," she finally muttered in some surprise. "I always thought Israel was in Africa." The producer's uncertainty had historical precedent. Russian-born, British-educated Chaim Weizmann became Israel's first president and was a veteran observer of Western ways of seeing. He remarked that reporters routinely passed through Palestine, ignoring its complicated history, and often left more ignorant than when they arrived.

Problems in Reporting the Israeli-Palestinian Dispute

When E. Clifton Daniel, the chief *New York Times* correspondent in the Middle East, completed his tour reporting the region's Arab-Israeli conflict, he observed that the words a reporter used invariably placed the correspondent on one side of the controversy or the other. Nearly sixty years later, his successors at the *Times* and other elite media were accused by each side of unfairly favoring the other. *New York Times* editor Daniel Okrent complained that media watchdog groups claimed the newspaper was "pro-Israeli" when it referred to Arab "freedom fighters" as "terrorists." The *Times* deputy foreign editor, Ethan Bronner, was criticized for being "pro-Palestinian" when the paper used the phrase "Israeli-occupied territories" instead of "disputed territories." The paper's former Jerusalem bureau chief, James Bennet, saw no easy way out of this "linguistically volatile" thicket when reporting news from the region.[3]

Michael Getler, writing in the *Washington Post*, worries that market pressures faced by the prestige press make it increasingly less likely that front page news on the Middle East and elsewhere will be reported objectively. Decisions about what to place "above the fold" are "complicated and subjective" because of the "circulation challenges newspapers face." Getler argues that "when many readers already know at least the basics about the big stories during the course of the day from television, radio or the Internet," the tendency for newspapers is to "showcase in-depth reporting" that is often interpretative. The *Post*'s managing editor, Phil Bennett, agrees that the nature of how "A1 stories" are reported is governed by the growing recognition that "the great majority of readers do not use The *Post* as their sole source of information." This pressures the paper to be provocative in its reporting on the Middle East. "We must balance our goals of being authoritative and credible," Bennett observes, "with our recognition that there is new in news." The paper's executive editor, Len Downie, says stories that can be portrayed through the frame of "conflict" and "change" tend to be "prominently displayed" because they are "of great interest to many, many of our readers." News of the Israeli-Palestinian struggle frequently lends itself to this frame.[4]

David Nes, a veteran observer of U.S. policy-making and the press, observed that "America's strongly emotional pro-Israel bias" was the "understandable aftermath" of "public revulsion over the Holocaust" and "American admiration for the Israeli success story." Israel's victories in the 1948 and 1967 wars seemed to clarify the image of "a people who are hard-working, technologically skilled, and militarily tough," Nes argued, "a people

Americans can easily admire and identify with."[5] Others saw the partisanship less sympathetically. Edward Said, a professor of English and Comparative Literature at Columbia University, was convinced that a long standing Western antipathy toward the Muslim world dating back to the Crusades was behind the warm embrace of Zionism. "Zionism and its supporters," Said argued, "have rationalized the eradication of the present reality in Palestine" and its majority Arab population. Said and critics after him would argue that the "uncritical support of Israel and Zionism" by the press had been critical in advancing Israel's standing in the first generation after its establishment.[6]

James Reston of the *New York Times* once observed that "you can put it down as a general rule that almost any criticism of our government's policies in the Middle East will be attacked and even rebuked these days either by Israeli officials or their friends in this country or both."[7] That began to change, however, after the October 1973 War and the Arab oil embargo, which cut oil supplies to the United States and other nations friendly to Israel. Peter Jennings, an ABC correspondent stationed in the Middle East at the time, noted that until then "American reporters were generally very misinformed about the Middle East, particularly about the Arab world. Very few reporters had had the opportunity to live in the Arab world. Now, more and more are having it." As a result, Jennings now saw less "bias" in American reporting on the Arab-Israeli conflict. "I think Americans for years have been largely ignorant of the Arab world. I don't think it's a deliberate bias, but an ignorant one." Lee Eggerstrom, correspondent for Ridder newspapers, concurred. There had been a "new discovery of the Arab nations by the American news media" following the October War. He felt certain that there had been as much reporting from Arab nations in the year following the war as there had been in the twenty-five years leading up to the war.[8]

Fouad Moughrabi, editor of *Arab Studies Quarterly*, notes that increased reporting reflected an important "shift in the definition of the conflict from Arab-Israeli to one that pits Israel against the Palestinians." By 1977, a majority of Americans supported the creation of a separate Palestinian state. By 1982 Americans supported the two-state solution for Palestine by a two- to- one margin. In that year, for the first time, a majority of Americans favored direct talks with the Palestine Liberation Organization, even over Israeli objections.[9]

The Web, the Intifada and 9/11

In September 2000 an escalation in violence erupted between Israel and the Palestinians. Three months of rock throwing, Molotov cocktails, and automatic weapon fire from mostly Palestinian youth and retaliation by Israeli forces had left 300 Palestinians and thirty Israelis dead. The "Intifada" or uprising received substantial coverage in the American press, which pointed out the level of sustained violence far surpassed Israeli-Palestinian clashes of the 1990s. Palestinian supporters went on-line to complain about press coverage. Fairness and Accuracy in Reporting, a pro-Palestinian media watchdog group, argued that while nearly a third of all stories filed in the 1990s on Palestine used the phrase "occupied territories," by the beginning of the next decade fewer than 10 percent did. This not only marked "a deterioration in the quality of reporting from the Middle East," but an avoidance of "an honest accounting of each side's grievances." The result, according to Seth Ackerman, author of the study, was that "instead of a war to end a military occupation" the conflict was portrayed "as simply an outburst of hatred."[10]

Palestinian supporters claimed that post-September 11 reporting increasingly framed the United States and Israel as allies in a common struggle against "Islamic terrorism," making it increasingly difficult to communicate a Palestinian point of view to the American public. Ahmed Bouzid, founder of Palestine Media Watch, argued that "Israeli officials, Israeli army spokespersons and Israeli civilians" saw their quotes widely published in America's prestige press after 9/11, while Palestinian voices were hardly heard. "The effort to be fair and balanced," Bouzid argued, "is negligible." Israeli actions were generally seen as "self-defense."[11] Fairness and Accuracy in Reporting agreed with Bouzid's analysis. America's War on Terror, it claimed, had made the nation's news networks "megaphones for official views."[12]

"Palestine Media Watch"

Ahmed Bouzin is a Philadelphia software developer who launched the Palestine Media Watch Website (www.pmwatch.org) in October of 2000 to address what he sees as anti-Palestinian bias in broadcast and print journalism and on the Web. In five years, the site claimed forty-two local chapters, whose mission has grown to include meetings with members of mainstream media for the purpose of promoting "a pro-Palestinian point of view."[13] The organization's letter writing, phone call and networking initiatives had made it not only a critic but a player in the competition to depict Israeli-Palestinian relations. Israeli critics Noam Chomsky of the Massachusetts Institute of Technology and Princeton's Norman Finkelstein praised the initiative as "immensely significant" in having the media contribute to a "durable peace" in the Middle East.[14]

The organization's point of view has appeared in the *New York Times*, *Washington Post*, *Washington Times*, *Chicago Tribune*, on the Cable News Network, National Public Radio, Voice of America and Pacifica Radio as well as the Associated Press, *Foreign Policy*, *American Journalism Review*, and *Columbia Journalism Review*.[15] The organization sends e-mailings to foreign desk editors, op-ed editors, media writers and Middle Eastern scholars designed to bring "healthy coverage to the Palestinian-Israeli conflict" through "constructive pressure." Its "media critique quick sheet" measures how many times United Nations or human rights reports are mentioned in coverage patterns; how many times the word "occupied" is used in a story; how many times the words "terror" or "terrorist" are used to describe Israeli actions; and how many times Israeli actions are depicted as a "response" or "retaliation" to Palestinian provocation. PM Watch is also alert to "how much personal detail" is given on Palestinian and Israeli "victims" and how many times Palestinians are quoted compared to Israelis.[16]

PM Watch members are instructed on how to contact and meet with editorial boards and opinion makers. Guidance includes "suggested language" and "things to harp on," some of these points were developed by the National Council of Churches at its April 2002 meeting.[17] The aim is for all PM Watch members "to adopt one common set of expressions and words" that will give editors a new "conceptual framework for thinking and talking" about the problems of Palestinians. The language is designed "to challenge the basic premise that underlies" coverage of the Israeli-Palestinian conflict. The object is to make the word "Israelis" become synonymous with "occupier" and "Palestinians" with the "occupied." Israeli "settlements" were to be called "colonies," and Israeli "settlers" should be called "Israeli colonizers." "Israeli Defense Forces" should be referred to as "Israeli Occupation Forces." "Security measures" in this lexicon becomes "collective punishment measures." Israel's "security fence" should be called an "Apartheid Wall." Editors and opinion leaders should be told that Israeli "military operations" were really "Israeli assaults against Palestinian civilians." Israel's "crack down on militants" should be described as "political assassinations." "Physical pressure" by the "Israeli military" should be called "torture" by "the U.S.-financed Israeli military." "Palestinian violence" by "militants" should instead read "the resistance of Palestinian fighters." Israel's claim to legitimacy should be challenged linguistically. "Jerusalem," Israel's capital, should be called "occupied Arab Jerusalem."[18]

Through its affiliation with a wide number of media watch groups — Al-Awda, Arab Media Watch, Honest Reports, If Americans Knew, FAIR, Inky Watch, Inside CNN, the Institute for Public Accuracy, Norman Solomon's Media Beat, PR Watch and Reclaim the Media — and cooperating news sources — the World Press Institute, The Maynard Institute, the Poynter Institute, the Palestine Chronicle, the Electronic Intifada, the Palestine Liberation Organization's Negotiating Affairs Committee, Yale University's Avalon Project, and Antiwar.com — Palestine Media Watch hopes not only to critique but "change U.S. policies" on the Palestinian West Bank, Gaza, and East Jerusalem.[19] Bouzin is convinced that their combined efforts "to end the Israeli occupation" will eventually "make a difference."[20]

"Honest Reporting"

During June 2005 organizers of HonestReporting.com, a Website dedicated to promoting greater "objectivity" in reporting on the Middle East and less "pro-Palestinian bias," hosted a "leadership mission" to Israel. The site's chief editor, Shraga Simmons, coordinated meetings with key government leaders and journalists as well as a tour of Israel's "security fence" and a live demonstration of the Israel Defense Force's "Initial Response Team." Participants spent a day at Israel's Foreign Ministry office, had a private meeting with Diaspora Minister Natan Sharansky, a famous Russian dissident, and visited "victims of Palestinian terror." The purpose of the event was to offer "advocacy training" to a "high-level group" who would "be inspired to act as Israel's ambassadors, committed to defending Israel worldwide."[21]

Simmons argues that "since October 2000, in addition to fighting an anti-terror war, Israel has been fighting a media war." Stepped up suicide bombings by Palestinian attackers and mounting Israeli casualties induced "HonestReporting.com" to organize "120,000 activists" who "scrutinize the media for anti-Israel bias, and then mobilize subscribers to respond directly to relevant news agencies."[22] In June of 2002 the *New York Times* reported that major editorial changes were made at Cable News Network after a long campaign by the Website and its affiliates to gain what they consider "better balance" in reporting on the Intifada. CNN officials denied that they were "appeasing" pro-Israeli forces by sending their chief news executive Eason Jordan to Israel in the aftermath of founder Ted Turner's claim that both the Palestinians and the Israelis were guilty of "terrorism." Published reports indicated that for weeks HonestReporting.com readers had sent up to 6,000 e-mails a day to CNN executives "effectively paralyzing their internal e-mail system." An Israeli cable company threatened to pull the plug on CNN, replacing the cable system with competitor Fox News. Jordan made staff changes and ordered the network's news desk to "go to extremes" to avoid any impression of moral equivalency between Israel's "terror victims and their attackers." CNN's Wolf Blitzer was then dispatched to Israel to file a series of reports on Israeli victims of terror attacks.[23]

"Alerting and mobilizing members via e-mail to respond to imbalanced reporting by contacting the media directly" is Honest Reporting's major mission. In addition to its New York and Jerusalem offices, the site's affiliate network in Canada, Brazil, Australia, in the Spanish, Russian and Italian speaking worlds, and on college campuses encourages members "to partner in Israel's fight against media bias."[24] The site targets not only major media outlets, offering contact details on hundreds of American newspapers, but also focuses on contacts with Jewish newspapers and a "Campus Watch" initiative that monitors campus newspapers.[25] The site's daily Web log enables subscribers worldwide to take action when they detect "anti-Israel bias."[26]

Simmons distributes to media monitors "seven principles of media objectivity" that guide their surveillance of reporting on the Middle East. Members are urged to be alert to "misleading definitions and terminology,' "imbalanced reporting," "opinions disguised as news," "lack of context," "selective omission," "using true facts to draw false conclusions," and "distortion of facts." The tendency of mainstream media to offer links to Websites relating to the Middle East is a source of particular irritation to Simmons' group. CNN.com, she notes, offered twelve Arab-related "general information sites," and none from Israel. Equally "insidious" was the perceived tendency of reporters to offer "balance" when doing the opposite. Honest Reporting's team is also on the lookout for "leading questions," "distorted photo captions," and the determination of the media "to choose to report certain events over others" that reflect a biased point of view. Like Bouzid, Simmons is convinced that "by being astute media observers, we can make a difference."[27]

Media Bias and the Gaza Withdrawal

In August 2005, Israel closed twenty-one Jewish settlements in the Gaza Strip, an area barely twice the size of Washington, D.C., that lies along the Mediterranean coast on Israel's southern border. Some 8,500 Israeli settlers, comprising 1,700 families, were evacuated from enclaves that were surrounded by 1.4 million Palestinians. Media coverage of the widely publicized event provoked a new round of competing claims that the press wasn't playing fair in reporting the region's latest conflict. Analysis of that coverage and the criticism it provoked demonstrate the difficulty of maintaining objectivity in a land dispute in which each side is certain that history is on its side.

Each side can point to deep roots in Gaza's sands. The first Jewish sovereignty in the area dates back to the time of the Maccabees, 150 years B.C., although the Jewish presence in Gaza can be traced to the tribe of Judah in the Book of Judges 1,300 years before that. The first Arab sovereignty occurred in A.D. 634, when Arab armies drove out what was then the largest Jewish settlement in Israel. In modern time, the Gaza Strip's borders followed the armistice lines between Egypt and Israel after the 1948 Arab-Israeli

War. The territory was captured by Israel in the 1967 Six-Day War and subsequently opened to heavily protected Jewish settlements. After the Oslo Accords in 1993, the Gaza Strip came under the control of the Palestinian Authority. In February 2005, the Israeli government voted to implement Prime Minister Ariel Sharon's plan for unilateral disengagement from the Gaza Strip, beginning on August 15, 2005.

In a rare moment of near unanimity, America's mainstream media overwhelmingly endorsed the Israeli action. Roger Cohen, long a critic of the Sharon government, wrote in the *New York Times* that the Israeli evacuation of Gaza reflected an "emergent democratic current" in the region that struck a blow at terrorist groups who used the impasse over Gaza to justify Jihad.[28] The *Times* editorially praised Sharon's "political courage," which had created "a new peace dynamic between Israel and the Palestinian Authority."[29] Alan Cowell reported from Ramallah that Mahmoud Abbas, the newly elected president of the Palestinian Authority, appeared poised to rein in Palestinian "militants" in Hamas, who threatened to use Gaza as a staging ground for attacks against Israel.[30] While warning that Sharon's "undisguised aim is to freeze the status quo indefinitely," the *Washington Post* editorially acknowledged the Gaza evacuation "brightened peace prospects," helping to create "the most hopeful moment in more than four years of bloody conflict."[31] The *Post*'s foreign service correspondent, John Ward Anderson, considered the disengagement plan "a major personal and political triumph for Sharon" over "Israel's ultranationalists and settler groups."[32] The *Post*'s syndicated columnist Charles Krauthammer hoped the Palestinians would soon "be forced to the collective conclusion that they cannot drive the Jews into the sea and must therefore negotiate a compromise for a permanent peace."[33] Ken Ellingwood, reporting from Jerusalem for the *Los Angeles Times*, thought the transfer of power and direct talks between the Israelis and Palestinians might offer "the possibility of a lasting cease-fire and the chance for a long-term solution to the conflict."[34] The paper's editorial board shared this sentiment, stating "this courageous move in the face of opposition" might well create "the basic framework to settle the Israeli-Palestinian clash."[35] The *Chicago Tribune*'s Cam Simpson reported that the Israeli action might pressure Palestinian President Abbas "to restructure and reform notoriously corrupt Palestinian institutions and jumpstart a Palestinian economy devastated by years of war and Israeli-imposed isolation."[36] The *Tribune*'s Jerusalem correspondent, Joel Greenberg, called the Israeli withdrawal "a remarkable turnabout for Sharon, a hawkish former general who for years was the architect of Israel's settlement drive."[37] Sharon's face-to-face meeting with President Abbas seemed to signal to Greenberg "the prospect of long-term quiet" in the violence-torn region.[38]

"It seemed as if the whole world was watching," *NBC Nightly News* anchor Brian Williams reported from Gaza on the evening of August 19, 2005, at the height of internationally televised clashes between Israeli soldiers and settlers. That dramatic coverage would be the basis of escalating complaints from each side that bias, and not facts, guided reporting. NBC's Middle East correspondent, Martin Fletcher, came under intense criticism for characterizing settlers in Neve Dekalim as "extremist Jews" who "pelted police with oil, turpentine, paint, even acid," injuring twenty-one policemen.[39] HonestReporting.com called "Fletcher's failure" to confirm the injury report as "NBC's misrepresentation of the situation in Gaza." Fletcher's emphasis on the "violence" of the settler response, in the Website's view, was a "baseless charge" that missed the "fundamental reality" that the disengagement had "gone smoothly" with much greater calm and efficiency than had been predicted. HonestReporting argued that "at this very sensitive time, journalists have a duty to be extra-cautious in presenting the story in a fair and accurate manner." It urged readers to write NBC, protesting their reporting.[40]

HonestReporting went on to criticize what it saw as three "media distortions" in reporting on Israeli withdrawal from Gaza. The first was the "media myth" that equated the forced evacuation of Jews from Gaza with the removal of Palestinian Arabs from their homes during and after Israel's War of Independence in 1948. Steve Kelley, an editorial cartoonist with the *New Orleans Times-Picayune*, portrayed a loud-mouthed Israeli settler bitterly complaining, "How can you just throw us off land where we've lived for so long?" Nearby the father of a Palestinian family quietly says, "You tell us." Chris Britt illustrated a similar sentiment in the *Springfield* (Ill.) *Journal-Register*. A bearded Jewish settler is being dragged away from his Gaza home by two soldiers wearing the Star of David on their backs. Britt has him exclaiming, "How can you force us out?! We love this place! We stole it fair and square!" Another settler witnessing the spectacle laments, "Doesn't 38 years count for nothing!" A Palestinian father holding the hand of his small son, can be seen saying, "We know the feeling." In the view of HonestReporting the comparison is historically inaccurate. Palestinians fled to Gaza, beginning in 1948, because they supported the losing side in "Arab-initiated wars." Israelis living in Gaza, on the other hand, "were evacuated in a unilateral effort to bring peace to the region."[41]

A second fault that HonestReporting found in reporting on the Gaza withdrawal was the claim by some in the press that "Palestinians are now receiving their 'native' Gaza back." The Website countered the claim by reporter Michael Matza in the *Philadelphia Inquirer* and Jeff Stahler in the *Columbus* (Ohio) *Dispatch* that Palestinian Arabs "had ever had sovereignty in Gaza before Israel took control of Gaza in 1967." The Website reported, "Egyptians ruled Gaza, and before them, the British," and for 400 before them, "the Ottoman Empire."[42] The Website urged readers to write letters to the *International Herald-Tribune* and other news agencies, whose coverage claimed "the Gaza withdrawal was an Israeli ploy to hold onto the West Bank." What particularly rankled HonestReporting was Patrick Chapette's editorial cartoon in the *Herald-Tribune* that depicted Israeli Prime Minister Ariel Sharon standing in front of a moving van that bore his name. A house from a Gaza settlement was being loaded in the front of the van, while at the back of the van, the same house was being taken over to the West Bank. "These portrayals distort the fact that Israel remains committed to halt settlement growth in the West Bank," the Website said. Portraying Sharon as "a mean-spirited, imperialistic conqueror" missed the sacrifice that Israelis were painfully making to encourage the peace process. Readers were urged to attack such "cynicism" by writing letters to offending papers.[43]

Palestine Media Watch excoriated news organizations for being far too sympathetic to Israeli settlers in what had been "the longest running occupation in modern history."[44] The Website stated that no "rational, empirically driven Martian" would be able to make sense of press reports portraying "the passive, peace-loving, and defenseless people of Israel."[45] ABC's Charlie Gibson described the Israeli evacuation of Gaza as a "wrenching drama on the road to peace in the Middle East." John Donvan, reporting for ABC from Neve Dekalim, interviewed settlers who were "praying for a miracle." They implored Israeli soldiers to allow them to stay in their homes. "How can you do this to us?" the settlers asked the soldiers, Donvan reported. "Aren't you a Jew? How can you just uproot kids? How can you reward terrorism with our land, with our homes?"[46]

To whom the land belongs lies at the heart of the Israeli-Palestinian dispute. That point is emphasized by Palestine Media Watch, which is convinced that Israel has illegally occupied land belonging to Palestinians. Its analysis of more than 1,300 stories filed by Associated Press depicting the Israeli-Palestinian conflict since the Intifada, or Palestinian uprising, beginning in September 2000, found only twenty-nine stories, barely 2 percent of the total, reported that Gaza and the West Bank were "Israeli-occupied territories." As a result, Palestine Media Watch claimed, readers are told of "fighting" and "violence" without understanding that Israeli occupation of Palestinian lands was at the heart of the conflict.[47] Jennifer Griffin, reporting for Fox News from the Jewish settlement of Marad, referred to Gaza as "land Palestinians want for a state that was captured by Israel in the 1967 War."[48] David Hawkins, reporting on the evacuation for CBS News, ignored the historical dispute over the settlements and portrayed the pullout in political terms. He quoted an Israeli official as saying "the evacuations had gone better than expected." That would mean, in Hawkins' view, "A big political victory for Ariel Sharon," who had "put his future and the future of his country on the success of the pullout."[49]

The Sons of Israel and the Sons of Ishmael

One morning while on my way to work in West Jerusalem, I stopped my car on a long and winding road near Mevassaret Zion nine kilometers west of the city. Above me children appeared to be playing on earthworks. I asked my companion, a veteran reporter in the region, if the old walls had any significance.

"They're Roman," he said casually. "About two thousand years old." In the Middle East the walls were seen as so recent that no one thought of them as museum pieces.

At that time, in the 1980s when I was reporting on the Israeli-Palestinian conflict, it was seen as highly controversial when the government of Menachem Begin named Jerusalem as the Israeli capital. Palestinian Arabs strenuously objected, claiming parts of Jerusalem were Israeli-occupied territory that belonged to a future Palestinian state. The Carter and Reagan administrations, aware of international opposition to the Israeli decision, refused to move the American embassy from Tel Aviv to Jerusalem. I asked Teddy Kolleck, Jerusalem's long-time mayor, what he thought of the American reluctance.

"How long has Washington been your capital?" he asked me.

"About 200 years," I answered.

"Well," he observed, "then Washington has been your capital for less than one-tenth of the time that Jerusalem has been Israel's capital."

Charlie Gibson got it right when he told American viewers, "For Israelis and Palestinians there is nothing like connection to the land. For the settlers in Gaza, each day was an inherently political statement."[50] The same, of course, is true of the Palestinian Arabs who celebrated the Israeli withdrawal from Gaza as a step in the creation one day of their own sovereign state.

The Palestinian celebration had historic precedent. That precedent, however, was Israeli. "Thanks be to God!" *The New Palestine* had proclaimed on November 30, 1947, following a vote by the United Nations to create separate Jewish and Arab states in Palestine. After a wait of 1,877 years a Jewish state, which the Roman Empire had destroyed in the year 70 of the Christian era, would be reborn in the Eastern Mediterranean, where the Star of David, the press reported, would fly next to the flag of other nations. The Zionist point person with the American press at that time was triumphant but slightly more pragmatic. "Victory at last!" Harry Shapiro wired chairmen of the American Zionist Emergency Council's nationwide committees. "Now has come a time to celebrate our achievement," Shapiro told them, even though "struggles and hardships remain ahead."[51]

Shapiro's warning was prescient. "The situation in Palestine has been a headache for me for two and a half years," President Truman wrote a friend on the eve of Israeli statehood, in words that could have been easily echoed by three generations of presidents who would follow him. "The Jews are so emotional and the Arabs are so difficult to talk with that it is almost impossible to get anything done. I hope it will come out alright, but I have about come to the conclusion that the situation is not soluble as presently set up."[52] Truman was not unaware of what succeeding presidents and members of the press would come to understand. The differences between Jews and Arabs in the Middle East go back long before Israel's struggle for survival in the post–World War II period. That was why Truman quipped to an advisor that he sorely wished that "God almighty would give the children of Israel an Isaiah, the Christians a St. Paul, and the sons of Ishmael a peep at the Golden Rule" so that the future of the region could be finally and peaceably settled.[53]

Given the region's long and complex history, modern reporters who rotate into and out of covering the Israeli-Palestinian struggle, can be forgiven their difficulty in reporting the conflict. Lacking language skills and a nuanced understanding of local cultures, they are often put in the position of one network news anchor, encumbered by these same difficulties, whose plane touched down outside Tel Aviv on the eve of battle just in time for him to do an immediate live satellite feed back to the United States. "The American people want to know what it feels like," his producer demanded. "Warm and moist," the anchor answered.

William Fulbright, long-time chairman of the U.S. Senate Foreign Relations Committee, observed in 1975 that since many Americans shared a European ancestry with Israeli Jews, and knew "the unique talents and tremendous energy of the American Jewish community" that this made it "natural" for Americans to identify closely with the Jewish cause in Israel.[54] But technology and immigration patterns have changed that picture in the generation since Fulbright made that statement. There are more Muslims living in the United States in 2005 than Jews, and the rise of the Internet and the World Wide Web now makes it possible for concerned citizens and media watchdog groups to organize across international borders. The result is that critics of press coverage of the Israeli-Palestinian dispute are better organized than ever, better able to make their case for "bias," and, arguably, better positioned to bring pressure to bear on reporters and their news organizations.

Each side claims "objectivity" is what it wants — balance, fairness, and impartiality. That means each wants better communication of its point of view. That's what makes media criticism in the digital age an exercise in public relations, whose real purpose is to mobilize public opinion in behalf of historic players whose conflict reaches back to the earliest records of human history. I was reminded of this when not long ago I was being driven to the airport in a Gulf State by an Arab educator deeply angered by what he saw as the "pro-Israeli bias" of the American mass media. It was a "crime," he was certain, that America and its journalists were allowing Israel to "illegally occupy Arab lands." Israelis were "murderers," he insisted, and the American news networks were "complicit in their crimes." Weren't these lands "disputed," I asked my host, going back to the time of David 3,000 years ago? My colleague wouldn't hear of it. He acted as if he could hardly imagine the suggestion. If Palestinians were determined to create their own state, living in peace beside their Israeli neighbors I asked him, why hadn't they launched that state in 1948, when the United Nations first proposed the two-state solution. Or why, I asked him, hadn't they created that state between 1948 and 1967 when Gaza and the West Bank were in Arab hands and under Arab control? These incidents, I told my Arab host, created the impression among many Israelis that what Arab states have in mind is not only the creation of a Palestinian state but the end of a Jewish one.

My colleague had been raised in the mediated world of the modern Middle East, where meaning for so many is shaped by the nightly news, the morning paper, the hourly radiocast, and, now, Web and satellite technologies that make meaning twenty-four/seven. History for many of these watchers is becoming a casualty to news narratives that subordinate context to conflict, while depicting the modern Middle East as beginning in the aftermath of the 1967 six-day war, ignoring an Israeli presence in the Holy Land that goes back to Biblical times. The result of this lack of understanding is the growth of a generation of media users who run the risk of being prisoners of their own propaganda. If newsmen and women are to give Israelis and Palestinians a picture of the world where peace is a possibility it will likely be through the creation of a digital space where the past is allowed to speak and in which media sensitize competing communities to the fears and suspicions of the other.

• POINTS OF VIEW •

Asper, I.H. *National Post* (Canada), October 31, 2002. http://christianactionfor israel.org/isreport/oct02/bias.html. "... [B]oth Israel and the honour of the news media are under grievous assault. And ... I regret to say, they are both threatened by the same cancer and have thus become inextricably linked. This is because DISHONEST REPORTING is destroying the trust in and credibility of the media and the journalists, and the same dishonest reporting is biased against Israel, thus destroying the world's favourable disposition toward it."

HonestReporting. http://honestreporting.com. This Website describes itself as "a fast-action Website that monitors Mideast media bias and ensures that Israel receives fair worldwide press coverage."

Kanazi, Remi. "Covering Israel/Palestine: US Media Bias." www.Countercurrents. org. "Every time a suicide bombing strikes Israel, mass coverage of the tragedy begins instantly. Whether landing on the front page of *The New York Times* or taking up the headline block on CNN.com, the pain Israeli people endure is shown endlessly. Israelis *do* suffer. Suicide bombings *are* horrific. Nevertheless, Palestinian pain occurs far more frequently, and yet often overlooked by the mainstream American media." Remi ,

Palestine Facts. www.palestinefacts.org. This Website describes itself as "a review of the historical, political and military facts behind the State of Israel and the Israeli-Arab Palestinian conflict." It argues that the media are biased against Israel.

Palestine Media Watch. www.pmwatch.org. This Website represents the Palestinian viewpoint.

NOTES

1. http://moncom.net/moncomworldeventsmsgs.asp?topictoview=7

2. "Israil 1991 to Present: Media Bias," http://www.palestinefacts.org/pf_1991to_now_media_anti_israel_bias.php

3. *New York Times*, 2 March 2005, Section 4, 2.

4. *Washington Post*, 13 February 2005, B6.

5. David Nes and William Fulbright, "U.S. Policy: Views from Abroad," *Journal of Palestine Studies* 5 (1975–1976): 243–244.

6. Edward W. Said, "Zionism from the Standpoint of Its Victims," *Social Text* 1 (1979): 7–12. See also, Edward W. Said, *Orientalism* (New York: Pantheon Books, 1978), 26–27, 107–108 and 306–307. Noam Chomsky, *Human Rights and American Foreign Policy* (London: Spokesman Books, 1978), 14–25. Avner Yaniv, *Dilemmas of Security* (New York: Oxford University, 1987), 20–23 and 44–50; and Yehoshafat Harkabi, *Israel's Fateful Hour* (New York: Harper & Row, 1988), 99–102.

7. Nes and Fulbright, "U.S. Policy: Views from Abroad," 245.

8. Edmund Ghareeb, "The American Media and the Palestine Problem," *Journal of Palestine Studies* 5 (1975–1976): 128–129, 132–133, 136, 138 and 142.

9. Fouad Moughrabi, "American Public Opinion and the Palestine Question," *Journal of Palestine Studies* 15 (1986): 56–57 and 63–64.

10. Seth Ackerman, "Al-Aqsa Intifada and the U.S. Media," originally appeared in the January-February 2001 issue of FAIR's magazine *Extra!* It was expanded and published under the same title is *Journal of Palestine Studies* 30 (2001): 61–74.

11. Adeel Hassan, "The Other War: A Debate — Questions of Balance in the Middle East," *Columbia Journalism Review*, May/June 2003, 54–56.

12. See FAIR's "Action Alert" commentary at www.fair.org, dated 18 March 2003.

13. "What Is PMWatch," www.pmwatch.org/pmw/cast/aboutomwatch.asp.

14. "What Are They Saying About PMWatch," www.pmwatch.org/pmw/cast/aboutpmwatch.asp.

15. "What Does PMWatch Do," www.pmwatch.org/pmw/cast/aboutpmwatch.asp.

16. "Media Critique Quick Sheet," www.pmwatch.org/pmw/tools/T_Critique.asp.

17. "Meeting Editorial Boards," www.pmwatch.org/pmw/tools/T_MeetingEditorialBoards.asp.

18. "Suggested Language for Talking About the Struggle for Self-Determination," www.pmwatch.org/pmw/language/index.asp.

19. "Media Watchgroups on the Conflict," www.pmwatch.org/pmw/index.asp.

20. "The Other War: A Debate," www.cjr.org/issues/2003/3/bias.asp.

21. "Leadership Mission to Israel," 20 March 2005, www.HonestReporting.com/YomYerushalayim.

22. "Honest Reporting is One of the World's Largest Media Watch Groups," www.honestreporting.com/a/About_us.asp.

23. Jim Rutenberg, "CNN Navigates Raw Emotions in Its Coverage from Israel," *New York Times*, 1 July 2002, Section C, 1.

24. "Info Sheet-PDF," www.honestreporting.com/a/About_us.asp.

25. "Contact Details for Major Media Outlets," aish.com/Israel/contacts.asp. "Contact Details for Hundreds of American Newspapers," search.yahoo.com.bin/search?p=Newspapers+U.S.+list. "Contact Details for Jewish Newspapers," ajpa.org/2/direct.html. "Campus Critiques," www.israelactivism.com/hrcampus/.

26. "Backspin: Media Realignment Project," www.backspin.typepad.com/backspin/about1.html.

27. "What Is Bias," www.honestreporting.com/a/What_is_Bias.asap.

28. *New York Times*, 6 March 2005, Section 4, 1.

29. Ibid., 24 February 2005, Section A, 22, and 1 March 2005, Section A, 18.

30. Ibid., 25 February 2005, Section A, 3.

31. *Washington Post*, 9 February 2005, A22, and 23 February 2005, A18.

32. Ibid., 21 February 2005, A20.

33. Ibid., 25 February 1005, A21.

34. *Los Angeles Times*, 10 February 2005, A3.

35. Ibid., 22 February 2005, B10.

36. *Chicago Tribune*, 2 March 2005, A4.

37. Ibid., 21 February 2005, A1.

38. Ibid., 14 February 2005, A3.

39. *NBC Nightly News*, 19 August 2005.

40. HonestReporting.com, "Media Critiques: Fletcher's Failure," 23 August 2005, http://www.honestreporting.com/articles/45884734/critiques/Fletchers_Failure.asp.

41. HonestReporting.com, "Media Critiques: Stripping Gaza of Its Myths," 31 August 2005, 1, http://www.honestreporting.com/articles/45884734/critiques/Stripping_Gaza_of_Its_Myths.asp.

42. Ibid., 2–3.

43. Ibid., 4–5.

44. Palestine Media Watch, "Press Media to Mark 38th Anniversary of the Israeli Occupation," 5 June 2005. http://www.pmwatch.org/pmw/mediocrity/displayCall.asp?essayID=290

45. Palestine Media Watch, "For U.S. Media, 'Calm' Means 'Calm for Israel,'" 27 February 2005. http://www.pmwatch.org/pmw/mediocrity/displayCall.asp?essayID=276

46. *World News Tonight*, 15 August 2005. *Nightline*, 15 August 2005.

47. Palestine Media Watch, "The Associated Press: Uprising Without Explanation," 17 June 2002, http://www.pmwatch.org/pmw/reports/ap/ap061702.html; and Palestine Media Watch, "The Associated Press: Business as Usual," 28 October 2003, http://www.pmwatch.org/pmw/mediocrity/displayCall.asp?essayID=207.

48. *Special Report with Brit Hume*, 15 August 2005.

49. *CBS News*, 19 August 2005.

50. *World News Tonight*, 15 August 2005.

51. Telegram from Shapiro to local emergency committee chairmen, dated 29 November 1947. File 1-4-17. American Zionist Emergency Council Papers. The Temple. Cleveland, Ohio.

52. Letter from Harry Truman to Eddie Jacobson, dated 25 February 1948. Papers of Harry S. Truman. Official File. 204 Misc. Box 774. Folder 1. Harry S. Truman Library. Independence, Missouri.

53. See the notes of David Niles following his conversation with Truman on 13 May 1947. PSF Subject File. Folder: Foreign-Palestine. Box 184. Truman Papers. Truman Library.

54. Nes and Fulbright, "U.S. Policy: Views from Abroad," 243 and 244.

2

Ideology

Michael Ray Smith

"Given the success of Fox News, the Wall Street Journal, the Washington Times, New York Post, American Spectator, Weekly Standard, New York Sun, National Review, Commentary, and so on, no sensible person can dispute the existence of a 'conservative media.' The reader might be surprised to learn that neither do I quarrel with the notion of a 'liberal media.' [But] It is tiny and profoundly underfunded compared to its conservative counterpart...."—Eric Alterman, *"What Liberal Media?"*[1]

"The trouble with politics and political coverage today is that there's too much liberal bias.... There's too much tilt toward the left-wing agenda. Too much apology for liberal policy failures. Too much pandering to liberal candidates and causes."—Bill Kristol, editor, The Weekly Standard[2]

A casual reading of the daily press or regular viewing of network news leaves many in the audience convinced that "conservatives" are behind the scenes, or "liberals," or even the notorious "left-wingers" or "right-wingers." Most Americans can be divided into one of three groups when it comes to arguments about the news media and ideological bias. The first group is comprised of those who think the media are biased to the left and cite as examples National Public Radio, the *New York Times*, and ABC's *World News Tonight*. The next group believes that the media are biased to the right and cite Fox News, radio talk shows such as Rush Limbaugh, and the *Washington Times*. The final group believes audience members are biased and practice selective perception by seeing and hearing only those views that confirm their bias and prejudice.

So, who's right?

No easy answers are evident, and the subject is often emotionally charged. To make matters worse, the very words "liberal" and "conservative" have many, often confusing, meanings. The labels are used casually to refer to a person's faith, politics, or lifestyle. Yet few take time to define the terms when it comes to media criticism. Questions of media bias colored by ideology can easily turn into a debate with each side assuming that the American press must tilt one way or another as a byproduct of hidden or deliberate worldviews that shape messages to promote a predetermined view of reality. As early as 1922, Walter Lippmann suggested this tendency in his seminal work, *Public Opinion*: "For the most part, we do not first see, and then define; we define first and then see."[3]

Adding to the confusion are organizations that only exist to highlight, often using Websites, the hidden ideology of news. On the conservative side are, for example, National Review Online, the Media Research Center, *Opinion Journal*, and www.smartertimes.com, a critique of the *New York Times*. On the liberal side are such critics as Fairness and Accuracy in Reporting (FAIR) and moveon.org, which among other things monitors Fox News for examples of its conservative, allegedly Republican content.

The simplest way to consider the issue of ideological bias is in terms of the liberal-conservative split. The issue is a complicated one, though, with different ways to approach it. So in the following discussion, we'll not deal simply with the liberal v. conservative debate but will pay particular attention to basic outlooks underlying the issue and the counter-claims of critics.

The Problem Is with the Journalists

Scholars often agree that the media play favorites, but they disagree on whether the ideological bias is Republican or Democrat, liberal or conservative, racist or Euro-centrist, and so on. So, who are the people who write the news, and how do they get their bent to represent reality from one side or the other?

Prior to the 1970s when journalists were not paid well, the idea of the ordinary person writing for the ordinary person suggested that reporters distrusted authority as much as readers did. However, as incomes increased in the following decades, reporters tended to abandon their working-class roots and transcended the "ordinary person" myth. Typically, reporters gained more education and greater incomes than their audience to become more like the elite class that they once were thought to police.

For David Horowitz, a left-wing activist turned conservative activist, ideological leanings begin in journalism schools. He argues that the faculty members of leading law and journalism schools are overwhelmingly liberal. Horowitz and fellow researcher Joseph Light examined voter-registration information of professors at some of the nation's leading law and journalism schools and found that most were registered Democrats. They found that at Columbia's journalism school, among the most notable in the nation, Democrats outnumbered Republicans 15 to 1 and at Berkeley's journalism school, 10 to 0.[4]

Nicholas Lemann, a *Columbia Journalism Review* writer who examined the study, suggested that journalism schools practice a type of teaching spawned in the nineteenth century called the "German model" of higher education, which insists scholars conduct disinterested research to rise above their personal passions. He argues, however, that the more recent view is that "there is no such thing as transcending one's perspective." The solution: Journalism schools should consciously create a balance of perspectives by hiring professors who represent a spectrum of political ideologies, and news organizations must follow suit. Nonetheless, Lemann concluded that for journalism educators "to build in liberal-conservative balance in every hire and every class would be to take us away from our core assumption, which is that reporting can get you meaningfully closer to the truth. Not a version of the truth — [but] *the* truth."[5]

Columbia Journalism Review itself may have provided just a month earlier some evidence in support of critics who claim the media are liberal. It is among the premier voices for criticism of the press. In an editorial criticizing conservative critics of the media — but not liberal ones — *CJR* in December 2005 challenged them: "Honest conservatives ... should consider a pair of New Year's resolutions: first, recognize that challenging political power and holding it to account is the legitimate role of the press in a democracy, not some liberal plot."[6]

Such views notwithstanding, does personal ideology color the news? Academics call this area of research the "socialization of the news culture," meaning that the people who are attracted to the news business often tend to approach life with the same mindset and personality. Journalists are debunkers, people who enjoy challenging authority and like to take risks. In addition, they sometimes share a philosophy of skepticism and a healthy distrust of anyone in power. This kind of wise-cracking character is part of the Hollywood-inspired folk tradition of the determined reporter who will stop at nothing in the pursuit of a scoop. A long line of this kind of journalist caricature can be seen in the likes of Hildy Johnson from Ben Hecht and Charles MacArthur's 1931 play, *The Front Page*, to countless other reporters depicted in film and fiction. These relentless pursuers of truth worship at the throne of the scoop, worth any sacrifice needed to get the job done.

In 1990, three researchers explored the background of journalists by conducting a survey of the most elite members of the press corp. They hoped to discover a link between a reporter's personal ideology and his or her actions. *The Media Elite: America's Power-brokers* — the seminal work of Dr. Linda S. Lichter of Columbia University; S. Robert Lichter of Washington University, and Stanley Rothman of Smith College — questioned the press corps of the nation's most respected newspapers about a variety of topics, including the regularity of their worship activities. The study includes a profile of the "typical" media worker: an upper-middle class, white, male college graduate earning $30,000-$50,000 a year, whose parents are college graduates, perhaps professionals. The authors report that 68 percent of the 240 journalists interviewed come from northeastern or north-central cities and have little sympathy for small-town America. Few attend church or synagogue.

The authors argue that journalists' regional and class prejudices determine their handling of the news — urban, nonreligious, and liberal. They concluded that the creators of news at prestigious newspapers and television networks in the Northeast share similar values on social issues such as abortion, but they do not represent the majority of Americans. Their research suggested that the press corps's personal value system, which is out of step with the mainstream of the nation's 290 million citizens, colors the news. The sociology of the newsroom at American's largest and most read periodicals is responsible for news content that challenges the values of middle-America, hence the news tends to favor a liberal agenda, they said.[7]

Once the findings of Lichter, Rothman, and Lichter were made public, two researchers, known for their use of Karl Marx's criticism of free-market economies as exploitative of labor, contradicted the "press is liberal" idea. Edward Herman and Noam Chomsky argued that news organizations are just another business guided by a profit motive and a desire to support the status quo of government, education, and business.

They are not alone. As early as 1979, for his book *Deciding What's News,* sociologist Herbert Gans studied how stories became news at *Newsweek* and CBS. He concluded that almost all the news stories he studied reflected six cultural issues often linked to the American way of life. The six values were ethnocentrism, altruistic democracy, responsible capitalism, individualism, leadership, and allegiance to maintaining the social order.[8]

For Gans, the press tells stories that support rather than challenge the dominant order. So most news articles celebrate rather than criticize United States' free-market economy. Yet, Gans had his critics, too. They argued that the press should reflect the values of the audience, a convention that is considered laudable if a news organization wants to be community-minded.

Gans focused on the values, professional standards, and external pressures that shaped journalists' judgments. The selection of content that becomes news is based on framing, the idea that dominant values shape the news. This "para-ideology" of the media works so that "the news is not so much conservative or liberal as it is reformist." In this sense, Gans agreed with Lichter, Rothman, and Lichter, that people who are attracted to journalism often are reform-minded individuals. This reformist tendency is the basis of the charge that mainstream journalism is often liberal, meaning critical of prevailing political policies and supportive of dramatic changes in the status quo.

In 1993, Indiana University scholars David Weaver and G. Cleveland Wilhoit found that jobs in journalism were declining. Furthermore, in their report, "The American Journalist in the 1990s," they said reporters had grown older, with the average age being thirty-six compared to an average of thirty-two in 1982. Finally, they found that the presence of minority reporters increased by at least 8 percent.[9] Journalists described themselves as 44 percent Democrat, 16 percent Republican, and 34 percent independent. More striking is that two decades earlier, Weaver and Wilhoit said, reporters described themselves as 36 percent Democrat, 26 percent Republican and 33 percent independent.

However, some polls also describe a sizable audience who consider the people who collect and report the news to be neither liberal nor conservative, just journalists trying to be fair and impartial. For example, a Gallup poll in the spring of 1998 asked respondents to judge the bias of seven types of news organizations, ranging from network news to local newspapers, and found that 36 percent rated the media as fair and impartial, while 18 percent had no opinion on the subject. In 2000, a Pew Research Center survey of presidential election news coverage found that the majority of respondents said both Democrat and Republican campaigns were treated fairly by news organizations.

In 2004, a Pew Research Center survey found that at national news outlets, liberals outnumbered conservatives 34 percent to 7 percent and at local outlets by 23 percent to 12 percent. That research seemed to agree with Lichter, Rothman, and Lichter and settle the matter, but it didn't. The sample included 547 journalists, most of whom were associated with 100 of the nation's largest newspapers. Nearly 1,470 newspapers are published daily. So the 100-newspaper figure tends to skew the survey results. Smaller newspapers of 20,000 circulation, the size of the average daily newspaper in the United States, vastly outnumber the metro newspapers, and these community newspapers may reflect their communities.

In Dunn, N.C., for example, the *Daily Record* newspaper regularly runs a preaching column by a female pastor, commentary by supporters of the NRA, and hometown news by the newspaper's founder, Hoover Adams. In 2001, the Audit Bureau of Circulation, an independent organization that measures circulation figures, found that the *Daily Record*, with 112 percent, has the greatest circulation penetration of any daily newspaper in the nation. That means it is being read by everyone in its circulation area and some readers are picking up a second copy, presumably at lunch time when the paper is available on newspaper racks. Each year the paper continues to exceed the 100 percent penetration mark. This kind of finding supports the idea that the smaller newspapers are not only popular, but readers gravitate to content that tends to reflect the values of the community, often considered conservative by social scientists.

In 2003, Tim Groseclose of UCLA and Jeff Milyo of the University of Missouri, in their study "A Measure of Media Bias," found a liberal bias by reporters [10] They defined the measure of bias in terms of the views of members of the U.S. Congress. Then they asked, for example, "Is the average article in *The New York Times* more liberal than the average speech by Tom Daschle?" or "Is the average story on Fox News more conservative than the average speech by Bill Frist?" They concluded that the mainstream media consistently show a strong liberal bias. The majority of news outlets — except Fox News' *Special Report* and the *Washington Times*— scored liberal, with *CBS Evening News* and the *New York Times* receiving a score far left of center. Outlets such as the *Washington Post*, *USA Today*, NPR's *Morning Edition*, NBC's *Nightly News*, and ABC's *World News Tonight* were moderately left. The most centrist outlets (but still left-leaning) were the *Newshour with Jim Lehrer*, CNN's *NewsNight* with Aaron Brown, and ABC's *Good Morning America*. Fox News' *Special Report*, while right of center, was closer to the center than any of the three major networks' evening news broadcasts.

Syndicated columnist Terry Mattingly found that journalists often reflect similar values and quoted journalist Peter Brown, who linked journalists to their neighborhoods. Brown said that anyone looking for journalists' attitudes should look in the neighborhoods that marketing experts describe with labels such as "Bohemian mix" and "money and brains." Journalists are much more likely to be single than married and with children. They read *Rolling Stone* instead of *Christianity Today*. They go to the theater, instead of yard sales. They eat sushi instead of Tater Tots. Mattingly, in the book *Building a Healthy Culture*, said most journalists simply do not speak the language of people who live in suburbs, and Brown thinks that they look down their noses at the lives of ordinary Americans.[11] *U.S. News and World Report* columnist John Leo agrees with Brown and Mattingly. He is convinced that "reporters tend to be part of a broadly defined social and cultural elite, so their work tends to reflect the conventional values of this elite. The astonishing distrust of the news media isn't rooted in inaccuracy or poor reportorial skills but in the daily clash of worldviews between reporters and their readers."

Brown told Mattingly when discussing the "disconnect" between mainstream newspapers and cultural conservatives: "Any business that doesn't understand or respect the lives of somewhere between 25 and 40 percent of its potential customers isn't a business that is very serious about growing or even surviving."

The Problem Is with the Labels

Among the old jokes in newsrooms is that everyone thinks he or she can do three things better than others. They are (1) make a fire, (2) make love, and (3) edit a newspaper. Critics go nearly blind with rage when they see obvious ideology leaking into news articles. Most readers understand the idea of opinion and commentary and look for that content to be labeled as such, but they are suspicious of articles that aren't labeled as commentary but seem distorted by a biased writer.

In *Bias: A CBS Insider Exposes How the Media Distort the News*, Bernard Goldberg calls Dan Rather "the Dan" to suggest the Don of the News Mafia.[12] For many viewers of Rather's 2004 coverage of President Bush's National Guard service, the bias charge could not be denied. For them, Rather's ideology as a liberal colored his news judgment. The problem here and elsewhere is the compression of concepts such as "liberal" and "conservative" into ideas that ordinary people assume possess the same meanings for everyone. When it comes to assigning labels such as "liberal," and "conservative," and "right-wing," and "left-wing," many people draw from a personal understanding and never bother to ask what is meant by those terms.

Nowhere is labeling more divisive than with media watchdog groups who toss the terms around. For instance, consider two books from 1990. In *And That's the Way It Isn't: A Research Guide to Media Bias,* authors L. Brent Bozell III and Brent H. Baker examine a 1985 survey of 621 newspapers.[13] They insist that most reporters are liberal. Yet *Unreliable Sources: A Guide to Detecting Bias in News Media* by Martin A. Lee and Norman Solomon examines the coverage of network and cable operations and the major newspapers and reports that the media are conservative.[14] How can two sets of authors be so opposite in their findings? Part of the answer is the tendency to label first and support with evidence later.

Lee is the publisher of the Fairness & Accuracy in Reporting's journal *Extra!*, and Solomon is the Washington coordinator for FAIR and a member of its advisory board. Bozell is well-known for his Media Research Center that regularly cites examples of liberal media bias. This center, in existence since 1987, includes sixty employees and a $6 million operating budget. For Bozell, liberal means Democrat. For Lee and Solomon, conservative means Republican. When the administration is Republican and the press coverage of foreign policy is supportive, Bozell rates that periodical as fair and balanced, but when a Democrat is leading the White House, the coverage, while positive of foreign policy, is unfair and unbalanced. The same formula works for Lee and Solomon.

Ideology colors perception. That's the assertion of both books, but note the evidence each presents to prove a point. Take Lesley Stahl. She began working as the White House correspondent for CBS News in 1989. She also worked on CBS's *Face the Nation. The Way It Isn't* suggests she is a liberal because she worked for New York City Mayor John Lindsay in the 1960s before working as a national affairs correspondent for CBS from 1982 to 1986. *Unreliable Sources,* however, sees Stahl guilty by association because she once greeted Republican Party's national chairman Frank Fahrenkopf with a kiss at an awards banquet. Lee and Solomon characterize Stahl as against liberals because she called union officials "special interests" during the 1988 Democratic convention. They also found her reference to Soviet leader Mikhail Gorbachev's "charmed offensive" to be supportive of America's defense industry and the government, suggesting her conservative tendencies.

Unreliable Sources is a quasi-attack on such works as *The Way It Isn't*. Both books suggest a kind of conspiracy of values at work, with *Unreliable Sources* citing the overlapping alliances between government agencies, corporations, and wealthy businessmen as evidence of back-room deal-mongering.

In the world of Lee and Solomon, everything is for sale, even the messengers in the media. Take Linda Ellerbee of Maxwell House coffee fame. She said she made a coffee commercial "for the money." She took the money to finance her new documentary production company and to avoid commercial pressures of corporate compromise. "It is necessary to destroy integrity in order to save it," Lee and Solomon write.

Critics such as Lee and Solomon argue that the press is liberal because it favors business and the status quo. Lee and Solomon find concentrated media ownership particularly odious. They intensely dislike General Electric, which owns NBC, because of its obsession with conservatism. They note that conservative icon Ronald Reagan was once on GE's payroll as a speaker against communism, labor unions, social security, and the like. They argue that the press is biased toward its own self-interest — an industry motivated by market and financial profits. Newspapers, critics argue, want writers to keep the bottom line clearly in view. Former *Washington Post* reporter Scott Armstrong said in *Unreliable Sources*, "I was never unaware ... that my principal job was to increase the return on investment for the Graham-Meyer family." Investigative journalism was allowed if it boosted sales, "but if protecting the First Amendment became more expensive than the return on investment, the First Amendment would be the loser."[15]

To some extent, readers and viewers agree with that criticism. In 1998, the American Society of Newspaper Editors conducted the Journalism Credibility Project and found that about 70 percent of those who responded thought that the cause of bias in news was a desire for higher ratings and readership, while only 10 percent thought it was due to political bias. Another way to state these findings is to say that audiences see media bias not as political bias but bias in favor of an approach favoring profits over reporting.

Charges of Bias Disappear When the Media Agree with Readers

It is a truism that we judge media bias from our own perspectives. Audience members often think articles that agree with their opinions are bias-free. In 2005, Tien-Tsung Lee, for example, found in "The Liberal Media Myth Revisited; An Examination of Factors Influencing Perceptions of Media Bias" that a person's personal bias is related to perceptions of media bias. His work suggests that audiences' ideologies and partisanship have a strong effect on how they view the media.[16]

A case study may help illustrate the point. On April 21, 1994, ABC's *20/20* broadcast an hour-long show about environmental threats to ordinary people, a show that was panned and praised. *Extra! Update*, a publication of Fairness in Accuracy in Reporting, which favors a liberal agenda, criticized the report because it "minimized or denied environmental concerns." It also argued that corporations such as ABC are bent on protecting the status quo and the interests of powerful people who support business.[17] However, Andy Gabron, writing in *MediaNomics*, a publication of the Free Enterprise and Media Institute, which favors a conservative agenda, praised the *20/20* report, saying that reporter John Stossel "looked at the cost of exaggerated fears." Gabron said the *20/20* program didn't press for more laws but urged the audience to use perspective to avoid "huge regulatory bureaucracies that not only take our tax money, they also take a little bit of our freedom."[18] He noted that the show topped the Nielsen ratings for its time slot, suggesting that big audiences mean successful programming. If an ideology existed, so the thinking goes, it is the kind of ideology that the majority of Americans accept.

Finally, the meaning of ideological bias may change with the times. Until the 1950s, bias was a synonym for partiality and usually implied a deliberate effort to distort events. Harold Ickes, Franklin Roosevelt's interior secretary, cited this kind of an example in 1939 when the press castigated the New Deal. In 1969, Vice President Spiro Agnew accused the press of practicing a kind of unconscious but menacing ideological slant as it railed against the Nixon administration. In each of these cases, the charge of ideological bias is used when the side that an audience member favors appears to be degraded by the news coverage. By contrast, when the side that the audience member favors receives a positive report, he or she tends to see the media coverage as free of bias.

• THE EVIDENCE •

These days the idea of media bias based on deliberate or latent ideology appears to be as accepted as some unavoidable racial bias, but the evidence used to make this claim often is linked to inaccurate reporting. Nonetheless, a Gallup News Poll from 2003 found that a little more than half of Americans trust the media when it comes to reporting the news fully, accurately, and fairly (although some other polls have found the percentage to be lower). Trust in the media, according to some polls, has not changed significantly over the last sixty years.

While this news is encouraging, journalists are more often registered as Democrat than Republican, with nearly half describing themselves as Democrats. Lichter, Rothman, and Lichter examined the media elite and found that journalists are not part of the middle class and are often registered Democrats. Weaver and Wilhoit found similar evidence. Horowitz found that journalism professors most often are registered as Democrats and suggested that political ideology leaks into the curricula at the nation's prominent journalism schools.

Others such as Lee and Solomon disagree and argue that most journalists may be Democrats and reflect a liberal bias, but the real power is in the board rooms where conservatives make policy and spread the ideology of free-market capitalism. These ideologues, critics say, preach that no government oversight is good.

Overall, we know that reporters tend to be registered Democrats, tend to be college-educated, and tend to see themselves as smarter than their audience. If for no other reasons, the potential for bias should be of concern. When journalists at the largest and more powerful news organizations look and sound less and less like the people to whom they are duty-bound to provide a faithful account of the day's news, then journalistic responsibility to the society as a whole will be weakened to the point of ineffectiveness.

• RESOLUTION •

The best reporters faithfully report, but they cannot shake their training, the culture, the deadline pressure, or the financial expectations embedded in the newsroom culture. Reporters can scrutinize their own work and perspectives, and editors, generally more experienced and knowledgeable than reporters, can do a diligent job of excising bias. But for all that, the real safeguard for the reader and viewer is to be aware of the complex nature of bias — the practice of mindless labeling and the equally mindless suspicion that when your side wins, the news finally got it right.

News reports that are misunderstood, for all the reasons listed in this chapter, will only aggravate the sense that the media are be unfair. Reporters must work harder to get information released that is timely, accurate, and relevant, and audiences must be willing to grant journalists some liberty as they work on deadline and against competing journalists. The job of the audience is to be discerning, not dismissive. Some reports will agree with an audience member's personal ideology; and some won't.

Ideological media bias probably won't go away anytime soon. In the meantime, here are some suggestions for audience members that may help to reduce its damage:

• Be vigilant in their media diet and monitor the intersection of Madison Avenue, Wall Street, Pennsylvania Avenue, and Main Street — recognizing the views and practices of everyone involved in the news process, including advertisers, business, government, journalists, and the public.

• Realize that as newspaper circulation goes up, the tendency for a liberal bias is more likely. A metropolitan newspaper is more likely to be seen as liberal, just as voters in a big city are more likely to be registered Democrat.

• Realize that average-size daily newspapers far outnumber large metropolitan newspapers. Smaller communities are often cautious about sweeping changes and value tradition. Newspapers in such towns are more likely to reflect the community and have a conservative bent.

• Finally, realize that the best diet of news is to seek a variety of sources. The idea of reading widely is often quoted as the best remedy to overcome a press mired in ideological values, and this remedy may prove the most useful for readers who want to be well informed.

Short of these measures, some media critics think reform in news coverage is inevitable. Writer Peggy Noonan predicted that the introduction of Fox News and the retirement of the old guard of network news opinion leaders such as Dan Rather and the growth of 500 channels of cable will mean more voices with more variety. "With our mass media busy with reluctant reformation," she wrote, "where does that leave us?" She predicted that audiences will demand news and information that reflect a kind of ideology-free content.[19] She is in good company. "News and truth are not the same thing," journalist and media critic Walter Lippmann once said. "The function of truth is to bring to light the hidden facts, to set them into relation with each other, and make a picture of reality on which men can act." Finding truth is a partnership between you and the best journalism you can find.

• POINTS OF VIEW •

Accuracy in Media [AIM]. http://www.aim.org. Describing itself as "Non-profit, grass-roots citizens watchdog of the media promoting fairness, balance and accuracy in the news," this Website represents the conservative point of view.

Alterman, Eric III. *What Liberal Media?: The Truth About Bias and the News.* New York: Basic Books, 2003. Alterman refutes charges of left-wing media bias by examining statements made by Ann Coulter, Rush Limbaugh, Bill O'Reilly, Sean Hannity, and others.

Breed, Warren. "Social control in the news room." *Social Forces* 33 (1955): 326–335. The decision-making process in a newsroom emphasizes the impact of time deadlines, space limitations, and the reliance of editors on their sense of their community's appetite for news. While Breed's research is dated, it is important as a backdrop to the debate that ideology is solely responsible for the content of news.

Buchanan, Pat. "Is liberal media bias a myth?" *Town Hall.Org.* June 16, 2002: http://www.townhall.com/columnists/patbuchanan/pb20030616.shtml. Buchanan responds to Alterman's book, *What Liberal Media?* Buchanan claims that all major networks operate from a liberal perspective and concludes that Big Media remains a "fortress of liberalism."

Fairness and Accuracy in Reporting [FAIR]. http://www.fair.org. Describing itself as "the national media watch group, [which] has been offering well-documented criticism of media bias and censorship," this Website represents the liberal point of view.

Goldberg, Bernard. *Bias: A CBS Insider Exposes How the Media Distort the News.* Regnery Publishing: Washington, D.C., 2002. Goldberg uses his twenty-eight years of work at CBS News to argue that senior-level producers and top anchors routinely allowed their personal ideology to distort the news. The national media typically shun conservative voices on social issues such as the role of stay-at-home mothers, abortion, and other politically charged debates.

Groseclose, Tim, and Jeff Milyo. "A Measure of Media Bias." September 2003. http://mason.gmu.edu/~atabarro/MediaBias.doc. Content analysis comparing media views with politicians' views shows "a very significant liberal [media] bias. All of the news outlets except Fox News' Special Report received a score to the left of the average member of Congress."

Lichter, S. Robert, Stanley Rothman, and Linda Lichter. *The Media Elite: America's Powerbrokers.* Huntington Beach, Calif.: Adler, 1986. A survey of the best of America's journalists depicts them as out of touch with their audience. The research is considered controversial and created widespread reaction, both favorable and unfavorable, particularly because it focuses on the most elite of America's press, which doesn't take into account all the small daily and weekly newspapers that tend to hire journalists who reflect traditional views.

McGowan, William. *Coloring the News: How Crusading for Diversity Has Corrupted American Journalism.* San Francisco, Calif.: Encounter Books, 2001. The mainstream press tends to cover "diversity issues" of immigration, race, gay rights, feminism, and affirmative action from an ideological framework. A misguided approach to covering news is shaped by multicultural orthodoxy meant to restrict debate.

Media Research Center (MRC). www.mediaresearch.org. The MRC describes itself as "a conservative media watchdog group dedicated to bringing political balance to the news and entertainment media."

NOTES

1. Eric Alterman, "What Liberal Media?" *The Nation*, 24 February 2003, http://www.thenation.com/doc/20030224/alterman2.

2. Promotional flier for *The Weekly Standard*. Quoted in Eric Alterman, *What Liberal Media?: The Truth About Bias and the News*. (New York: Basic Books, 2003), 3.

3. Walter Lippmann, *Public Opinion* (New York: Free Press, 1965), 54–55.

4. Nicholas Lemann, "At the J-Schools: the Case Against Ideological Engineering," *Columbia Journalism Review*, January/February 2006, 16–17.

5. Ibid., 17.

6. Editorial, "Defining Bias Downward," *Columbia Journalism Review*, http://www.cjr.org/issues/2005/1/editorial.asp

7. S. Robert Lichter, Stanley Rothman and Linda Lichter, *The Media Elite: America's Powerbrokers* (Huntington Beach, Calif.: Adler Publishing Co., 1986).

8. Herbert J. Gans, *Deciding What's News: A Study of CBS Evening News, NBC Evening News, Newsweek, and Time* (Chicago, Ill.: Northwestern University Press, 1979).

9. David Weaver and G. Gleveland Wilhoit, "The American Journalist in the 1990s: Traits, Education, Work, and Professional Attitudes," paper presented to the Newspaper Division, Association for Education in Journalism and Mass Communication national conference, Kansas City, Kansas, August 1993.

10. http://mason.gmu.edu/~atabarro/MediaBias.doc

11. Terry Mattingly, "Reform of Professions and Elite Fields: Journalism," in Don Eberly, ed., *Building a Healthy Culture: Strategies for an American Renaissance* (Grand Rapids, Mich.: W.B. Eerdman's, 2001).

12. Bernard Goldberg, *Bias: A CBS Insider Exposes How the Media Distort the News* (Washington, D.C.: Regnery Publishing Co., 2002).

13. L. Brent Bozell III and Brent H. Baker, *And That's the Way It Isn't: A Research Guide to Media Bias* (Alexandria, VA.: Media Research Center).

14 Martin A. Lee and Norman Solomon, *Unreliable Sources, A Guide to Detecting Bias in News Media* (New York, N.Y.: Carol Publishing Group, 1990).

15. Ibid., 20.

16. Tien-Tsung Lee, "The Liberal Media Myth Revisited: An Examination of Factors Influencing Perceptions of Media Bias," *Journal of Broadcasting & Electronic Media* 49:1 (March 2005): 43–65.

17. Karl Grossman, "Victor Neufeld's Anti-Environmental Spin Continues," *Extra! Update* (1994): 1.

18. Andy Gabon, "Reporter Hype Fears, Ignores Facts," *MediaNomics* 2:6 (June 1994): 1.

19. Peggy Noonan, "Not a Bad Time to Take Stock: Thoughts on the decline of the liberal media monopoly and the future of the GOP," *WSJ.Com Opinion Journal*, January 21, 2006, http://www.opinionjournal.com/columnists/pnoonan/?id=110007835

3

Political Partisanship

Debra Reddin van Tuyll and Hubert P. van Tuyll

"Fight Pro-Republican Media Bias.... The corporate media favor Bush and the right wing, and work against liberals and Democrats. Endless unfair media attacks against the Clintons, Al Gore and now Sen. Kerry bias the political process. We don't have to take it any more, but media bias won't fix itself. We must fight back."— Democracy Means You Website[1]

"Why is the mainstream media allowed to go unchallenged attacking Republicans while simultaneously giving the Democrats a free ride?... This one-sided reporting is getting tiresome and makes one question the value of the freedom of the press. The mainstream media is controlled, the news is censored and spoon fed. They are giving solace and encouragement to our enemies and putting our troops in danger. This is not a game."— Fight the Bias Website[2]

Politicians moan about media bias on a regular basis. Pundits fret about it, and authors clamor about it for pages on end. Republicans have complained about liberal bias for at least forty years, and while Democrats only recently entered that conversation, they are convinced that liberal media bias is a myth. Democrats, however, have no difficulty believing that conservative media bias is very real and very dangerous.

Today's parties are closely identified with conservative and liberal ideologies. It is almost impossible to separate partisan and ideological biases. "Democrat" and "liberal," and "Republican" and "conservative," are routinely used as synonyms.

This chapter examines what prominent Democratic and Republican pundits have to say. We call the commentators who write about partisan bias "pundits" because few of them are scholars. Mostly, they're either media people or political operatives.

Partisan bias is one of the most controversial aspects of media bias, but it is difficult to determine exactly when it exists. Some writers, including David Niven, author of *Tilt? The Search for Media Bias* (2002), believe it is difficult, if not impossible, to determine whether coverage is biased because it is difficult to define what fair coverage would be. Is equal coverage the only fair and unbiased method of reporting? Or does equal coverage itself constitute a form of bias? Many journalists do seem to accept that partisan bias exists. So do many politically engaged citizens, and so do the pundits of both sides.

Most reporters are more liberal than most Americans. In 1992, Bill Clinton beat George H. W. Bush by 5 percent among voters but, according to a Roper poll, by 82 percent among journalists. Left-leaning reporters, however, do not automatically equate with left-leaning coverage. After all, reporters are only the starting point for stories. Most articles have to go through a progression of editors — and some, maybe even the publisher — before they get on the air or onto the printed page. Employees at powerful corporate heights skew to the right rather than the left and tend to be closer to the political leanings of the general public.

The issue of partisan bias has been around a long time, perhaps ever since the media claimed to be nonpartisan. The first systematic examination, however, was Edith Efron's *The News Twisters* (1971), alternatively seen as a piece of hack journalism that offered no proof of anything, or as a serious treatment of a serious problem plaguing American democracy. The book was essentially a response to the perceived "Eastern liberal establishment" hold on the press, a contention that liberals/Democrats dispute.

Perhaps the best definition of partisan bias is Niven's: when a member from one party is treated differently from the member of another party. This sort of bias is easily recognized by most media consumers and is not a great problem because it is easily and readily corrected. A more insidious form of bias is the one that is shaped not by the up-front treatment of a candidate, politician, or issue, but by careful word choices made intentionally to color the media consumer's interpretation of the information.

The many allegations of media bias, particularly liberal Democratic bias, made today may actually be good news for those like the proponents of the public journalism movement who are concerned about the disengagement of citizens with public life. Studies have indicated that media bias is most often alleged by those who have distinct political leanings. Their criticisms of the media are usually based on their political ideologies. If that research is correct, then the ever-increasing allegations of partisan bias could be evidence of growing partisanship (i.e., civic engagement) by Americans. If press coverage — good or bad, biased or not — of politics has contributed to a reawakening of interest in politics, then the media have indeed fulfilled their primary mission: to bring citizens together to debate and decide public issues. Of course, the study also shows that people with the most extreme views are the most sensitive to negative portrayals of their views since they feel a stronger connection to them. So perhaps the allegations of bias are only another piece of evidence of growing partisanship and intolerance for opposing perspectives. It may be, too, that simply being aware of bias is a starting point for diffusing its effect.

The Republican Assault

Republican dissatisfaction with the media goes back at least to the 1960s. The delegates who nominated Arizona Senator Barry Goldwater for president at the 1964 Republican Convention reacted with some passion when former President Dwight Eisenhower criticized the media. That they were primed to respond suggests that contemporary grass-roots attitudes about the media had earlier antecedents. Perhaps these could be traced all the way back to the New Deal of the 1930s and the emergence of the modern liberal-conservative debate. At least one medium — television — was viewed with grave suspicion before 1964. Two prominent Republicans — Joseph McCarthy and Richard Nixon — had gone down in defeat as a result of their TV performances. However, 1964 was different. Although Goldwater suffered a defeat of historic proportions, his party laid the basis for future victory. The deep South voted Republican for the first time since Reconstruction. Republicans were poised to make the transition from opposition party to majority party. With the Republicans' emergence from fringe status after 1966, charges of press bias became much more prominent. It became a target for partisan attacks by the Republicans, especially during the Nixon administration when Vice President Spiro Agnew would denounce journalists as "nattering nabobs of negativity." (This phrase was coined by Nixon speech writer William T. Safire, who later joined the nabobs as a columnist for the *New York Times.)*

The Nixon years had a lasting effect on Republican attitudes toward the media for two reasons. First, Republicans moved from vague dissatisfaction to specific and sustained criticism. For example, Edith Efron and Joseph Kelly published book-length studies alleging liberal media bias. Second, Republican criticism of the media became more organized through the establishment of special-interest groups such as Accuracy in Media (1969).

Ironically, a trend of even greater import was the media's growing mistrust of government — mirroring, incidentally, Republican mistrust of big government. Watergate left many reporters feeling that they had not adequately watched the administration. To make up for this oversight, they became much more adversarial. At the national level, this attitude initially translated into being more adversarial toward Republicans — four of the five post-Nixon administrations were Republican — thereby fueling Republican mistrust of the press as well as big government.

Most Republican commentators claim bias, but beyond that there are significant differences among them. The rise of the Republican-led conservative movement amidst alleged liberal media bias has caused a few commentators to moderate their position. Nevertheless, the existence of some liberal bias is almost taken as a given, as can be seen in an examination of sources. For this chapter, we will look only books and articles. Most TV and radio commentary consists of statements with little analysis and few facts — the result of the inherent shortcomings of electronic media.

Major sources on bias include publications from Accuracy in Media and The Media Research Center (established in 1987). They provide a constant flow of ammunition and advice for Republicans and conservatives seeking to criticize the media. High-profile commentators such as Ann Coulter, Larry Elder, and Bill O'Reilly routinely include media criticism in their comments. Occasionally an insider denounces his organization, as did CBS correspondent Bernard Goldberg in *Bias* (2002). Then there are less well known critics, such as Bob Kohn, who methodically critique media outlets or, as in Kohn's case, one outlet (the *New York Times*). Established scholars such as Thomas Sowell also join the debate.

There is, however, disagreement regarding the extent of bias. Coulter is far more virulent than O'Reilly. Commentators do not agree on the cause of the bias. Most reject the notion of a conspiracy. They are more likely to see the media as populated by people with a liberal world view. A few see something more nefarious, but most do not, because the strongest piece of evidence in Republican hands is the "innocent" explanation: most rank and file reporters are liberal. Within that generalization there are quite a few nuances. Reporters are most liberal on social issues, less so on political, and even less on economic matters. Still, no Republican president has been elected with a journalistic majority.

To correct this situation requires a national effort, according to Brent H. Baker's *How to Identify, Expose and Correct Liberal Media Bias* (1994). This book was intended as a manual for local conservatives to ferret out and respond to liberal-minded journalism. Baker and the MRC recommend a thorough approach, as exemplified by their own massive computerized database of news stories and broadcasts. Baker explicitly denies the existence of a conspiracy but argues that media decision makers have little contact with conservatives. Rather than a conspiracy, the problem is that news reaches the nation through a fairly small number of major outlets. Baker lists the *New York Times, Washington Post, Los Angeles Times, Wall Street Journal,* Associated Press, the three primary broadcast networks, and CNN. (His book preceded the Fox News Channel).

Speaking for the MRC, Baker draws three conclusions. First, he rejects the traditional journalistic view that personal perspective doesn't influence reporters' work. Second, he points out that not everything that is hostile is biased. Editorials and opinion columns don't count because they openly and properly advocate a particular perspective. A story that makes conservatives look bad but is accurate is also proper. Stories that do not involve policy matters don't require a balanced approach. Third, he notes that while there are many stories with a pro-taxation and regulation theme, there are very few that blame national problems on taxation, regulation, welfare, centralized control, a decline in moral values, and lenient judges. In other words, story selection matters. Baker also provides a practical list of types of bias: commission, omission, story selection, placement, source selection, spin, labeling, and policy reaction or condemnations within a story.

Kohn's 2003 critique of the *New York Times*—*Journalistic Fraud: How the New York Times Distorts the News and Why It Can No Longer Be Trusted*—is more focused and effective than most of his cohorts' efforts. He wrote without relying on the invective that, while popular among Republicans, certainly persuades no one else. He also made substantial use of the comments of *Times* employees disillusioned with trends at the paper as well as criticism from media observers (one of whom compared the paper to Britain's *Guardian*). He also benefited from having some college-level journalism training.[3]

So what does Kohn, a lifelong *Times* reader, find? He provides a long list of methods for slanting the news (in fact, his book is an excellent manual for propagandists). One of his most persuasive arguments is a cogent critique of the modern style of "interpretive" reporting. In the past, newspapers relied on an "inverted pyramid" approach in which the salient facts were compressed in the "lead" or opening of the story. Nowadays, news stories often begin with "interpretive" comments that, Kohn argues, can easily slant an entire story. He methodically demonstrates how each aspect of the lead—the who, why, what, where, when, and how—can be slanted to reflect a particular perspective. Headlines can also be used to hype a paper's views, as part of a crusade, to downplay a story, or, in his most interesting set of examples, to not reflect the story at all. In an age when many people only have time for the headlines, this is not a small consideration.

But what about the facts? So long as facts are reported in the article, can any real harm be done? According to Kohn, a great deal. Key facts may be omitted; they may be distorted; they may be falsified; or, cleverly, insignificant facts may be emphasized at the expense of the ones that matter. Were such events "random," a reader might conclude the cause was incompetence, not bias; but Kohn believes that misuse of facts in the *Times* always seems to benefit the liberal perspective. The same is true of the use of opinion within articles. Obviously, a writer could seek opinions that happened to bolster his/her perspective, among other methods. Kohn also devotes a great deal of space to the use of language and the practice of labeling (relying at times on Ann Coulter's examples), whether by calling one commentator "conservative" without noting another being "liberal," or using the term "extreme" more on one side of the spectrum than the other. The *Times* also uses its staff to support its crusades; and, Kohn notes, *every* article during the period he studied was against going to war in Iraq — a perspective that its readers probably applauded, but that should give one pause.

Occasionally, the ideology behind the book does emerge. For example, Kohn refers to Bob Woodward and Carl Bernstein as "two young Washington Post reporters who were out to take down President Nixon."[4] This is a remarkably revisionist piece of history. A bigger issue than ideology is evidence. Kohn's examples are solid. Do they add up to proof? Critics of his perspective point to a lack of quantification and scientific analysis in books of this type. A more telling point is that an ideologically minded researcher will almost always find what she/he is looking for. The great power of the media has given new meaning to the phrase, *quies custodies ipsos custodes,* "who guards these guardians," but that also applies to media critics.

To some Republicans, however, the liberal bias of the media is so prevalent that calls for a more "scientific" approach miss the point. Ann Coulter makes use of the fact that Democrats are the overwhelming majority of editors, national correspondents, news anchors, and reporters. Republican commentators are only "grudgingly tolerated within the liberal behemoth." To Coulter, there is no objective reporting to analyze, scientifically or otherwise. She argues in *How to Talk to a Liberal* that Democrats just cannot grasp the distinction between opinion journalism and objective news. Going further than Kohn, she claims that "journalists definitely promote the left-wing agenda." Fraudulent reporters like Jayson Blair got away with malfeasance because their writings "fit preconceived views." The *New York Times* is "a sort of bulletin board for Manhattan liberals." The lack of Republican reporters results from "media discrimination."[5]

Coulter lives on the edge and likes it there. No innocent explanations for her. Others are more restrained. Larry Elder views liberal media bias as the result of journalists' political leanings. In his book *The Ten Things You Can't Say in America*, he cites data concerning journalists' own opinions and gives numerous examples, including a period during which the *Los Angeles Times* referred seventy-one times to "hardline conservatives" but used the adjectives only twice for liberals — and one of those references was to Soviet leader Mikhail Gorbachev! He also blames ignorance, in particular journalists' lack of economic knowledge. As with Kohn, Elder's ideology sometimes has unfortunate results. He cites the work of AIM and the MRC without divulging their leanings. He also bashes Arizona Senator John McCain, a conservative who challenged the Republican party establishment — leading to reactions, including Elder's, that show that while conservatives demand that conservative views be heard, that demand does not extend to all conservative views.[6]

Fox News commentator Bill O'Reilly is more concerned about the effects of media bias and the role that media play in shaping values. Cultural corruption, he writes in *Who's Looking Out for You?*, is not dealt with by the mainstream media (echoing somewhat the views of the MRC). Newspaper editors tend to be too "politically correct" to make moral judgments on trends unless a trend runs counter to their (liberal) ideology.[7] O'Reilly, however, does not reserve his venom for liberals alone. While he lambastes Bill Moyers for pretending to be objective and derides PBS and NPR as "outright liberal house organs," he concedes that talk radio is mostly Republican and adds that "if you disagree with that you risk being labeled a 'wacko' or some such." He is also friendly toward some media icons, such as Mike Wallace and Peter Jennings. Significantly, he worries about growing corporate power in the media, which he sees as a restrictive force. Interestingly enough, he is moderate in his criticisms of CBS. Rather than seeing the network and its famous ex-anchor, Dan Rather, as biased, in his book *The No Spin Zone* he deplores their lack of investigative reporting on the "establishment" and believes that Dan is a pragmatist who understands that there is corruption built into the system and is willing to live with it.[8]

No such moderation can be found in Bernard Goldberg's insider account of life at CBS, *Bias: A CBS Insider Exposes How the Media Distort the News*.[9] His account is not totally one-sided. He concedes that bias is largely in the eye of the beholder. The major network anchors simply do not understand what "liberal bias" is. He does not ignore the existence of conservative media. However, he gives no ground on two issues; the existence of bias, and its impact. Liberal bias comes naturally to most reporters, and this is exacerbated by the isolation of many leading media figures. They talk only to people like themselves. There is also a strong tendency, he argues, to follow the lead of major organs such as the *Washington Post* and *New York Times*. Journalists are overwhelmingly liberal and Democrat; only 4 percent admit to being Republican. Polling data cited by Goldberg shows how Washington journalists' politics differs from the country as a whole. In the 1992 presidential election, for example, here is how the public and journalists voted:

Candidate	Electorate	Journalists
Clinton	43%	89%
Bush	37%	7%
Perot	19%	2%

Nor was this difference just a one-time event. Golberg's biggest criticism is not so much related to party as to cultural and social issues (mirroring O'Reilly). There "we often sound more like flacks for liberal causes than objective journalists."[10] Like Kohn, he focuses on word choice as a way to influence perception — using as an example the word "scheme" instead of "proposal" for publisher and Presidential candidate Steve Forbes' flat tax plan.

Is Goldberg merely a disgruntled employee? All insider exposés are written by disgruntled employees. Happy workers are not likely to rush into print with their complaints because, by definition, they don't have any. What about his evidence? From a pragmatic political perspective, it hardly matters. Republicans find their views reinforced — especially because the target is CBS. Accusations make news; few people delve into the details. In the wake of CBS's publicizing of fake Bush military service records, and the subsequent removal of Dan Rather as news anchor, the network has not been in a position to defend itself.

Goldberg's attack on CBS is bolstered by the frequent attacks on the network from one of the *bona fide* scholars on the right — Thomas Sowell of Stanford University. He has accused CBS of frequent and methodical bias and probably reached the height of invective when he awarded a "Joseph Goebbels Award" to Rather for the Bush military records fiasco.[11] Like Larry Elder, Sowell sees more ignorance than conspiracy, describing reporters as "usually poorly informed about science, uninformed about history and misinformed about economics."[12] Sowell is important because his credentials give him credibility. He effectively supports Republican charges of media bias on sociocultural issues.[13] He also has tackled the definition of "objectivity," ridiculing those who believe it requires "neutrality" when referring to the likes of, for example, Saddam Hussein. "Objectivity refers to an honest seeking of the truth, whatever that truth may turn out to be and regardless of what its implications might be. Neutrality refers to a preconceived balance, which subordinates the truth to this preconception."[14] It will not escape the reader that this definition contains an implicit defense of media bias along with the explicit criticism.

The Democrat Response

Democrats have begun returning fire. Republican-turned-Democrat David Brock offers the archetypal Democratic argument in his most recent book, *The Republican Noise Machine: Right Wing Media and How it Corrupts Democracy* (2004). According to Brock, the right-wing media are perverting American democracy and threaten to undermine all that is good and right about America by making it impossible to debate any political issue fairly. Those commentators who have offered the Democratic defense have also been successful, to some degree, at using media to put forth the more liberal ideologies that some within the Democratic party have adopted, but only Michael Moore's movie *Fahrenheit 911* and a handful of books have made any sort of big splash. Perhaps out of frustration with the greater success, they argue, of the Republicans in finding media support, some of the more radical Democrats and liberals have hinted that they suspect a conspiracy might be afoot — and might have been afoot for the last thirty or forty years — to accomplish a right-wing take-over of the press so as to sweep aside opposing viewpoints. Brock made this argument in his earlier book, *Blinded by the Right: The Conscience of an Ex-conservative* (2002).

Those who have taken on the job of responding to the Republican media, like Al Franken in *Lies (and the Lying Liars Who Tell Them)*,[15] argue overwhelmingly that there is no such thing as liberal bias, that such claims are, and have been from the beginning, nothing more than a smoke-screen effectively promulgated by Republicans who want to stimulate distrust of mainstream and elite media — the *New York Times*, the *Washington Post*, the three major over-the-air networks, NPR, and PBS. Democratic pundits argue that these media, as opposed to right-leaning outlets like Fox News and most talk radio, are the only ones that are fair, accurate, and objective, and that the prestige press and the three networks (the very same media that conservatives criticize for bias) aspire, as David Brock argued in his book *The Republican Noise Machine,* "to the universal standards of objective, non-partisan journalism."[16] W. Lance Bennett, for example, in his book *News:*

The Politics of Illusion, points to the "icy relations between the Clinton staff and the Washington press corps."[17] They claim that George W. Bush got better coverage than President Clinton and Vice President Gore, and they offer this as evidence of the lack of bias. Equally important to the Democratic response, though, is the issue of objectivity.

The Democratic cadre of spokesmen hold up the ideal of objectivity as the hallmark of journalism. They seek fairness, accuracy, and balance in reporting, they say, and consider any other kind of reporting to be inferior. This ideal of objectivity was a mainstay of twentieth century journalism. Contrary to what these writers would ask readers to believe, however, objectivity is a relative newcomer to American journalism and may be more of an effect of society on the press than an innate journalistic norm or an example of perfected practice. Others have argued that objectivity was one of the great fallacies of twentieth century journalism that allowed men such as Joseph McCarthy and Adolf Hitler to do great harm. These authors have argued that a new kind of journalism was necessary, one that did not insist on reporting only facts accurately. Instead, they proposed what has been called "interpretative reporting." It requires journalists to explain to readers or viewers what a story means, why certain facts are more important than others, and why one perspective is more efficacious than another. Richard H. Reeb, Jr., in his book *Taking Journalism Seriously: "Objectivity" As a Partisan Cause,* took this argument a step further with his contention that journalism is inevitably partisan. "Journalism," he argued, "never takes place in a vacuum but is constituted by a point of view."[18]

Objectivity's Democratic defenders point to the repeal of the Fairness Doctrine during the Reagan administration as the beginning of the descent into a right-wing media hell where they are confronted on television with the likes of Bill O'Reilly and John Stossel; on radio with Rush Limbaugh, Michael Reagan, and their clones; and in print with a countless multitude of voices that advocate Republican party principles. The Fairness Doctrine was a long-standing policy of the Federal Communications Commission that grew out of the idea that the broadcast airwaves belong to the public and thus must be used for public service. It required television and radio news stories to represent all different sides of a story. However, the growth of the cable industry allowed a proliferation of voices to reach most Americans, and in 1987 the FCC determined the Fairness Doctrine was no longer necessary to ensure access to all different ideologies. The decision laid the groundwork for opinion-based broadcasts by people like Rush Limbaugh and Al Franken.

Brock has been one of the shrillest voices denying liberal bias and claiming that the reverse is true. In his two books he stops short of alleging a conspiracy, but not by much. A former Republican and *Washington Times* staffer, he argues that ideology is by far more important than accuracy for right-wing media, and he hints that his former colleagues will stoop to almost anything to spread their ideas and gain adherents. He supports this claim with the allegation that "in twelve years of right-wing journalism, my work had never been fact-checked,"[19] a claim that seems impossible given the editing processes used at most newspapers.

Like most of those who defend the Democrats, Brock dates the beginning of the Republican assault on the press as the publication of Efron's *The News Twisters,* which was published the year after Agnew's assault on the media . Brock hints, though, that the conspiracy might go even further back. He argues that every Republican presidential candidate from 1932 to 1988 (with the exception of Goldwater) received a majority of newspaper endorsements.

In *The Republican Noise Machine* Brock accuses the media of changing the United States into a conservative nation where Republicans control all three branches of government, leading the mainstream press to tilt overwhelmingly to the right. Further, he argues, the right-wing press has been able to garner power only because it has the backing of "right-wing billionaires, foundations, and self-interest groups." He postulates that many Americans are incapable of recognizing the power of the right-wing media and that the gap between those who can and those who cannot threatens our democracy. Brock's argument, though, is weakened by his inability to understand that Republican media might just be influential because they resonate with a large number of Americans. President Bush did, after all, win enough votes in 2004 to earn a second term in the White House. Given that outcome, one must wonder who exactly is out of touch with American politics.

Brock's arguments are unconvincing for another reason as well: his own biases are sufficiently obvious to call into question his commitment to fairness and accuracy. He may have learned how to dish out political polemics by working for the *Washington Times* and the *American Spectator*, but he certainly did not leave the techniques behind when he became a Democrat. For example, he contends that right-wing bias — but *only* right-wing bias — results in journalistic malpractice. He does not explain how a right-wing bias in media could result in "distortions, misrepresentations, and outright lies," without the same thing being true of a left-leaning bias.[20] He makes an equally questionable argument when he contends that conservative media "censor" news that they fail to pick up from the prestige press. News media have no obligation to pick up stories from the Associated Press daybook or the *New York Times* front page. In fact, that practice is frowned upon and is disparagingly referred to as "pack journalism."

Brock does concede one very important point, and that is that bias, most often, is in the eye of the beholder. Media consumers are more likely to see bias in stories that attack their views than they are when they see stories that support their positions. He also asks a question that is well worth pondering: Is "equal coverage" the same thing as "balanced coverage"? He believes the right's calls for equal coverage is a smoke screen that masks questions about the quality of ideas presented and which ones represent truth and which ones do not.

Ultimately, Brock's position boils down to discontent with the Republican party and the media that support its causes because they have reinvigorated the old partisan press system. He argues that Democratic commentators, unlike Republicans, are not tied to particular political movements. He also believes that liberal columnists and pundits are more independent and less partisan than their conservative counterparts.

Eric Alterman makes many of the same points in his book *What Liberal Media: The Truth about Bias and the News*. Like Brock, he is unconvinced by claims of liberal bias in media; and, also like Brock, he is pretty sure that there is, instead, a bias that favors Republicans. He points out that even Republican operatives such as Pat Buchanan, James Baker, and William Kristol have conceded that there's not much to the "liberal bias" charge. Further, he argues that the right's claims of a "liberal media" are nothing more than a means of controlling political debate. Republicans, he says, gain when the public believes the mainstream press has a liberal bias because then readers and viewers are more likely to go to conservative media, which present themselves as more "fair and balanced," than liberal media. The Republican press is not only unfair and unbalanced, Alterman argues; but some of it is even inaccurate. He points to the work of Ann Coulter and Bernard Goldberg as examples.

Moreover, Alterman argues that Republicans are getting a foothold in left-leaning media by getting hired there, and he claims this is particularly true for publications like the *New Yorker* and the *Nation*. He points to the ubiquity of Republican columnists and commentators who, he argues, fill up so many newspaper op-ed pages. He is particularly concerned about the domination of broadcasting by Republican commentators since the reach of that medium is so great. He argues, probably rightly so, that the television and radio shows of Republican commentators strengthen their party's positions.

Of all the authors who have attempted to frame a Democratic response to the Republican critique of the press, David Niven has been one of the few to go after hard, quantitative evidence. For his book *Tilt?*, he examined hundreds of newspaper articles, published between September 1, 2000, and August 31, 2001, to find out whether any sort of bias exists in media. Hia conclusions are a bit unexpected. He contends that some kinds of media bias do exist, but partisan bias is not one of them. But the media, ironically, see things differently. News stories dealing with the question of media bias are twelve times more likely to allege liberal bias, and, further, nine out of ten journalists believe their personal views affect their coverage of politics. Since most reporters are Democrats, the expectation would be for their bias to be liberal.

Niven devised an interesting and unusual methodology for his study. Rather than looking at coverage of the two major parties' candidates in an election, he looked at the ways different presidents have been covered in similar situations. Specifically, he looked at how media covered presidents with regard to the unemployment rate, a perennial "hot issue" for most Americans. He asked the question, "Does a Democrat president with a high unemployment rate get better or worse coverage than a Republican president with a high unemployment rate?" He examined coverage during the presidencies of George H. W. Bush and Bill Clinton in periods when the unemployment rate was the same. He found 6 percent more coverage of Clinton, but the articles were 5 percent shorter. Further, stories about Bush were slightly more likely to be on page one. In essence, Niven found that in similar situations, both presidents produced similar coverage, thus lending credence to those like David Brock who argue that partisan bias is in the eye of the beholder. Niven's findings held up for politicians at all levels. From Congress to governors to mayors, there was no evidence of partisan bias. He offers an interesting explanation for the absence of partisan bias. He points out that politicians have enough power to attract press attention so that they can quickly and easily counteract biased reports.

Despite these findings, Niven did find evidence of three kinds of media bias, and one of those, negativity, might explain the perceptions of partisan bias. As any first-year newswriting student knows, the press does have a decided preference for stories with negative outcomes. Stories involving conflict will always get higher billing than the so-called "brights" pioneered some twenty years ago by *USA Today*. Niven's study documented this preference for negative news. In months when the unemployment rate was higher, Niven found more coverage of the president, and that coverage was more likely to be negative, an indication that the news Americans get about the president may be skewed, not by partisan bias but by a preference for negativity.

In the final analysis, Niven argues that findings of bias are impossible to sustain without a baseline against which they can be measured. He claims that different levels of coverage do not necessarily represent bias. If the traditional quantitative yardstick is thrown out, something else must take its place. Niven's suggestion of coverage of similar situations with different office holders has an intuitive logic to it, and his empirical study did find support for this method.

• THE EVIDENCE •

Republicans see clear evidence of bias going back at least to the 1960s and, occasionally, even farther — to the debate of the New Deal, which spurred the emergence of today's conservative and liberal ideologies. Their criticisms are particularly aimed at the elite press organs. Democrats see these organs as objective and note the existence of numerous conservative media outlets today. Ann Coulter, in her book *How to Talk to a Liberal,* even proposes a compromise, under which Fox News would admit its Republican slant if other media agreed to confess their Democratic leanings.

Most Republican accusations are based on cases and examples, not statistical analysis. Statistical studies have failed to confirm the existence of bias. However, media bias is a difficult phenomenon to study for two reasons. First, its practice can be subtle, involving stories not covered, choices of persons to ask for comment, and word choice. Second, the bias may not be intentional. One person's "mainstream" view may be another's liberal or even radical perspective. It might be more instructive to think of journalists and their work product as *influenced* by environment, education, background, Ideology, etc., rather than *biased,* which immediately assumes that there is an objective way to cover every story. W. Lance Bennett, in *News: The Politics of Illusion*, believes it is "a fantasy" for news media to be less biased because "[t]he kind of bias that most people have in mind is really in the eye of the beholder."[21] That sort of bias is not particularly harmful, according to Bennett, because people can recognize it and determine for themselves whether to accept or reject the reporter's perspective. Intentionally or not, Bennett is endorsing the popular view that partisan media bias exists — a view abetted, ironically, by the major media, which faithfully report accusations of bias and give credence to the charges.

Much of the Democratic response reads as if it has been cribbed from the same sources — bias is in the eye of the beholder; there is no such thing as liberal bias; but conservative bias is real and dangerous. Either the Democratic perspective is narrowly tailored, or its apologists have agreed on a set of talking points. Given that the commentators have been able to mount unified arguments, it is curious that the Democratic party has not been able to get the same level of political mileage that the Republicans have gotten from their pundits.

• RESOLUTION •

What can be done to resolve the problem of partisan media bias? Perhaps nothing, for three reasons. Media outlets sensitive to criticism might become reluctant to publish stories. Second, if there is liberal media bias, it has not had much political effect if political elections are the measure. No self-proclaimed liberal Democrat has been elected president in the last forty years. Republican views dominate national politics. Despite an unpopular war, an anemic economy, and an inarticulate presidential candidate, the Republican party won an across-the-board victory in the 2004 national elections (although they lost control of congress in 2006). Finally, what many call "bias" may be something different entirely.

The press has been closely aligned with parties twice in American journalism. Once was when Hamilton's Federalists were battling Jefferson's Republicans over issues such as the size of government, interpretations of the Constitution, relations with Britain and France, the Sedition Act, the national bank, and the national debt. Andrew Jackson rekindled partisanism in the press in order to get elected in 1828. That era of partisan journalism lasted most of the nineteenth century. In the twentieth century, new ideas about journalistic professionalization and ethics, as well as market forces, paved the way for reporting based on nonpartisanism and objectivity.

Unfortunately, journalists and academics became so enamored of this twentieth century model that they saw it as the end-point in the evolution of American journalism. But the end of American journalistic history had not been reached. Journalists no longer believe that their jobs are just to provide facts. Today, they are taught that they should interpret those facts. This has opened up the press to allegations of bias. The Merriam-Webster Dictionary defines "to interpret" as "to understand according to individual belief, judgment, or interest." In a word, interpretation includes bias. The question is whether this seemingly apparent media bias is real, or whether it heralds the beginning of a new partisan press period.

If we have entered a new partisan press period, why is this so? American society has become polarized. John Kerry and John Edwards were right in their 2004 campaign speeches when they claimed that there were two Americas, but they focused on socioeconomic concerns. America is also divided along ideological lines. This was true in earlier partisan press periods as well. Through the early part of the twentieth century, Americans moved closer to consensus as they united to support the nation through two world wars, the Korean War, and the Cold War. In the second half of the century, however, the consensus ruptured over the Vietnam War, civil rights, and the women's movement, leading journalists to conclude that they could not tell the stories about these issues using "traditional," objective methods of journalism. Perhaps America cycles between unity and division, and perhaps its press is likewise destined to cycle between objective and partisan journalism.

Should the media attempt to avoid all bias or work to change the perception of bias? A partisan press has its advantages. Readers and viewers know instantly what their news source's viewpoint is. In addition, a partisan press might mean more news sources and therefore more media diversity. Those who consider partisan media anathema have a difficult task. Public opinion is hostile toward the media. Fair behavior is not always perceived as such. Media outlets that make few bones about their views are sometimes the most popular and successful (consider Fox). Viewers and readers are not troubled by biases that reflect their own points of view. Of course the analytical comments that reporters make are often highly irritating to viewers and readers. So those kinds of "interpretive" comments could be left out. That might address the major bias claims. But would it work for the well-intentioned media outlet? We will let Bill O'Reilly have the last word.

In contrast to some other Republican commentators, he does not think that CNN is particularly biased. Instead, he claims, in *Who's Looking Out for You?*, that CNN has "little cohesive point of view."[22] This, he thinks, is precisely the former cable-news leader's problem — and also why technology may make partisan media more popular: In the age of instant news access via the Internet, a bland reciting of the facts is obsolete.

• POINTS OF VIEW •

Alterman, Eric. *What Liberal Media?: The Truth About Bias and the News.* New York: Basic Books, 2003. Alterman contends liberal bias is a myth made up by Republicans to gain political power.

Baker, Brent. *How to Identify, Expose and Correct Liberal Media Bias.* Alexandria, Va.: Media Research Center, 1994. Foreword by Brent Bozell III. Baker offers this book as a training manual for those who would like to counter what they perceive as liberal bias in their local media.

Barone, Michael. "Our Partisan Media." *The American Enterprise Online.* http://www.taemag.com/issues/articleid.16375/article_detail.asp. It is "nonsense" for journalists to claim that the news media are objective. They have a strong anti-conservative bias.

Bennett, W. Lance. *News: The Politics of Illusion,* 3d ed. White Plains, N.Y.: Longman, 1996. An academic analysis of how news coverage distorts citizens' understanding of American politics.

Boehlert, Eric. *Lapdogs: How the Press Rolled Over for Bush.* New York: Free Press, 2006. "The news media have too often been afraid of the facts and the consequences of reporting them, instead rolling over like lapdogs for President Bush, his administration, and conservative pundits."

Brock, David. *The Republican Noise Machine: Right Wing Media and How It Corrupts Democracy.* New York: Crown Publishers, 2004. Right-leaning media have the power to destroy the American democracy.

Coulter, Ann. *How to Talk to a Liberal (If You Must): The World According to Ann Coulter.* New York: Crown, 2004. In this attack on liberalism and the liberal media, Coulter argues, unlike other conservatives, that the media's promotion of "the left-wing agenda" is deliberate.

Elder, Larry. *The Ten Things You Can't Say in America.* New York: St. Martin's, 2000. Elder, a black conservative, uses numerous examples to confirm the AIM/MRC view of America media.

Franken, Al. *Lies (and the Lying Liars Who Tell Them: A Fair and Balanced Look at the Right).* New York: Dutton, 2003. In addition to defending mainstream media from charges of bias, Franken focuses on right-wing media and accuses them of being uninterested in the truth.

Goldberg, Bernard. *Bias: A CBS Insider Exposes How the Media Distort the News.* Washington, D.C.: Regnery, 2002. Goldberg, a former CBS correspondent, reveals what he considers to be the systematic liberal bias in the news division of this network.

Kick, Russ, ed.. *You Are Being Lied To: The Disinformation Guide to Media Distortion, Historical Whitewashes and Cultural Myths.* New York: The Disinformation Company, 2001. A collection of essays by left-leaning and moderate authors who believe there is no such thing as liberal bias and that conservatism is dangerous for America.

Kohn, Bob. *Journalistic Fraud: How the* New York Times *Distorts the News and Why It Can No Longer Be Trusted*. Nashville, Tenn.: WND Books, 2003. An analysis of liberal bias in America's most prominent prestige newspaper.

Niven, David. *Tilt? The Search for Media Bias*. Westport, Conn.: Greenwood Press, 2002. This academic study of whether there is bias in the press concludes that there is, but not of a partisan nature.

Parenti, Michael. *Inventing Reality: The Politics of Mass Media*. New York: St. Martin's Press, 1986. Once one of America's most famous radicals, Parenti attacks the media as defenders of the establishment and favorable to right-wing views.

Reeb, Richard H., Jr.. *Taking Journalism Seriously: "Objectivity" As a Partisan Cause*. Lanham, Md.: University Press of America, 1999. Journalism always involves taking sides if there is any serious attempt made to find out the truth of a matter.

O'Reilly, Bill. *The No Spin Zone*. New York: Broadway Books, 2001. Author has much to say about the problem of self-censorship, whether caused by political correctness or as a byproduct of media mergers.

O'Reilly, Bill. *Who's Looking Out for You?*. New York: Broadway Books, 2003. Author is surprisingly complimentary of many major media figures but particularly despises commentators who pretend to be objective while supporting partisan causes.

NOTES

1. http://www.democracymeansyou.com/article108.php

2. http://www.fightthebias.com/Mission/Mission.htm

3. Bob Kohn, *Journalistic Fraud: How the* New York Times *Distorts the News and Why It Can No Longer Be Trusted* (Nashville, Tenn.: WND Books, 2003).

4. Ibid., 139.

5. Ann Coulter, *How to Talk to a Liberal (If You Must): The World According to Ann Coulter* (New York: Crown, 2004), 180–83, 185, 197, 202.

6. Larry Elder, *The Ten Things You Can't Say in America* (New York: St. Martin's, 2000), 101–104, 106–114, 123–24.

7. Bill O'Reilly, *Who's Looking Out for You?* (New York: Broadway Books, 2003), 71, 78, 80.

8. Bill O'Reilly, *The No Spin Zone* (New York: Broadway Books, 2001), 153, 158.

9. Bernard Goldberg, *Bias: A CBS Insider Exposes How the Media Distort the News* (Washington, DC: Regnery Publishing Co., 2002).

10. Ibid., 22, 125.

11. Some of his criticisms can be found in three articles in *Capitalism Magazine* on October 28 and December 26, 2004, and May 17, 2005. Available at http://www.CapMag.com.

12. Thomas Sowell, "Newsweek: Too Good to Check," *Capitalism Magazine*, May 17, 2005. Available from http://www.CapMag.com..

13. Thomas Sowell, "No Media Bias?" *Human Events*, July 14, 2003, 667.

14. Thomas Sowell, "Media Confusion Between Objectivity and Neutrality," *Capitalism Magazine*, January 6, 2004. Available at http://www.CapMag.com.

15. Al Franken, *Lies (and the Lying Liars Who Tell Them: A Fair and Balanced Look at the Right)* (New York: Dutton, 2003), 1–2.

16. David Brock, *The Republican Noise Machine: Right Wing Media and How it Corrupts Democracy* (New York: Crown Publishers, 2004), 2, 111.

17. W. Lance Bennett, *News: The Politics of Illusion*, 3rd ed. (White Plains: Longman, 1996), 102.

18. Richard H. Reeb, Jr., *Taking Journalism Seriously: "Objectivity" as a Partisan Cause* (Lanham: University Press of America, 1999), 118–120, 4.

19. Brock, *Blinded by the Right*, 295.

20. Brock, *The Republican Noise Machine*, 11.

21. Bennett, *News: The Politics of Illusion*, xiii.

22. O'Reilly, *Who's Looking Out for You?* 78–79.

4

Religion

Katie H. Porterfield

"It hardly needs to be said that Western media is biased against Islam and Muslims: every Muslim who reads the daily newspaper(s) in his city, watches television or listens to the radio is well aware of this.... [But] we can reduce the noise of the anti–Islamic and anti–Muslim chorus in the media and increase the pro–Islamic and pro–Muslim material appearing there and thus gradually change the image of Islam in the West."—Ahmad Shafaat, web-based writer on Islamic topics[1]

"'The little nut from the Christian group.' That's how a staff editor at CBS News' Washington bureau described presidential candidate Gary Bauer in April 1999. It was an inside conference call, but it was going out to CBS News bureaus all over the country.... [T]he bureau chiefs participating in the discussion met it with dead silence. No one protested. What that tells you is that this reflects an attitude prevalent in much of the major media. A shrug of the shoulders and 'Doesn't everybody think so?' It is OK to slur fundamentalist Christians. But anyone making a similar disparaging comment about any of the 'politically correct' minority groups would have been dismissed."—Wes Vernon, NewsMax.com[2]

"Branch Davidian sect led by David Koresh
die in fire at compound near Waco"

"San Francisco court rules Pledge of Allegiance
unconstitutional because it includes 'under God'"

"Media expose Catholic Church sexual abuse cover-up"

"Consecration of gay Episcopal Bishop ignites
debate about role of homosexuals in Church"

"Muslims claim their faith is a peaceful religion"

"Christian conservatives support President Bush's
proposed ban on same sex marriage"

These are just several of countless religious issues that have made headlines since the early 1990s. While similar stories regularly appear on evening news programs, newspaper front pages, and news magazine covers, critics question the validity of such stories. Were they reported to the public objectively, or were they influenced by media bias?

In 1993, the First Amendment Center in Nashville, Tennessee, produced a report, *Bridging the Gap: Religion and the News Media*, written by John Dart, a journalist who specializes in religion, and Jimmy Allen, a Baptist minister. The report assessed the division between religious organizations and the news media. This division, Dart and Allen said, resulted because religious leaders were unhappy, not only with the limited amount of religious news coverage, but also with the quality of such coverage, which they believed exhibited bias. Journalists, however, denied that they were biased but expressed feelings of uncertainty about reporting religious stories.[3] In 2000, Dart added an introductory update to the report, asserting that progress had been made, just in those seven years, in "bridging the gap." He measured progress by an increase in the amount of religious news coverage and religious news reporters. However, data regarding whether critics were happier with the quality of coverage or believed the media had become less biased was not available.

Dart reasoned that despite changes in the religious climate, misunderstandings between organized religion and the news media, which often lead to bias or accusations of bias, will most likely never disappear. Some observers have argued that religion and journalism, because they have exactly opposite views on reality, can never co-exist peacefully. The result is that critics of the media claim that bias is inherent in journalism, while journalists claim that they have no bias and that critics simply are dissatisfied because reporting does not blatantly favor religion.

The debate over bias involves such issues as whether the media are biased for or against certain religions or specific Christian denominations; whether journalists maintain a principle of objectivity; and whether bias is anti-religious bias, liberal bias, or secular humanist bias (or anti–Christian bias). While religious critics are convinced bias is widespread, supporters of the media argue that such biases do not exist. Some contend that an anti-religious bias is a myth, others argue that the appearance of bias results from the fact that the media cover stories that represent conflict, and others say the media approach religious news with Judeo-Christian values or a series of moral values that exalt religion. Because Christianity predominates in the debate, this chapter will focus mainly on it.

Anti-Religious Bias

One of the most common arguments regarding the coverage of religion is that the news media demonstrate an anti-religious bias. Critics argue that such a bias is evident because most media outlets do not have fulltime religious reporters. This point of view is expressed, for example, by Bernard Goldberg, former CBS News Correspondent and author of *Arrogance: Rescuing America from the Media Elite* and *Bias: A CBS Insider Exposes How Media Distort the News*. In an interview published on Townhall.com (2003), he asserts that religion is one of the most important institutions in America — yet, he asks, "who's covering religion for CBS News? Or NBC News? Or I think even ABC News? I know they had a religious correspondent, but I'm not sure what the status of that is."[4]

In an article in *Christian Century* (2001), John Dart reports the "status" of ABC's religion news correspondent. He writes that although Peter Jennings hired Peggy Wehmeyer, the first and only religious correspondent on network television, in 1994, her contract was not renewed in 2001. "Just as the booming economy helped news media 'get religion,'" Dart writes, "the current downturn in advertising has forced staff cutbacks in both print and broadcast media." He quotes Charles Haynes of the Freedom Forum's First Amendment Center in Arlington, Virginia, as saying, "ABC's decision 'sends the message that religion coverage is unimportant and expendable.'"[5]

Also in the Townhall.com interview, Goldberg makes what he calls a "bigger point" about religious bias in the newsroom. Surveys indicate, he says, that journalists are not religious people, a fact that is certain to affect their coverage of religion. "Journalists somehow think that they are the only species on the planet who can keep their biases in check because they're professionals," he says. "Well, I don't think that's true."

Bruce Bartlett, a senior fellow with the National Center for Policy Analysis, agrees with Goldberg in "The GOP's Secret Weapon ... Yes, it's the 'New York Times,'" an article published in *The Weekly Standard* (2002). He asserts that most reporters are agnostics and those who are affiliated with a religion belong to mainline or liberal churches and denominations. He points out that "the return to fundamentalism and the return to orthodoxy have been the most important religious trends of the last three decades." Thus, he writes, if a newspaper does not have a reporter who is a religious conservative, "what is going to trigger his editor's interest in covering the deeply religious when neither has much knowledge of that community in the first place?"[6]

For years, critics have cited a 1980 survey conducted by S. Robert Lichter, Stanley Rothman, and Linda Lichter, discussed in their book *The Media Elite* (1986). They interviewed 238 journalists systematically selected from the *New York Times*, *Washington Post*, *Wall Street Journal*, *Time*, *Newsweek*, *U.S. News and World Report*, CBS, NBC, ABC, and PBS. Their study found that half of those interviewed said they were not affiliated with a religion, and 86 percent said they seldom or never attended religious services. Other statistics — such as 84 percent of the media elite interviewed strongly opposed state control over sexual activities, 75 percent disagreed that homosexuality is wrong, and 54 percent did not regard adultery as wrong — led the authors to conclude that "members of the media elite emerge as strong supporters of sexual freedom, and as natural opponents of groups like the Moral Majority."[7]

In an analysis of the point of view commonly supported by the Rothman-Lichter study, Stewart M. Hoover, in his book *Religion in the News* (1998), writes, "This idea, that the natural inclination of media decision makers is to be either anti-religious or at least irreligious, is widely shared. The implication is that those who determine the construction of 'the religion story' in the nation's newsrooms have a natural disinclination to do it well or to do it fairly." Critics, Hoover asserts, deny the idea that professional journalistic values can overcome personal preferences and attitudes in an attempt to give religious coverage fair treatment. In fact, Hoover says, not only do critics believe that journalists are incapable of ignoring their aversion toward religion, they also contend that media attitudes and practices regarding religion result in suspicion and hostility.[8]

Secular Humanist Bias

Such hostility, critics — especially conservative Christian critics — say, is associated with a secular humanist bias. Marvin Olasky, a journalism professor at the University of Texas, has become perhaps the most vocal Christian conservative voice on issues related to religion in the media. In a June 1998 *Moody* magazine article, he writes that evangelicals take issue with press coverage because it is "the result of a materialist world view hostile to Christianity.... Most journalists see leftist guerillas, homosexual parades, and anti–Christian textbooks as the good news of our era."

Olasky's critique is part of a broader one that he argues in his book *Prodigal Press: The Anti-Christian Bias of the American News Media* (1988). He asserts that a humanistic perspective has replaced a God-centered one and dominates media coverage of religious issues. His argument is rooted in the history of American journalism, as he believes the American press practiced a Christian form of journalism until the mid-nineteenth century when the penny press drove religiously inspired publications from the field, and journalists became influenced by anti–Christian humanism and pantheism. Now, Olasky says, conflict between journalists and Christians is inevitable. "God shows Christians that He exists independently of our minds by acting on our minds from outside," he writes. "Yet, if a person who has not had that experience is unwilling to accept the testimony of others, and thus assumes internally-generated psychological change rather than God's grace, he will see Christian fact as imagination and Christian objectivity as subjectivity." Thus, Olasky believes journalists ignore "Christian fact[s]" and "Christian objectivity," yielding an anti–Christian bias.[9]

In an article headlined "Bias is Back" in *World Magazine* (2002), Olasky dissects four news stories from June 2002 to illustrate the print media's anti–Christian bias. He writes of a story about Rev. Jerry Vines, pastor of the First Baptist Church of Jacksonville, Florida, who, at the Southern Baptist Convention's annual gathering, said, "Islam was founded by Muhammad, a demon-possessed pedophile who had 12 wives — and his last one was a 9-year-old girl." While Olasky contends Vines' statement was "very tough language," he explains that it "arguably had a factual base" because in Islam, the Hadith-stories of Muhammad's life do say that he had many wives, one of whom was nine years old. "Whether that made Muhammad a pedophile," Olasky reasons, "could be debated among psychologists, and whether he was demon-possessed has been debated among theologians for almost 1,400 years — Muhammad himself at one point thought he might be — but there was no reason for journalists to be shocked, shocked that Mr. Vines, a former SBC president, took a strong stand against Islam." Despite this, Olasky says that the *New York Times* referred to Vines' statements as "'hate speech against Muslims' that has 'become a staple of conservative Christian political discourse.'"[10]

Olasky also cited stories about Vines from other media, including the Associated Press and the *Washington Post*. The AP, he says, quoted an Islamic Studies professor as saying, "The Vines statement 'makes me wonder what's the hateful religion right now that we should be worried about.'" Olasky says this story demonstrates how journalists emphasized subjectivity and failed to determine objective fact.

Liberal Media Bias

Other critics say that when it comes to covering religious conservatives, the media demonstrate a liberal bias. In fact, the Lichter-Rothman study found that most of the journalists interviewed considered themselves liberal and supported Democratic candidates. The authors say that psychological tests show that "media outlooks can unconsciously operate to shape their [journalists'] conceptions of the news." In selecting sources, for example, journalists make choices in accordance with their perspectives on issues.[11]

The liberal media bias argument finds an unlikely ally in liberal Eric Alterman, whose book *What Liberal Media* (2003) argues that the bias of the media is conservative. Despite his book's overall premise, however, he writes, "If religion were the only measure of bias then conservatives would have a strong case." He contends that journalists are more comfortable with the secularist Democratic party than the Republican party of evangelical and fundamentalist Christians. He cites an article titled "Our Secularist Democratic Party" from *Public Interest* (2002), in which Louis Bolce and Gerald De Maio write that the *New York Times* published twice as many stories on the power of fundamentalist Christians in the Republican party in 1992 than the *Times* and the *Washington Post* published together on secularists in the Democratic party during the entire 1990s. Alterman writes that the media consider the Democratic position to be the "normal" one and that "it is so normal, it does not occur to anyone to point it out." As a result, he writes, "conservatives might wish to argue, if the media is secular and the Democrats are secular, the two are quite naturally allies against the faithful on those issues where religion plays a role in the public sphere."[12]

In a *Journal of Media and Religion* article titled "The Framing of Fundamentalist Christians: Network Television News, 1980–2000," Peter A. Kerr illustrates conservative Christian claims of a liberal bias in coverage of religion. He quotes Tim LaHaye, coauthor of the *Left Behind* novels, as saying: "It's no secret to any of us how the liberal media manages the news and helps to set the national agenda on public debate. They report the news in such a way as to promote the political goals of the left. The censorship of Christian principles and ideas covers many more issues than abortion and the homosexual lifestyle. The media slants what is reported in the areas of national defense, the budget, school prayer, and Soviet expansion in Central America, among others. The truth in all these areas is being hidden." Kerr also quotes Jerry Falwell, televangelist and founder of the Moral Majority, as saying, "Far from reflecting what the public thinks, the press reflects what it thinks. No wonder those who are trying to call America back to her moral and spiritual traditions and heritage are so often ravaged by the columnists and excoriated by network reporters."[13]

In the study *Bridging the Gap*, Dart and Allen assert that many traditional religious groups blame the liberal press for skewed reporting. They cite a survey response they received from Father Francis E. Butler, a Catholic priest in Montgomery, Alabama. He wrote, "The media [have] a liberal agenda, i.e., abortion, homosexuality, pro-pornography, etc., and the authentic ministers of God's Words are on opposite sides of the issues."[14] Dart and Allen included many other quotations indicating Christian skepticism toward what many believe is a liberal, secular press that exercises its biases everyday.

General Anti-Christian Bias

Regardless of whether critics believe the media exhibit an anti-religious bias, a secular-humanistic bias, or a liberal bias, one thing is certain — the majority of clergy believe the media are biased against them and their causes. In the survey that Robert Wyatt conducted for the First Amendment Center, clergy were asked to respond to the statement, "Most religion coverage today is biased against ministers and organized religion." Published in the Dart and Allen study *Bridging the Gap*, the results revealed that 58 percent of mainline Protestant clergy, 70 percent of Catholic priests, and 91 percent of conservative Protestant ministers agreed either strongly or somewhat.[15]

The Dart-Allen study also found that members of the Christian clergy and media critics often complain about the fact that conflicts make news, while reporters pass over other, non-controversial but important actions and events. "When conflict," the authors write, "flares within religious denominations over women's ordination, gay rights, abortion, papal authority, etc.— clergy and other religious leaders have despaired at the 'negative' image given to their denomination."[16] It is often during such conflicts that religious groups point to bias against them. The Catholic Church, for example, claimed an anti–Catholic bias in coverage of the priest sexual abuse scandal, one of the biggest religious stories in recent years. The *Boston Globe* reported in 2002 that a Vatican-approved journal, *La Civilta Cattolica*, accused the American news media of blatant bias and asserted that they are driven by "'morbid and scandalistic curiosity.'"[17]

Anti-Religious Bias as Myth

Just as critics contend the news media are biased, others argue that there is no bias. They refute the idea of an anti-religious bias; claim that journalists approach their beat with Judeo-Christian morals; dispute the claim of "liberal media" bias; and argue that both fundamentalist Christians and Catholics are simply wrong in their contentions that the media are biased against them.

John Dart, in his "Update 2000" to *Bridging the Gap*, reports on a mail survey conducted in 1999 indicating that the number of newspapers with fulltime and part-time religious editors and reporters has increased since 1993. Twenty-one percent of all newspapers in the United States responded to the survey. Of these, nine reported assigning a fulltime editor to religion, and thirty reported assigning a part-time editor to the beat. In addition, the number of fulltime religion reporters has increased from 57 to 92, with the number of part-time religion reporters increasing from 95 to 163.[18]

The terrorist attacks on September 11, 2001, led to an economic downturn that caused many newspapers and TV outlets to reduce staff members. Despite such cutbacks, John Hafner writes in a *University of Montana Journalism Review* article (2002) that newspapers are successfully reporting on religious issues. In addition, he writes, "Associations for religion reporters are leading the way toward craft improvement by helping reporters define and report issues accurately and objectively."[19]

In *Bridging the Gap*, Dart and Allen contend that an anti-religious bias in the media is a myth. First, they dispute the popularly cited Lichter-Rothman survey, which found that journalists are irreligious. The authors argue that although the Lichters and Rothman surveyed only 240 East Coast respondents, the study has been used to reflect the religious views of journalists as a whole. The survey, Dart and Allen believe, hardly represents an adequate sample of journalists.[20]

They argue that the Lichter-Rothman survey conflicts with data collected in their own survey, conducted by First Amendment Center representative Robert Wyatt. He polled 266 newspaper editors nationwide and found that 72 percent said that religion had meaning in their lives. Three-fourths of the religion writers surveyed indicated that faith was very important in their lives, while only 9 percent of the editors and 4 percent of the religion writers responded that they were not religious.[21] In his introduction to the study, John Seigenthaller writes, "Because the misconception created by Lichter-Rothman is so widespread, it is hoped that this refutation will be widely circulated by the secular news media. A misled public needs to know that journalists harbor no ill will toward religion."[22]

Dart and Allen also point to other surveys conducted through the years that have also contradicted the Lichter-Rothman survey. In a *Newspaper Research Journal* article (1988), Judith Buddenbaum, a professor from Colorado State University, states that only 10 percent of reporters surveyed in 1985 at large and small newspapers across the country said they were not affiliated with a religion.[23] In addition, in a study published in *Journalism Quarterly* (1987), Earnest C. Hynds, a journalism professor from the University of Georgia, reports that he surveyed religion writers at newspapers with a circulation of 100,000 and found that 78 percent claimed they belonged to a church, synagogue, or other religious body.[24] Finally, Dart and Allen introduce results from a survey conducted by David H. Weaver and G. Cleveland Wilhoit (1992) that indicated that 71.8 percent of religion writers and editors surveyed claimed religion was either very important or somewhat important.[25]

After clarifying what they believe to be discrepancies associated with the general religious makeup of American journalists, Dart and Allen continue their defense of journalism by asserting that the media are not biased against religion or religious practitioners. "We found, in general," they write, "that rather than exhibiting an overt bias or disinterest in religion stories, most news professionals were simply reluctant to go much beyond the familiar formula stories of religion on celebrities, sectarian tragedies, sexual scandals and offbeat claims of supernatural activity." Although their survey indicates that the majority of the clergy polled believe the media are biased, unfairly negative, and too sensational in their religious coverage, it also indicates that journalists reject this notion. Journalists do, however, acknowledge responsibility for errors. Thus, when the press' religion reporting fails readers — which Dart and Allen believe the press does — they attribute the failures to misunderstanding and ignorance about religion.[26]

Such unfamiliarity, misunderstanding, and ignorance result, Dart and Allen say, not from "a thoughtless secularism that slides easily into anti-religious treatment by the media," but from a secular approach that involves "a dispassionate treatment of religious claims and movements that regards everyone fairly." Because journalism is empirical in nature, reporters value facts and clarity and, Dart and Allen say, "may find the basis of religious knowledge too subjective, intuitive and unverifiable in ordinary ways." Covering religious matters, therefore, is often foreign territory for journalists. As a result, they are uncomfortable with religious coverage and fear not only making mistakes, but also the wrath of religious representatives when such mistakes are made. Dart and Allen turn to Bill Moyers, a PBS commentator who often covers religious stories, to summarize this idea. "Mainstream journalists mostly ignore religion because they don't understand it and because they are worried about misinterpreting it," Moyers says. "They do know it's a subjective series of subcultures for which there is no common language. It's the Tower of Babel to a mainstream journalist — everybody's speaking in tongues."

Dart and Allen find support in their argument against the presence of an anti-religious bias in former journalist Doug Underwood. In his book *From Yahweh to Yahoo!* (2002), Underwood discusses the results of his survey, conducted with Keith Stamm, that sought to make sense of the conflicting data regarding journalists' approach toward religion. In 1998, Underwood and Stamm mailed questionnaires to 1,413 daily newspaper journalists across the United States and Canada and received 432 responses. They found, like Dart-Allen, Buddenbaum, and Hynds, that reporters are more religious than critics acknowledge. Eighty-five percent of religion reporters said religion was important or very important to them, as did 73 percent of investigative reporters and 67 percent of the other reporters surveyed.

No Secular Humanist or Anti-Christian Bias

With his survey, Underwood also sought to test the hypothesis that journalists' ethics and morals are rooted in Judeo-Christian values and that these values are reflected in the outlooks of even the most agnostic and irreverent journalists. The journalists surveyed tended to support the hypothesis; for although they could be categorized according to varying religious affiliations and beliefs, the majority of them were found to put traditional Judeo-Christian values into practice in their profession. Thus, Underwood says, the results indicated that "unspoken and unconscious religious impulses tend to motivate members of the journalism profession, including those who think of themselves as nonreligious."[27] Underwood, then, counters not only the idea that reporters are irreligious or exhibit an anti-religious bias, but also Olasky's contention that journalists approach religious issues with a secular, humanistic outlook that results in an anti–Christian bias.

Before Underwood conducted his study, Mark Silk published his book *Unsecular Media: Making News of Religion in America* (1995), in which he asserts that the media serve to exalt religion rather than to destroy it. "When the news media set out to represent religion," writes Silk, "they do not approach it from the standpoint of secular confronting the sacred." The media interpret events according to a "series of moral formulas, or topoi, that shape the way religion stories are conceived and written." He asserts that seven topoi guide religion journalism. They include good works, tolerance, false prophecy, hypocrisy, inclusion, supernatural belief, and declension (decline of religious values in society). Each of these moral formulas resonates a common, cultural understanding used when discussing religious issues. Thus, Silk concludes, "Ignorant of religion, even hostile to it, some news professionals may be; but the images of religion they put on display reflect something other than their personal ignorance or hostility."[28]

Silk's theory, like Underwood's, denies the idea that the media exercise an anti-religious bias or approach religious issues with a secular outlook. In fact, Silk and Underwood imply that journalists approach religion with a pro-religious, or pro–Christian, bias.

No Liberal Bias

Underwood asserts that despite conservative contentions that the "liberal" media are more sympathetic to liberal groups, "The press's fixation on conflict appears to go some way in explaining why the press coverage of the 'religious Right' or 'Christian conservatives' vastly outweighs the coverage of 'liberal Christians' or the 'religious left.'" He references a Nexis search that showed there were four times more daily news stories involving Christian conservatives than stories involving Christian liberals. In addition, a similar search revealed that there were twice as many stories about the Christian Coalition, the lobbying organization associated with Christian conservatives, than stories about the National Council of Churches, the religious organization identified with liberal causes. Despite this, Underwood asserts, if there is a liberal bias, it is "only up to a point" because press coverage of both organizations relied on involvement in political controversy. "Whatever the press' political orientation," Underwood writes, "the first rule seems to be to cover religion largely through the prism of public disputes."[29]

Fairness and Accuracy in Reporting (FAIR), a liberal media watchdog organization, issued a report by Jeff Cohen titled "Media Coverage of Religion: An Overview (1999)" that asserts that mainstream media are not hostile toward Christian conservatives and the organized church. In fact, Cohen argues, "coverage is often so embarrassingly soft that it seems to be pandering to believers." To demonstrate his claim, he cites a FAIR survey that examined religious cover stories from *Time*, *Newsweek*, and *U.S. News and World Report*. Journalistic balance, Cohen argues, is noticeably absent in such articles. For example, an article from *Time*, titled "Does Heaven Exist?," did not provide one point of view contending that heaven does not exist. In addition, Cohen claims, the media even provide Religious Right advocates such as Jerry Falwell with constant opportunities to express their points of view.[30]

According to Dart and Allen's *Bridging the Gap*, "religion writers staunchly affirm that they have no agenda of causes to promote." Dart and Allen refer to Quentin J. Schultze, a professor of communications at Calvin College, who argues that even though journalists may have little understanding of religion they are working within a pervasive conservative culture. "Except for a few columnists and broadcast editorialists," Schultze says, "journalists and other media professionals are intellectual and religious eunuchs. In fact, a number of studies suggest rather convincingly that news is inherently conservative because it rarely challenges the underlying assumptions of the prevailing political and economic institutions in the United States." But Dart and Allen contend that perhaps the issue is not about liberalism or conservatism. It may be, they say, that the tension between media and religion results from the press' need to assimilate into changing culture, while religious believers resist change that goes against traditional morals or beliefs.[31]

What Anti-Christian Bias?

Peter Kerr published two studies, one about the print media and the other about the broadcast media, arguing that the media are not biased against fundamentalist Christianity. The first, conducted by Kerr and P. Moy and published in *Journalism and Mass Communications Quarterly*, was titled "Newspaper Coverage of Fundamentalist Christians, 1980–2000 (2002)."[32] The second, "The Framing of Fundamentalist Christians: Network Television News, 1980–2000 (2003)," was published in the *Journal of Media and Religion*. While the studies reveal that coverage of fundamentalists is slightly negative, the evidence does not conclude that the media are adverse to fundamentalists. Kerr writes, "This research confirms that fundamentalists have been a bit unreasonable in their deprecation of the 'secular humanistic media.'... "[33]

As for the charges of anti–Catholic bias in coverage of priests and sexual abuse, many journalists and media analysts reject the allegation. One such naysayer is Peter Hart, a writer for FAIR. In an article published in *Insight on the News* (2002), he states, "It's a mistake to conflate 'bad news' with media bias.... [T]he most extensive coverage of the scandal has been provided by prominent Catholic figures within the mainstream media," such as NBC's Tim Russert and Fox's Bill O'Reilly. Such coverage, Hart says, demonstrated "an impulse to reform and rehabilitate the church, or to act as constructive critics from within the church walls." He quotes church representatives, such as Sister Mary Ann Walsh, a spokeswoman for the U.S. Conference of Catholic Bishops, who says, "in most areas the church has been given a fair shake."[34]

Michael Paulson's *Boston Globe* article, "Crisis in the Church; Jesuit Journal Raps U.S. Media's Church Coverage," presents arguments against *La Civilta Cattolica's* claim that the American news media have exhibited an anti–Catholic bias. Paulson quotes James M. Naughton, practicing Catholic and president of the Poynter Institute, as saying, "It's certainly true that most religious organizations have seldom been subjected to the kind of scrutiny that the Catholic Church is being subjected to now, but it's not at all clear that any of them have covered up abuses by clerics to the same extent." In the same article, Mark Silk is quoted as saying, "The truth of the matter is that this is the biggest religion story in the history of the mass media, and it is a huge scandal, and the amount of piling on has been minimal."[35]

• THE EVIDENCE •

The conflicting data regarding whether journalists are religious people reveal weaknesses in both arguments. The Rothman-Lichter survey, for example, has been used not only to support the charge of irreligion among journalists but also to claim anti-religious media bias. Although the survey was conducted nearly three decades ago, its staying power has been remarkable. However, because the researchers polled only individuals from the "media elite"— top media outlets on the East coast — it is difficult to extend results to a larger population of journalists. To do so would mean accepting the premise that these "media elite" dictate the attitudes of all media outlets across the nation. That assumption is questionable.

Through the years, several surveys, most recently that of Underwood and Stamm (2002), have supposedly refuted the Rothman-Lichter study by concluding that the majority of journalists polled do, in fact, value religion. However, the fact remains that these surveys polled only newspaper journalists, with particular attention to religion reporters, while the Lichter-Rothman survey polled journalists not only from newspapers but also from magazines and television stations. In fact, Rothman and Lichter pointed this out in a response to Dart and Allen's critique of their survey in a letter to the *New York Times* in 1993. They asserted that the data from Wyatt's 1993 survey, which Dart and Allen used, were not directly comparable to their own. The Lichter-Rothman data were based on a survey conducted with several staff members of the print and broadcast "media elite," while the 1993 survey polled only religion writers and managing editors at newspapers in small to medium-sized cities. Additionally, Rothman and Lichter contend that the questions on the two surveys were not comparable. Stewart explains, "The most often statistic cited from their [Rothman and Lichter] research — the 86 percent figure — was for religious service attendance, a question not included in Wyatt's survey. Thus, as Rothman and Lichter put it, 'Without this information, we cannot know how [journalists'] professional attitudes relate to their behavior.'"[36]

With several surveys representing different samples of journalists, what is one to make of, first, the religious makeup of the media and, second, the extent to which this makeup contributes to media bias? First, it is important to recognize that Wyatt, Buddenbaum, Hynds, Weaver and Wilhoit, and Underwood all surveyed newspaper journalists. While some surveyed religion writers, others surveyed daily reporters, and still others surveyed both, each found that the majority of journalists surveyed were either affiliated with a religion or valued religion in their lives. This indicates that newspaper journalists may be more religious than critics contend. It may also disprove the notion that journalists are hostile toward religion. It does not necessarily eliminate the possibility that the media, even newspapers, are biased.

In fact, if these surveys are accurate and newspapers are more religious than commonly thought, could we not conclude that they are biased toward religion? Underwood broaches this idea, concluding with his survey not only that the majority of newspaper journalists value religion, but also that they use these values, rooted in Judeo-Christian tenets, in their professional activities. This theory and a similar one proposed by Mark Silk suggest that the media are biased toward Christianity. This argument contrasts with that of Marvin Olasky and others, who assert that the media approach religion with a secular, humanist perspective that results in an anti–Christian bias.

Both arguments have validity. While it is certainly not difficult to look at America and the media and see materialistic, corporate (basically non-religious) values at work, there is also evidence of Judeo-Christian values. The American culture and media do promote and uphold many morals that stem from Judeo-Christian tenets. Consider the Ten Commandments, for example. Although there is debate about their constitutional role in society, if a public figure, religious or not, breaks almost any of them, whether society supports or rejects that public figure, such actions become news. Media coverage of President Bill Clinton's adultery is just one example.

In addition, if one looks for either liberal or conservative bias in religious coverage, he or she can most likely find it. Much of the material, though, that fundamentalist Christians and Roman Catholics claim is biased may be the result mainly of the media's propensity to emphasize conflict, controversy, and the negative. Episodes of sexual abuse by priests in the Catholic Church, for example, received great coverage because, among other things, they contained exactly the types of news values that the media delight in. Media bias, whether liberal or conservative, is not synonymous with negative coverage. In addition, perhaps unfortunately, the general public has demonstrated interest in such conflict. Conflict sells papers and increases ratings, and like other businesses, the media must make money to survive.

Perhaps even more relevant, however, is that while journalists claim not to promote agendas and may strive to achieve balance in all coverage, they are, after all, only human. They have values and ideals — and whether such values and ideals are liberal or conservative, or rooted in Judeo-Christian tenets or not, they will at the very least unconsciously affect something as emotionally charged as coverage of religion. Those values play out in judgments and decisions about what topics to cover and which sources to choose.

Still, despite the arguments that one can make that bias does not exist in the coverage of religion, we must recognize that a large segment of the religious population believes that it does. It is difficult to dismiss their complaints out of hand. Furthermore, the charges of bias differ from denomination to denomination, with conservative Christians most concerned about bias against them. The exact nature and extent of bias are debatable, but if it does exist, it should be a concern for not only devoutly religious people but for journalists also.

• RESOLUTION •

What then, can journalists do to avoid such bias? The first step for any journalist is an obvious one. He must recognize that he is only human and that he has biases. If he is aware of such biases, he can work to keep them in check. In an article titled "Covering Conventional and Unconventional Religion: A Reporter's View" published in the *Review of Religious Research* (1997), John Dart offers suggestions for "combating ignorance about religions small and large," for it is this ignorance that commonly leads to bias or accusations of bias. He recommends that religion reporters seek continuing education opportunities, such as fellowships, seminars, and conferences, and maintain contact with religious experts. He also encourages religion reporters to work with professional societies, such as the American Academy of Religion, for suggestions regarding knowledgeable sources on various subjects or denominations. Finally, Dart says, "reporters should approach any group, small or large, the same way."[37]

• POINTS OF VIEW •

Bartlett, Bruce. "The GOP's Secret Weapon ... Yes, it's the New York Times." *The Weekly Standard*, November 25, 2002. http://www.weeklystandard.com/Utilities/printer_preview.asp?idArticle=1920&R=527D36E32. The religious trend throughout the past three decades has been fundamentalism and a return to orthodoxy; yet if a newspaper does not have anyone on its staff who is a religious conservative, "how is that paper going to have any clue about what is going on among those who share such beliefs? ... [W]hat is going to trigger the editor's interest in covering the deeply religious when neither has much knowledge of that community in the first place?"

Dart, John, and Jimmy Allen. "Bridging the Gap: Religion and the News Media." Nashville, First Amendment Center, 2000. Freedomforum.org, http://www.freedomforum.org/publications/first/bridgingthegap/Bridgingthegap.pdf. Instead of exhibiting an explicit bias toward religious stories, most journalists were "reluctant to go much beyond familiar-formula stories on religious celebrities, sectarian tragedies, sexual scandals and offbeat claims of supernatural activity."

Hart, Peter. "Q: Are the media guilty of anti–Christian bias in covering the church sex scandals? No: The media have performed a service by exposing the crisis and pushing for reform." Insight on the News, July 29, 2002, 41. Hart, a media analyst for Fairness and Accuracy in Reporting (FAIR), a liberal organization, concludes that the news media were not biased in covering the sex scandal in the Catholic Church.

Hoover, Stewart M. *Religion in the News: Faith and Journalism in American Public Discourse*. Thousand Oaks, Calif.: Sage, 1998. Media treatment of religion is an indicator of the broader role and status of religion in contemporary public discourse.

Kerr, Peter A. "The Framing of Fundamentalist Christians: Network Television News, 1980–2000." *Journal of Media and Religion* 2:4 (2003): 203–235. Fundamentalists who maintain that the broadcast media are unduly biased must look elsewhere for substantiation, for the networks have done a fair job of reporting objectively.

Kerr, Peter A., and P. Moy. "Newspaper Coverage of Fundamentalist Christians, 1980–2000." *Journalism and Mass Communications Quarterly* 79:1 (2002): 54–72. Fundamentalist Christians are incorrect in their accusations that newspapers are biased against them.

Olasky, Marvin. *Prodigal Press: The Anti-Christian Bias of American News Media*. Wheaton, Ill.: Crossway Books, 1998. Olasky, a conservative columnist, argues that a secular humanist outlook replaced a God-centered one in the nineteenth century, causing today's media to exhibit an anti–Christian bias.

Silk, Mark. *Unsecular Media*. Chicago: University of Illinois Press, 1995. News coverage in America is an expression of values that stem from religious traditions; thus the American media present religion from a religious rather than a secular point of view.

Underwood, Doug. *From Yahweh to Yahoo: The Religious Roots of the Secular Press*. Chicago: University of Illinois Press, 2002. Journalists not only value religion but approach their professional responsibilities with Judeo-Christian values.

Zempel, Ryan. "Liberal Media Bias, part II." Townhall.com, December 15, 2003, www.townhall.com/columnists/GuestColumns/Zempel20031215.shtml. Zempel interviews Bernard Goldberg, who states that there is media bias in relation to religious issues because journalists are not religious people and religion is one of the major institutions in America; yet few major networks have religious correspondents.

NOTES

1. Ahmad Shafaat, "Western Media's Bias: We Are Not Helpless Against It," http://www.themodernreligion.com/assault/media-bias.html

2. Wes Vernon, "CBS's Goldberg Exposes Leftist Media Bias," http://www.newsmax.com/archives/articles/2001/12/3/215106.shtml

3. John Dart and Jimmy Allen, *Bridging the Gap: Religion and the News Media* (Nashville, Tenn.: First Amendment Center, 2000).

4. Ryan Zempel, "Liberal Media Bias, part II," Townhall.com, December 15, 2003, www.townhall.com/columnists/GuestColumns/Zempel2003215.shtml.

5. John Dart, "Downs and Ups for TV Religious News," *Christian Century,* June 20, 2001.

6. Bruce Bartlett, "The GOP's Secret Weapon... Yes, It's the 'New York Times,'" *The Weekly Standard*, November 25, 2002.

7. Robert Lichter, Stanley Rothman, and Linda Lichter, *The Media Elite* (Bethesda, Md.: Adler & Adler, 1986).

8. Stewart M. Hoover, *Religion in the News: Faith and Journalism in American Public Discourse* (Thousand Oaks, California: Sage Publications Inc., 1998).

9. Marvin Olasky, *Prodigal Press: The Anti-Christian Bias of the American News Media* (Westchester, Ill.: Crossway Books, 1998).

10. Marvin Olasky, "Bias Is Back," *World Magazine*, August 17, 2002.

11. Lichter, et al., *The Media Elite* , 294–295.

12. Eric Alterman, *What Liberal Media? The Truth About Bias in the News* (New York: Basic Books, 2003), 104.

13. Peter A. Kerr, "The Framing of Fundamental Christians: Network Television News, 1980–2000," *Journal of Media and Religion* 2 (4, 2003): 209.

14. Dart and Allen, *Bridging the Gap...*, 19.

15. Ibid., 45.

16. Ibid., 18.

17. Michael Paulson, "Crisis in the Church; Jesuit Journal Raps U.S. Media's Church Coverage," *Boston Globe*, 31 May 2002, A1.

18. Dart and Allen, *Bridging the Gap...*, ii.

19. John Hafner, "Reviving Religion Coverage," *University of Montana Journalism Review* 31 (2002).

20. Dart and Allen, *Bridging the Gap...*, 53.

21. Ibid., 54.

22. John Seigenthaler in the Introduction to Dart and Allen, *Bridging the Gap...*, I.

23. Judith Buddenbaum, "The Religion Beat at Daily Newspapers," *Newspaper Research Journal* 9 (Summer 1988): 57–70.

24. Ernest C. Hynds, "Large Daily Newspapers Have Improved Coverage of Religion," *Journalism Quarterly* 64 (Summer/Autumn 1987): 44–48.

25. David H. Weaver and G. Cleveland Wilhoit, *The American Journalists: A Portrait of U.S. News People and Their Work* (Indianapolis: University of Indiana University Press, 1991).

26. Dart and Allen, *Bridging the Gap*, Update 2000, i and 6.

27. Doug Underwood, *From Yahweh to Yahoo!* (Chicago: University of Illinois Press, 2002), 133–135.

28. Mark Silk, *Unsecular Media: Making News of Religion in America* (Chicago: University of Illinois Press, 1995), 55 and xii.

29. Underwood, *From Yahweh to Yahoo!*, 256–258.

30. Jeff Cohen, "Media Coverage of Religion: An Overview, "Fair.org, December 1999, http://www.fair.org/articles/media-religion.html.

31. Dart and Allen, *Bridging the Gap...*, 19–20.

32. Peter Kerr, "Newspaper Coverage of Fundamentalist Christians, 1980–2000," *Journalism and Mass Communication Quarterly* 79 (1, 2002): 54–72.

33. Kerr, "The Framing of Fundamentalist Christians...," 230.

34. Peter Hart, "Q: Are the media guilty of anti–Catholic bias in covering the church sex scandals?; NO: The media have performed a service by exposing the crisis and pushing for reform," *Insight on the News*, 29 July 2002, 41.

35. Michael Paulson, "Crisis in the Church; Jesuit Journal Raps U.S. Media's Church Coverage," *Boston Globe*, 31 May 2002, A1.

36. Hoover, *Religion in the News...*, 60–61.

37. John Dart, "Covering Conventional and Unconventional Religion: A Reporter's View," *Review of Religious Research* 39 (2, December 1997), 150–151.

5

Abortion

Stephen E. Stewart

*"National news outlets have occasionally shown themselves willing to deal
with the painful reality of abortion for women and the tragedy of unwanted
children — but usually only when discussing abortion policies of foreign governments.... The Los Angeles Times devoted 28 column inches to exploring the
question, 'Can Woman Reporters Write Objectively on Abortion?'—without
pondering whether male reporters can."—Tiffany Devitt, Fairness and Accuracy
in Reporting*[1]

*"The news media hit a new low in bias against the Pro-Life Movement with
its lopsided coverage of the murder of Florida abortionist David Gunn. The ...
coverage, particularly by the broadcast media, has been appalling, twisting the
truth of the pro-life message beyond recognition. The truth is, to be pro-life is to
be anti-violence.... But for the media, that truth doesn't fit their fiction of what
'pro-life' means. So they ignore it."— Nancy Myers, National Right to Life News*[2]

Journalists have marched in pro-choice rallies. Publications have introduced abortion graphics that emphasize the woman, rather than the fetus. The situation has given
media critics enough ammunition to allege that the media have a pro-choice bias. On
the other hand, journalistic values often determine what stories are written and which
quotes are published. Perhaps abortion coverage is based solely on journalistic traditions
rather than an inherent bias.

People with opposing opinions on whether abortion should be legal cannot even agree
on what to call each other. Are the proponents of legality "pro-abortion"? Many of them,
perhaps most, would say not. They prefer to be called "pro-choice," emphasizing a woman's
right to choose whether to give birth or terminate a pregnancy. Those who oppose legal abortion like to call themselves "pro-life," emphasizing their belief that the unborn child is a person and abortion is murder. But to call these people "pro-life" implies that those on the other
side are against life — an assertion they would hotly dispute. Any effort to avoid bias on abor-

tion — or to assess the media's fairness, as in this chapter — must heed the advice of linguistics professor George Lakoff. He told National Public Radio in 2004 that "you have to be able to create a discourse in which you talk about the way things are framed and why that matters."[3] In exploring the issue of abortion bias, then, one must decide what words to use. Ultimately — not unlike a reporter making an honest effort to deliver a neutral story — the writer must make a choice, knowing that some people will see bias in that choice. The decision here is to use "pro-choice" and "anti-abortion." "Pro-choice" does not judge the morality of abortion; "anti-abortion" does not say whether an abortion destroys a human life.

The apparent abortion bias of the media has shifted through history. In *The Press and Abortion, 1938–1988*, Marvin Olasky said that newspapers' nineteenth-century abortion coverage emphasized horrors of abortion, but the press avoided hard-hitting exposés. In the early twentieth century, doctors successfully pressured newspapers to refuse abortion advertising, but news coverage focused on the notion that legalizing abortion would best address corruption. "As pro-abortion public relations emerged, reporting of abortion became neutral and a new set of cozy relationships developed. Newspapers from mid-century on both set a pro-abortion agenda and were used by those setting agendas."[4]

Pro-Choice Bias

After legalizing most abortions with *Roe* v. *Wade* in 1973, the Supreme Court gave states more power to regulate abortions in *Webster* v. *Reproductive Health Services* (1989). By mid-1990, the fairness of abortion news coverage was controversial enough to spawn a four-part series of daily articles in the *Los Angeles Times* by media critic David Shaw.

Shaw wrote that "a persuasive case can be made that abortion opponents received more favorable coverage than did abortion advocates, at least on television," between *Roe* and the months immediately preceding *Webster*. Abortion was legal and not under imminent threat during that period, Shaw wrote; so the abortion-rights movement was dormant while the other side was active. But things changed after *Webster*.[5]

Shaw's one-column headline on the July 1 front page said, "Bias Seeps into News on Abortion." His article described the *Times*' comprehensive study of major newspaper, television, and newsmagazine coverage during the previous eighteen months. More than 100 interviews were conducted with journalists and activists on both sides of the abortion debate. The results, Shaw said, confirmed that pro-choice bias often exists. He acknowledged that responsible journalists try to be fair and that many accusations of bias are not valid. But in examining stories, Shaw had found "scores of examples, large and small, that can only be characterized as unfair to the opponents of abortion, either in content, tone, choice of language, or prominence of play." He summarized his findings with these points:

• The news media consistently use language and images that frame the abortion debate in terms that implicitly favor abortion-rights advocates.

• Abortion-rights advocates are often quoted more frequently and characterized more favorably than abortion opponents.

• Events and issues favorable to abortion opponents are sometimes ignored or given minimal attention.

• Many news organizations have given more prominent play to stories on rallies and electoral and legislative victories by abortion-rights advocates than to stories on rallies and electoral and legislative victories by abortion rights opponents.

• Columns of commentary favoring abortion rights outnumber those opposing abortion by a margin of more than 2 to 1 on the op-ed pages of most of the nation's major daily newspapers.

• Newspaper editorial writers and columnists alike, long sensitive to questions of First Amendment right violations and other civil liberties in cases involving minority and anti-war protests, have largely ignored these questions when Operation Rescue and other abortion opponents have raised them.

"[T]hroughout the media, print and broadcast alike, coverage of abortion tends to be presented — perhaps subconsciously — from the abortion-rights perspective," Shaw wrote. He said ABC News described *Webster* as "a major setback for abortion rights." He asked: "Couldn't it also have been called 'a major victory for abortion opponents'? Yes. But most reporters don't identify with abortion opponents."

In his third article, Shaw cited the *Washington Post*'s sparse coverage of a "Rally for Life" in Washington on Saturday, April 28, 1990, as "a classic case study" of Richard Harwood's observation a month earlier that the *Post*'s news coverage "has favored the 'pro-choice' side." Harwood was the *Post*'s ombudsman. The paper's rally coverage angered its own managing editor, Leonard Downie, who considered it inadequate. Shaw said *Post* reporters and editors "don't seem to have many friends or colleagues who oppose abortion." So they were not aware of the magnitude of the rally "even though various low-level people on the Metro desk had been alerted to it three times in the course of the week."[6]

Shaw's series is perhaps the most often-cited critique of media abortion coverage — cited by both anti-abortion and pro-choice writers. In his 2003 book *What Liberal Media? The Truth About Bias and the News*, self-described liberal Eric Alterman conceded that Shaw gave "dozens if not hundreds of examples that any fair-minded person who is not a partisan of one side or the other would have to agree are slanted in the direction of the side that favors legal abortions.... [T]he point ends up being undeniable."[7]

Shaw's work is almost sixteen years old. Has media bias changed since 1990? William McGowan's answer is no. In *Coloring the News: How Political Correctness Has Corrupted American Journalism* (2002), McGowan said Shaw's series had little lasting effect. "The dynamics Shaw described in 1990," McGowan said, "could still be seen at work in the controversy over the Partial Birth Abortion Ban Act of 1997, in which journalists who should have been trying to help the public sort through a complex and deeply felt issue struck poses and insulted those they deemed to be on the wrong side."

As if to show that the first and second criticisms on Shaw's bulleted list still apply, McGowan said that the *New York Times* lumped the Partial Birth Abortion Ban Act together with a dozen other efforts to roll back abortion rights, sponsored by Christian conservatives. A June 1995 *Times* story by Gerry Gray quoted no supporters of the legislation, McGowan wrote, but "allowed abortion rights activist Kate Michelman to say that the ban on third-trimester abortion was an effort to 'sensationalize' and distract from the real issue in the debate: 'who should decide' — women or the government?" In "the most egregious misrepresentation of the issue," McGowan said, CBS correspondent Ed Bradley quoted one doctor who called "partial birth abortion" a "propaganda term." Bradley parroted "the abortion lobby's insistence that partial birth abortion was largely reserved for cases of catastrophic fetal deformity."[8]

John Carroll, editor of the *Los Angeles Times*, lent credence to the enduring validity of Shaw's second point with a memo to subordinates on May 22, 2003. Carroll's memo, as quoted by Fox News commentator Bill O'Reilly, criticized liberal bias in a front-page story about Texas abortion legislation. The legislation required abortion doctors to tell patients that they might be risking breast cancer. Only in the last three paragraphs did the story quote a scientist who believed the abortion-cancer connection was valid, the editor's memo said, and the scientist was quoted on his political views, not his scientific ones. "Apparently, the scientific argument for the anti-abortion side is so absurd that we don't need to waste our readers' time with it."[9]

Jeb Byrne, in a 1995 article in *Commonweal*, found mainstream journalism's response to Shaw's series "disappointing." It should have received more media attention and should have been addressed by *Columbia Journalism Review* and *Washington Journalism Review*, he wrote. He also found it curious that the Pulitzer Prize jury awarded Shaw a Pulitzer but maneuvered to avoid basing it on the abortion series, which was part of the work for which the *Los Angeles Times* had nominated him. "There are indications," Byrne wrote, of improvements "here and there" in the media. "But the ideological pro-choice drumbeat remains detectable behind much of the reporting. In the commentary it is overpowering." He said the media covered the Supreme Court's *Rust* v. *Sullivan* decision (1991) as a free-speech issue because it dealt with restrictions on counseling in federally-funded family-planning clinics. This observation is consistent with Shaw's final bullet point that editorial writers and columnists are insensitive to the free-speech rights of abortion opponents, even if it does not directly confirm it.[10]

In 2002, John Leo wrote in *U.S. News & World Report* that Shaw's "apparently explosive report provoked no self-examination, no panel discussions.... Privately, lots of reporters and editors said it was true, and a few articles appeared. But in general, journalists reacted as if the Shaw report had never happened." Leo said that when he became a member of *Columbia Journalism Review*'s advisory board a year later, he pushed for *CJR* to examine Shaw's findings, but "[e]veryone was determined to look the other way." The reason? "Feminists in the newsroom would not stand for this issue to be aired."[11]

In a tribute to Shaw published on National Right to Life's Website after Shaw died in 2005 at age sixty-two, Dave Andrusko said he did not sense a sudden change in the journalistic paradigm as a result of the Shaw series, nor an end to sloppiness and arrogance.[12]

Some studies have supported Shaw's conclusion of media bias in favor of abortion rights.

Frederick Fico and Stan Soffin conducted a content-based study of eighteen public issues in eighteen newspapers during February 1991, published in 1995 in *Journalism & Mass Communication Quarterly*. They found abortion among the issues on which stories were most out of balance. "The reporting of various issues involving abortion tended from extremely one-sided to nearly balanced," they wrote. "... By and large, stories favored pro-choice sources by a wide margin, although 90 percent of the stories included statements from both sides."[13]

Seven years later, Tim Graham and Clay Waters presented an overview of five years of studies. They wrote a report for the Media Research Center — an organization that describes itself as "documenting, exposing and neutralizing liberal media bias."[14] The report, *"Roe* Warriors: The Media's Pro-Abortion Bias (Updated and Revised)," cited multiple studies and examples.[15] They concluded with a five-point summary (paraphrased here) of the media's abortion tilt:

• Abortion advocates are rarely labeled as liberal, while abortion opponents are often described as conservative. The former are described the way they prefer, as advocates of abortion rights, while abortion opponents are never described as "pro-life," their preferred term.

• In the 1996 elections, networks reported sixty television stories about Republicans fighting over abortion platform, but only one story about Democrats debating the same issue.

• Almost one-third of reporters' stories on "partial-birth abortion" contained inaccurate claims and statistics.

• Pro-lifers' annual March for Life on the anniversary of *Roe* v. *Wade* has been largely ignored on network newscasts, while liberal protests and marches draw more attention.

• Network newscasts presented more than 500 stories on violence against abortionists after the 1993 shooting of David Gunn, a doctor who performed abortions, while ignoring the violence of abortion and the violence and harassment committed by abortion advocates and abortionists.[16]

In their 2002 book *Shaping Abortion Discourse: Democracy and the Public Sphere in Germany and the United States*, Myra Marx Ferree, William Anthony Gamson, Jürgen Gerhards, and Dieter Rucht reported on their content analysis of articles about abortion. The *Los Angeles Times* and *New York Times* (as well as two German newspapers) published these articles between 1962 and 1994 (the study had some time gaps). A total of 5,770 U.S. articles were published, and 1,243 were sampled. The researchers classified 11,686 idea elements within these articles and found that 47.5 percent were framed in a pro-choice direction; 33.5 percent, anti-abortion; and 19 percent, neutral. Thus, a plurality was pro-choice, but a majority was either anti-abortion or neutral.[17]

Measuring the presence of speakers with opposing views in the same article, the scholars found that 58 percent of U.S. articles contained speakers with only one viewpoint. Within this 58 percent, almost twice as many had pro-choice speakers as anti-abortion speakers: 35 percent of the whole, versus 19 percent, with 4 percent taking a neutral viewpoint.[18]

Some believe that media bias results from journalists' own pro-choice opinions and the opinions of people they associate with, particularly other journalists. Shaw reported in 1990 that "most major newspapers support abortion rights on their editorial pages, and two major media studies have shown that 80 percent to 90 percent of U.S. journalists personally favor abortion rights." He added that some reporters took part in a pro-choice march in Washington in 1989, and the American Newspaper Guild, a journalists' union, had officially endorsed "freedom of choice in abortion decisions."[19]

The Pew Research Center for the People & the Press reported in 2004 that "news people — especially national journalists — are more liberal, and far less conservative, than the general public." Thirty-four percent of national journalists and 23 percent of local journalists described themselves as liberals in a Pew survey as compared with 19 percent of the public. "Just 7 percent of national news people and 12 percent of local journalists describe themselves as conservatives, compared with a third of all Americans." In a 2002 Pew Research Center survey, 58 percent of the public said belief in God is necessary to be a moral person, but 91 percent of national journalists and 78 percent of local journalists said it is not necessary.[20]

A Pew Research Center poll of 1,405 adults dated March 8–12, 2006, showed the public in the middle on abortion, although leaning toward choice. Fifty-eight percent opposed a national law that, like a proposed law in South Dakota in 2006, would ban abortion in all cases except to save the life of the mother; 34 percent favored such a law, and 8 percent were unsure. As to whether to make it more difficult for a woman to obtain an abortion, 56 percent opposed or strongly opposed this; 37 percent favored or strongly favored it; and 7 percent were unsure. An Associated Press-Ipsos poll of 1,001 adults conducted in 2006 found 51 percent saying abortion should be legal in most or all cases; 43 percent saying it should be illegal in most or all cases; and 6 percent unsure.[21]

"For most journalists," McGowan wrote in 2002, "opposition to abortion is not a civilized position, and this view gives them the right of way to caricature pro-lifers as religious zealots, while abortion rights activists, no matter how radical and inflexible, are described with respect, and in many cases with adulation."[22] Stephen Hess, senior fellow for governance studies at the Brookings Institution, commented during a Washington forum in 2004 that "when you look at issues like abortion or homosexuality, they [journalists] cover it or don't cover it because, of course, everybody they know has that position and it never enters their mind to do the same sort of balance that they are very scrupulous about doing when they're on a political story."[23]

Ferree and co-authors wrote about Flip Benham's exasperation with ABC News' coverage of the 1995 baptism of Norma McCorvey, who was Jane Roe in *Roe* v. *Wade*. Benham was with Operation Rescue, an anti-abortion group. He presided over the baptism and offered an exclusive story to ABC because ABC had Peggy Weymeyer, a born-again Christian, covering religion. She "knew what was going on," in Benham's opinion. However, her boss, Peter Jennings, saw the story as a political shift while Benham saw it as a change in a person's relation to God. Jennings "just doesn't have a clue. That is the media," Benham said.[24]

In a sidebar to his 1990 series, Shaw noted that abortion is a more personal issue for women reporters than for men and explored whether women can write objectively about it. "Most women reporters say they're able to do this," he wrote. "But many say they have to work harder to do so on abortion than on any other issue. Some fail." He cited a 1989 study by the Center for Media and Public Affairs; it found that "women reporters for five major news organizations quoted supporters of abortion rights twice as often as they quoted abortion opponents in their stories," in Shaw's words.[25]

In *Nieman Reports* (1998), Jan Collins described a content analysis of 224 print and broadcast news stories about abortion in 1991 and 1992. The Center for Media and Public Affairs conducted the analysis. It showed that in stories reported by men, most opinions quoted were anti-abortion, while in stories reported by women, most opinions were pro-choice.[26]

A dozen years after that study, Myrna Blyth was of the opinion that elite women journalists exhibited pro-abortion bias. In her 2004 book *Spin Sisters: How the Women of the Media Sell Unhappiness — and Liberalism — to the Women of America*, she said abortion was "the binding pledge of their sorority. The issue on which there can never be any equivocation or discussion." Politicians cannot keep the Spin Sisters' support if they stray from the Planned Parenthood position, Blyth wrote, nor can fellow writers.[27]

No Pro-Choice Bias

The most prominent argument tending to refute the alleged pro-choice bias of the news media is the assertion that journalists try to be fair. Another rebuttal — but a rare one — is that the media are biased in the other direction, or at least that they will give prominent coverage to anti-abortion opinions and facts that put abortion in a bad light. Other writers, while conceding that news coverage may be slanted, attribute it to reasons other than ideological bias — usually the dynamics and news values that shape reporting. Finally, there is an argument that although the American media might not achieve the elusive standard of fairness, while striving for it they allow diverse and dissenting voices to be heard — more so, at least, than in Germany, which was the other country in a comparative study.

One might accuse David Shaw, the *Los Angeles Times* reporter whose landmark 1990 series alleged pro-choice bias and documented it, of promoting his own anti-abortion agenda. That assumption would be wrong, according to his friend Russ Parsons. On August 2, 2005, the day after Shaw's death, Parsons published a tribute that said Shaw was personally pro-choice. "As a journalist, that he wrote the series the way he did is what impresses me the most. And that was pure Shaw — searching and intellectually honest no matter whose ox might be gored."[28]

Shaw wrote, "Reasonable critics of the media generally concede that most journalists try to be fair" and that they are usually successful in putting personal biases aside.[29] He noted that journalists specializing in abortion had done work that was "both fair and comprehensive." He quoted Nancy Myers, communications director for the National Right to Life Committee, as saying that reporters who frequently cover abortion come to know more about its subtleties and complexities and the sincerity of the people involved, which results in fairer coverage. Some newspapers without abortion beat reporters won praise for specific stories, Shaw said.[30] He also found abortion coverage, in general, becoming more fair: "Activists on both sides say media coverage has generally improved of late, but they still think critical issues go largely uncovered. Many reporters agree."

Shaw's series inspired self-examination among fair-minded journalists, according to William Powers' comments published in *National Journal* three days before Shaw died. The series provided one of journalism's occasional "moment[s] of blinding clarity about itself," Powers wrote. The series "dramatically shifted the paradigm of abortion coverage, overnight," as he told it. "For American journalism, it was a giant head slap, as in: My God, he's right. And the series quietly resonates today. Mainstream coverage of abortion is far more careful and fair. The sloppiness and unconscious arrogance Shaw found to be so common in 1990 are now uncommon."[31]

Powers did not cite any evidence to support his assertion, though he did quote Karen

Tumulty, *Time* magazine's national political correspondent, who was covering abortion for the *Los Angeles Times* when it published the Shaw series. "David forced everyone to do basic journalism again," she said, "and the first thing you do in basic journalism is check your preconceptions at the door."

As noted earlier, Andrusko's article for National Right to Life was skeptical that Shaw had changed the journalistic paradigm or ended sloppiness and arrogance. But Andrusko admitted: "Yet it would be not only ungenerous but also inaccurate to believe that Shaw's exhaustive examination did not help to level the playing field. How could it not? ... What is unquestionably different is that the average pro-lifer now has many more outlets in which to speak his or her mind, on the one hand, and that there are many, many journalists and commentators who are pro-life, on the other hand."[32]

Andrusko's comments relate to the contrast that Ferree and co-authors drew in 2002 between Germany and the United States. The Ferree group, as noted earlier, had found framing and the selection of speakers in U.S. media more sympathetic to the pro-choice position than the abortion opposition. By contrast, in Germany they found a plurality (45.7 percent) of stories framed in the anti-abortion direction and anti-abortion speakers quoted more often than pro-choice.[33] However, they gave U.S. journalists credit for a climate more conducive to fairness than in Germany. They observed that "the theme of fairness, balance, and freedom from bias" is "prominent in the metatalk of American journalists." U.S. media, they wrote, allow more noninstitutional, dissenting voices to be heard. They offer "popular inclusion, empowerment, and the avoidance of premature closure." U.S. journalists are much more sensitive than their German colleagues to accusations of unfairness. This creates "greater opportunities for the voices of grass-roots actors to be heard, notwithstanding the advocates' own sense of being shut out or misrepresented." The United States fits with the concept of "popular inclusion," while "elite dominance" is a better fit for Germany, they said. U.S. journalists pursue "a content-based standard of fairness," quoting people from both sides, "hoping to find fairness procedurally via the clash of their opposing arguments.... American journalists, then, are doomed to an endless quest for the holy grail of a frame-free standard of fairness that is unattainable." By contrast, in Germany the political parties are more clearly identified with anti-abortion and pro-choice positions, and the media's goal is proportionality, "the allocation of space to reflect the share of party seats in the legislature and role in government." In Germany, therefore, people do not talk about media fairness on abortion, and "the consequence of journalistic practice for the exclusion of less institutionalized, grass-roots actors goes unnoticed." Also, in United States media coverage, "[g]overnment decisions do not force an artificial end to efforts by mobilized citizen groups to achieve policies that they consider better." Narratives illuminate the personal consequences of decisions.[34]

Tiffany Devitt, writing in 1992 for Fairness & Accuracy In Reporting, remarked on a television graphic that emphasized the fetus rather than the woman. This may have been evidence that television journalists changed their behavior because of Shaw. Shaw had written that when the networks broadcast an abortion story, they often used the word "abortion" as a backdrop with the first "O" stylized into the biological symbol for female. "The networks could just as easily stylize the 'O' to represent a womb, with a drawing of a fetus inside. But they don't," Shaw said.[35] About two years later, Devitt said TV was using a graphic that consisted of "a late-term fetus hanging in space, with no connection to a pregnant woman." She saw this as consistent with the media's tendency to "push women out of the public's mental picture of the abortion issue."[36]

Eric Alterman wrote in 2004 that Shaw had a "profound influence" on coverage of abortion: "Shaw won a Pulitzer Prize. His findings were accepted and editors, reporters, and producers alike did their best to implement changes in their coverage. Today journalists are constantly on alert for bias in the pro-choice direction." Alterman said that abortion clinics had trouble interesting the media in anthrax threats and attacks that they were receiving in 2001, and by 2002, "it was possible ... to wonder if the balance on abortion coverage had not tipped entirely in the opposite direction." As an example of such a possible tilt, he noted that in 2002 the *Washington Post* endorsed a nominee for a federal judgeship whom Senate Democrats considered conservative on abortion.[37]

In 2002 McGowan, who is generally of the opinion that the media are pro-choice, used Ruth Padawar as a rare example of a journalist who employed "old-fashioned legwork and basic mathematics" to set the facts straight about partial-birth abortion (as abortion opponents call it). It was "too little, too late," he wrote, but fourteen months into the story, this reporter at the *Bergen* (N.J.) *Record* actually called doctors in her state who performed the procedure. She calculated that, contrary to pro-choice activists' claims that no more than 500 partial-birth abortions were performed nationally in any year, more than 1,500 took place in New Jersey alone. Her findings also refuted claims that almost all of these procedures are done only in cases where the woman's life is in danger or the fetus is extremely abnormal; only a minuscule number had been performed for medical reasons, as McGowan told it. He said *Washington Post* medical reporter David Brown echoed these findings on a national scale in a story titled "Late Term Abortions: Who Gets Them and Why." McGowan said Brown also refuted the fallacy that the fetus felt no pain, quoting researchers to the contrary.[38]

Another critic who gave the media credit for setting aside their own opinions and providing fair coverage occasionally, if not all the time, is Blyth (2004). She commended *Marie Claire* magazine for balanced reporting that included "personal stories from a variety of women with different views." Yet *Marie Claire* made clear in an editorial that its own position was pro-choice, and it invited readers to sign a pro-choice petition on its Website.[39]

The third story in Shaw's series, while finding fault with the *Washington Post*'s coverage of the 1990 Rally for Life, cited a half-dozen examples of media that gave the rally prominent coverage and said there were others. The ABC, CBS, and NBC evening news programs made the rally their lead story, Shaw said, and it was atop page one in the *New York Times*, *Los Angeles Times*, *Boston Globe*, and "several other major papers."[40]

One of the few published comments alleging anti-abortion bias in the media concerned coverage of another rally, on the opposite side of the issue, fourteen years later. The March for Women's Lives on April 25, 2004, was perhaps the largest protest in the history of Washington, D.C., with as many as 1.15 million participating, according to Julie Hollar. The march supported women's reproductive rights. But she commented later that year in an article for Fairness & Accuracy In Reporting that "media muted those voices by downplaying the size and significance of the event, and largely ignoring the issues that marchers attempted to bring back into the public discourse." FAIR conducted a Nexis search comparing this march with the Promise Keepers' Washington march in 1997. Promise Keepers, described by Hollar as "an evangelical men's organization with an anti-feminist and anti-gay theology," drew fewer demonstrators — 750,000 at most — but received far more coverage.[41]

Shaw had found that op-ed commentaries were predominantly pro-choice. But Garance Franke-Ruta, in a March 2006 article in the online edition of *The American Prospect*, reported that in the two years prior, "not one op-ed discussing abortion on the op-ed page of the most powerful liberal paper in the nation was written by a reproductive-rights advocate, a pro-choice service-provider, or a representative of a women's group." He was speaking of the *New York Times*, which reminded him of poet Robert Frost's quip that a liberal is a man too broad-minded to take his own side in a quarrel. Eighty-three percent of the *Times*' 124 op-ed pieces that mentioned abortion during that time were written by men, Franke-Ruta said. The writers were mostly "pro-life or abortion-ambivalent men, male scholars of the right, and men with strong, usually Catholic, religious affiliations." By contrast, in 1991–1992, out of 129 op-ed mentions of abortion, forty-six (36 percent) were written by women.

Ferree and co-authors quoted Kim Gandy of the National Organization for Women as saying that while beat reporters tend to support abortion rights and women's rights, the owners and managers of newspapers, television stations and networks have "a very strong bias against women's rights.... They tend to be certainly anti-feminist if not anti-women." Rosemary Candelario of the Reproductive Rights National Network told these authors that she saw a bias toward not the pro-life side but "the mainstream approach." Leaders of advocacy groups on both sides expressed their frustration with the media, saying they had to use other means to get their messages out.[42]

In her 1992 article, Devitt complained that the media often report on the politics of abortion without consulting or quoting the people most affected by it — women. If so, the media are showing a bias against the concept that the most important consideration in an abortion is the woman's right to choose. (Abortion opponents might ask why a woman's point of view is more important than the interests of the unborn child.)

As for dynamics and news values that shape reporting, Shaw wrote that "journalists say they interview the people they find the most relevant, articulate, available, and outspoken on a given story." He quoted L. Brent Bozell, III, chairman of the conservative Media Research Center. Bozell said he did not think that the media were representing pro-abortion bias when they used anti-abortion sources whom readers might see as extremists. "'It has nothing to do with agenda,' he [Bozell] says. 'I think it has everything to do with ... journalism. The raunchier the quote, the better it is; the more fire and brimstone, the better the story comes out.'"[43] Elsewhere, Shaw wrote: "[T]he threat of sudden, drastic change on an emotionally volatile issue always makes a good story. It gets reportorial adrenaline flowing. It gets television ratings. It sells newspapers and magazines. That may help explain why abortion clinic blockades by Operation Rescue and shrill pronouncements by leaders on both sides are given heavier coverage than, say, new medical developments."[44]

Shaw also said that editors of papers where he found imbalanced reporting on anti-abortion rallies "insist that it was not bias but inattention or poor news judgment under deadline pressure that explains their coverage."[45]

In her 1997 master's thesis at the University of Alabama, Laurie Ann Lattimore offered two reasons other than bias for the variations in network news coverage of controversial issues. She said the media concentrate on governmental events where journalists "are comfortable with the level of conflict and have easier access to all viewpoints." To a lesser degree, she said, "aberrational events" attract the media, "but they devote most of their coverage to proponents for whose side obvious progress was made." Her random sample of 105 abortion stories on network nightly news programs from 1988 had shown that "television's attention to a position on a controversial issue goes through cycles," although she had found "a generally pro-abortion view in the news media."[46]

In a 2003 *Columbia Journalism Review* article titled "Re-thinking Objectivity," Brent Cunningham showed how a pro-choice journalist can be influenced to write stories that help the other side. He was a statehouse reporter for the *Charleston Daily Mail* in West Virginia in the early 1990s. Year after year, bills restricting access to abortion were sent by a pro-choice House speaker to the health committee, chaired by a woman who was also pro-choice. Most committee members were pro-choice, too, and the bills always died. The legislative process never had the chance to run its course. This is how reporter Cunningham reacted: "Once I understood, I eagerly wrote that story, not only because I knew it would get me on page one, but also because such political maneuverings offended my reporter's sense of fairness. The bias, ultimately, was toward the story.... Reporters are biased toward conflict because it is more interesting than stories without conflict; we are biased toward sticking with the pack because it is safe; we are biased toward event-driven coverage because it is easier; we are biased toward existing narratives because they are safe and easy. Mostly, though, we are biased in favor of getting the story, regardless of whose ox is being gored."[47]

• THE EVIDENCE •

Most people believe the media are biased in favor of choice, but there is not enough empirical evidence to prove it.

The most impressive effort to make a fair and factual evaluation of the media's abortion coverage was Shaw's 1990 four-part series in the *Los Angeles Times*. The *Times* did what it described as an eighteen-month "comprehensive" study of newspapers, television, and newsmagazines, including more than 100 interviews. Shaw quoted numerous knowledgeable and authoritative sources of both facts and opinions. But his was not an academic study. The *Times* provided no charts or sidebars giving quantitative or qualitative details beyond what was in the text of Shaw's stories. He had plenty of anecdotal material but not much evidence of quantitative analysis. And, of course, his study is sixteen years old. The recent report that Shaw was pro-choice enhances the credibility of his findings and also shows that he knew what it means to put personal bias aside. But, ironically, the facts that he wrote the series and that the *Times* published it also enhance one's faith that the news media do achieve fairness on occasion — which weakens the general applicability of Shaw's conclusions.

The most impressive scholarship comes from Ferree and her team of American and German researchers who looked at abortion discourse in both countries. They developed what they called "an unusually complicated data set, using multiple methods, including content analysis of newspapers and organizational documents, a survey of organizations, and intensive interviews." Details in their book show that this description is accurate. This is valuable research as far as it goes, and it supports the idea of a modest pro-choice bias in the media while giving the media credit for trying to be accessible and fair. However, media fairness was not the focus of the study, and the content analysis ended in 1994.

Graham and Waters' report cites or alludes to about a dozen studies and one Nexis search. But these are of less usefulness because they come from an organization with admittedly anti-liberal bias and because supporting details are not provided so that the conclusions and methodology can be evaluated.

Other writers cited a limited amount of empirical evidence. Fico and Soffin's study provided some data regarding eighteen newspapers published during a single month of 1991. Collins cited a 1998 content analysis. Alterman's assertions were rhetorically skillful but short on evidence. Franke-Ruta's study of *New York Times* op-ed pages was data-driven but limited to one publication and a two-year span. Lattimore performed a six-year content analysis of network nightly news.

We do not have a rigorous, thorough, recent study of the bias or fairness in the news media's abortion coverage. What we need is someone who will make the effort Shaw did to evaluate overall abortion coverage, using research methods that provide a sound basis for generalizations.

Most knowledgeable people say the media have had a pro-abortion tilt in recent years, but when under criticism or in a self-analytical mood, the media tend to try harder to be fair. The Pew survey and other evidence show that journalists are more liberal on social issues than the public is. This evidence, though, contains few specific mentions of abortion. Nonetheless, it is reasonable to infer that journalists are predisposed to favor choice and that their interaction with fellow journalists reinforces this mind-set.

• RESOLUTION •

What can be done to make abortion coverage fairer? Journalists must seek Ferree's elusive holy grail of fairness, and partisans on all sides must keep the pressure on by demanding to have their points represented in stories and complaining publicly when they aren't. In recent years, the Internet has made it easier to bring journalists' bias or oversights to public attention.

From a conservative perspective, Graham and Waters offered the following four "recommendations for future fairness":

1. Portray the abortion debate as something with two equally ideological, passionate, or "extreme" sides....

2. Report on the abortion debates going on within both political parties....

3. Apply investigative journalism to the abortion debate and the abortion industry....

4. Try to cover pro-life storylines as well as pro-abortion storylines.[48]

These are good suggestions, though the second one seems designed more to put the Republican Party in a positive light than to promote fair abortion coverage, and the third one must be applied equally to both sides and not used only to expose abuses by abortion providers. Also, any portrayals should reflect facts, not spin.

Collins advocated covering abortion according to a "humanity" principle: "How is this particular story affecting people?" She added: "In the case of abortion, I hope that journalists remember to include the woman — the living, breathing woman who is at the heart of every agonizing decision to terminate a pregnancy."[49] This "humanity" principle is good if expanded to include the interests of the unborn child and other humans affected by every abortion decision.

Both the public and journalists seem to lean toward the pro-choice position — journalists more so than the public. But abortion is not simply a matter of public opinion. It has political, medical, moral, social, personal, legal, religious, and sexual dimensions, to name a few. As reporter Eileen McNamara of the *Boston Globe* told Shaw, "At base, abortion isn't about politics, and it isn't about the law. It's about philosophy and it's about morality and it's about your world view, and newspapers are ill-equipped to deal with those issues."[50] However ill-equipped they may be, journalists should make an honest effort to cover all of the complexities fairly and to enlighten societal and personal decision-making.

• POINTS OF VIEW •

Alterman, Eric. *What Liberal Media? The Truth about Bias and the News.* New York: Basic Books, 2004. Journalists' reaction to David Shaw's 1990 *Los Angeles Times* series shows that they make an effort to be fair in covering abortion.

Blyth, Myrna. *Spin Sisters: How the Women of the Media Sell Unhappiness — and Liberalism — to the Women of America.* New York: St. Martin's Press, 2004. Members of the female media elite believe that reproductive rights — abortion — is the issue that all women must care and agree about, and they spin their content accordingly, biasing it in favor of abortion.

Cunningham, Brent. "Re-thinking Objectivity." *Columbia Journalism Review* (2003). www.cjr.org/issues/2003/4/objective-cunningham.asp. When the author was covering the West Virginia legislature, he reported how pro-choice legislators were thwarting anti-abortion legislation — not because of any bias he had for or against abortion, but "because such political maneuverings offended my reporter's sense of fairness."

Fico, Frederick, and Stan Soffin. "Fairness and Balance of Selected Newspaper Coverage of Controversial National, State, and Local Issues." *Journalism & Mass Communication Quarterly* 72 (1995): 621–633. Content-based study of 259 stories on eighteen issues in eighteen newspapers during February 1991 found abortion to be one of the issues where stories were most imbalanced — in favor of abortion.

Graham, Tim, and Clay Waters. "*Roe* Warriors: The Media's Pro-Abortion Bias (Updated and Revised)." Media Research Center report, 1998. secure.mediaresearch.org/specialreports/news/sr19980722.html. Five years of studies showed that the media tilt abortion coverage in favor of choice in five ways.

Lattimore, Laurie Ann. "Rise to Prominence: News Media Attention to Issues of Controversy." Master's thesis. Tuscaloosa: University of Alabama, 1997. This study offers explanations other than bias for variances in network television coverage of abortion — specifically, that most stories originate from institutions previously "legitimated" through media coverage and that the media tend to cover stories involving conflict.

Leo, John. "With Bias Toward All." *U.S. News & World Report*, 18 March 2002, 8. Privately, many reporters and editors said David Shaw's four-part series finding bias in press coverage of abortion was true, but they largely ignored it.

McGowan, William. *Coloring the News: How Political Correctness Has Corrupted American Journalism.* San Francisco: Encounter Books, 2002. The pro-choice biases identified by David Shaw still existed years after his 1990 series was published.

Olasky, Marvin N. *The Press and Abortion, 1838–1988.* Hillsdale, N.J.: Lawrence Erlbaum Associates, 1988. Nineteenth-century press coverage fueled anti-abortion campaigns, but by the latter half of the twentieth century, newspapers were setting a pro-abortion agenda.

Powers, William. "Look Back in Wonder." *National Journal*, 30 July 2005, 2474–2477. David Shaw's 1990 *Los Angeles Times* series made a difference: mainstream coverage of abortion is now far more careful and fair, with less sloppiness and less unconscious arrogance.

Shaw, David. "Abortion Bias Seeps into News." *Los Angeles Times*, 1 July 1990, A1. An eighteen-month study of newspapers, television, and newsmagazines found them unfair to opponents of abortion in such matters as language, framing, whom they quoted, selection of events to cover, and prominence given to stories. This was the first in a series of four daily front-page articles by Shaw, including "Abortion Foes Stereotyped, Some in the Media Believe," 2 July; "'Rally for Life' Coverage Evokes an Editor's Anger," 3 July; and "'Abortion Hype' Pervaded Media after *Webster* Case," 4 July.

NOTES

1. Tiffany Devitt, "Abortion Coverage Leaves Women out of the Picture," http://www.fair.org/index.php?page=1483.

2. Nancy Myers, "Hitting a New Low in Bias," http://www.gargaro.com/abortionbias.html.

3. "Term Paupers," National Public Radio "On the Media" transcript, www.onthemedia.org/transcripts/transcripts_121704_frame.html.

4. Marvin N. Olasky, *The Press and Abortion, 1838–1988* (Hillsdale, N.J.: Lawrence Erlbaum Associates, 1988), xii.

5. David Shaw, "Abortion Bias Seeps into News," *Los Angeles Times*, 1 July 1990, A1.

6. David Shaw, "'Rally for Life' Coverage Evokes an Editor's Anger," *Los Angeles Times*, 3 July 1990, A1.

7. Eric Alterman, *What Liberal Media? The Truth about Bias and the News* (New York: Basic Books, 2004), 108.

8. William McGowan, *Coloring the News: How Political Correctness Has Corrupted American Journalism* (San Francisco: Encounter Books, 2002), 124, 125.

9. Bill O'Reilly, "An Internal Memo from The L.A. Times...," Fox News report, 29 May 2003, www.foxnews.com/story/0,2933,88059,00.html.

10. Jeb Byrne, "The News Media and Abortion: Where Objectivity Fails," *Commonweal*, 25 October 1991, 602–604.

11. John Leo, "With Bias Toward All," *U.S. News & World Report*, 18 March 2002, 8.

12. Dave Andrusko, "David Shaw: RIP — Part Two," National Right to Life report dated 8 August 2005, www.nrlc.org/News_and_Views/August05/nv080805part2.html.

13. Frederick Fico and Stan Soffin, "Fairness and Balance of Selected Newspaper Coverage of Controversial National, State, and Local Issues," *Journalism & Mass Communication Quarterly* 72 (1995): 627.

14. Media Research Center home page, www.mrc.org.

15. Tim Graham and Clay Waters, "*Roe* Warriors: The Media's Pro-Abortion Bias (Updated and Revised)," 1998 Media Research Center report, secure.mediaresearch.org/specialreports/news/sr1998 0722.html.

16. Media Research Center's summary of Tim Graham and Clay Walters, "*Roe* Warriors: The Media's Pro-Abortion Bias (Updated and Revised)," secure.mediaresearch.org/specialreports/news/ ROE2.html.

17. Myra Marx Ferree, William Anthony Gamson, Jürgen Gerhards and Dieter Rucht, *Shaping Abortion Discourse: Democracy and the Public Sphere in Germany and the United States* (Cambridge: Cambridge University Press, 2002), 47, 111.

18. Ibid., 240.

19. Shaw, "Abortion Bias...."

20. "How Journalists See Journalists in 2004: Views on Profits, Performance and Politics," report by Pew Research Center for the People & the Press, people-press.org/reports/pdf/214.pdf.

21. "Abortion and Birth Control," PollingReport.com report, www.pollingreport.com/abortion. htm.

22. McGowan, *Coloring the News...*, 124.

23. "The Biennial Pew Media Survey: How News Habits Changed in 2004," transcript of a Brookings/Pew Research Center Forum held 8 June 2004, www.brookings.edu/comm/events/20040608.pdf.

24. Ferree et al., *Shaping Abortion Discourse...*, 277.

25. David Shaw, "Can Women Reporters Write Objectively on Abortion Issue?," *Los Angeles Times*, 3 July 1990, A23.

26. Jan Collins, "Covering Abortion from the 'Humanity Principle,'" *Nieman Reports* 52 (1998): 85–87.

27. Myrna Blyth, *Spin Sisters: How the Women of the Media Sell Unhappiness — and Liberalism — to the Women of America* (New York: St. Martin's Press, 2004), 273.

28. Russ Parsons, "Abortion Series Was Pure Shaw," Poynter Forums posting dated 2 August 2005, poynter.org/forum/view_post.asp?id=10031.

29. Shaw, "Abortion Bias...."

30. David Shaw, "'Abortion Hype' Pervaded Media after *Webster* Case," *Los Angeles Times*, 4 July 1990, A1.

31. William Powers, "Look Back in Wonder," *National Journal*, 30 July 2005, 2474–2477.

32. Andrusko, "David Shaw: RIP...."

33. Ibid., 240.

34. Ferree et al., *Shaping Abortion Discourse...*, 111, 240, 273, 282–283, 301, 253, and 254.

35. Shaw, "Abortion Bias...."

36. Tiffany Devitt, "Abortion Coverage Leaves Women Out of the Picture," 1992 Fairness & Accuracy In Reporting report, www.fair.org/index.php?page=1483.

37. Alterman, *What Liberal Media?...*, 108–109.

38. McGowan, *Coloring the News...*, 125–126.

39. Blyth, *Spin Sisters...*, 277, 279.

40. Shaw, "'Rally for Life'..."

41. Julie Hollar, "Muting the Women's March: Media Lose Focus When Women Protest in Washington," Fairness and Accuracy In Reporting report dated August 2004, www.fair.org/index.php?page= 1966.

42. Ferree et al., *Shaping Abortion Discourse...*, 278.

43. Shaw, "'Rally for Life'...."

44. Shaw, "'Abortion Hype'...."

45. Shaw, "'Rally for Life'...."

46. Laurie Ann Lattimore, "Rise to Prominence: News Media Attention to Issues of Controversy," Master's thesis, University of Alabama, 1997, 65, 63, 14.

47. Brent Cunningham, "Re-thinking Objectivity." 2003 *Columbia Journalism Review* article, www.cjr.org/issues/2003/4/objective-cunningham.asp.

48. Graham and Waters, "*Roe* Warriors...."

49. Collins, "Covering Abortion...."

50. Shaw, "'Abortion Hype'...."

6

Homosexuality

Dave Cassady

"Statements of this sort [from a story in the Boston Globe] leave no doubt about the presumed relationship between a gay orientation and sexual abuse of children: the argument explicitly presented is that gay priests are responsible for the sexual abuse scandal."— Glenda M. Russell and Nancy H. Kelly, Subtle Stereotyping[1]

"There's this assumption [by the media] that we're going in this 100 percent pro-gay direction and no one's going to stop it. The media is trying to establish a sense of inevitability, which causes anxiety in people.... Hollywood and Broadway have always attracted a homosexual element.... These folks are low on religious observance, highly educated, and they think that what they think is what all highly educated people think."—Tim Graham, Media Research Center[2]

Media coverage of homosexuality has changed drastically in the past twenty years. Prior to the 1980s the media generally treated homosexuality as an unacceptable behavior. They saw it as a matter of people choosing to indulge in perverted behavior.

That changed as gay activists mounted their own campaign similar to the women's and the civil rights movements. The mainstream media, which had a long history of supporting such efforts, began to cover the gay rights movement in the same way they had covered civil rights efforts. They focused on the positive and pro-active aspects of the groups and their efforts. They rarely sought to report information that would reflect negatively on the groups.

Today, the media no longer portray homosexuality as an illness, a reversible life choice, or a crime against nature. Mainstream publications, such as *Time* and *Newsweek*, no longer refer to it as abhorrent, criminal, depraved, deviant, or perverted.[3] They now frame it as biologically determined and influenced by genetics. Reproachful words have been replaced by gay, lesbian, homophile, and transgender.

As acceptance of homosexuality increased in both the media and society, so did the public debate about the media's treatment of it.

To the anti-gay forces, the media's so-called "objective coverage" was not unbiased reporting. They viewed it as prejudiced support because news outlets made no effort to seek out and report any "negative" aspects of homosexuality. Just as it had been impossible to successfully point out "negative characteristics" of the feminist movement or to try to single out any "negative" aspect of simply being black, it was difficult for the anti-gay groups to get the media to accept and publicize what they saw as the negative aspects of homosexuality.

So, the critics said, the media, in covering the activities of the pro-gay and lesbian groups, were in a sense supporting their efforts. It wasn't so much a matter of the media publishing or broadcasting positive stories that most frustrated the anti-gay forces as it was, in many cases, the media's not including negative images.

The AIDS epidemic of the 1980s provided a watershed moment that at once complicated and solidified the coverage. Originally identified in gay men and presented as a "gay disease," AIDS was a convenient subject for those opposed to homosexuality. It was, they argued, the obvious result of abhorrent conduct. But, as the disease spread to non-gay victims through blood transfusions and other means, anti-gay activists lost a strong avenue of attack. Any hope they had that the media would report AIDS as a significant evil melted in the shadow of the images of children and other "innocents" dying of the disease.

A sizable number of people still oppose homosexuality, and much of the opposition is found in the large conservative religious population. They believe that religious doctrine prohibits homosexuality. As with other "clearly defined" moral issues, they see positive coverage of homosexuality as biased. Even more so than issues like abortion (for which most anti-abortion groups allow some exceptions), those opposing homosexuality argue that there is no positive context for it. Therefore, there is no place for coverage that is positive or even that is not negative.

On the other hand, for those looking for societal acceptance of homosexuality, the media are dragging their feet, failing to provide forceful action in support of the movement as they have supported other oppressed minorities. For those who believe that homosexuality is acceptable, the media have remained tools for gay opponents, afraid to take stands that question traditional values and prejudices. The media, the critics argue, carry too much material that questions the homosexual lifestyle. The media would not, they argue, publish material similarly critical of such issues as civil rights; and thereby the media demonstrate that they treat homosexuals in a biased and negative manner.

The Media Are Pro-Homosexual

For generations, the vast majority of Americans viewed homosexuality as wrong, as a crime against nature. Until the latter part of the twentieth century, a person could successfully sue for defamation if wrongly identified in the media as being homosexual, and most states outlawed homosexual activity. Homosexuals in the military were discharged.

Since the 1980s, though, anti-homosexuality critics claim the media have gone in the opposite direction and today lend support to gay issues and lifestyles. They have pointed to such evidence as surveys that find that journalists think homosexuality is acceptable. For example, researchers Stanley Rothman and Amy Black reported in the spring 2001 issue of *The Public Interest* that their survey found that 73 percent of journalists agreed with the statement that "homosexuality is as acceptable a lifestyle as heterosexuality" (including 40 percent who agreed strongly).[4]

Critics point to two incidents that occurred in 1998 within a week of each other as examples of the biased coverage. In Wyoming a gay college student, Matthew Shepard, was beaten, robbed, and left to die in Laramie, ostensibly because he was gay. In Prairie Grove, Arkansas, a 13-year-old boy named Jesse Dirkhising was kidnapped, sexually tortured, and suffocated by tape placed over his mouth. His assailants were two openly homosexual men.

The contrasting coverage of the episodes drew harsh censure from anti-gay critics. Shepard became a martyr in most mainstream media, a representative of the anti-gay abuse that was allegedly rampant in the country. By playing the story the way they did, critics said, the media aided gay activists, who were pushing for the inclusion of sexual orientation in hate crimes laws locally and nationally.

Dirkhising's murder drew far less coverage. His abductors were homosexual, and his torture had been sexual in nature; but, according to the critics, the matter received minimal coverage for that very reason. Homosexuals could be seen as victims by the media but could not be presented as the perpetrators of serious crime — especially crime based on sexual orientation. Andrew Sullivan pointed out the disparity in the amount of coverage. A Lexis-Nexis search in August of 2005 showed 3,007 articles on Shepard in the month after his death and only forty-six about Dirkhising.[5]

In the conservative media, critics claimed that Shepard had been at least partially responsible for his fate, that he had a habit of cruising bars looking for sexual partners. They claimed the mainstream media (particularly *Newsweek*) were aware of this but made little effort to fully investigate or report the information. Tim Graham of the Media Research Center said the disparity in coverage was because "Nobody wants to say anything negative about homosexuals. Nobody wants to be seen on the wrong side of the issue."[6] Dorthea Cooke, also of the MRC, was even more critical. The coverage of the cases, she said, "illustrates how organizations have become mouthpieces for gay rights activists."[7]

Additionally, they charged, the media used the Shepard murder to further their own pro-gay agenda. By heavily covering the incident and promoting it as a hate crime based on sexual orientation, the mainstream media were simply promoting gay efforts to include sexual orientation in hate crime legislation, further legitimizing the gay lifestyle as something that needed to be protected.

Critics point to other examples of how media coverage of "news events" is simply a thinly veiled effort to push the gay agenda. For instance, when *Time's* Jonathan Gregg claimed that the reason the Shepard murder was covered was because it "touches on a host of complex and timely issues: intolerance, society's attitudes toward gays and the pressure to conform, the use of violence as a means of confronting one's demons" and that the reason "the Dirkhising story received so little play is because it offered no lessons" and because "Dirkhising's death gives us nothing except the depravity of two sick men," critics responded that Gregg was simply throwing up a facade to justify media bias. Reed Irvine and Cliff Kincaid of Accuracy in Media, for example, argued that the sadomasochistic violence of the Dirkhising murder did not simply reveal something about his two killers but instead was representative of a common aspect of homosexuality.[8]

Another recent significant issue involving homosexual overtones was the Catholic church's sexual abuse scandal involving priests and boys. The homosexual aspect of the scandal was rarely presented in the discussion of the issue. Mary Eberstadt claimed, "There is no outbreak of heterosexual child molestation in the American church, " and "this crisis involving minors — this ongoing institutional horror — is almost entirely about man-boy sex."[9]

Rather than shedding light on the homosexual nature of the abuse, John Corry argued, "the media decline to recognize this, and instead practice journalistic sleight of hand. Thus the scandal is never about predatory male homosexuals. The dominant culture protects them and the scandal is supposed to be about something else." Eberstadt argued that the media have directed the controversy away from shock over the homosexual molestation of boys to shock over the lack of responsibility on the part of the Catholic church in how the matter was handled.[10]

One the most contentious issues regarding homosexuality has been same-sex marriages. Opponents have used a number of ways to try to prevent gays and lesbians from marrying. States have attempted to pass laws defining marriage as one man, one woman; and, on the national level, a constitutional amendment defining marriage the same way received majority support in both the U.S. Senate and House of Representatives (although not the two-thirds vote necessary for approval).

Critics claim that, despite strong opposition to same-sex "marriage," much of the media coverage has been blatantly pro-gay marriage. Some states, and cities such as San Francisco and Portland, Oregon, have issued marriage licenses for gay couples and have held highly publicized marriage ceremonies that the media have covered. Critics argue that the tone of the coverage of the ceremonies is a thinly disguised support for them. The couples, male and female, have been shown as average looking, generally middle-aged and older, exchanging vows, smiling, and enjoying the congratulations of their friends and family. The extensive amount of coverage and the positive nature of it have critics calling for more balance, more coverage of the other side.

The Media Are Anti-Homosexual

Despite what critics call unbalanced coverage in favor of the gay movement, members of that movement have criticized the media for lack of action. Many times coverage is criticized as weak, not forceful enough. The pro-gay forces are looking for activism on the part of the media and bristle when the media present stories or editorials that are not actively supportive.

Chicago gay rights activist Richard Garcia, commenting on a murder investigation involving a gay victim, claimed, "Police did not take the murder seriously until community activists raised hell and got media attention. If there isn't any public attention to these things they aren't taken care of properly. Any minority community doesn't have the best relations with the police. Unless there's attention, nothing gets done." The *Chicago Sun-Times* quoted the comments in a sympathetic editorial. "Like it or not," it declared, "minority communities must rely on the media to help turn up the heat on issues that might otherwise be ignored."[11]

Some gay supporters, however, claim that the demand for media activism has, in fact, been detrimental to the gay rights effort. Much as racial minority reporters have long been expected to be "sensitive" to the "minority perspective" and female reporters have been expected to present "the women's angle," gay reporters are being expected to represent the "gay perspective." Some gay reporters have complained that they are pressured to be gay first and reporters second. Gay activists pressure them to cover stories from a sympathetic "gay perspective," and they say this prevents them from providing a diverse and complete discussion of the issues. This, they argue, hurts gay rights efforts because it allows critics to focus on the biases and omissions in the coverage. They question whether gay reporters are serving less as news people and more as apologists for radical homosexual groups.

As a result, the question the quality of the journalism involved, wondering if the effort to become more "gay friendly" in the newsroom and in the pages of the papers has led to coverage that is too positive or, as John Gallagher, a reporter for the gay-oriented newsmagazine *Advocate*, put it, "sort of spongy. I don't know if it's because newspapers don't want to offend their gay and lesbian readers — [but] you see it even in the gay press."[12]

Achy Obejas, a lesbian reporter in Chicago who worked in the gay press and now works for the *Chicago Tribune*, said ,"There is a sense among the [gay community] leadership that the gay and lesbian media was there to protect them and if you asked tough questions, you were an asshole traitor."[13] In a presentation at a convention of the National Lesbian and Gay Journalists Association (NLGJA), the panelists, all gay journalists, argued that the biggest effect of the tendency toward positive stories was to misinform both mainstream America and the gay community itself.

Mark Fitzgerald, writing in the professional journalism publication *Editor and Publisher*, agrees. "Most newspapers, especially metro dailies," he writes, "are striving to present themselves as 'gay friendly' both in their offices and their pages. As more news about gay people and organizations gets into the paper, however, some gay and lesbian journalists are beginning to question the quality of coverage. Put bluntly, they say, it's simply too positive."[14]

Others see any kind of negative coverage as something to avoid. Jeorfdan Legon, a gay reporter for the *San Jose* (Calif.) *Mercury*, pointed out that the press was not being critical of the gay community because of the past stigmatization and marginalization it had endured. "It brings back a very bitter taste to the gay community and can be perceived as gay bashing. There is a feeling the mainstream press owes us for marginalizing the community."[15] Such coverage was especially true of the AIDS epidemic, critics argue. In the beginning it was presented as a "gay" disease, evident mainly in the homosexual community. Many anti-gay forces pointed to the epidemic as an inevitable consequence of the gay lifestyle; and mainstream media, with little evidence being presented to show the full spectrum of AIDS victims, fed into the idea by simply not printing much information to counteract the idea.

But another gay reporter, Bettina Boxall of the *Los Angeles Times*, has a different perspective. "The organized gay community," she argues, "is not interested in news, it's interested in propaganda — particularly if you are a gay reporter."[16]

Many in the media see it differently. They believe access to newspapers and TV is an opportunity for activism. Leroy Aarons, founder of the NLGJA, which boasts 1,300 members, argues, "Many of us are out in our newsrooms fighting publicly and courageously in behalf of getting the true story, the accurate one, out to America."[17]

Similarly, because gay right issues are generally equated with other forms of social equality, civil rights, women's issues, and so forth, the media face pressure in a broader sense to be "socially responsible." Within the journalism profession, for example, rules have been established over how and when to deal with a person's sexual orientation just as they have been for addressing gender, race, and ethnicity. Kelly McBride of the Poynter Institute recommends that gays should be allowed to determine themselves whether their sexual orientation is relevant to a story and that coded phrases like "domestic partner" and references to two people as "a couple" be avoided.[18] But it is this type of seemingly oversensitive guidelines that has critics on both sides. Those who see the media as pro-gay argue that such an approach is another example of the media going out of their way to protect a specific group of people, while pro-gay critics of the media see it as unnecessary deferential treatment that sets gays apart when they shouldn't be.

• THE EVIDENCE •

Critics who say the media have a pro-gay bias have some justification for their complaints. It is not necessarily true that the media are pro-gay. The appearance of such bias is more an issue of avoidance. By using the justification that they are simply covering important, relevant events, the media are able to avoid becoming personally involved in the controversy. Pronouncements by respected journalistic organizations such as the Poynter Institute put coverage of gays in the same category as the efforts to make reporting of race and gender neutral. The development of a "stylebook addition" by the NLGJA further institutionalizes this practice.

Gregg's explanation of the massive difference in the coverage of the Shepard and Dirkhising cases is a prime example of the positioning of the coverage of gays as having broader social implications than the coverage of other types of events. The Shepard case offered "broader lessons." The Dirkhising case did not. Most of the criticism of Shepard was a strained effort to blame him for the attack. In the argument over Dirkhising, Irvine and Kincaid relied on unsupported allegations that violent sexual behavior was inherent in being homosexual. On the other hand, the statistics cited above by Andrew Sullivan showing the gross imbalance in the number of articles on the two cases gives fodder to the arguments of preferential treatment.

But those who criticize the coverage of gays in these contexts often try to skew the argument.

In the criticism of the Dirkhising coverage, Irvine and Kincaid try to make the point that Dirkhising was violently, sexually abused by two gay men, ignoring that media reports of sexually violent assaults on women by heterosexual males generally don't emphasize the criminals' sexuality.

Additionally, anti-gay critics have tried to take characteristics and behaviors (especially deviant sexual behaviors) and imply that only gays participate in such actions and that the mainstream media ignore them as such. But critics face a different kind of problem here. The detail they provide on their Websites and specialty publications are not something that mainstream media will print or broadcast to a wider audience.

Six years after the two men accused of murdering Shepard were convicted and sentenced, an ABC news program analyzed the incident. Carl Rerucha, the chief prosecutor in the case, said the emphasis the media placed on Shepard being the victim of a hate crime overshadowed the real facts of the case. Aaron McKinney, one of two men convicted of killing Shepard, said the motive for the crime was robbery and that Shepard was killed in a methamphetamine induced rage. Anti-gay critics point out that the "simple robbery" concept wasn't even considered in the reporting of the crime immediately after it happened. The media rarely, if ever, focused on that aspect of the case. It was universally presented simply as a matter of two homophobic young men killing an openly gay victim.

The question of finances definitely has some impact on the coverage of gays. In controversial issues such as the Catholic church abuse scandal, part of the media motivation may have been not to antagonize the largest religious denomination in the country. As Corry and Eberstadt correctly point out, despite the fact that virtually all of the sex abuse scandal involved male priests molesting young boys, the issue has never been presented as a homosexual issue. (By the same token, however, little mention is made of the fact that a significant portion of sexual predators and pedophiles are white heterosexual males.)

Anti-gay activists continue to attack the mainstream media for what they see as a cover-up of the "truth" about homosexuality. Faced, however, with a dominant journalistic attitude that isn't critical of homosexuality, they have found that their own difficulty in defining their "truth" about homosexuality beyond conservative religious philosophy has made it difficult for them to get their arguments into the media. That difficulty may, of course, provide evidence that their criticism is correct.

• Resolution •

Faced by significant potential audiences on both sides of the issue, the media look for creative ways to present the topic. Instead of addressing the morality of it head-on, they cover it by focusing on the public debate over issues such as same sex marriage, hate crimes legislation, and discrimination.

While public pressure has led the media to seek out and accept openly gay people in the newsrooms, this same pressure has hindered them from maintaining a critical and balanced approach. There, obviously, has been no push to hire or accept people with opposing viewpoints into the newsroom. And, with the pressure to be included, gay reporters have also felt pressured in the newsroom and in the community to provide positive, activist coverage of gay issues.

It is unlikely that the media will resume an approach that people would consider anti-gay. With an increasing acceptance of homosexuality in the general population and the inability of the anti-gay forces to find effective arguments against it, it is likely the media will continue to cover events, statements, and issues in a factual manner, offering little critical evaluation.

• Points of View •

Anderson. Peter B., Akram Fakhfakh, and Mary Alice Kondylis. "Attitudes Toward The Media's Portrayals of Gays and Lesbians." *Electronic Journal of Human Sexuality* 2

(July 1, 1999). www.ejhs.org. In an academic study that is generally favorable toward homosexuals, the authors conclude that, rather than media content specifically, "individual beliefs and values, specifically their [the audience's] level of religious beliefs, are the determining factor in their rating of the media's portrayal of homosexuality...." The authors ask whether "the extremely negative [media] portrayals of homosexuality in the past have helped suppress some homosexual behaviors in addition to open communication about homosexuality."

Bennett, Lisa "Fifty Years of Prejudice in the Media," *Gay and Lesbian Review Worldwide* 7:2 (Spring 2000): 30–34. An overview of the presentation of homosexuality in *Time* and *Newsweek* from 1947 to 1997 argues that the media were biased against homosexuals. The coverage has softened as homosexuality has become more acceptable in society.

Brennan, Phil. "Media Push Homosexuality as Part of P.C. Agenda," NewsMax.com, February 9, 2002. http://www.newsmax.com/archives/articles/2002/2/8/165348.shtml "The mainstream media is trying to force feed the homosexual agenda to the American people."

Curry, Erin. "Media Overlooks Possible Hate Crime Perpetrated by Homosexual in Chicago," in *BP News* (2002): n. pag. http://www/sbcbaptistpress.org/bpnews.asp?Id=14794. In the media's eyes, some victims — those who are homosexual — are more important than others.

Duin, Julia. "Homosexuality Seen as Accepted by Media." *Washington Times*, 30 July 2003. "[A]nalysts say an almost casual acceptance of homosexuality pervades the media."

Fitzgerald, Mark, "Are Newsrooms Too Gay Friendly?" *Editor and Publisher*, 28 September 1996, p. 12 A discussion including comments by a variety of mainstream gay journalists over the question of whether the media, in their efforts to seem more gay friendly, are going too far.

Kincaid, Cliff, "Poll Finds Values Gap Between Media and Public," *Human Events* 9 (June 1995: 19. A vast majority of the national media (83 percent) feels homosexuality should be accepted while only 41 percent of the public feels it should.

LaBarbera, Peter, "Homosexual Journalists: How Biased Are They?" *Human Events* 8 (December 1995): 5–6. The growing number of homosexual journalists at major newspapers is resulting in a skewed and pro-gay coverage of the issue.

McBride, Kelly, "How Do You Say He's Gay," *Poynteronline*, 11 August 2003. http://www.poynter.org/column.asp?id=53&aid=43961. Journalists generally should identify an individual's homosexuality only if the person agrees.

McBride, Kelly, "Writing About Gays and Lesbians," *Poynteronline*, 24 January 2004. http://www.poynter.org/content/content_print.asp?id=59795. The news media should present a variety of points of view on issues related to homosexuality.

McGowan, William. *Coloring the News: How Crusading for Diversity Has Corrupted American Journalism*. New York: Encounter Books, 2001. Journalists with good intentions to promote "diversity" have become mouthpieces for the homosexual agenda.

"Media Pushes Homosexuality — But Backlash May Come." Traditional Values Coalition, 2003. http://www.traditionalvalues.org/modules.php?sid=1084 "Big Media's commitment to increase the number of homosexual reporters and editors has succeeded.... [The media's positive treatment of homosexuals] is more than mere 'coloring of the news.' It is outright dishonesty — propaganda disguised as reporting."

Sheldon, Rev. Louis P. "Some Victims of Hate Murders Are More Equal Than Others," Traditional Values Coalition, 2004. http://www.traditionalvalues.org/modules.php?name=News&file=article&sid=648. Sheldon looks at the way the media report on crimes involving gays and concludes that when a gay person is killed, he or she is seen as a martyr.

Sullivan, Andrew. "Us and Them." *New Republic,* 2 April 2001, p. 8. Addresses assertions by anti-gay critics that two murders involving gays in 1999 were covered in a biased manner defending homosexuals. While Sullivan claims many of the charges are not warranted, he concludes that some of the criticisms leveled at the media by the anti-gay forces do have merit.

NOTES

1. Glenda M. Russell and Nancy H. Kelly, *Subtle Stereotyping: The Media, Homosexuality, and the Priest Sexual Abuse Scandal* (a study sponsored by the Institute for Gay and Lesbian Strategic Studies), http://64.233.161.104/search?q=cache:7fb4OajG1I0J:www.iglss.org/media/files/MediaStereotype.pdf+the+argument+explicitly+presented+is+that+gay+priests+are+responsible+for+the+sexual+abuse+scandal&hl=en&gl=us&ct=clnk&cd=1&client=safari.

2. Quoted in Julia Dunn, "Homosexuality Seen as Accepted by Media," *Washington Times* website, http://www.washtimes.com/national/20030729-112753-3972r.htm.

3. Lisa Bennett, "Fifty Years of Prejudice in the Media," *Gay and Lesbian Review Worldwide* Vol. 7, No. 2, Spring 2000.

4. Stanley Rothman and Amy Black, "Media and Business Elites: Still in Conflict?" *The Public Interest* (Spring 2001).

5. Andrew Sullivan, "Us and Them," *New Republic,* 2 April 2001, p. 8.

6. Quoted in abstract of article by Joyce Howard Price, "Who Was Jesse Dirkhising?" *Washington Times* on Covenant News, http:www.covenantnews,com/dirkhising,htm.

7. Quoted in abstract of article by Andy Davis, "Media Coverage of Trial Still Lacking," *The Arkansas Gazette* on Covenant News, http:www.covenantnews,com/dirkhising,htm.

8. Reed Irvine and Clifford Kincaid, "Homosexuality is Not Normal," http:www.covenantnews,com/dirkhising,htm.

9. Quoted in John Corry "Blinded by the Bias" *American Spectator* 34:2 (July/August 2002).

10. Ibid.

11. Laura Washington, "Gays Split on Coverage of Brutal Boys Town Murder," *Chicago Sun-Times,* 12 April 2004, p. 43.

12. Quoted in Mark Fitzgerald, "Are Newspapers Too Gay Friendly?" *Editor and Publisher,* 28 September 1996, p. 12.

13. Fitzgerald, ibid., 13.

14. Ibid.

15. Ibid.

16. Ibid., 13.

17. Quoted in Peter LaBarbera, "Homosexual Journalists: How Biased Are They?" *Human Events,* 8 December 1995, p. 5.

18. Kelly McBride, "How Do You Say He's Gay?" *Poynteronline,* 24 January 2004, http://www.poynter.org/content/content_print?id=43961.

7

Gender

Ginger Miller Loggins

"If the elite media had a pro-feminist bias, women and their issues should be everywhere on the news. Are they? Decidedly not.... [W]hen women do appear on network 'ideas' programs, on op-ed pages and on cable shows, ultra-conservative women are more likely than feminists to give the female perspective.... Overall, when the media covers feminism, it focuses on how dead the women's movement is, when it died, and how it will never rise again."—Caryl Rivers, Women's eNews[1]

"Media bias is especially strong on cultural issues. While most Americans are believing Christians, most people in the mainline media are not, and overwhelmingly they are pro-feminist and pro-choice on abortion. Hence the breathtakingly one-sided coverage of Anita Hill's charges against Clarence Thomas (the media reported over and over that 'women' were outraged by Hill's charges even as their own polls showed that most women believed Thomas)...."—Michael Barone, The American Enterprise[2]

Women constitute just over 50 percent of the population in the United States. Yet most commentators seem to agree that the media act against women's interests. On one side of the debate are political conservatives who blame the bias against women on feminism. On the other side are people who often critique the media from a feminist perspective and suggest that women and women's issues are underrepresented in both the coverage and the makeup of the media. In the end, both sides may see two halves to a distinctive gender bias against women in the media.

Those who suggest that the media have a feminist bias point to the liberal, feminist viewpoints of most journalists as proof. In this analysis, journalists bias the news because they view feminist ideas as mores that everyone accepts. These journalists do not fathom that their views are actually well to the left of most Americans. The argument additionally suggests that in trying to support the feminist movement, the news often shows disparaging portrayals of men and women in ways that unfairly strengthen the argument for feminism.

Those arguing from a largely feminist perspective point to a dearth of media coverage that includes women. They use this lack of coverage as evidence of a sexist bias against women. They also point to the lack of women in journalistic management and to the content of the news itself. This analysis suggests that when the mostly male managers do decide to cover women or women's issues, they often portray their subjects stereotypically or make generalizations that inhibit women's progress in society.

Feminist Media Bias against Men

Examining the conservatives' claims, no one appears to argue that women are over-represented in the news, and few suggest there are valid reasons for a dearth of female voices. However, some have claimed that the bias exists because the media pander to a liberal, feminist minority. A number of authors comment on this bias, but the argument that William McGowan presents for a feminist bias in the media's coverage of the military serves as a good introduction. In his book, *Coloring the News* (2001), McGowan addresses the feminist standpoint that the media reveal when they report on the military. His evidence centers around three major complaints: the media ignore the danger of allowing women into the military when they cannot meet the traditional physical tests of military recruits, the media portray women who have ignored military rules as victims instead of criminals, and the media ignore the rampant sexual activity present in the military since women first entered the armed forces.[3]

West Point's 1997 choice as "Master of Sword" serves as an example of McGowan's first complaint. West Point chose a female lieutenant colonel as the head of the Office of Physical Education that year. McGowan points out that the media covered the new appointment, but did not discuss whether the standards for the position were lowered so that a woman could be appointed. For McGowan, this story forms but one example of how the media look to the difficulties experienced by women who are entering the military instead of the leniency the military shows toward women, whom it wants to recruit and retain because of new, possibly misguided, government policy.

More dangerous examples of such leniency include the cases of Navy Lieutenants Kara Hultgreen and Carey Lohrenz. McGowan points out that not only did the media ignore the idea that gender-norming may have led to the problems caused by these women, but they asserted that the women were victims. Military records show that both women were unprepared as fighter pilots.

Lt. Hultgreen paid for her lenient training with her life — an internal Navy report suggests that her plane crashed because she failed to respond appropriately to engine trouble. The Navy's initial press release, however, said engine failure caused her training accident. Despite the media's traditional distrust of the military, the press quickly and widely reported the engine failure as the culprit. When one newspaper uncovered the internal report pointing to pilot error, other media outlets ignored this lead. Although the Navy's report suggests that Hultgreen's final errors were consistent with errors she had made in the past, the media did not investigate whether leniency toward women allowed Hultgreen to become the first female pilot assigned to combat duty.[4]

Lieutenant Lohrenz was grounded by her supervisors before her poor training and inability actually endangered herself or other personnel aboard her carrier. While her flying abilities were clearly below par, Lohrenz claimed that male pilots who made equivalent errors were not singled out. McGowan said that the media showed their usual bias by siding with Lohrenz, "as a feminist hero fighting the forces of male domination," and paid more attention to the theft of her service records than the substandard performance evident within these records.

McGowan's third complaint is the media's failure to cover the rampant sexual activity prevalent following the entry of women into the military. McGowan points to a run on birth control pills and condoms at American military establishments in Bosnia as evidence of this trend. He also points to the free ride the press gave Second Lieutenant Kelly Flinn when the service threatened her with a court-martial for fraternization and adultery. Such violations can damage unit cohesion and morale, but the press downplayed the seriousness of the violations in Flinn's case. The media took such violations more seriously, however, when General Joseph Ralston was considered as the new assistant chairman to the Joint Chiefs of Staff. Despite the fact that Ralston's adultery had occurred many years ago during a marital separation, the press claimed the military was changing the rules by not treating Ralston as it had Flinn.[5]

The media again ignored the devastating impact of military fraternization when *Time* magazine covered the first co-ed Navy ship to sail at sea.[6] *Time* noted the pregnancies and fraternization on board. Despite the rampant fraternization, it claimed the *USS Eisenhower* was performing as well as it had with an all male crew, if not better.

McGowan used each of these examples to show a media bias in favor of a gender integrated military and to demonstrate that the press buries legitimate investigations because of a defensive feminist environment. Two factors helped create this feminist climate — a fear of providing fuel for a conservative backlash, and a fear of being illegitimately blackballed as sexist. McGowan reviewed conversations he had with reporters to support the influence of those two factors and pointed to an occurrence at the *New York Post* to show how reporters can be illegitimately blackballed. In 1997, Scott McConnell wrote an editorial questioning the push for Puerto Rican statehood that some readers denounced. They claimed that the essay included numerous stereotypes. The paper fired McConnell in response to these claims. McGowan argued that this served as an example for those who want to critique any idea backed by women or minorities.

Bernard Goldberg generally agreed with McGowan's claims regarding the defensive feminist climate within the media. In his book, *Arrogance* (2003), Goldberg published an interview with sportscaster Bob Costas regarding the influence of feminism on coverage of Title IX and the Augusta golf club. Title IX mandated that elementary and secondary schools provide women sport opportunities equivalent to the opportunities and funding afforded to men's sports. According to Costas, a defensively feminist stance in the press has blocked discussion on changing Title IX to provide for more equitable sports for both men and women. Costas also challenged the media's coverage of the Augusta Golf Club's refusal to admit women. Costas said, "There is a good case to be made [for the inclusion of women at Augusta], and on balance I find it persuasive," yet Costas objects to the way the press automatically gave excluding women the "moral equivalency" of excluding African Americans.[7]

Those who see a feminist bias in the news also express concern, even without an environment that stifles opposing viewpoints, that a smaller and smaller variety of viewpoints are held by journalists. McGowan, the author of *Coloring the News* (2001), argued that affirmative action for women and minorities has increased superficial diversity while limiting intellectual diversity in the newsroom.[8] Both he and Myrna Blyth suggested that this limited diversity has led towards the silencing of conservative dissenters within the media. Blyth, a conservative feminist and the former editor in chief at the *Ladies Home Journal,* continually referred to the uncomfortable political conversations she had with other women's magazine reporters and editors in her book, *Spin Sisters* (2004).[9] They constantly assumed that a liberal, feminist agenda represented the only rational outlook. Their assumption that no one could possibly disagree seemed to have kept her from doing just that in each conversation that she relates. McGowan reported similar accounts of discomfort among the journalists that he interviewed. They talked to him about a liberal bias in the press, but asked him at the time or later to not use their names.

The way the media handle Hillary Clinton is also frequently used as an example of limited intellectual diversity within the press. Although Goldberg claimed that some members of the press treated an interview with Clinton like a "love fest," he admitted that she faced more hard questions than any other First Lady. Goldberg also suggested, however, that no other First Lady in office deserved such tough questions, and that the press became "lapdogs" during her Senatorial campaign.[10] In *Spin Sisters,* Blyth made a pointed comment about writer Ann Douglas, who interviewed Clinton for *Vogue* magazine the same day the press learned that the President would testify in front of a grand jury. Long before interviewing the First Lady, Douglas wrote *The Feminization of American Culture.* According to Blyth, the book discussed how Victorian women used their femininity and apparent powerlessness as weapons. In her book, Douglas apparently suggested that women would kill errant husbands with kindness and loyalty in order to gain power. Blyth thought it was ironic that Douglas would criticize Victorian women for this trait and not relate the trait to Clinton's reaction to her husband's adultery. Instead, Douglas' published interview with Vogue praised the First Lady for her confidence, intelligence, and sense of humor.[11]

The media's coverage of daycare issues described by Goldberg in his book, *Bias* (2002), also serves as a prime example of the press' refusal to present a story that may contradict feminist values. Goldberg pointed to evidence from social scientists, medical journals, and government institutes to show that a rise in working mothers and the use of daycare facilities is related to rising rates of child abuse, teenage drug abuse and pregnancy, child aggression, childhood hospitalizations for respiratory infections, and low academic scores. That may seem like too many ailments to blame on working mothers and their inability to personally supervise their kids while at work, but Goldberg presented logical arguments for each connection.

The relation between aggression and extended time in daycare originated from the National Institute of Child Health and Human Development. According to Goldberg, the April 2001 study found that 17 percent of kids in daycare "argue a lot, demand a lot of attention, act cruelly, show explosive behavior, talk too much, and get into lots of fights" even if the daycare is one of the most highest rated in quality. Goldberg suggested that Dan Rather called the study "controversial" only because it would make a large portion of the *CBS Evening News'* audience feel guilty—working mothers. CBS did not give the study much credence because it was too lazy to see if daycare might actually be a problem for kids, because such stories are not particularly attractive in the visual medium of television news, because the idea that "some very young children behave aggressively when they're way from their mothers for long stretches of time" would offend some of its audience, and because the organization, like most news organizations, refuses to attack feminists.[12]

This bias towards the feminist movement and liberal agendas concerning minorities has even influenced reporters to consider abandoning objectivity. McGowan said many reporters see objectivity as a "White Guy Objectivity" that leaves out the point of views of women and minorities. McGowan further suggested that such a lack of objectivity has alienated traditional newspaper readers by injuring the press' credibility while failing to draw in new minority readers.[13]

The feminist bias damages the press' credibility and lowers readership with its tendency to rely on stereotypes of men as violent and women as victims. Goldberg presented multiple examples throughout his books of how the press paints men as "putzes."[14] Although the traditional implication of putz may be harmless, Goldberg painted a much more derogatory definition of the term through a press that exaggerates men's role in domestic violence, vilifies divorced fathers as deadbeat dads, and generally suggests that men create problems throughout society by victimizing women.

To support his contention in *Bias,* Goldberg points to the extremes exhibited in various headlines and morning talk shows. Such stories suggest that man is "one of the most persistent and frustrating problems in evolutionary biology," that women are better off without them, and that castration may be a reasonable punishment for grooms who do not show up at the chapel. Goldberg suggests these extremes are allowed because the media believe they have a license to overkill the oppressors — to get away with anything they say about the patriarchy and the men who represent it, without being held accountable for inappropriate comments or blatant untruths. This license to overkill is why the media know that castration is funny, but cutting off breasts is not. It means that while the press portrays deadbeat dads as a pressing problem in society, it is not concerned that courts are also forcing men to financially support children to whom — according to DNA evidence — they have no relation.[15]

An additional example from McGowan's coverage of the press' feminist bias against the military shows how the press paints men as violent oppressors. Reports on the Aberdeen sex scandal discussed drill sergeants having consensual and coerced sexual relations with trainees. The sergeants reportedly competed for having sex with the most trainees and many trainees boasted of their relationships, using them to get preferential treatment. Instead of looking at the problem as one between men and women, McGowan reports that the press portrayed it as representing "a military culture deeply alien to women, one in which protections against sexual harassment were weak and ineffective, and where the exclusion of women from important combat related positions left them in a second-class status." The press insisted on presenting the story as a sexual harassment problem that involved men forcing themselves on women instead of addressing the possibility that it could simply point toward the problems with putting men and women together in military training situations. When ABC News talked to Congress on the issue, it spoke to feminist Senator Olympia Snowe, a Republican known for her criticism of the military and did not bother to mention the viewpoints of those in Congress working to eliminate co-ed basic training.[16]

Those who argue that a feminist bias exists in the news assert that while the media stereotype men as Neanderthals, they also paint women as their innocent victims. Blythe spends a lot of time in *Spin Sisters* pointing out this victimization portrayal. She argues that feminism uses the women's magazines in particular, and other media in general, to convince women they are victims and still need the feminist movement and the government to protect them from patriarchal ills. Her content analysis examining the cover lines of five women's magazines published from 1990 to 2002 presented a world in which women's situations got worse over the years despite their gains in equality. Blyth finds the media coverage of "me-time" particularly disturbing. According to magazines and other media, me-time is a serious problem for the modern woman who needs a little self indulgence to survive the demands of both her work life and her family life. Blyth argues that feminism has created this "victim virus" by encouraging such unimportant self-indulgences and downplaying the importance of motherly responsibilities.[17]

In *Arrogance*, Goldberg generally summed up these arguments for a feminist bias by asserting that feminism has stolen journalism; the feminist bias of the press means it does not examine extreme and unsupported claims from feminists that again show women as victims and men as violent aggressors. For example, Gil Garcetti worked as the district attorney for Los Angeles and spoke at a feminist news conference in Pasadena, California, that year's Super Bowl location, in January 1993. According to Goldberg the bulk of the press quoted Garcetti as saying that "domestic violence goes up tremendously [on Super Bowl Sunday] it's a fact" without investigating his claim.[18] One reporter investigated the claim, and discovered that the Abuse Bowl was a myth. Christina Hoff Summers of the *Washington Post* could find no evidence that domestic violence rates increased anywhere during the Super Bowl. Goldberg concluded that while the media always express doubts about claims from the National Rifle Association or the Christian Coalition, they take feminist claims at face value.

Media Bias against Women

Caryl Rivers offered a direct reply to Goldberg's claim of a liberal, feminist bias. In a Women's eNews article, "Pro-Feminist Media Bias? Show Me the Women!" Rivers asserted that five months after September 11 the news was more likely to show an Afghani woman than allow an American woman on a Sunday morning talk show. Only 11 percent of guests on such shows were female. Rivers also pointed towards the observation of the *Washington Post* that when women are invited on Sundays they usually come from a small Washington-based conservative group. And while the same group had fourteen opinion pieces in three national papers during 1995, those papers published no commentary from significantly larger feminist organizations, such as the National Organization for Women or the Feminist Majority Foundation. Rivers said that although young women are living feminist lifestyles by going to college or competing in marathons, contact sports, and for good careers, the media can only talk about feminism in the past tense — as a dead movement rejected by today's young woman.[19]

She disputed the claims in *Bias* that the media ignore stories about daycares that might make mothers feel guilty. Instead, she suggests that the bias goes in the opposite direction — the media largely ignore positive stories about daycares. When the press does pay attention to a story, as it paid attention to the study Goldberg discussed that related daycares to child aggression, the negative information ends up in the headlines and any positive information gets scant mentions. In this example, the same study also found a link between daycares and kids' cognitive skills, but that connection was not highlighted by the press.

As for Goldberg and others' claims that the press did not critically evaluate Hillary Clinton, Rivers points out that she found fifty references to Clinton as a "witch" or as "witchlike" and one story that likened Clinton to Glen Close's "Fatal Attraction" character before Monica Lewinsky's relationship with the president became news. After those headline's broke, Clinton was more likely to be characterized as weak-willed and passive. Rivers suggested that all such descriptions are inappropriate and would certainly never be applied to a sitting president.

River's argument also parallels Myrna Blyth's argument in *Spin Sisters*. They appear to agree that the media portray women as weak. However, where Blyth argued that the media's stereotypical portrayal brings new members to the feminist movement; Rivers suggests that the media's portrait of female weakness works against feminism. She sees media portrayals of women as furthering one of two dichotomous myths: "the Myth of Female Weakness and the Myth of Female Strength." [20] Whereas Rivers suggests that the media portray working mothers as mythical Wonder Women, Blyth points to the same portrayals and sees the media showing women as victims of too many demands.[21]

One of Rivers' examples of the vulnerable woman shows how the media's victim virus does not always support a feminist movement that suggests women have a right to a career and marriage late in life. Rivers debunks the 1980s media myth that single women over the age of 35 are more likely to be killed by terrorists than married. According to Rivers, the media did not report that the statistic only holds true for women over 35 who limit their mates to men two or three years older than themselves. Otherwise there is no shortage of eligible men. Rivers also refers to more recent, unpublicized research indicating that women are more likely to marry when they get more education in order to point out how such fear-inducing statistics about women discourage them from advancing their careers. After all, if they do not forgo the career to snag a man, they might turn into old maids.[22] All of Rivers' examples point to an antifeminist bias in a press that devalues women's worth and presence.

The authors of *Women, Media and Sport* find the same bias in sports journalism. Through surveys and experiments as well as content, historical, and contextual analyses, the authors suggest that the feminine stereotype of women has held women back in sports coverage and has been reinforced by sports journalism. They suggest a bias similar to the one Rivers' suggested — that the media consistently build female athletes up with an Artemis archetype only to ruin the feminist message with inadequate comparisons to male athletes.[23] In other words, while they use the Artemis myth to build woman up as strong and athletic, they always limit her strength and athleticism with poor verbal comparisons to man's strength and athleticism.

Linda Williams' historical analysis suggested that although African-American women did not have the stigma of femininity keeping them from sports, they were virtually excluded from mainstream press coverage. For example, in an unpublished content analysis she conducted with Angela Lumpkin, only five of more than 1,800 *Sports Illustrated* covers featured Black women. However, her historical analysis of various media showed that virtually excluding female athletes is not the only model for the press. She found that the black press featured black sportswomen much more frequently than the mainstream media.[24] So a better media representation of women is possible, but the mainstream media refuse to allow it.

The book's editor, Pamela Creedon, conducted a number of experiments concerning the coverage of athletic women. She found that while people who wanted to learn a sport were willing to learn from athletes of either gender, women in competitive sports did not change perceptions of the inferiority of female athletes. Spectators preferred watching men in competitive sports and women in more gender appropriate sports like figure skating.[25] These spectator biases and reactions suggest that the media reinforce the feminine stereotype through their sports coverage.

Mary Jo Kane and Susan L. Greendorfer followed Creedon's chapter by asserting athletics as a vehicle for male masculinity and media as the driver. The media have worked as a fundamental challenge to the feminist message inherent in women's athletics. Reviewing a number of academic articles on women in the sports media, Kane and Greendorfer concluded that women are underrepresented in sports journalism despite their prevalence in many types of sports. When female athletes are featured in journalism, the media emphasize and exaggerate the athletes' femininity or provide contradictory messages ultimately denying the women the power and prestige given to male athletes.[26]

Sunday talk shows and sports media are not the only places where studies have found that women are underrepresented in the press. The *San Francisco Chronicle* conducted a content analysis of its own paper following a reader's complaint. In his commentary, "Numbers Offer Guide to Better Coverage" (February 25, 2004), Dick Rogers reported that over a one-month period the paper came closest to representing women in photographs according to their proportional population in the reading area in the Datebook section's front page with an almost 60–40 percent balance of men to women. The Bay Area and front page sections followed with about 30 percent of their front page content featuring women. The Business section featured women in only 25 percent of its front page photographs, and the Sports section came in last with 10 percent female photographs.[27]

Similar findings have been revealed in recent academic studies of gender parity in the media's use of news sources. John Sutcliffe, Martha Lee, and Walter Soderlund discussed one such study in their article, "Women and Crisis Reporting," published in the *Harvard International Journal of Press Politics* (2005). They found that televised news reports of the Caribbean showed an over-reliance on male sources and male reporters.[28] Eric Freedman and Frederick Fico reported similar findings in their study that examined newspapers' sources in gubernatorial races. They published their study, "Male and Female Sources," in *Mass Communication and Society* (2005).[29] A *Media Report to Women* (2005) article, "Rice Lifts Numbers...," pointed out that the proportion of female protagonists in print and television news still does not reflect the proportion of women in the population.[30]

Those who argue the media are biased against women also point to the lack of women in the profession. This can be seen in Sutcliffe and colleagues' article,[31] as well as articles written for a general audience. Sheila Gibbons discusses the lack of female cartoonists in her article, "Dearth of Female Editorial Cartoonists Isn't Very Funny," published in the *Media Report to Women* (2005).[32] The *Columbia Journalism Review* examined the editorial fallout after one newspaper reader demanded more space for herself and other women in the op-ed page of the *Los Angeles Times*. As the article's title "Where the Girls Aren't: Population Trends in Op-ed Land" suggests, women are not prevalent in the newspaper editorial business. The author argues, however, that a wealth of female editorial writers are available.[33]

Others also suggest that because women are not evident in managerial positions, topics and information important to them do not get as much coverage. Carol Stabile and Deepa Kumar suggest in their study, "Unveiling Imperialism," published in *Media, Culture and Society* (2005) that normally the oppression of women in Afghanistan would not get any media coverage. They suggest that the only reason that issue got front page status was to justify American intervention in Afghanistan. The media did not cover this topic because of a newfound interest in women, but because of their traditionally masculine point of view.[34] John McManus and Lori Dorfman published their study, "Functional Truth or Sexist Distortion?" in *Journalism* in 2005. They found that the media did not cover violence perpetrated against women with the frequency or depth given to stories about similar violent acts.[35] An article published in the *Newspaper Research Journal* written by Koang-Hyub Kim and Philip Meyer, "Survey Yields Five Factors of Newspaper Quality" (2005), provides evidence showing why the gender of managers may matter. Their study suggests that women place less importance on spot news and more importance on background pieces than men.[36] When women are in the top spots, the types of stories that matter to women are less likely to be ignored.

Herbert Gans book, *Deciding What's News* (1979), may contain outdated data, but its reasoning for the lack of women in television news and news magazines still has relevance. Based upon two decades of content analysis and time as a participant observer, Gans concludes that the media have a bias toward those in power. This bias results in fewer women getting featured in news stories. Women will generally only be featured as unique and different from the men in power predominately when they try to assimilate into the power structure. Women, and ethnic minorities, who are not interested in assimilating will receive very little media coverage.[37]

Mary Douglas Vavrus suggests a more modern interpretation of the media's power-related gender bias in her book, *Postfeminist News: Political Women in Media Culture* (2002). Vavrus suggests that postfeminism — a movement negating the gains of traditional feminism — creates the gender bias. The media use a postfeminist slant to attract and target a small group of elite, heterosexual, White women. The postfeminist media takes the traditional goals and methods of feminism and revises them to promote "private, consumer lifestyles rather than ... a desire for public life and political activism."[38]

Vavrus also asserts that a postfeminist press suggests that feminism has achieved its goals of equality and now women only need to take advantage of what has been gained. The press reinforces this by focusing on women when they say "I'm not a feminist" while ignoring the "but" that follows the statements and asserts the desire to achieve a traditional feminist goal. Such coverage suggests that despite many women's feminist goals, they no longer need the movement to achieve those goals. Postfeminist media make it appear that the need for feminism has ended, so that any problems women face are individual problems. Women's struggles to join the work force then seem limited by personal choice instead of societal roadblocks.[39]

Vavrus' allegations of a postfeminist bias are related to Robert McChesney's ideas concerning a neoliberal democracy in his 1999 text, *Rich Media, Poor Democracy*. McChesney's neoliberal democracy describes America as an institution where debate means little and corporate solutions receive privilege over other possibilities.[40] Vavrus' postfeminist perspective accordingly suggests that the media claim change is unnecessary, making debate meaningless. This postfeminist media give women false expectations that they can buy everything and assume that they have the money to do so. Feminist aims that support corporate goals are promoted while any that oppose consumerism are shunned. The perspective encourages consumerism to solve problems, thereby catering to successful and professional women, while ignoring the needs of women still struggling financially.[41]

Vavrus' analyses of the Clarence Thomas hearings in 1991, the 1991–1992 election "Year of the Woman," the influence of "soccer moms" in the 1996 presidential campaign, and Hillary Clinton's 2000 run for congressional office show that the media's coverage of women at those times further emphasized personal choice over patriarchal barriers. During the Thomas hearings Vavrus asserts that the media struggled with Anita Hill's claims. Any conflicts brought to the forefront by the hearings were subverted by the press' claim that the 1991–1992 political elections represented the "Year of the Woman." Similarly a focus on Hillary Clinton's congressional campaign in 2000 diverted attention from the largest number of women ever to run for Congress that year. Vavrus says such coverage "disconnected [Clinton] from the rest of these candidates *and* from feminism as a social movement — despite her very clear articulation to a platform composed of the traditional 'women's issues.'"[42] The postfeminist media showed Clinton's individual success but did not allow feminist critiques of her coverage or discussion of whether her future constituents' needs related to feminist goals.

• THE EVIDENCE •

The bias against women as feminists is more heavily and widely documented than a pro-feminist bias. A large number of academic works document the disproportional prevalence of men in the news. Although content analyses like Blyth's have provided evidence that a feminist bias exists,[43] the argument for a feminist bias rests more on anecdotal evidence than on content analyses.

The fact that one argument generally comes from the academic press and the opposing argument usually comes from the popular press points to an additional disconnect between the two sides. Work emphasizing a feminist bias in media that frequently target men could benefit from more academic study. Goldberg suggests, however, that scholars may have no more desire than journalists for providing evidence opposing feminism. He details a journalism student's struggle to reject an assignment that assumed sexism was a prevalent problem in society. When the student suggested that the assignment had an inherent bias based upon the professor's assumptions, the professor assigned her an additional essay on sexism and told her, "you make me not want to teach."[44] This story suggests that academic studies on a media bias in favor of feminists are not likely to come from universities. Although there may be scholars who disagree with contentions that the media inappropriately exclude women, they may simply not have a strong interest in the area. Conversely, studies dealing with the issue of gender bias probably are conducted mostly by individuals who have a feminist agenda. This point brings into question the credibility of even supposed "scholarly" studies.

Another weakness in the argument that comes from both sides is that they exaggerate their claims. Rivers, for example, found from her study of talk shows and opinion pieces evidence that casts doubt on the accusations of critics of feminism. However, the opposition provides evidence that the media exhibit bias in more stories than day care. Goldberg also discussed the media's inability to research claims of high abuse during Super Bowl Sunday and also referred to phony statistics on consequences of domestic abuse.[45] Conservative arguments also point to the media's framing of military gender integration and other biased coverage. Rivers and other feminist scholars have not refuted these additional arguments.

Even if those who argue for a feminist bias are wrong, it does not necessarily mean that arguments of an anti-feminist bias in the media should be accepted at face value. Although content analyses revealing a lack of female coverage largely come from the academy, even one newspaper has conducted a content analysis and admitted its own deficiencies. The *San Francisco Chronicle*, however, did not take the analysis as conclusive proof of bias. Rogers admitted that more women are probably involved in Bay Area businesses than their coverage in the paper implies, but cautioned that statistics should not govern journalistic integrity and decision making—a justification for allowing continued disproportionate coverage.[46]

The evidence that women are not proportionally represented as news reporters, editorial writers and cartoonists, sports reporters, general news sources, general news subjects, and sporting news subjects appears too overwhelming to be disputed. But, as Rogers suggests, such an imbalance does not necessarily mean the media are biased against women. The media may very well reflect a societal bias against women, and the question of whether the media reinforce such a bias or have no choice but to reflect such a bias needs more evidence to be answered.

While both sides have weakness in their arguments, neither argument appears completely unfounded. It appears that media professionals show a bias against feminist ideas when they disproportionately ignore women and women's issues and may over-correct for that tendency by doing things such as framing military integration from feminist standpoints and uncritically accepting inaccurate information from feminist groups. There may be legitimate reasons for the virtual exclusion of women in many news items, but surely the exclusion does a disservice to the media's role in portraying an accurate representation of all of society. Alternatively, the media may portray women as victims and men as victimizers in ways that fit a feminist frame while ignoring more conservative viewpoints, but as Vavrus argues that does not necessarily promote a truly feminist agenda.

Both sides may be showing one small part of the whole picture; and, in fact, Goldberg inadvertently suggests this possibility. When addressing the coverage of minorities in the press, he suggests that the media like minorities and liberal platforms aimed at improving equality for minorities, but does not actually care to feature minorities.[47] Such an attitude about women could be what is driving the promotion of some feminist goals on the one hand, such as the seriousness of domestic abuse against women or the integration of the military, and the unfeminist exclusion of women from most news coverage in general.

However, there are equally valid arguments on the other side that suggest the bias toward feminism does not always promote the movement. Analyses of sports may be the most telling on this count. As *Women, Media and Sport* suggests, women are entering the previously male dominated arena of sport in droves. Mary Jo Kane and Susan Greendorfer point out that at the college level there are five times as many women participating in sports today than before the passage of Title IX. They now constitute one-third of all collegiate athletes, as opposed to the 15 percent of athletes they represented in 1971.[48] However, the book shows that women are not getting 33 percent of the college athletics coverage and that the coverage they do get promotes stereotypical images of women, no matter how competitively the athletes play.

Blyth's arguments and the arguments of other conservatives suggest that the media are hostile to women in their frequent characterization of women as weak. Rivers and the authors in *Women, Media and Sport* would agree with this assessment, and they would even probably agree that men's portrayals as violent villains can be exaggerated. However, they see it as related to the media's bias against women as opposed to an influence of feminism's need for new members. After all, the dearth of women in the media suggests that the media somehow oppose representing women accurately and would appear to be a perfectly legitimate way to emphasize the need for feminism all by itself.

Vavrus' analysis of media as a postfeminist tool for corporate structure may come closest to explaining the apparently contradictory bias in media that occasionally champion women's causes on one hand, such as domestic abuse, military integration, and sexual harassment, while victimizing women and diminishing their influence on the other.[49] The corporate influence is certainly evident in Blyth's analysis, which includes chapters on such topics as the "Feminine Physique" that argue women's magazines try to convince readers they can buy happiness with the right lipstick, clothes, and cosmetic surgery.[50] Vavrus' interpretation of the problem also allows for Blyth's assessment that the media consist of women who grew up with the feminist movement and still agree with it, but may not actually empower women with their journalistic endeavors.

• RESOLUTION •

Authors on both sides of the debate imply a number of ways the media can improve their coverage. Goldberg specifically presents twelve ideas in his latter book, *Arrogance*. These ideas basically are aimed at increasing intellectual diversity in the newsroom. Such a goal appears to be called for by people on both sides of the gender bias issue. If media outlets recruited from impoverished and rural areas as Goldberg suggests, a more vocal conservative group inside the press might appear as well as a more vocal feminist group.

In addition to recruiting more intellectually diverse professionals, the media need to work at making minority opinions easier to express. While extended, philosophical conversations about what is news and what is balanced coverage may not have a place in the day-to-day flurry of producing a newspaper or a newscast, such conversations can be encouraged in news meetings at the beginning or end of each day.

Such conferences could easily be adapted to encourage all employees to comment on any excluded stories they thought should have been broadcast or printed and any included stories they thought presented a biased viewpoint. Such discussions should allow coworkers to take time explaining the merits of particular story ideas and their relevance to all members of the community, male and female. Limiting such conversations to weekly meetings would mean that the stories can still be covered the next week and still be timely. Less frequent yearly meetings might mean that a particular story will never get covered, but will also mean that all news workers have a better understanding of the differing viewpoints when a similar story comes along.

Discussing different viewpoints does not necessarily mean that any viewpoint deserves as much attention as any other. Journalists should make an informed decision about each viewpoint when they decide which ones to include and not to include, and how much coverage each viewpoint deserves. Sometimes a decision may depend upon an estimation of how much acceptance and agreement there is behind the viewpoint or the relevance of this view to most people in society.

In such discussions, the main concern should not be whether an idea came from liberals or conservatives, feminists or sexists, Republicans or Democrats, corporations or the unemployed, or how the desires of such groups relate to the journalist's own self-interests. Then, when they select the viewpoints that they can cover and the importance of that story, journalists should do their utmost to ensure each fact is considered critically, no matter its impact on their own lives or perspectives. They must also ensure a viewpoint is valued based upon the evidence that supports it and its legitimacy in modern society, not on a reporter's opinions about the source of the viewpoint. Combing through stories, viewpoints, and information in such a way continues the journalistic tradition of objectivity. Despite its occasionally flawed application in the press, journalists would do well to remember the tradition and work hard to live up to that ideal no matter whether it is truly achievable.

Living up to objectivity means that even if the newsroom is diverse, the individual reporter should also diversify his or her information. No matter how diverse a newsroom may be, personal introspection on others' viewpoints can help communication with people from other backgrounds and broaden one's understanding and respect for their positions.

• POINTS OF VIEW •

Billings, Andrew C., James R. Angelini, and Susan Tyler Eastman. "Diverging Discourses: Gender Differences in Televised Golf Announcing." *Mass Communication & Society* 8:2 (2005): 155–171. Although a gender bias persists in golf, it is expressed differently in golf than in other sports

Blyth, Myrna. *Spin Sisters: How the Women of the Media Sell Unhappiness and Liberalism to the Women of America*. New York: St. Martin's Press, 2004. The feminist perspective of most magazine writers results in a media emphasis on all the problems for and weaknesses of the modern woman.

Creedon, Pamela J., ed. *Women, Media and Sport: Challenging Gender Values*. Thousand Oaks, Calif.: Sage, 1994. Women do not have adequate representation in the media, and the representation that does exist limits women's advancement in sports and society.

Gans, Herbert J. *Deciding What's News: A Study of CBS Evening News, NBC Nightly*

News, Newsweek, and Time. New York: Pantheon Books, 1979. After studying the work environment and resulting news product, a sociologist concludes that the media's bias toward those in power creates a bias against women, particularly if those women are not interested in assimilating into traditional society.

Goldberg, Bernard. *Bias: A CBS Insider Exposes How the Media Distort the News*. Washington, D.C.: Regnery Publishing, 2002. A CBS reporter claims that liberalism biases the media against men as jerks and deadbeat dads

McGowan, William. *Coloring the News: How Crusading for Diversity Has Corrupted American Journalism*. San Francisco: Encounter Books, 2001. Because of a feminist bias in the news, the press does not critically evaluate or fully discuss stories that impact a feminist viewpoint, resulting in less public information about cultural problems.

Schlafly, Phyllis. *Feminist Fantasies*. Dallas, Tex.: Spence Publishing, 2003. This collection of writings explains the opposing viewpoints that Schlafly and others claim the media do not portray because of feminist bias.

Vavrus, Mary Douglas. *Postfeminist News: Political Women in Media Culture*. Albany: State University of New York Press, 2002. The media's postfeminist portrayals of the world bias content against women.

NOTES

1. Caryl Rivers, "Pro-Feminist Media Bias? Show Me the Women!" http://www.womensenews. org/article.cfm/dyn/aid/822/context/archive.

2. Michael Barone, "Our Partisan Media," *The American Enterprise Online*, http://www.taemag. com/issues/articleid.16375/article_detail.asp.

3. William McGowan, *Coloring the News: How Crusading for Diversity Has Corrupted American Journalism* (San Francisco, Calif.: Encounter Books, 2001).

4. Ibid., 129–130.

5. Ibid., 130, 138, 143.

6. Ibid., 131.

7. Bernard Goldberg, *Arrogance: Rescuing America from the Media Elite* (New York: Warner Books, 2003), 153.

8. McGowan, *Coloring the News*, 226.

9. Myrna Blyth, *Spin Sisters: How the Women of the Media Sell Unhappiness and Liberalism to the Women of America* (New York: St. Martin's Press, 2004).

10. Goldberg, *Arrogance*, 147–151.

11. Blyth, *Spin Sisters*, 169–171.

12. Bernard Goldberg, *Bias: A Cbs Insider Exposes How the Media Distort the News* (Washington, DC: Regnery Publishing, 2002), 172.

13. McGowan, *Coloring the News*, 231, 245–248.

14. Goldberg, *Bias*, 132.

15. Ibid., 134, 138–141.

16. McGowan, *Coloring the News*, 132, 133.

17. Blyth, *Spin Sisters*, 46, 75.

18. Goldberg, *Arrogance*, 131.

19. Caryl Rivers, *Pro-Feminist Media Bias? Show Me the Women!* [World Wide Web] (Women's eNews, February 20 2002, accessed April 22 2006); available from http://www.womensenews.org/ article.cfm/dyn/aid/822/context/archive.

20. Ibid.

21. Blyth, *Spin Sisters*, 57.

22. Rivers, *Pro-Feminist Bias*(accessed).

23. Pamela J. Creedon, ed., *Women, Media and Sport: Challenging Gender Values* (Thousand Oaks, Calif.: Sage, 1994), 293.

24. Ibid., 51, 54.

25. Ibid., 14.

26. Ibid., 33, 36–39.

27. Dick Rogers, "Numbers Offer Guide to Better Coverage," *San Francisco Chronicle*, February 25 2004.

28. John B. Sutcliffe, Martha F. Lee, and Walter C. Soderlund, "Women and Crisis Reporting: Television News Coverage of Political Crises in the Caribbean," *Harvard International Journal of Press/Politics* 10, no. 3 (2005).

29. Eric Freedman and Frederick Fico, "Male and Female Sources in Newspaper Coverage of Male and Female Candidates in Open Races for Governor in 2002," *Mass Communication & Society* 8, no. 3 (2005).

30. "Rice Lifts Numbers of Women in News, but Overall Coverage of Women Still Lags," *Media Report to Women* 33, no. 2 (2005): p. 3.

31. Sutcliffe, Lee, and Soderlund, "Women and Crisis Reporting."

32. Sheila Gibbons, "Dearth of Female Editorial Cartoonists Isn't Very Funny," *Media Report to Women* 33, no. 2 (2005).

33. "Where the Girs Aren't: Population Trends in Op-Ed Land," *Columbia Journalism Review*, May/June 2005.

34. Carol A. Stabile and Deepa Kumar, "Unveiling Imperialism: Media, Gender and the War on Afghanistan," *Media, Culture & Society* 27, no. 5 (2005).

35. John McManus and Lori Dorfman, "Functional Truth or Sexist Distortion?," *Journalism* 6, no. 1 (2005).

36. Koang-Hyub Kim and Philip Meyer, "Survey Yields Five Factors of Newspaper Quality," *Newspaper Research Journal* 26, no. 1 (2005).

37. Herbert J. Gans, *Deciding What's News: A Study of CBS Evening News, NBC Nightly News, Newsweek, and Time* (New York: Pantheon Books, 1979), 28 & 62.

38. Mary Douglas Vavrus, *Postfeminist News: Political Women in Media Culture* (Albany, NY: State University of New York Press, 2002).

39. Ibid., 20, 21.

40. Robert Waterman McChesney, *Rich Media, Poor Democracy: Communication Politics in Dubious Times*, The History of Communication; (Urbana: University of Illinois Press, 1999).

41. Vavrus, *Postfeminist News*, 23, 33, 29.

42. Ibid., 34, 149.

43. Blyth, *Spin Sisters*.

44. Goldberg, *Arrogance*, 213.

45. Ibid.

46. Rogers, "Numbers Offer Guide."

47. Goldberg, *Bias*, 161.

48. Creedon, ed., *Women, Media and Sport*, 32.

49. Vavrus, *Postfeminist News*.

50. Blyth, *Spin Sisters*, 81–110.

8

Race and Ethnicity

Tamara K. Baldwin and Henry M. Sessoms

"Race bias is still a fact in America, and media too often facilitate it. We are still haunted by notions of racial hierarchy because the United States has yet to confront the complex legacy of slavery. Progressive activists must remind themselves that a true struggle for media democracy demands they continually challenge the conventional wisdom of white supremacy."—Salim Muwakkil, In These Times Website[1]

"[Your African-American columnist] has to be the most negative thinking, bigoted, sour and color-seeing racist I have ever come into contact with. He sees nothing but black vs. white.... The color barrier will stay up as long as there are people such as him fueling the flames of racism.... How can he take something as innocent as a 6-year-old planting a garden and turn it into something so twisted as abuse? Let children be young for as long as they can be, or they may turn out to be like [your columnist]."—Letter to the Tuscaloosa (Ala.) News[2]

Discussions of race and ethnicity frequently center on how the media deal with the issues. Are the media free of bias when it comes to depictions of race and ethnicity, or are they biased? At issue is whether non-white individuals or groups — including but not limited to African Americans, Hispanics, Asian Americans, and Native Americans — are treated in the media the same as the white majority.

Both sides on this issue offer compelling arguments. Critics' major claims of bias can be grouped into three positions:

1. Stories about people of races and ethnicities other than white are often missing from the media

2. Stereotypical images and language remain a part of media coverage of people from non-white races and ethnicities

3. Media workplace practices and economic realities contribute to the continuation of a negative media bias in regard to race and ethnicity.

Viewpoints of those who argue that media are not biased against minorities can be summarized under three major positions:

1. The efforts the media have made recently have rid them of bias that may have existed in the past;

2. If any media bias exists, it is a pro-minority bias rather than an anti-minority one;

3. Claims that the media are biased against minorities are often exaggerated by critics with their own agendas or biases.

The Media Are Biased against Minorities

Viewpoint 1: People of races and ethnicities other than white are often missing from the media. A major criticism of the news media has been their lack of inclusion of minorities. This exclusion has permeated the media from their earliest days, and the effects are far from benign, according to Clint C. Wilson II, Félix Gutiérrez, and Lena M. Chao in their book *Racism, Sexism, and the Media*. Being left out, they argued, indicated the place in society that was accorded to members of non-white groups by whites, and "lack of coverage of peoples of color in mainstream news media had the effect of asserting their lack of status, a powerful psychological message delivered to Whites and non-Whites alike."[3] They contended that this exclusion determined the way the news media treated people of color thereafter, and that it also "established a legacy that permeates American news media into the 21st century." Some twentieth century examples they offer of the media's initial interest in a minority included the way the media dealt with the influx of Mexican immigrants (or "wetbacks" as they were often referred to) into California in the 1950s, the 1980s, and the 1990s and the way the media referred to Latinos as illegal aliens.

Joan Byrd examined the *Washington Post* to determine if it carried photographs of African Americans. In "Blacks, Whites in News Pictures" she wrote that of the 1,500 photographs the newspaper ran in a month-long period, photographs of whites outnumbered those of African Americans by more than three to one. The difference, she wrote, was not the product of any conscious racism on the part of the newspaper or its journalists, but rather was the result of the way news has been defined and judged through the years. She noted, however, that the collective message sent to African Americans is that the newspaper is racist.[4]

The absence of minority faces from the entertainment media has been noted by some. Hispanics made up only 2 percent of all of the prime time characters in television programs that aired during the 1994–95 season, according to a study conducted of ninety-six prime-time programs on ABC, CBS, NBC, Fox, UPN, and the WB.[5] In an article describing the "flight" of television programs featuring minorities from the four major networks for the 1996 television season, Christopher Farley described how only six minority-themed programs were offered by the Big Four networks (CBS, ABC, NBC, and Fox) during the 1996 season, down from twelve that were offered by the Big Four three seasons earlier. Minority programs, he noted, appeared instead on the newer networks at the time, UPN and WB, which were trying to build viewership and make a name for themselves.[6]

Viewpoint 2: Stereotypical images and language remain a part of media coverage of people from non-white races and ethnicities. Language and images that portray minorities in stereotypical terms can still be found in news coverage, according to Wilson, Gutiérrez, and Chao. They cite the cover of the November 16, 2002, issue of *Time* magazine as visual evidence of an image that they consider stereotypical. The words "Look Who's Cashing in at Indian Casinos," with the sub-headline "Hint: It's not the people who are supposed to benefit," appeared across the middle of the page. The lower half of the cover featured a photograph of the inside of a casino, while in the top half of the page *Time* editors featured a photograph of a Native American man with "war" paint on his face and torso rowing a canoe, clearly, they contend, a resurrection of the "noble savage" stereotype begun two centuries earlier.

Wilson and his co-authors also describe a "stereotypical news selection process" (akin to the gatekeeping function described in mass media research) used in determining what types of stories involving people of color ultimately make it into the media. The selection process involves, they argue, reports that neutralize "White apprehension with regard to non-Whites while accommodating the presence of people of color." Information about minorities/people of color that conforms to attitudes of whites about them is included in the news and repeated often enough that it becomes a theme of sorts. They cite what they call "success" stories, or stories that detail how a person of color overcomes the hardships of his or her "… (choose one) reservation, ghetto, barrio, Chinatown, or Little Tokyo," coverage that makes clear the status of both the white audience and the minority audience.

People of color, when portrayed in the news media, often appear, critics argue, in a small range of roles or as exhibiting certain characteristics. The coverage they often receive was noted by Robert Entman and Andrew Rojecki in their book *The Black Image in the White Mind.* Their content analysis of videotapes of network evening news programs from 1990–91 and 1997 led them to make conclusions about how "the outlines of the way media help construct the prototypical Black person, that is, the traits characterizing the most representative member of the category. He or she is an entertainer, sports figure, or object of discrimination." Their analysis of sound bites used in stories, they concluded, detected a pattern of lack of African-American and other minority voices in sound bites. Few if any people of color were featured in sound bites for stories dealing with economics, foreign affairs, electoral politics, science or education, or a number of other topics.[7]

Entman's and Rojecki's research revealed what they termed a "dearth of Blacks in stories that have as their central theme either blacks as positive contributors to American society or as people whose racial identity is incidental." Their analysis of transcripts of ABC news reports from the 1990s indicated that the network mainly discussed "Blacks as such" when they suffered or committed a crime or otherwise fell victim and required attention from the government. They claimed that "by tying appearances of Blacks so frequently to narratives of crime and victimization, the news constructs African Americans as a distinct source of disruption." In a chapter dealing with violence and stereo-types, they argued, based on an analysis of television news in Chicago, that the "news business can unintentionally produce subtle images that may stimulate negative emo-tions." Among the things they noted was coverage that included more mug shots for Blacks than for others and more shots of African Americans in handcuffs than others under arrest.

Teun A. van Dijk, in an essay titled "New(s) Racism: A Discourse Analytical Approach" described several types of racism (new racism, symbolic racism, everyday racism, indirect racism, and subtle racism) and noted minorities' lack of access to the media and lack of control over many of the items and practices that are a large part of the newsmaking process. The opinions of minority members are asked for less frequently or are found less credible or newsworthy, van Dijk argued, because "most journalists (and virtually all editors) are white." When the media cover stories about immigrants and racial minorities, he said, the treatment is usually restricted to a list of "usual suspects" in regard to topic choice. Some of the "takes" or story angles that he listed included the following: the arrival of illegals into the country, the social problems experienced by the immigrants, the response of the public or community to the new arrivals, how the new arrivals are different culturally, and the political response to the influx of immigrants. He noted the possibility for a negative connotation to be given to stories involving topics such as immigration and described certain word choices that he contends can become "code words" and lead to stereotypical portrayals. His examples include terms such as "Welfare mother," "illegals," "terrorist" used mostly in referring to Arabs, and "drug baron," reserved to describe a Latin American or South American person accused of drug crimes, but never used to describe a white man from the United States heavily involved in drug trafficking.[8]

Viewpoint 3: Media workplace practices and economic realities contribute to the contin-uation of media bias. A prevailing viewpoint of critics is that the climate of the media workplace — including newsroom practices — and the economic realities of the media business bear part of the responsibility for media bias.

Studies done as part of the Kerner Commission Report of 1968, commissioned by President Lyndon Johnson, found that newsrooms were predominantly a "white" world and called for aggressive actions on the part of news organizations to hire African Amer-icans and to begin to pay attention to and report news about the black community. At the time of the report, fewer than 5 percent of U.S. journalists were African American, and African Americans held fewer than 1 percent of supervisory positions in newsrooms. These figures included African American newspapers.

In the decades following the report, newsrooms and news organizations added African Americans and other minority group members to their staffs. However, many critics argued that, despite the efforts, little improvement in reporting of minorities has occurred.[9]

Learning newsroom practice and procedure when much of it is not formalized, as noted by Warren Breed in his 1955 study about newsroom policy ("Social Control in the Newsroom),[10] can be difficult for any reporter, but more so for a reporter who is also a member of a minority. The added difficulty faced by minority reporters in the newsroom in picking up newsroom policy was the focus of Clint C. Wilson II's article, "The Paradox of African American Journalists." He noted that the Kerner Report prompted the American Society of Newspaper Editors (ASNE) to set a goal of hiring a percentage of minority journalists employed equal to the minority population in the U.S. by 2000. While the percentage of African American journalists in the U.S. increased, the increase failed to keep up with the increase of minority representation in the U.S. population. By 1998, their percentage in the journalism field grew to 11.46, less than half that of minority representation in the U.S. population (26 percent). Wilson cited the nature of newsroom organization, journalistic practices, and the socialization process for journalists as possible factors contributing to this. He reported, "Placing Black journalists in the almost total racial and cultural isolation of the newsroom where operative news values, procedures, and policy have been long ingrained to exclude the African American perspective obviates their effectiveness as agents for change."[11]

Other critics cite as factors that can contribute to media bias deeply entrenched, even institutionalized, newsroom workplace habits, practices, and procedures, as well as traditional definitions of what constitutes and qualifies as "news."[12] Without fundamental change here, there argue, there is little hope for change without major shifts in thinking and in society. Christopher P. Campbell, in his book *Race, Myth , and the News*, claimed that despite efforts to change things, America's racial myths still endure. He attributed some of the responsibility to the media. The very nature of the news media and society, he argued, "may not allow [the media] to function in a manner that will contribute to more accurate portrayals of life outside the mainstream. That would require newsroom processes and social processes to be systematically questioned and altered."[13]

Another "reality" that contributes to media bias, critics claim, is the capitalistic nature of the media. From this perspective, the media are money-making entities increasingly concerned with their ability to compete and make a profit in a media-saturated society. Wilson noted that the ability "to show 'a successful bottom line' is directly related to a medium's proficiency at delivering a desirable audience to its advertisers,"[14] and people from minority groups, he reasoned, are often missing from that desired demographic. Some critics have concluded that the under-representation of minority groups in the higher socio-economic levels leads to their being "shortchanged" in news coverage.[15] Campbell argued that this preoccupation with the profit incentive on the media's part presents a "a major barrier to more racially comprehensive news coverage in the media."[16]

Some critics have cited the economic realities for television news programs, which are concerned with the need to achieve satisfactory ratings figures, as one explanation for the lack of coverage of minorities. In an article titled "The Color of Ratings," Av Weston explored the issue of coverage of minorities in prime time news. He conducted interviews with more than 100 professionals in the television news business, ranging from production assistants to executives and producers from five commercial networks, PBS, four station chains, and the syndicated program *Inside Edition*. Weston concluded that "Every week — every day — stories about African-Americans, Hispanics, and Asians are kept off the air." His interviews revealed that viewer demographics and ratings often determine whether a story will make the news or not. "Viewer demographics (demos) reveal an audience's age and racial composition, and as one former executive told me, '[Blacks] don't get the demo.' Indeed, 'They are bad demos' is a euphemism for 'Avoid stories about African-Americans.'"[17]

Media Bias Is Non-existent or Minimal

Viewpoint 1: The efforts the media have made in recent years have rid them of bias that may have existed in the past. Those who believe that no media bias exists regarding race and ethnicity argue that the media today are free of the biases that may have existed in the past. One of the areas where support for this view can be found is in current and recent television entertainment programming. The fall 2005 lineup included more diversity, according to Gail Pennington, television critic for the *St. Louis Post-Dispatch*. She wrote in "Network Shows Face Up to Pledge on Color Coding" that the diversity of the prime time schedule reflects networks' efforts to rid programming of their "lily-white" state of earlier years. She cited the multi-cultural cast of the popular *Lost*, which features African-American, Korean, Iraqi, Indian, and Hispanic characters among its cast. She also noted diversity in the characters of two other popular series: ABC's *Desperate Housewives* features an African-American couple and a Latino couple among its regular characters, and NBC's *Grey's Anatomy* has Japanese-American actor Sandra Oh playing one of the lead characters. On the comedy side, Pennington mentioned *Everybody Hates Chris*, a situation comedy based on the childhood of African-American comedian and star Chris Rock. This situation comedy, developed and narrated by Rock, was picked up in 2005 by UPN and features an all-black cast except for one white person who is a regular character. Pennington noted that the improvements made in recent years to television's offerings were the result of an outcry in 1999 made by the NAACP about the lack of diversity in television's programming. "Since signing a 2000 pledge to do better," she wrote, "the networks are trying, appointing executives to monitor diversity, setting up mentoring programs for writers and holding acting showcases for various minority groups."[18]

In addition to the programs mentioned by Pennington, fall 2005–2006 television listings included two programs featuring Latinos in leading roles, both on ABC. *George Lopez*, starring comedian George Lopez, is a situation comedy about a Latino family, which ABC added to its schedule in 2002. In 2005 ABC began airing another comedy about a Latino family, this one titled *Freddie*, starring Freddie Prinz Jr., who plays a young bachelor whose female relatives move in with him.

Even before the most recent diversity-aware entertainment programs appeared among the major networks' offerings, those who argue that media bias is minimal found evidence of their position in television's offerings as early as the 1980s. In the book *Annual Editions, Mass Media 03/04*, John McWhorter took the view that the history of blacks on television was a clear sign that "the color line is ever dissolving in America," a viewpoint he stated in his review of Donald Bogle's book *Primetime Blues: African Americans on Network Television*. McWhorter argued that portrayals of blacks in situation comedies and dramas on television were by 2001 a major improvement over their portrayals in the 1950s. He cited as evidence a number of highly successful programs featuring blacks in the starring roles: *The Cosby Show*, *A Different World*, *Sanford and Son*, *The Parkers*, and others. "If you put an African American of the 1950s before a television set in 2001," he argued, "he would surely be stunned and elated by the evidence of progress that would pass before his eyes."[19]

Adherents of this position also claim that improved print coverage of minorities has been evident in recent years. In the article, "Covering the Invisible 'Model Minority,'" William Wong noted that print coverage of Asian Americans has "become increasingly nuanced, textured and true to life, thanks in part to greater numbers of Asian American journalists, some of whom are bringing more informed coverage." He cited as the biggest reason for improved coverage of Asian Americans the growth and complexity of the Asian American population in the U.S., noting that since 1970, the population of Asian Americans has tripled, growing to eight million.[20]

Also improved is the coverage of Latinos in newspapers, according to Mercedes Lynn de Uriarte. In her essay "A Problematic Press: Latinos and the News," she identified the *Los Angeles Times* and the *Dallas Morning News* as the leaders among newspapers in coverage of Latinos, citing them for "providing not only consistent coverage, but also doing a much better job at covering Latino politics." Both newspapers, she noted, include minority news staffs of at least 20 percent of their totals, and both have minority members, including Latinos, in positions of leadership and decision making, qualities that, she argued, mitigated the problems of traditional gatekeeping that restricted newspaper coverage of Latinos. Coverage of Latinos, she noted, has increased and has moved beyond stories about crises or stories about culture and often include "the insightful stories as urged by the Kerner Commission."[21]

Viewpoint 2: If any bias exists on the part of the media, the bias is a pro-minority bias rather than an anti-minority one. Some critics cite a media bias but maintain that the bias favors the minority over the mainstream, or white audience. This bias, they contend, often results in a distorted view of reality or results in an awkwardness in news reporting, one that favors the minority in a positive way or manner. Valarie Basheda addressed this concern in an article titled "When Should You Quote Minority Sources?" She discussed the practice of "mainstreaming," which some major newspapers, including the *Detroit News* and those belonging to the Gannett chain, have instituted that requires reporters to seek out a person of a minority to be quoted in a story, even stories in which a minority figure may have little or no interest or involvement. While some view this practice as a way of ensuring that minority viewpoints are represented, others argue that it can lead to a distorted picture of the issues and often makes the minority figure a "token voice."[22]

Still others argue that minorities have been favored over those in the majority (mainly white males) in recent years by many of the programs and initiatives offered in efforts to encourage diversity in newsrooms and the media business. White reporters and others in the media professions feel that they are being overlooked or passed over in favor of the minority colleagues. Supporters of this view point to the various programs and initiatives that major networks, newspapers, news organizations, and university journalism programs have instituted to aggressively work toward achieving diversity and eradicating past biases in coverage of minorities. The intent is to encourage members of minorities in particular to apply for positions.

Two such initiatives are the Poynter Institute on Diversity and the Freedom Forum, which fosters diversity through the efforts of its Newsroom Diversity programs. The Poynter Institute's Diversity Website offers information about upcoming seminars in diversity, tip sheets on diversity issues, a bibliography on diversity issues, and links to articles about coverage of minorities by the media.[23] One article linked to the site addressed efforts to encourage young Native Americans to consider journalism as a career. "Hiring — and Nurturing — Native Journalists" by Jodi Rave described a partnership between the Missoula, Mont., *Missoulian* and the Western Montana Fair Board that hires teenagers from the local high school to write stories about the fair. One of the teens hired was a young Native American whose experience working at the paper made her seriously consider journalism as a career. This kind of program, Rave wrote, could be implemented by other newspapers around the country — especially those around Native American communities — to foster interest in journalism careers.[24]

The Website for the Freedom Forum's Newsroom Diversity initiative states that the Freedom Forum "works aggressively to identify, recruit, and train people of color for journalism careers."[25] In addition to hosting a Summer Diversity Institute in 2003, the Freedom Forum promotes diversity through a number of ongoing efforts, which include maintaining a Diversity Institute at Vanderbilt University, offering the Chips Quinn Scholarship program, which offers young people of color scholarships of $1,000, and establishing a $1 million partnership with the American Society of Newspaper Editors, the Associate Press Managing Editors, and the Al Neuharth Media Center to promote diversity.[26]

CBS's efforts to increase the presence of minorities in the television industry are detailed in its Diversity Mission Statement, found online at http://www.cbsdiversty.com/mission.shtml. CBS, according to its mission statement, "is committed to building and nurturing a diversified environment throughout the entire company, as well as the entertainment industry at large."[27] One of the initiatives of the CBS Diversity Institute is a Writers Mentoring Program, which focuses on helping minorities to succeed at writing dramas and comedy series. A similar initiative on the news side of CBS is also available for minority participation. CBS News announced in 2002 that it was instituting a program that it hoped would lead to greater diversity in the newsroom. The program, called the CBS News Development Program, was created to encourage more people of color to enter the news business by identifying and supporting minority journalists. Andrew Heyward, president of CBS News, was quoted as saying, "By identifying up-and-coming producers and reporters of color and providing them with new opportunities, we hope to offer these rising stars a meaningful experience that helps their careers and also helps us."[28]

Viewpoint 3. Claims that the media are biased against minorities are often exaggerated by critics with their own agendas or biases. A third viewpoint expressed by some is that claims of bias against minorities are often exaggerated by critics with their own agendas or biases. One such agenda they point to is political correctness. Robert Novak addressed the issue in his essay "Political Correctness Has No Place in the Newsroom." He blamed PC for newspapers adopting policies regarding language use that tend to go overboard to avoid the appearance of bias. He used as examples the *Los Angeles Times*' prohibition against using the term "Dutch treat," which might be seen to be disparaging of people of Dutch descent, and the word "Indian" to refer to Native Americans. He argued that political correctness in language not only destroys meaning but also demeans the people who are meant to be protected. People who believe in the real dignity of the individual, no matter of what race, sex, ethnicity, or other condition," he argued, "shouldn't embrace political correctness because it is bad philosophy; and reporters shouldn't do so either because it is bad journalism."[29]

In addition to political correctness, critics have argued that liberalism is another agenda or bias that has been used to exaggerate claims about negative media bias. William McGowan, in his book *Coloring the News: How Crusading for Diversity Has Corrupted American Journalism*, wrote that some news organizations have made holding liberal values a requirement for employment, not through any active mechanism, but rather through what he called an "invisible liberal consensus." This invisible layer has affected open discussion of diversity issues in newsrooms, with some feeling they cannot question how diversity issues are handled without running the risk of suffering hostility. He also criticized the diversity agenda that he contends opened the door to "ethnic, racial and gender cheerleading," which he claimed can occur when objectivity is lost. He also blamed the crusade for diversity as having unintended consequences for the media, including driving down morale, increasing attrition, and driving away many white, middle-class readers because of ideologically skewed reporting. The worst disservice, he argued, is the oversimplification of complicated issues and the undermining of the spirit of cooperation on the part of the public, two qualities "without which no multiethnic and multiracial society can survive."[30]

Tim Chavez echoed concerns about the diversity agenda and claimed that other agendas are being served in the name of diversity. In "Rethinking Diversity," he argued that the efforts of diversity champions have been "co-opted into an agenda more intent on protecting a racial spoils system and perpetuating an intimidating atmosphere of political correctness." He cited as an example the manner in which the *New York Times* allowed reporter Jayson Blair, an African American, to break newsroom policy rules regarding accuracy and attribution in his stories numerous times until the problems came to light with Blair's firing "*Times*' then-editor Howell Raines," Chavez wrote, "admitted to Southern guilt as a white man in allowing Blair, a black reporter, to repeatedly break the rules on accuracy and attribution that others get called on, and fired. Blair got promoted."[31] Diversity in the *Times* newsroom, Chavez claimed, was more important than accuracy. He argued that the message sent by affirmative action — that some discrimination, in college admissions or employment standards for minorities because they have been painted as less qualified or capable — has set diversity back in a harmful way and that it would fall to Hispanics or Latinos to change perceptions and work toward empowerment instead of entitlement.

• THE EVIDENCE •

Scholars, as well as society itself, are divided on the issue of racial and ethnic bias in the media. Some view the media as being biased in their coverage and portrayal of minorities, while others view the media as being free of bias. Both sides make compelling arguments and cite sound evidence to support their positions. While there might be more material, quantitatively speaking, on one side or the other, assessing the respective arguments and viewpoints requires more than simply counting the number of books and articles that have been written.

Virtually all scholars and critics, no matter which side of the issue they come down on, ultimately agree that present-day media treatments of the race and ethnicity issue are more even-handed and bias-free than at any time in the past. This is the case whether the particular topic of discussion is the amount of attention devoted to minorities (all agree that it is greater); the extent to which stereotypes are used (all agree it is less pervasive); or the utilization of minorities in the nation's newsrooms, entertainment venues, and media organizations (all agree that more minority voices are included). Most critics from both sides of the issue focus on advances made in African-American representation in the media, while much less evidence is provided on other minorities.

• RESOLUTION •

In any case, a lively debate can still be generated if one proposes that the media are now bias-free. One's position is likely to be determined subjectively. One's own race, political leanings, age, and income level may all affect one's attitude on the issue. Obviously there is no clear-cut answer to the question of whether or how the media are biased with respect to race and ethnicity. Some seemingly objective evidence can be viewed as supporting either side of the debate, depending upon one's own predilections. For example, the number of popular television entertainment programs featuring African Americans and Latinos offered on major networks in recent years can be cited as evidence that bias no longer exists. On the other hand, others can argue that the number of television programs featuring African Americans and Latinos is not proportional to their numbers in the country at large. Particularly troublesome in this connection is the fact that, even as a growing number of minorities are found in American society, less attention has been devoted to their place in the media. Native Americans, Asian Americans, and Arab Americans, for example, remain underrepresented.

In the final analysis, the question of media bias with respect to race and ethnicity is probably one that will go unresolved to the satisfaction of everyone. Valid and convincing evidence and arguments exist on both sides of the issue. No matter how much progress has been made and can be documented in this area, it may be unrealistic to expect that everyone will agree on a statement assessing the state of the media being bias free when dealing with race and ethnicity. Most people will, however, be more likely to agree that the media have a responsibility to strive to be as bias free as is practicable. Sensitivity to issues of fairness in treatment of ethnic and racial minorities should be practiced in all facets of the media. It is not necessary to embrace "political correctness" in reporting on minorities in order to present an equitable picture. It requires merely that the media be even-handed in their representations of all citizens, regardless of their race and ethnicity.

• POINTS OF VIEW •

Cropp, Fritz, Cynthia M. Frisby, and Dean Mills, eds. *Journalism Across Cultures*. Ames: Iowa State Press, 2003. This volume offers a collection of essays designed to help journalists improve the coverage of minorities and to increase understanding of the diverse cultures that make up American society.

Dines, Gail, and Jean H. Humez, eds. *Gender, Race, and Class in Media*, 2d ed. Thousand Oaks, Calif.: Sage, 2003. This all-encompassing text/reader includes seventy essays exploring media content and biases and practices based on gender, race, and class.

Dixon, Travis L., and Daniel Linz. "Overrepresentation and Underrepresentation of African Americans and Latinos as Lawbreakers on Television News." *Journal of Communication* 50 (2000): 131–151. Television news is biased because African Americans are portrayed as perpetrators of crime more frequently than they appear in police records.

Eberle, Bobby. "Media Bias Glaring in Racial Coverage." *Intellectual Conservative*, October 13, 2003. http://www.intellectualconservative.com/2003/media-bias-glaring-in-racial-coverage/. The media, because of their liberal bias, did not cover racial epithets that Louisiana Democrats used.

Holtzman, Linda. *Media Messages: What Film, Television, and Popular Music Teach Us About Race, Class, Gender and Sexual Orientation.* Armonk, N.Y.: M.E. Sharpe, 2000. Holtzman includes two chapters dealing with the mass media and racial biases that offer comprehensive overviews of the way race has been portrayed in the media.

Jacobs, Ronald N. *Race, Media and the Crisis of Civil Society: From Watts to Rodney King.* Cambridge, England: University of Cambridge Press, 2000. This work focuses on issues raised by the coverage of the Watts riots of 1965, the 1991 Rodney King beating, and the 1992 Rodney King trial verdict aftermath as covered by mainstream newspapers and African American newspapers.

McGowan, William. *Coloring the News.* San Francisco: Encounter Books, 2001. Pro-diversity bias has resulted in slanted rather than unbiased coverage.

Wilson II, Clint C., Félix Gutiérrez, and Lena M. Chao. *Racism, Sexism and the Media: The Rise of Class Communication in Multicultural America,* 3d ed. Thousand Oaks, Calif.: Sage, 2003. The authors examine the many media issues connected with the complexity and diversity of the U.S. population.

Witosky, Tom. "Mainstreaming and Diversity Are Gannett's Core Values: But these programs are not without controversy." *Nieman Reports*, Fall 2003, 39–41. Gannett newspapers have instituted programs to reduce inherent content biases found in white male dominated newsrooms, including a diversity program begun in 1984 to bring more minorities into the newsroom where content decisions are made.

NOTES

1. Salim Muwakkil, "Racial Bias Still Haunts Media," http://www.inthesetimes.com/site/main/article/478/.

2. *Tuscaloosa* (Ala.) *News*, 5 July 2006.

3. Clint C. Wilson II, Félix Gutiérrez, and Lena M. Chao, *Racism, Sexism and the Media: The Rise of Class Communication in Multicultural America* (Thousand Oaks, Calif.: Sage, 2003), 117.

4. Joan Byrd, "Blacks, Whites in News Pictures," in Shirley Biagi and Marilyn Kern-Foxworth, eds., *Facing Difference: Race, Gender, and Mass Media* (Thousand Oaks, Calif.: Pine Forge Press, 1997), 96.

5. National Council of La Raza, "Don't Blink: Hispanics in Television Entertainment," in Biagi and Kern-Foxworth, ibid., 29.

6. Christopher John Farley, "TV's Black Flight," in Joan Gorham, ed. *Mass Media 1997/98* (Guilford, Conn.: Dushkin/McGraw Hill, 1997), 143.

7. Robert Entman and Andrew Rojecki, *The Black Image in the White Mind* (Chicago: University of Chicago Press, 2000), 63–64.

8. Teun A. van Dijk, "New(s) Racism: A Discourse Analytical Approach," in Simon Cottle, ed., *Ethnic Minorities in the Media* (Philadelphia: Open University Press, 2000), 37–39.

9. Kenneth F. Irby, "What's Missing in This Picture?" Posted July 1, 1999, Poynteronline (http://poynteronline.org/content-view.asp) and "30 Years After Kerner Report, Some Say Racial Divide Wider," Posted March 1, 1998, CNNInteractive (http://www.cnn.com/US/9803/01/kerner.commis sion/). For information from the 2005 newsroom employment census conducted by the American Society of Newspaper Editors, see "News Staffs Shrinking While Minority Presence Grows," Posted April 12, 2005, ASNE Online (http: www.asne.org/index.cfm?id=5648).

10. Warren Breed, "Social Control in the Newsroom: A Functional Analysis," *Social Forces* 33:4 (1955): 326–335, also reprinted in Wilbur Schramm, ed., *Mass Communications*, 2nd ed. (Champaign.: University of Illinois Press, 1960), 178–197.

11. Clint C. Wilson II, "The Paradox of African American Journalists," in Cottle, *Ethnic Minorities and the Media*, 87, 97.

12. See Ben H. Bagdikian, *The Media Monopoly* (Boston: Beacon Press, 1983) and Gaye Tuchman, *Making News: A Study in the Construction of Reality* (New York: The Free Press/Macmillan, 1978).

13. Campbell, *Race, Myth and the News*, 136.

14. Wilson, "The Paradox of African American Journalists," 96.

15. Wilson, Gutiérrez, and Chao, *Racism, Sexism and the Media*, 125.

16. Campbell, *Race, Myth and the News*, 32.

17. Av Weston, "The Color of Ratings," in Joan Gorham, ed., *Mass Media 03/04* (Guilford, Conn.: McGraw-Hill/Dushkin, 2003), 34–35.

18. Gail Pennington, "Network Shows Face Up to Pledge on Color Coding," *St. Louis Post-Dispatch*, 12 October 2005, E1.

19. John McWhorter, "Gimme a Break! Blacks, Television, and the Decline of Racism in America," in Gorham, *Mass Media 03/04*, 40, 45.

20. William Wong, "Covering the Invisible 'Model Minority,'" in Biagi and Kern-Foxworth, *Facing Difference*, 98.

21. Mercedes Lynn de Uriarte, "A Problematic Press: Latinos and the News," in *Journalism Across the Cultures* (Ames: Iowa State Press, 2003) 57.

22. Valarie Basheda, "When Should You Quote Minority Sources?" in Biagi and Kern-Foxworth, *Facing Difference*, 140.

23. Poynter Institute on Diversity. http://www.poynterinstitute.org.

24. Jodi Rave, "Hiring — and Nurturing — Native Journalists," Posted September 22, 2005 on Poynter Institute Website (http://www.poynter.org/content/content_print.asp?), 1–3.

25. "Newsroom Diversity," Freedom Forum Online. http://www.freedomforum.org/diversity/default.asp.

26. "Diversity Programs," Freedom Forum Online. http://www.freedomforum.org/templates/document.asp?documentID=12803.

27. "Diversity Mission Statement," CBS Diversity Institute (http://www.cbsdiversity.com/mis sion.shtml.) Accessed date October 30, 2005.

28. "CBS News Development Program," Posted August 4, 2004 (http://www.cbsnews.com/sto ries/w2004/08/03/broadcasts/printable633770.shtml).

29. Robert Novak, "Political Correctness Has No Place in the Newsroom," in Joan Gorham, ed. *Mass Media 96/97* (Guilford, Conn.: Dushkin/Brown & Benchmark, 1996), 62.

30. William McGowan, *Coloring the News: How Crusading for Diversity Has Corrupted American Journalism* (San Francisco: Encounter Books, 2001), 31, 34.

31. Tim Chavez, "Rethinking Diversity," *Hispanic* 16 (2003): 80.

9

Crime

Kay Best Murphy

"'A scary orgy of violent crime is fueling another public call to action.' That's the way U.S. News & World Report began its cover story on 'Violence in America' early this year. In typical fashion, the magazine spoke of 'escalating crime numbers,' 'the wave of violence' and 'the upward spiral of violent crimes.' It's standard crime coverage: attention-grabbing, assertive, scary ... and inaccurate."—Jeff Cohen and Norman Solomon, JeffCohen.org[1]

"Much has been made ... about the perceived tendency by news reporters to focus on missing or murdered white women and children while ignoring missing or murdered women and children of color.... As the managing editor of a mid-sized daily newspaper, I assure readers that the color of the victim is of absolutely no importance to news decisions, except in crimes where race is central.... I'm more interested in the extraordinary circumstances. The 10th fatal mugging at a midnight subway platform by a gangster is less intriguing than the discovery of a grandmother's corpse in a public park and the realization that her 4 grandchildren are now missing. Which would you put on the front page?"— Ron Franscell, Under the News blogger[2]

Readers of the *News & Observer* in Raleigh, N.C., gathered at a community forum in January 2006 and accused the newspaper of over-representing crime in neighboring Durham. Business and civic leaders said the biased crime coverage conveyed a negative image of their city and threatened to stifle business growth and deter people from moving into Durham neighborhoods. The newspaper, responding through staff writer Ted Vanden in an opinion-page column a week later, denied the coverage was biased. He said "it would be irresponsible and a disservice to *N&O* readers, in Durham and elsewhere, to downplay or sugarcoat that truth. If anything, it's the newspaper's role to make sure that the public and politicians are facing up to the issue and taking steps to deal with it."[3]

In her 1980 book, *Crime News and the Public,* Doris Graber concluded that some newspapers devoted as much as 22 to 28 percent of their coverage to crime and justice issues while local television news programs devoted about 20 percent of air time to them.[4] Graber said "social scientists, as well as citizens in general, have complained a good deal in recent years about coverage of crime news. Crime news, it is claimed, is too plentiful in the press and on television." She contends that other news is slighted because too much attention is given to crime and that the crime coverage offered is biased or distorted. Other works—including a college textbook, *Writing and Reporting News: A Coaching Method,* by Carole Rich—deny that the media are biased by explaining how journalists gather and select news content, including crime.[5]

Do some crimes warrant more coverage than others? Is there the presence or absence of bias in the selection process or for crime news in the manner in which it is gathered? Does the media's coverage of crime accurately and fairly reflect the social reality of crime and the perpetrators of that crime? This chapter will discuss opposing arguments about the presence or absence of bias in the media's coverage of crime by exploring views on crime news content, news gathering techniques, and scholarly studies that compare news content to the social reality of crime. Since the publication of Graber's book on media crime coverage, other studies have tried to answer similar questions. Their conclusions fall on both sides of the bias issue, and they shed light on the reasons why bias does or does not exist.

Guilty of Bias

Those who accuse the media of bias have an enormous amount of scholarly research and opinions on which to base their claims. Doris Graber and other media critics who examine news products and compare them with actual crime statistics contend that the media inaccurately reflect crime in society. For example, the media disproportionately give more attention to murders than burglaries.[6] In addition, scholarly research by Travis Dixon, Christopher Campbell, and others shows the media unfairly depict the perpetrators of that criminal behavior. Specifically, African Americans are portrayed as crime perpetrators more often than they are arrested for those crimes.[7] Scholars also offer their opinions on why the media are biased.

Figures: Facts or Fiction?

Critics most often suggest that the media (1) do not accurately reflect the social reality of crime through their crime news content and (2) give too much attention to crime in general when compared to the total news content. Many scholars contend that systematic biases—systems or methods used in the selection of news—exist in the reporting of crime news and distort the social reality of crime. In a 1987 article in *Media, Culture and Society,* Jack Katz wrote that "the picture one obtains about crime from reading the newspapers inverts the picture about crime one gets from reading police statistics."[8]

Graber agreed that the picture is inverted in the press because murder is one of the least frequent crimes that occur in social reality but one of the more prevalent in crime news stories. She said "[crime news] presents a distorted image of the relative incidence of various types of street crimes by exaggerating murder, rape, and assault and under-representing robbery, burglary, and theft."[9]

Graber compared the crimes written in Chicago police records to the corresponding crimes covered in the *Chicago Tribune* from January 1976 to January 1977 and found a poor match. Graber said murder constituted 26 percent of all crime mentions in the *Tribune* during her one year study even though murder constituted only 0.2 percent of all crimes in the police index. Nonviolent crimes like theft and car theft, which appeared more often in the police index at 47 percent of all crimes, represented only 4 percent of all crimes mentioned in the *Tribune.*

Just as murder gets more than its fair share of crime news, crime news gets more than its fair share of overall news content. Some scholars, including Graber, contend extensive crime coverage displaces the coverage of other news topics, such as state government and health when comparing overall news content. Newspaper space and television news airtime is limited, which means the addition of any story leads to the elimination of another.

Graber's study analyzed the entire content of four newspapers (including the *Chicago Tribune*), two local network stations and three national networks from January 1976 to January 1977. The study also included four audience panels, who kept diaries, to recall stories and answer questions with regard to their perception of crime based on media reports. All members of the audience panels claimed to pay attention to the mass media — newspapers and television newscasts — to get information about crime and the justice system.

In examining news content, Graber compared the frequency of crime stories to nine other story topics, including elections, state government, and health and medicine. Graber said crime and justice topics averaged 25 percent of all content in newspapers, 20 percent of local television content, and 13 percent of national television content. Of that, 9 percent featured individual crime stories in newspapers, 8 percent in local television, and 4 percent for national television. Graber said "crime news receives ample coverage and display. By certain social significance criteria, it is excessive."

In examining crime coverage in the *Tribune,* Graber said stories on individual crime received almost three times as much attention as the presidency, the U.S. Congress, or the state of the economy, and it received almost four times as much coverage as state or city government. In examining national television coverage, Graber concluded individual crime news was as extensive as coverage of the presidency and the U.S. Congress.

Jack Katz agreed with Graber in his 1987 article "What makes crime news?" Katz analyzed the content of daily crime news stories from the *New York Times* and *Newsday* from mid-1974 to 1978 while he was employed by the Eastern District of New York. He found that biases cause crime news distortion because the media give more emphasis to unusual crimes like murder. "There are systematic biases in the reporting of crime news," he said, "at least in the respect that crime as presented in the daily news differs consistently from crime as described in official police statistics.... In study after study, the content of crime news has been found to diverge widely from the patterns available in official statistics. The relationship does not appear to be random or incoherent: in many respects, the picture one obtains about crime from reading the newspapers inverts the picture about crime one gets from reading police statistics."[10]

When the media inaccurately portray crime, the public gets an inaccurate picture of the social reality of crime. Dennis T. Lowry, Tarn Ching Josephine Nio, and Dennis W. Leitner in a 2003 article in the *Journal of Communication* said the public's perception of crime as an important national issue spiked in 1994 after television network news gave more attention to crime stories. Scholars, however, did not find a related spike in crime offenses in police records during that time.[11]

Lowry and the other researchers used survey figures collected in Gallup Poll reports to determine what people thought were the most important problems facing the nation. They also collected crime figures from the FBI Uniform Crime Reports and news content figures from the Center for Media and Public Affairs to determine which topics were being shown by three network television evening newscasts — ABC, CBS, and NBC. They published their conclusions in an article titled "Setting the Public Fear Agenda: A Longitudinal Analysis of Network TV Crime Reporting, Public Perceptions of Crime, and FBI Crime Statistics." In that article, they concluded that the network newscasts' number one topic in the 1990s was crime. This focus resulted in a public belief that crime was one of the most important problems facing the country. In fact, Lowry reports that only 2 percent of those surveyed believed crime was an important national issue in April 1990, but those numbers grew to 37 percent in January 1994 and 52 percent in August 1994.

"This study provides strong confirmation for earlier studies that have also found positive statistical relations between crime news coverage and public perceptions about crime," Lowry's study said. "Given the research design used in this study, with longitudinal survey data and network TV news data both preceding and following the big scare in 1994, the agenda-setting results seem somewhat striking."

The Structure of Bias

News media organizations, like other businesses, have operating structures. The media have developed organizational structures to routinize news gathering, helping the media increase efficiency in gathering, sorting, and producing news.[12] One of these structures is the "beat" system, which designates one or more reporters to seek information about a particular topic.

Graber contends that the beat system, specifically the "cops beat" or "police beat," is inherently biased because it places the importance of gathering crime stories above issues that fall outside of the beat system. "News from these beats is allotted space and air time according to fairly regular patterns...," she said. "Events occurring remote from these beats, by contrast, are often ignored, except when they are sensational in nature, or when a reporter's whim has suddenly cast them into the limelight of attention as a feature or special investigative report.... [T]he structure of the beat system would seem to preordain substantially more coverage of street crime, particularly the more violent and bizarre incidents, than coverage of more routine crime occurrences, including white-collar crime."[13]

The beat system is a media personnel structure aimed at efficiency and predictability, where a reporter is designated to gather crime news as opposed to other news topics. This structure reserves the center stage for crime stories, allotting space and airtime to that topic, Graber said.

The media's organizational level also pushes crime toward center stage. In his book *Rich Media, Poor Democracy: Communication Politics in Dubious Times,* Robert McChesney, a liberal critic, said the media offer more stories about crime, shoot-outs, and court cases because they are inexpensive and easy-to-cover. Investigative and in-depth stories are more expensive to produce than covering single events, like individual crimes. According to McChesney, "the main concern of the media giants is to make journalism directly profitable." Network newscasters' expensive stories, like international news of the 1970s, have been replaced with less expensive news, like crime, in the 1990s. "The annual number of crime stories on network TV news programs tripled from 1990–92 to 1993–96," McChesney said. "Not only are such stories cheaper to cover and air, they hardly ever enmesh the parent corporation in controversy, as do 'hard' news stories."[14]

Officially Biased

News reports based too heavily on government officials, critics claim, cause bias in crime reporting because the viewpoints of law enforcement officials are given more attention than those of the accused. In her 1980 book, Graber pointed out that crime reporters rely heavily on police blotters for news, shaping news content into a "steady, constant stream" of crime stories based on official viewpoints.[15] Her conclusion was followed up in 2004 by James Simon and Sean Hayes, who agreed official sources dominate crime stories. They discuss their analysis of juvenile crime stories in their 2004 article "Juvenile Crime Stories Use Police Blotter without Comment from Suspects," published in the *Newspaper Research Journal.* Simon and Hayes said "researchers have long recognized that reporters, in constructing crime stories, follow certain patterns in deciding what sources to quote." Those patterns emerged in their study of juvenile crime stories, which examined stories printed in the three largest newspapers in Connecticut between January and March of 2002. They found 81 percent of stories included police comment but only 8 percent contained comment from the suspect's point of view. "Despite the presumption of innocence until proven guilty, the point of view of the juvenile, his or her attorney and family members was included in only 8 percent of the overall stories" Simon and Hayes concluded. The results of their study said that "not much has changed since Graber first documented the shortcomings of crime reporting more than two decades ago."[16] They said journalists rely heavily on police information in first-day crime stories and do not make a great effort to provide the viewpoint of those outside law enforcement, such as that of the accused.

Long-term relationships between reporters and sources can also bias stories because the reporter might feel sympathy for a source's problems or the reporter might feel a sense of responsibility for the success of the sources' programs. Herbert Strentz, author of the 1989 book, *News Reporters and News Sources,* said journalists may favor information provided by authorities if there is a strong relationship between the reporter and source. Strentz said "the reporter must be sensitive ... to any relationship with news sources that lessens the journalist's control of news content or threatens credibility with the audience and other news sources."[17]

Racial Bias

Researchers who compare police crime statistics to the frequency of news stories often find African Americans are over-represented in crime stories. In other words, African

Americans are portrayed as criminals more often than they are listed as criminals in police records. Critics contend this bias is prevalent in the media's crime coverage.

Christopher P. Campbell, author of the 1995 book *Race, Myth and the News*, said routine news coverage is biased because it advances stereotypes instead of social reality by casting non-White Americans in aggressive and criminal roles. Campbell contends local television newscasts continued "traditional racist stereotyping" into the 1990s. "The stereotypes," he said, "are not as blatant as their predecessors in the mass media; rather than minstrels and Sambos, we see a more subtle mythology about minority life — the product of majority culture stereotyping that is inadvertently communicated by TV journalists. ... I agree the journalists who produce and report stories that feed mythical notions about race rarely, if ever, do so as part of some 'intentional' or diabolical' plot." The absence of African Americans portrayed in stories outside of crime news is part of the distortion by the media, Campbell argued. "[C]riminal activity is portrayed as the endeavor of choice among African Americans, while everyday life outside of the white community is largely invisible."[18]

Campbell and Graber contend that much of crime news is focused on individual acts of crime rather than stories that show the social complexity of crime. Focusing on individual crimes is one of the patterns of newsrooms, and that cycle perpetuates the focus on individual crimes. The routinization of news gathering limits the need for more profound thought processes, which means reporters fail to consider crime stories in the complex framework of society. Campbell contends the media fail to consider the historical, economic, political, or social factors when writing stories, and it results in unbalanced stories that distort reality and promote racial stereotypes.[19]

Campbell said one reason newspapers fail to portray African Americans in a fair and balanced manner is because minorities have little to do with news-decision making in newsrooms. According to Campbell, newspapers are controlled mostly by white male executives who are less sensitive to racial stereotyping than minority employees. In daily print newsrooms, African Americans and other minorities fill less than 8 percent of the jobs and half the daily newspapers employ no minorities. Campbell based his conclusion on 1992 statistics from the American Society of Newspaper Editors.[20]

Other researchers agree. In a study published in the *Journal of Communication* in 2000, Travis Dixon and Daniel Linz contend that African Americans were more likely to be portrayed as perpetrators of crime on television news (37 percent) than to be arrested (21 percent, according to crime reports) for those crimes. That discrepancy grows larger when considering felonies. African Americans were more likely to be portrayed as felons on television news (44 percent) than to be arrested for felonies (25 percent). Researchers said both examples are statistically significant.[21]

Dixon and Linz, whose study included only Los Angeles-based stations, contend that the reason African Americans are over-represented as criminals is in part due to ethnic discourse and in part as an outgrowth of unconscious stereotyping. "News editors and reporters," they argued, "are not exempt from this phenomena. As a result, they may make decisions about the newsworthiness of events based on a discourse rooted in unconscious stereotypical assumptions. Under such circumstances, Black perpetration of crime, particularly if Whites are victims, may be deemed highly newsworthy by news gatherers who may unconsciously conform to these ethnocentric, discursive practices."[22]

Dixon and Linz also contend that the media pay more attention to blue-collar crimes that involve face-to-face impersonal force than to white-collar crimes that are nonviolent-economic crimes. White-collar crimes include some degree of fraud, collusion, or deception, and lack of face-to-face interpersonal force. This structural constraint on news gathering results in less coverage of white perpetrators, who commit more white-collar crimes than African Americans.

Innocent of Bias

Not everyone sees bias in crime news. While readers of the *News & Observer* (Raleigh, N.C.) claimed the newspaper's coverage was biased, the newspaper said it was not. In an opinion-page article "Durham sees red over crime," published in January 2006 in the *N&O*, staff reporter Ted Vaden wrote about reader criticism at a community forum hosted by the newspaper. At that forum, readers accused the newspaper of over-representing crime coverage in Durham. Vaden defended the newspaper's crime coverage, saying the newspaper would not "sugarcoat" the truth and would continue its crime coverage. Vaden wrote that "the truth is ... that Durham does have a murder crime problem, disproportionate to its population size and more troublesome than that of Raleigh and other North Carolina cities." The newspaper's publisher, Orage Quarles III, was quoted as saying, "we're going to keep talking about crime and the newspaper will keep raising hell until you all say enough is enough" and address the problem.[23]

Like the *News and Observer*, most media and journalism advocates plead not guilty when the media are accused of bias. They use modern journalism values and paradigms to explain why the media give more attention to some stories, such as crime, than to others.[24] In their defense, journalism advocates point to changes and improvements in the ever-evolving industry that are aimed at eliminating areas of potential bias.

In his 1997 book *Journalism Ethics*, John C. Merrill said journalists in the second half of the twentieth century placed a greater emphasis on journalistic responsibility and on the goal of fairness and balance, a movement spurred by the 1947 Hutchins Commission report and media responses to it. The commission took journalists to task, warning that the First Amendment would not protect the mass media from governmental control if the media persisted in being irresponsible. In the 1950s and 1960s, journalism responded with codes of conduct and better education for media workers. This evolution has moved journalism away from the apprentice model of training and toward a more professional level of skill involving more of a college-educated, rule-bound workforce. Journalists contend part of their job is to avoid bias.[25] That concept applies to crime reporting as well.

While the public and scholars may say the media are biased, the media contend they are fulfilling their roles as "gatekeepers" when they decide to publish a murder story rather than a house burglary. Gatekeepers determine what news is important enough to appear in the media. This is not biased coverage, they contend, because media audiences expect journalists to prioritize the news. Even though news reports may not reflect crimes in the frequency in which they occur in social reality, audiences still get an accurate picture of crime news because audiences understand the media will give unusual crime, like murder, more attention than less violent crimes.[26] As for racial bias, some news organizations have gone to great lengths to eliminate news structures conducive to it. These include hiring more racial minorities to diversify news decision-making, rethinking news-gathering paradigms, and reconsidering the selection of news content.

"Gatekeepers"

Journalists act as "gatekeepers" of news, deciding which information is passed beyond the gate to news audiences. As with other news topics, crime coverage many times covers the unusual crime rather than the most common. In her book, *Writing and Reporting News: A Coaching Method*, Carole Rich explains the criteria journalists use in selecting news content.[27] Many college students use Rich's textbook to learn how journalists select news content based on a series of journalistic criteria. That criteria, called "the qualities of news stories for hard- and soft-news stories" by Rich, include: timeliness, proximity, unusual nature, human interest, conflict, impact, helpfulness, entertainment, and issues or problems in the community. By Rich's definition, a local murder merits media coverage because of its proximity, unusual nature, conflict, and community-issue relevance. In his 2005 opinion article "In crime coverage, does status matter?" Ted Vaden said the "unusual nature" of murder makes it more newsworthy to readers. He said "[there is] nothing wrong with meeting readers' interests, as long as the coverage is appropriate to the importance of the news."[28]

Graber said audiences, to a certain extent, filter news stories by comparing them with their own existing attitudes and perceptions. In other words, audiences use their own judgments when consuming news. Graber said "this explains why sensational crime coverage does not automatically lead to panic reactions among most people. However, jolting evidence that disconfirms the audience's mental status quo may lead to rapid reshaping of perceptions. This study also provides evidence of more gradual incremental reshaping that occurs through the combined impact of media and other stimuli over extended time periods." This gradual process changes news audience's perceptions over time, thus supplying a new "mental status quo" to be used to when judging the value of news consumption.[29]

Mark Warr of Washington State University conducted a study in the mid 1970s that supported Graber's belief that the public evaluates crime news and, therefore, can gain an accurate idea of crime. In his 1980 *Social Forces* article "Accuracy of Public Beliefs About Crime," Warr found the public's perception of crime was fairly accurate.[30] He surveyed adult residents of a major metropolitan area, asking them to estimate which crimes happened most frequently and which least. They accurately answered that theft was more prevalent than murder, even though theft received less media coverage. He said that "the results, then, do not support the contention that the public grossly misperceives the official incidents of criminal offenses.... The data presented here belie the argument that media coverage of crime leads to distorted public perceptions of the incidence of offenses."[31] Warr said statements made by critics of the news media, including comments on crime news sources, news linkages, story accuracy, and the rationality journalists exhibit, have all too often been based on presumption rather than evidence. Warr said "the results of this study demonstrate a remarkable degree of correspondence between official information and public perceptions, a finding which runs counter to the literature on media coverage of crime."

Structure: Method Not Bias

Three things in life are certain for journalists: death, taxes, and deadlines. Over the last century, journalists have developed organizational structures to help them gather and produce news efficiently. Graber and other critics have blamed the beat system for contributing to the distortion of news content, because the system leads to the over-representation of beat topics, such as crime.[32] In his 2000 *Newspaper Research Journal* article "Why does the beat go on?" Lee Becker and other scholars conclude journalists employ such structures to differentiate tasks. Becker said such systems are necessary to gather news in a timely, orderly, and efficient manner.[33] Journalists use beats as a method for deciding which reporters will talk with which sources in gathering the types of news that routinely appear in the news media. In their study, Becker and his partners surveyed three different-sized newspapers in 1998 in the southeastern United States and found five types of beats are common regardless of the size of the newspaper. They are courts, crime, education, government, and hospitals. Becker said "beats seem to exist because they do represent an efficient means of gathering the types of news newspapers want." As slaves to daily deadlines, journalists rely on this structure to produce news fast enough for production schedules. Not all media rely on beats. According to Becker, television newsrooms generally have fewer reporters than print media and do not rely heavily on the beat system. Television news collection method relies more on reporter enterprise and leads from newspapers.[34]

One journalism textbook for college students recommends the "crime beat" be changed to the "violence beat." In their mini-course text *Reporting Violence*, Jane Ellen Stevens, Ester Thorson, and Lori Dorfman contend expanding the nature of the beat to include all violence, not just crime reports, would place the media focus more on public health issues rather than individual crimes.[35] Stevens and her co-authors said crime coverage under this new beat topic would expand to emphasize crime prevention, the status of violent crime, crimes that go unreported, and the response to crime by public health officials.

Although beats have dominated media production systems for decades, another system is emerging. In their 2003 *Journalism & Mass Communication Quarterly* article "Changing the Newsroom Culture: A Four Year Case Study of Organizational Development at the St. Louis Post-Dispatch," Peter Gade and Earnest Perry said that media beat systems are giving way to a more modern structure, the team system, which shifts news collection decisions from one person to a team of journalists.[36] Some newspapers adopted the system about ten years ago, and others have followed the trend.

Gade said that although some journalists resist this new system, team-based work offers flatter corporate hierarchies and shared decision-making that breaches traditional barriers and diversifies content. As the team structure takes the place of the beat structure, it also eliminates one area of crime bias criticized by Graber and others.

Not Officially Biased

Although some criticize the press for relying too heavily on official sources, journalists need them to lend credibility to stories. Stephen Buckley, a national correspondent for the *St. Petersburg Times*, explained in an online tip sheet for reporters that spending time with police sources will help them get more information about crime.[37] Buckley said "tell them a little about yourself. Ask them about their families. And of course, ask them about work." Reporters who establish good sources, people who are willing to give them information, produce good stories. In his book *Journalism Ethics, Philosophical Foundations for News Media* (1997), John C. Merrill said there should be no inherent biases in dealing with sources as long as journalists understand that journalistic objectives are different from those of their sources. Merrill said sources are needed to provide expert knowledge and credibility in the area of the story. Although these sources may try to introduce their biases into stories, reporters avoid this. Merrill said "the good reporter will want to diminish this subjectivity as much as possible. Bias is a constant threat, and the reporter can never really know the representiveness [sic] of a source without considerable and sophisticated research." "Good reporters" do more than relay information from sources. Merrill said they apply ethics. Merrill devised a formula to highlight characteristics usually considered essential for a good reporter. That formula is TUFF, which stands for Truthful, Unbiased, Full, and Fair.[38]

Editors, too, realize the danger of strong ties between reporters and sources. Becker said that's why they sometimes rotate reporters between beats so that journalists don't get so familiar with the people they report on that they can't be objective.[39] According to Donna Shaw, who wrote "Dilemma of Interest" in a 2006 issue of *American Journalism Review,* journalists understand law enforcement and other government officials sometimes attempt to use the media for their own gain or to promote their own agendas.[40] Shaw said journalists avoid this when making publication decisions. Shaw's article deals specifically with the vague crime investigation term "person of interest" and how journalists are responsible for making their own judgment calls rather than automatically printing any information passed on by law enforcement officials.

Shaw quotes other journalists to make the point that police and the media have different missions, purposes and obligations. Kelly McBride, ethics group leader at the Poynter Institute and former reporter, said in Shaw's article that when police call someone a "person of interest" they often "are trying to scare the person into confessing, drum up more information about the person and kind of otherwise smooth over cracks in their case. As journalists, we have to treat that term with increased skepticism."[41]

Racially Unbiased

Despite what critics say, there are studies and examples of media reform that show the media accurately portray African Americans in crime stories and do not advance stereotypes of African Americans as criminals. A study published in the *Journal of Broadcasting & Electronic Media* in 2003 by Travis L. Dixon, Cristina L. Azocar, and Michael Casas contradicts prior research studies that charge network television news programs with over-representation of African Americans as criminals. The 2003 study yielded a content analysis of 128 of the network news' 30-minute programs during 1994–1997. The analysis of the samples was compared with crime reports and official records. The results of Dixon's study show perpetrators of crime, both White and African American, were accurately represented on network television newscasts. The study showed African Americans were no more likely to be depicted as criminals on network news (27 percent) than to be arrested (30 percent, according to crime reports). Concerning violent crime, African

Americans were no more likely to be portrayed as criminals (38 percent) than to be arrested for violent crimes (42 percent). Dixon and his group said in the study "perhaps it is possible that this signals a change in the way that news broadcasts report race."[42]

Some broadcast news media have made changes in news content recently, specifically reducing the number of crime stories shown, according to a study produced by the Project for Excellence in Journalism by the Columbia University Graduate School of Journalism. Tom Rosenstiel, Carl Gottlieb, and Lee Brady explain in their 2000 *Columbia Journalism Review* article "Time of Peril for TV News" that "better news content" helps stations maintain or increase viewership. The study compares news content to ratings. Although the study did not address race specifically, it targeted the use of crime stories, which some media critics said are biased in their portrayals of African Americans as criminals. Part of "better news content" means airing fewer crime stories and fewer stories targeted at demographic subsets of your audience, the study said. The study looked at thirteen TV stations for three years and determined that those with quality news content were able to increase or sustain their ratings.[43]

Newspapers also have made structural changes that correct inherent biases noted by Christopher Campbell in his book *Race, Myth and the News.* Campbell claimed news content was unfair to African Americans because they were over-represented in the media as criminals. Gannett media corporation made such a change in 1984. In his 2003 article "Mainstreaming and Diversity Are Gannett's Core Values: But these programs are not without controversy," Tom Witosky said Gannett initiated an employment program in 1984 that mandated newspaper editors hire more minorities, including African Americans, to bring the perspectives and values of minorities into the news decision-making process.[44] Bringing more minorities into the decision-making process would decrease the racial bias that Campbell said was inherent in newsrooms where white managers made the decisions, including content decisions concerning crime. Witosky said Gannett raised its ratio of minority journalists on staffs in the last two decades to 17.1 percent of the company's newsroom workforce.

Graber attributes some racial biases to society rather than the media. Her study contends that readers employ their own social prejudices when processing information from the media to reinforce their own mental images of criminals' demography. Graber evaluated public perception of crime through interviews with panelists. Graber concluded the panelists' views of criminals did not match what was portrayed in the media. "One can say that the press does not depict criminals and victims largely as nonwhite, poor, and lower class," she concluded, "but the panelists do.... Panel members who identified criminals demographically viewed crime largely as the work of young males, black or belonging to other minority races. The *Tribune*, in turn, identified 70 percent of the criminals as white, past 25 (years of age), and somewhat better balanced sexually than was true of the panel's images."

In the end, Graber said the public is not a "mere blotter for media images." Instead, the public uses its own stereotypes to interpret gathered information. Graber said "it is the public, rather than the media, that perceives both criminals and victims as largely flawed in character, nonwhite, and lower class." Graber's study showed that audiences select mass media crime and justice information to reinforce their own attitudes, and they reject information that clashes with their own perceptions about crime. Graber also said media consumers, not the media, are more focused on blue-collar (violent) crime than on white-collar (nonviolent) crime. She concluded that white-collar crime was "well and prominently" covered by the media. However, members of the audience panels, when asked about which crimes they had heard of or read about, mentioned almost exclusively stories about street crimes.[45]

• THE EVIDENCE •

Journalists and researchers have different viewpoints on whether the media give audiences a fair and balanced picture of crime. Some offer research and explanations to back their claims. The question is how strong or weak are their arguments. Which are more valid?

In terms of scholarly research, media critics would win their claim that statistics show the media do not treat all crime stories as equally important. The media do over-represent murder in overall crime news content. Graber's analysis on murder provides evidence that journalists give more coverage to murder (26.3 percent of crime stories published, for example, in the *Chicago Tribune*) than murder as listed in police records (0.2 percent). Much weight must be given to Graber's conclusions, for her research covers many media outlets over a full year. However, long-range studies are necessary because the impact of crime and other news is cumulative. "[L]ooking at crime news for brief, selected time periods," Graber points out, "or assessing its impact in one-stage interviews fails to capture reality. It makes it impossible to judge the completeness of news coverage or to gauge the repetition rates of various stories and themes."[46]

Katz's conclusion in his article "What makes crime 'news'?" offers the weaker argument that crime news inverts reality. Although he conducted a content analysis of newspaper content, he did not break down the numbers and compare them with police statistics in the manner Graber did.[47] Neither did he include TV networks in his analysis.

In Rich's book, journalists concede that more significance is placed on stories of unusual nature and conflict, such as murder.[48] But are the reports biased? Scholars and journalists don't share the same definition of "fair and balanced crime stories"; they judge them by different standards. Journalists do not factor the percentage of a certain crime's frequency in social reality and then set aside that percentage of news space or airtime in crime coverage for that type of crime.

Media critics make a good argument that news structures, including the beat system, cause news content to be biased, but they fall short of proving it beyond a reasonable doubt. Graber's evidence shows empirical evidence of news content distortion, but her argument that structure is the cause of that bias appears to be based on reason rather than evidence. Graber claimed the beat system of gathering news keeps topics like crime on center stage at the expense of other topics outside the beat system.[49] However, TV networks normally don't use the beat system, and some newspapers are turning away from it in favor of the team system.

Regarding the use of official sources in crime stories, the evidence shows that the media rely heavily on official sources without getting the viewpoint of those accused of crime. Is there a potential for news bias in favoring official sources? Yes. But there is no empirical evidence to substantiate the specific claims that reporters allow their relationships with officials to cloud or bias news content.

Although there is conflicting evidence regarding African Americans and crime coverage, one must logically conclude some bias has been present because the media have taken steps to correct it. The 2000 study of Los Angeles-based television stations by Dixon and Lenz showed African Americans were more likely to be portrayed as perpetrators of crime on television news than were shown in police reports. However, the 2003 Dixon, Azocar, and Casas study showed perpetrators of crime, both white and African American, were accurately represented on network television newscasts. Graber agreed, saying the press did not depict criminals largely as nonwhite. A weakness of the 2000 Dixon-Lenz and 2003 Dixon-Azocar-Casas studies is they reflect only television news and do not include newspaper figures.

• RESOLUTION •

Taken in total, the evidence suggests biases are widespread in crime reporting, especially in the amount of news coverage devoted to unusual crime. The biases exist in crime reporting, just as there are biases throughout journalism. To suggest that the media will ever be completely free of bias is ludicrous. What's important is that journalists make every effort to avoid it. Merrill wrote that "we will never be totally free of bias, of course, because all reporters have values and their own ways of selecting and structuring information. Good reporters, though, can refrain from putting intentional bias into their stories."[50] As Graber said, the media can minimize the biased nature of crime reporting by offering more in-depth stories that place single-event crime stories into perspective.[51] Journalists could investigate crime patterns and could explain how a single-event crime fits into the overall reality of criminal activity. This would offer a more accurate account of the frequency and nature of crime, and it would reduce artificially produced crime waves not supported by actual crime statistics. As the semi-profession of journalism continues to evolve, journalists must be aware of the bias accusations lodged against them and keep them in mind when deciding crime news content. Just as journalists reacted to the 1947 Hutchins Commission report with a flurry of professional codes, today's journalists must make commitments to produce more fair and balanced crime stories. Journalists should

1. Evaluate how much of their medium's overall news content is devoted to crime and decide whether crime receives too much attention.

2. Devote more time to in-depth crime issues rather than focus on individual crime occurrences.

3. Monitor crime news content for unintentional racial bias and establish policies for hiring and placement that ensure minority voices and opinions are included in newsroom decisions, such as crime content.

4. Be sure that crime stories are as fair and balanced with regard to sources and viewpoints as with any other topic covered by the press.

5. Explain through editorials, Websites, and other consumer-producer communication why certain stories receive more attention than others, allowing the public to make a better assessment of the crime news they read and view.

• POINTS OF VIEW •

Dixon, Travis L., Cristina L. Azocar, and Michael Casas. "The Portrayal of Race and Crime on Television Network News." *Journal of Broadcasting & Electronic Media* 47 (2003): 498–523. Television news networks accurately represented African Americans in crime stories when comparing the frequency they were portrayed as criminals to the frequency they were named in crime reports.

Katz, Jack. "What Makes Crime 'News'?" *Media, Culture and Society* 9 (1987): 47–75. There are systematic biases in the reporting of crime news, at least in the respect that crime as presented in the daily news differs consistently from crime as described in official police statistics.

Lowry, Dennis T., Tarn Ching Josephine Nio, and Dennis W. Leitner. "Setting the Public Fear Agenda: A Longitudinal Analysis of Network TV Crime Reporting, Public Perceptions of Crime and FBI Crime Statistics." *Journal of Communication* 53 (2003): 61–73. TV network news shows aired more crime news in 1994 than real world crime figures showed, causing the public to believe incorrectly there was a crime wave.

Shaw, Donna. "Dilemma of Interest." *American Journalism Review* 28 (2006): 56–61. Journalists understand that law enforcement and other government officials sometimes attempt to use the media for their own gain or to promote their own agendas; journalists avoid this bias.

Simon, James, and Sean Hayes. "Juvenile Crime Stories Use Police Blotter without Comment from Suspects." *Newspaper Research Journal* 25 (2004): 89–94. Crime news stories are biased because reporters rely heavily on police blotters and official sources to verify story content without seeking the perpetrator's point of view to balance the article.

Vaden, Ted. "In Crime Coverage, Does Status Matter?" *News & Observer* (Raleigh, N.C.), 22 May 2005, A27. The "unusual nature" of murders gives newspapers a legitimate reason to give them more attention than more common crimes, despite accusations that such preference is biased.

NOTES

1. Jeff Cohen and Norman Solomon, "'Crime Time' News Exploits Fears," http://www.jeffcohen.org/docs/mbeat19940608.html

2. Ron Franscell, "Crime News as a Cultural Ink-Blot," Under the News, http://underthenews.blogspot.com/2006/06/crime-news-as-cultural-ink-blot.html

3. Ted Vaden, "Durham Sees Red Over Crime," *The News & Observer* (Raleigh, N.C.), 22 January 2006.

4. Doris Graber, *Crime News and the Public* (New York: Praeger Publishers, 1980), 24, 33.

5. Carole Rich, *Writing and Reporting News: A Coaching Method* (California: Wadsworth/Thomson Learning, 2003), 25–29.

6. Graber, *Crime News and...*, 39.

7. Travis L. Dixon and Daniel Linz. "Overrepresentation and Underrepresentation of African Americans and Latinos as Lawbreakers on Television News," *Journal of Communication* 50 (2000): 151.

8. Jack Katz, "What Makes Crime 'News'?" *Media, Culture and Society* 9 (1987): 57.

9. Graber, *Crime News and...*, 42.

10. Katz, "What Makes Crime...," 57.

11. Dennis T. Lowry, Tarn Ching Josephine Nio, and Dennis W. Leitner. "Setting the Public Fear Agenda: A Longitudinal Analysis of Network TV Crime Reporting, Public Perceptions of Crime and FBI Crime Statistics," *Journal of Communication* 53 (2003): 62, 70.

12. Graber, *Crime News and...*, 21.

13. Ibid.

14. Robert W. McChesney, *Rich Media, Poor Democracy: Communication Politics in Dubious Time* (Chicago: University of Illinois Press, 1999), 54.

15. Graber, *Crime News and...*, 42.

16. James Simon and Sean Hayes, "Juvenile Crime Stories Use Police Blotter without Comment from Suspects," *Newspaper Research Journal* 25 (2004): 90, 91, 92.

17. Herbert Strent, *News Reporters and News Sources: Accomplices in Shaping and Mis-Shaping the News* (Iowa State University Press, 1989), 111, 115, 6.

18. Christopher P. Campbell, *Race, Myth and the News* (California: SAGE Publications, Inc., 1995), 69, 82, 115, 127.

19. Ibid., 83, 115.

20. Ibid., 127.

21. Dixon, "Overrepresentation and underrepresentation...," 145, 146.

22. Ibid., 148, 149.

23. Vaden, "Durham sees red...," A27.

24. Rich, *Writing and Reporting...*, 23–29.

25. John C. Merrill, *Journalism Ethics: Philosophical Foundations for News Media* (New York: St. Martins Press, Inc., 1997), 17–21, 91–106, 166, 167, 195.

26. Mark Warr, "The Accuracy of Public Beliefs About Crime," *Social Forces* 80 (1980): 466, 467.

27. Rich, *Writing and Reporting...*, 23–29.

28. Ted Vaden, "In Crime Coverage, Does Status Matter?" *The News & Observer* (Raleigh, N.C.), 22 May 2005, A27.

29. Graber, *Crime News and...*, 122.

30. Warr, "The Accuracy of Public...," 467.

31. Ibid., 464, 466.

32. Graber, *Crime News and...*, 20, 21.

33. Lee Becker, Wilson Lowrey, Dane Claussen, and William Anderson, "Why Does the Beat Go On?" *Newspaper Research Journal* 21 (2000): 3,4.

34. Becker, "Why Does the Beat...," 3.

35. Jane Ellen Stevens, Ester Thorson, and Lori Dorfman, *Reporting Violence* (Berkeley: Berkeley Media Studies Group, 2001), 6.

36. Peter Gade, and Earnest L. Perry, "Changing the Newsroom Culture: A Four-Year Case Study of Organizational Development at the *St. Louis Post-Dispatch*," *Journalism and Mass Communication Quarterly* 80 (2003): 329, 330.

37. Stephen Buckley and Chip Scanlan, "Tips for Covering Cops," Poynter Online column, http://www.poynter.org/column.asp?id=52&aid=11804, 3 May 2006.

38. Merrill, *Journalism Ethics...*, 195, 187.

39. Becker, "Why does the beat...," 9.

40. Donna Shaw, "Dilemma of Interest," *American Journalism Review* 28 (2006): 59, 60.

41. Ibid.

42. Travis L. Dixon, Cristina L. Azocar, and Michael Casas. "The Portrayal of Race and Crime on Television Network News," *Journal of Broadcasting & Electronic Media* 47 (2003): 514, 516.

43. Tom Rosenstiel, Carl Gottlieb, and Lee Ann Brady, "Time of Peril for TV News: Quality Sells,

But Commitment — and Viewership — Continue to Erode," *Columbia Journalism Review,* November/December 2000, 84, 88.

44. Tom Witosky, "Mainstreaming and Diversity Are Gannett's Core Values: But These Programs Are Not Without Controversy," Neiman Reports, Fall 2003, 39–41.

45. Graber, *Crime News and...,* 122, 54, 55, 66, 63.

46. Ibid., 2.

47. Katz, "What makes crime...," 48, 49, 57.

48. Rich, *Writing and Reporting...,* 26, 27.

49. Graber, *Crime News and...,* 21.

50. Merrill, *Journalism Ethics...,* 177.

51. Graber, *Crime News and...,* 128.

10

The Environment

Kim Cross

"Within the U.S., news coverage of the [1997 Kyoto climate] talks was extremely sparse, and at times misleading. Despite the high stakes involved in global warming, and the U.S.'s central role in it— both as the most powerful country at the negotiating table and as the world's biggest polluter— there's a good chance that Americans relying on mainstream U.S. media remain unaware of the anti-environmental demands made in their name.... [T]hanks to the U.S. media, most Americans hardly even knew the talks were happening, much less what was at stake."— Rachel Coen, Fairness and Accuracy in Reporting[1]

"Activists and regulators depend on public fear and outrage over air pollution to maintain and enhance their power and budgets. As the polls show, their phony gloom and doom stories have been all too successful in misleading Americans to overestimate the risks we face. The exaggerations and fabrications have now been repeated so often that they have become 'common knowledge.' Journalists should be acting as a check on these distortions, but they are not. Journalists, like much of the public, consider environmentalists and regulators to be virtuous guardians of the public good."— Joel Schwartz, Heartland Institute[2]

Reporters covering the environment are among the most experienced and best trained journalists in the newsroom, yet they continue to fight a stigma that has existed since the beat began: green bias. There is an assumption among many readers, sources, and even some fellow journalists that environmental reporters are environmentalists. "Whenever I walk into a meeting with industry officials, people assume I'm an environmentalist," says Mark Schleifstein, an environmental reporter for the *New Orleans Times-Picayune*. "I'm a reporter who covers the environment. I'm not an environmentalist who works for a newspaper."[3]

Schleifstein, who has spent more than two decades covering environmental issues ranging from hurricane protection to industry pollution, says accusations of bias are lobbed from opposing sides. Environmental activists accuse the media of overlooking environmental problems in favor of industry interests. Meanwhile, "It's a frustrating problem for reporters on the beat," says Schleifstein, who is on the board of directors of the Society of Environmental Journalists, a professional organization. "People on both sides think you're biased."

Even more troubling are attitudes within the newsroom, as discussed in Bud Ward's *Nieman Reports* article "Environment Journalists don't Get Much Respect." "There's a perception of bias in the newsroom that seems to be unique to the environmental beat," one reporter said at an annual meeting of the SEJ. She had never encountered this perception when she worked on other beats. It seems that no matter how much environmental journalists swear by the principles and practices of independent journalism, they frequently find themselves fighting the perception that they are not objective reporters but "greens with press passes."[4]

In the highly politicized and controversial realm of environmental coverage, reporters disagree about whether they should be passive observers or advocates of change. Regardless of which stance they take, most share a deep concern for the environment and an interest in its health. If they appear to care too much, however, they are chastised, subject to a debilitating double standard. "Covering environmental issues is not like covering crime," says Schleifstein. "No one thinks crime stories are biased." Rocky Barker, an environment reporter for the *Idaho Statesman*, echoes that view. "When you care about education, you're not accused of being pro-education or pro-children," Barker says. "But when you care about the environment, you become a lightening rod."[5]

Whether or not the accusations are true, journalists realize that the *perception* of bias is almost as detrimental as bias itself. "We can't have a reporter walk into the office of a CEO of a timber company or the CEO of a nonprofit advocacy group and be automatically perceived as representing a persuasion," says Len Reed, a science and environment editor at the (Portland) *Oregonian* in the Paul Rogers article "Complexity in Environmental Reporting is Critical to Public Decision-Making." "Half of environmental journalism is having the story, half is having credibility."[6]

While there seems to be a general consensus that some bias exists, people disagree about the nature and source of that bias. Some say that journalists are inherently biased — consciously or subconsciously — in favor of the environment. Others say that environment reporters are as objective as any of their colleagues, but may be more vulnerable to manipulation by scientists and biased sources attempting to exploit them. Some argue that bias is inadvertent, a result of institutional factors such as news values and production cycles. A few reporters not only admit they are pro-environment, but argue that they have a responsibility to act as advocates for the environment. Many more, however, say they have a responsibility to be balanced and fair but admit that covering the environment without bias is a challenging endeavor.

Where bias does exist, it is not easy to determine whether it is intentional or inadvertent, individual or institutional, primary or secondary, specific to environmental coverage or present in all areas of coverage. As with most environmental issues, there are no simple answers. When it comes to green bias, there are many shades of gray.

Green Bias: A Lopsided Version of Reality

In 2001, Bjorn Lomborg, a Danish statistics professor, published a seminal work that provides evidence of a fundamental, systematic bias in media coverage of the environment. His 500-page statistical tome, *The Skeptical Environmentalist: Measuring the Real*

State of the World, draws the dissident conclusion that the state of the environment is not nearly as bad as the media suggest. Like other critics, Lomborg claims the media tend to overstate environmental problems, sometimes to the point of sensationalism. Unlike many critics who accuse the media of crusading, however, Lomborg is no right-wing conservative. He is a self-proclaimed "old left-wing Greenpeace member" who overturned his own green bias by methodically examining all the scientific data he could find about the environment. With the heart of an environmentalist and the mind of a statistician, he concluded that environmental conditions in many cases are *improving* (though they're not necessarily good) while the media continue to report otherwise.[7]

Lomborg blames the fundamental disconnect not on biased reporters but rather inherent problems in the communication process. As the results of science get passed on through environmental organizations, textbooks, the news media and other channels, the information gets warped, taken out of context, and sometimes intentionally abused by individuals or groups attempting to further an agenda. The result is what Lomborg calls "the Litany," the gloomy yet comfortingly familiar images and messages that resound from newspapers, television, politicians, and water cooler conversations, all chronicling what appears to be the steady deterioration of the environment. Lomborg contends that the Litany, which the public has come to accept as common knowledge and self-evident truth, is really an artificial — and largely biased —"reality" based on misconceptions and erroneous ideas promulgated by the media.

Few refute Lomborg's claims that the media present a "lopsided version of reality." News is not a representative sample of events, but rather a subjective selection of incidents filtered through news values that favor immediate crises over long-term developments and environmental trends that are stabilizing or slowly improving. Deadlines and short production cycles introduce a bias toward certainty in a field that takes great pains to avoid it. Scientists present their findings as conditional and hedged in uncertainty "since knowledge is developing and liable to change with tomorrow's results," say David Murray, Joel Schwartz, and S. Robert Lichter in their book, *It Ain't Necessarily So: How Media Make and Unmake the Scientific Picture of Reality.*[8] Yet the media, which favor clarity and conclusiveness, often state those results with unwarranted certainty. Limited news holes offer little room for scientific qualifiers and in-depth explanations, increasing the opportunity for misinterpretation.

Lomborg acknowledges that the complexity of most environmental issues exceeds the capacity of the media to explain them with scientific accuracy to a nonscientific readership. Yet the media could, and should, be able to present a simplified yet accurate "big picture" of fluctuating systems instead of the consistently negative predictions that prevail. Many environmental journalists dismiss Lomborg as a Pollyanna. They argue that environmental problems are in fact underreported, understated, and regularly overshadowed by other news deemed "more important" by editors and readers. But they admit that he is right about one thing: environmental news is almost always bad news.

Bias Toward Doom

As the old saying goes, *no news* is good news. When it comes to environmental coverage, it sometimes seems as if *no* news is *good* news. Global warming. Disappearing species. Air pollution. Chemical spills. Most environmental coverage suggests the environment is in a state of imminent crisis, even when science suggests a different reality. While journalists often are aware of stabilizing or improving trends, those stories rarely get covered.

"I plead guilty," says Schleifstein, of the SEJ and the *New Orleans Times-Picayune*. "We report on chemical plants when they blow up. We don't always report on them when they reduce emissions." He admits that the public does not understand a lot of the improvements that have been made in the last fifty years, such as the cleaning of the Mississippi River and reductions in air pollution around the country. "A reason for that is because when guys like us do our jobs, we're doing daily stories," he says. "We're doing stories on what's happening day to day, not stepping back and looking at the whole picture."

The bias toward doom is not necessarily intentional, but likely a result of "framing," the news industry's inherent gate-keeping procedure of "selecting and highlighting some features of reality while omitting others, as discussed in R.M. Entman's article "Framing: Toward clarification of a fractured paradigm."[9] From a reader's perspective, the result is an unbalanced picture, biased heavily toward negative news about the environment. Professor Anders Hansen of the Centre for Mass Communication Research at the University of Leicester points out in her article "The Media and the Social Construction of the Environment" that the media's coverage of certain environmental issues often has little or no correlation with the immediacy and gravity of those problems. "Just as it would be a mistake to assume that the jump to the forefront of media ... is a simple reflection of a sudden deterioration of the environment," he writes, "so too would it be misleading to assume that those environmental issues ... are necessarily the most immediately threatening or serious (as defined for example by scientists or environmental activists).[10]

One factor that contributes to the problem is the incongruity between the news industry, which demands immediacy, and the nature of environmental problems, which tend to develop gradually. The world's most potentially catastrophic environmental problems, such as climate change, accrue slowly and almost imperceptibly over time. In the absence of a major news event, such issues would not be covered if journalists operated strictly under the traditional standards of newsworthiness.

Holly Stocking and Jennifer Pease Leonard emphasize the challenge of covering gradually developing environmental problems in the *Columbia Journalism Review* article "The Greening of the Press." "It ain't news unless it's new," they say. Without obvious news pegs, journalists must continually search for new angles in order to keep important long-term issues, such as global warming, in the news. "It allows persistent, and growing, environmental problems to slide out of sight if there is nothing 'new' to report," they say. Current problems get more coverage than future problems, even if the future problems are potentially much greater.[11]

As a result, ongoing environmental problems are covered in seemingly arbitrary fits and starts. Hansen provides a perspective that suggests an explanation. Unlike other news events, environmental problems manifest slowly over a time-scale that does not match the news production time frame. As he puts it, "environmental issues do not ordinarily articulate themselves." Consequently, many issues "only become known because someone makes claims about them." Or, journalists must arbitrarily force these issues if they are to be covered on a scale of importance relative to other "breaking" news. This helps explain why some issues fade in and out of prominence with little link to actual events.[12] It's no coincidence that the environment re-surfaces in the news during a lull in major breaking news.

Insufficient context is another way in which framing can lead to bias. The way the media frame a problem signals to readers the cause of that problem, and some critics argue that a type of bias can occur when journalists avoid — consciously or unconsciously — certain links between environmental problems and factors that exacerbate the presumed causes of those problems. For example, Michael T. Maher argues in his article "How and Why Journalists Avoid the Population — Environment Connection" that population growth is a contributing factor in nearly all environmental problems, but the media's failure to frame stories within that context has resulted in the public's ignorance of that relationship.[13]

More often, however, the bias is towards trends. Environmental coverage tends to be biased towards "established" problems and issues. Coverage of "new" issues tends to emerge in special interest publications before being picked up by the mainstream press. Issue salience is periodical and not necessarily tied to news events, suggesting the slant toward those issues is largely arbitrary. What the press deems of "imminent" import may not necessarily be, according to the *Journal of Communication* article "Media Roles in a Social Movement."[14]

Finally, news values, human interest, and sometimes corporate agendas can shape the way journalists frame environmental coverage. Alison Anderson conducted a qualitative research study published in *Media, Culture and Society* in 1991 that suggests that there is story-selection bias in British environmental coverage toward those issues that satisfy particular news values. For example, the media heavily covered a "seal plague" that involved widespread deaths among a species that, by its "cuteness," happens to be very conducive to the visual aspects of the media. (By contrast, a species of beetles driven to extinction would never enjoy so many headlines.) One newspaper, the *Daily Mail*, had already decided to start a wildlife campaign with a human interest angle, and when the seal story emerged it fit the bill, resulting in a "Save Our Seals" campaign that lasted more than a year. It's a good example of the media arbitrarily influencing the issue salience to further their own agenda instead of simply reporting the news.[15]

Bias Against Environmental Coverage

Some say that the media are actually somewhat biased *against* environmental coverage. Everette E. Dennis says in *Media and the Environment* that the media do not cover the environment as extensively as they do other topics because most environment stories often lack the human interest angle and just "aren't sexy enough" to push out other news.[16] Philip Shabecoff, a long-time former environmental reporter for the *New York Times*, suggests the bias against environmental stories comes from within news organizations, often promoted by editors themselves. Why? The macro-issues associated with environmental problems do not lend themselves to news values that emphasize new events, new angles, and distinct developments. In such an atmosphere, environmental stories tend to get buried or left behind. Shabecoff was ultimately taken off the environment beat by editors who insinuated that he was biased, and left the Times to found Greenwire, an online daily digest of environmental news.

Journalist and historian Eric Alterman III says in *What Liberal Media?: The Truth About Bias and the News* that he believes most journalists have a personal pro-environment bias, but he argues that the media have failed to challenge either the left or the right. Alterman's argument is that the news industry — from management structure to economic and social influences — is "organized to communicate conservative views and push our politics to the right — regardless of how 'liberal' any given reporter may be."[17]

In *Inventing Reality: The Politics of News Media*, Michael Parenti goes so far as to say that the media are so pro-capitalist that damning environmental stories about industries (e.g. poisonous waste dumpings by companies or nuclear plant accidents) are a rare instance in which the media cast businesses in a negative light. However, he says those stories typically only "scratch the surface" of the actual magnitude of the problems.[18]

Charles Alexander, a retired journalist who worked for *Time* magazine for twenty-three years, says in a *Nieman Reports* article that journalists are not over-reporting environmental problems, as many charge, but under-reporting them. "There is a strong case to be made that journalists *are* missing the environmental story," he says, "and if we don't do a better job of telling the story, devastation of the environment will be partly our fault."[19] Alexander argues that it is not only acceptable but *imperative* for journalists to be environmental advocates.

Alexander's view reflects one side of the great debate that has continued among the media ever since the inception of the environmental beat roughly three decades ago. Are environmental journalists biased? And if so, do they have a right to be?

Personal Bias and a Green Agenda

There is some evidence that suggests that environmental coverage is one area in which journalists tend to have a particularly strong pro-environment bias. The charges come from both the left and the right, from industry officials as well colleagues in the newsroom. They suspect that environment reporters are pursuing a personal agenda to fight for the environment.

It appears that even some environmental journalists themselves believe they are "too green." A 2001 Brigham Young University survey of environment reporters at 108 newspapers and 87 television stations in eight western states showed that 28 percent agreed that they and their peers were "too green" in orientation. Thirty-eight percent agreed that environment-beat reporters "sometimes should be advocates for the environment."[20]

Another study suggests it is not only environment beat reporters, but journalists in general, with a slight green tilt. A 1998 self-administered survey by Fairness & Accuracy in Reporting (FAIR) indicated that the one area in which journalists were "slightly left of the general public" was in their attitudes toward environmental regulation. Respondents were asked whether stricter environmental laws and regulations "cost too many jobs and hurt the economy" or "are worth the cost." The vast majority of journalists — 79 percent — said they think such laws are worth the cost, while 21 percent disagreed. By comparison, an October 1996 poll by the Pew Research Center reported only 63 percent of the public said they believe such laws are worth the cost, while 30 percent disagreed.[21]

In a similar vein, researchers at the Media Research Center, a media watchdog organization, surveyed journalists about their attitudes toward various social issues, and they found that most of them to be "strong supporters of environmental protection." As discussed in *And That's the Way It Isn't: A Reference Guide to Media Bias,* less than 20 percent agreed with the statement, "Our environmental problems are not as serious as people have been led to believe." Only 1 percent strongly agreed with the statement, and 54 percent strongly disagreed.[22]

If bias is more prevalent in environmental coverage than in other beats, it's probably no coincidence. It is one of the hazards of covering a highly technical subject. All science reporting requires a high level of education, knowledge, and training to ensure that journalists do not become stenographers for scientists. While the scientific method is designed to eliminate subjectivity, not all studies are equally valid, and journalists must be knowledgeable enough to discern which studies are the most reliable and relevant. "Good environmental coverage isn't merely reporting what one scientist says and then finding a scientist who disagrees and reporting what that person says," says (Louisville) *Courier-Journal* reporter James Bruggers in the *Nieman Reports* article "The Best is Tougher One Today." "When they interview sources, environmental journalists need to be able to determine how the information they are being told should be weighted in the context of the story."[23] Reporters need to know enough about science to understand the complexity of environmental issues and to be able to investigate the claims of scientists just as they would "check out" their sources' facts on any other beat.

In short, environmental journalists must be experts. While expertise should make a reporter aware of differing points of view — and therefore reduce the potential for bias — it also may cultivate strong opinions on controversial issues. Covering contentious issues with a point of view is not the same thing as outright advocacy, but some fear that it toes the line. "You want reporters who have expertise in certain topics, but when you have expertise, you run the risk of having strong opinions," says Lynn Cunningham, assistant to the editor of the *New Orleans Times-Picayune* in a unpublished interview.[24] As experts, environmental reporters must walk a fine line between informed reporting and advocacy.

The environment beat is also an easy place for reporters to become enchanted with the wonders of science — and scientists. Consequently, there may be a tendency to take their side. In her 1987 study "Selling Science: How the Press Covers Science and Technology," sociologist Dorothy Nelkin warned that science reporters — a category that includes environmental reporters — had gotten too close to their scientific sources. "Many journalists are, in effect, retailing science and technology rather than investigating them, identifying with their sources rather than challenging them," Nelkin wrote.[25] If environmental reporters approach scientific sources with less skepticism than they would on other beats, that opens the door to bias. The number of scientific findings reported with an unjustifiable air of certainty suggests this is a problem. As Murray, Schwartz and Lichter point out, cancer has been cured so many times — that is, according to the media — that it's a longstanding joke among the scientific community. "Too often, research that is either preliminary or inconclusive (or both) receives almost reverential treatment in the press," they authors say.[26]

Some point to monetary or institutional factors that could lead to personal bias. Robert Lee Hotz, a science reporter for the *Los Angles Times,* points out that nearly half of all journalists in the National Association of Science Writers are freelancers who must supplement (or subsidize) their journalistic work with more lucrative corporate and university assignments. Working for the same organizations you cover is a likely recipe for conflict-of-interest, but it is an unfortunate reality for most freelancers because it is difficult to make a living strictly on newspaper and magazine articles, which don't pay as well as corporate work. In that situation, it is feasible that writers could become biased — consciously or unconsciously — in favor of certain institutions with which they have a relationship. "They are not in a position to easily bite the hand that feeds them," Hotz says.[27]

Others believe it is possible for financial bias at an institutional level to seep into the newsroom. A 1989 study by the Media Research Center found that funding recipients received more coverage from the newspaper that donated to their cause than from other competing newspapers. For example, the Environmental Defense Fund, which received $21,000 from the New York Times Company Foundation, received 123 mentions in the *Times*, compared to 70 mentions in the *Los Angeles Times* and 46 in the *Washington Post*, neither of which contributed to the EDF. A similar pattern occurred for other environmental organizations supported by one of the three newspapers.[28]

"Just the Facts"

While many journalists admit that environment is one of the trickiest subjects to cover objectively, most are adamant that it can and should be covered with the same principles and standards that apply to other beats. Though they disagree about the elusive ideal of "objectivity" versus the more practical goals of "balance" and "fairness," most environmental reporters say they are able to cover the beat without bias. Schleifstein, says he believes this is true for most members of the SEJ. "The vast majority of our members believe they are not biased and that they attempt to approach environmental stories in an objective, traditional journalistic fashion," Schleifstein says. The organization is so staunch about this attitude that it will revoke the membership of any journalist who crosses the line. "If they write a press release, they're out," Schleifstein says.[29]

While there are advocate-reporters who work for special interest environmental publications, most mainstream environmental journalists share Schleifstein's view that they are reporters who cover the environment, not environmentalists who work for the media. "Let's get one thing straight: There are environmental journalists. And there are environmentalist journals. But ... except for those few columnists and editorial writers who write from a 'green' perspective, can there also be 'environmental*ist* journal*ists*?'" asks Bud Ward, a founding editor of *Environment Writer*, a newsletter. "This pairing of words strikes me as an oxymoron." Yes, Ward says, there are environmentalist writers. Many of them work for special interest publications, not the mainstream media. But the idea of environmentalist journalists is not acceptable by the strict definition of journalism. "The effort to inform and to separate fact from fiction in the forever-elusive pursuit of 'truth' or accuracy comes first," he says.[31]

With these values in mind, most journalists are very aware of the seductiveness of environmental concerns, which can easily be assimilated into one's personal point of view. But they are also aware of the dangers of slipping into partiality in their professional work. They know it can injure their credibility, and that damaged credibility can ruin a career. "There is a fundamental rightness to the environmental goal and we all believe in that," says Phil Kavits, an executive with the National Wildlife Federation and a former television reporter for nearly a decade. He is quoted in Lou Prato's *Covering the Environ-*

ment Beat: An Overview for Radio and TV Journalists. "But those who immerse themselves so thoroughly sometimes run the risk of getting on a soap box and they become
zealots. They may take a point of view but they should be fair."[31]

Kavits raises an interesting point. It's hard to be completely neutral about the environment, whose health is fundamentally important to human existence and prosperity. No
one takes an *anti*-environment stance. Even the critics who condemn the press as biased
are not opposed to a healthy environment; they simply argue that the media overlook the
economic costs and benefits associated with many environmental regulations. It seems
unreasonable to expect environmental journalists to maintain a completely neutral attitude
toward a topic that everyone — at least in theory — supports. But is it possible to approach
a story with a point of view but still cover that story fairly? Many say yes. "Even if environmental journalists are pro-environment, it's very important to prove the other side's case,"
says Roy Peter Clark, vice president of the Poynter Institute, a school for journalists.[32]

Boyce Rensberger, the director of the Knight Science Journalism Fellowships program at the Massachusetts Institute of Technology, adds that fair coverage does not necessarily allocating equal space to each side of an issue. It requires a reporter who knows
enough about the issue to weed out the wheat from the chaff. "Balanced coverage of science does not mean giving equal weight to both sides of an argument," he says. "It means
apportioning weight according to the balance of evidence."

Lou Prato says this is a gray area. On one extreme, "endorsing a position with little or no objectivity, fairness, or balance, and disregarding or denigrating information
that conflicts with the chosen position" is clearly advocacy. At the other extreme, advocacy can appear as "the presentation of a conclusion or opinion after conflicting arguments have been fairly presented."[33] The latter, according to some definitions, could be
construed as writing with a point of view, not bias.

A Duty to Be Advocates

Perhaps the strongest factor affecting bias among environmental journalists is the
human instinct to care. As Ronald Baily points out in *Eco-Scam: The False Prophets of
Ecological Apocalypse,* the process of highlighting bad news encourages journalists to cross
the line of objectivity to become environmental advocates.[34] Moreover, a sense of duty
and a desire to help avert human-induced environmental problems drives some journalists to do so openly and with a clear conscience.

Environmental coverage is one of a very few areas in which some journalists believe
it is acceptable to abandon objectivity and cross the line into advocacy. This camp argues
that environmental journalists have not only a right but a *duty* to act as advocates for the
environment. The health of the environment is so central to human survival that it should
be a rare exception to the journalistic ideal of objectivity, they say.

"Because of the concern by some activists and scientists that the media are not doing
an adequate job, a few have called on the media to abandon their traditions of 'objective'
reporting," says Jim Detjen, founding president of the SEJ in *Media and the Environment.* "They say that the global environmental problems faced by society during the coming decades are so staggering, and will require such fundamental shifts in the way people
live, that traditional approaches are no longer enough."[35]

The strongest argument for this case is the belief that the media have a crucial responsibility to educate the public to induce those changes. "Any deficiency in public understanding of the current state and probable future of the environment could be solved by continuous and massive press coverage," says Everette E. Dennis, co-author of *Media and the Environment.* "Many environmentalists and environmental experts — whatever their point of view on other matters — believe this. So do environmental journalists and other communicators, whether they adhere to the cant of objectivity or prefer advocacy journalism."[36]

Dennis points out other instances in which the media have willingly, and effectively, engaged in advocacy for a social cause: the civil rights movement and the war on drugs. "As one who believes that objectivity is more an ideological icon in our media than an operational reality, I still recognize how deep the passions on this topic go," says Dennis in *Media and the Environment.* "In earlier decades, reporters argued that human rights were so important that they could not and should not be impartial about the civil rights struggle. More recently, some newspapers and television stations have fashioned themselves as warriors in the war on drugs and have not only covered the story, but helped develop informational campaigns to promote drug-free schools...." If it is acceptable for the media to act impartially on these issues, why not for the environment?

Some reporters, including Rocky Barker of the *Idaho Statesman*, argue that journalists who assume passive roles in the pursuit of objectivity are missing the point. Barker says he is was part of the environmental movement — not as an environmentalist in the way that a Sierra Club officer is, but rather as a an informed individual who wishes to make a difference. Readers want accuracy and fairness. But they also want independent analysis. And independent analysis is not the equivalent of bias. "Accuracy is more than just getting the names and facts right," says Barker's boss, *Statesman* executive editor Carolyn Washburn, who was initially skeptical about Barker's approach, but now supports him fully. "It's about fully reflecting the issue."[37]

Lester Brown, founder of the Worldwatch Institute, a research organization that promotes environmental sustainability, argues that it's a matter of time. "We don't have time for the traditional approach to education — training new generations of teachers to train new generations of students — because we don't have generations, we have years," he says. "The communications industry is the only instrument that has the capacity to educate on the scale needed in the time available.[38]

Reporters who promote environmental advocacy do not believe that a lack of "balance" has resulted in media 'bias,' because they don't consider balance to be the issue. "They want a better argument, not a bigger one, and in trying to fashion that argument that have broken from the accepted lexicon of journalistic debate and asked for something truly radical: the freedom to arbitrate the arguments they construct," Dennis says. "It's not articulated as such, but the advocates feel it is their duty to teach, and the objectivists are constitutionally unable to join this argument except by dismissing it."[39]

Ultimately, members of this camp are driven not by ulterior motives other than a genuine desire to help. "I'm in this business to make an impact," Barker says. "I'm not some scribe sitting on the sidelines."

But even supporters of environmental journalists' right to be advocates say that balance is still imperative. "I don't think advocacy journalism is the answer," says Detjen. "I believe that advocacy journalism, if it means one-sided and unfair reporting, is misguided and in the long run counterproductive. If major newspapers, magazines and broadcast stations adopt an advocacy philosophy, the media will be treading on dangerous ground that could alienate readers and viewers and cause them to stop trusting the media."[40]

Second-hand Slant: Source Bias and Biased Sources

Many critics of the media point claim environmental journalists slant the news — intentionally or inadvertently — through the sources they choose. Kevin Decorla-Souza, an intern at the media watchdog group AIM, argued in a post on the Accuracy in Media Website that the media give increased attention to the alarmist claims of environmental groups, particularly on the issue of global warming, while ignoring the claims of skeptical scientists who refute the environmentalists' claims.[41] Likewise, Alison Anderson, author of *Media, Culture and the Environment,* argues that an over-reliance on biased sources, such as the environmental activist group Greenpeace, can lead to a green slant in environmental coverage.

In one study, social scientists interviewed 240 journalists about their backgrounds, voting habits, and attitudes on social issues to search for patterns that illustrate how these factors influence the news. The researchers concluded that in most areas of coverage, including environmental coverage, journalists tend to choose liberal (pro-environmental) sources more frequently than conservative (pro-business) sources. Two out of three journalists chose environmental activist groups and individuals as sources on pollution and environment stories, and nearly as many cite activist federal regulatory agencies. "These activist public and private-sector groups eclipse all others as favored sources of information," say S. Robert Lichter, Stanley Rothman, and Linda S. Lichter in their book, *The Media Elite.*[42]

Interestingly, others have found source bias in the opposite direction. Rosalind Jackson, an environmental sciences major at the University of California at Berkeley, conducted a content analysis study of major newspapers in the San Francisco Bay Area to quantify environmental coverage in the Bay Area. She concluded in a report called "Source Use in Environmental Coverage of San Francisco Bay Area Newspapers" that certain sources, particularly governmental and business sources, are cited more frequently in environmental coverage, resulting in bias.[43]

In examining environmental coverage in the Swedish press, Geoffery D. Gooch found evidence of source bias in favor of authorities over environmental groups. However, he argues in a *European Journal of Communication* article that the amount of bias is irrelevant because it is the quantity of stories about a given issue — not the quality of those stories — that affects public attitudes. He concludes that the influence of environmental media coverage on the Swedish public's attitudes is actually quite weak.[44]

On the other side of the fence is another, especially insidious type of source bias: biased sources.

Just as journalists struggle with their sometimes conflicting roles as independent reporters versus conscientious human beings, so do scientists. And that can blur the safeguard of trusting scientists for the cold, hard, objective facts. If scientists editorialize, how can even the most diligent reporter avoid bias entering her work?

In their popular book *It Ain't Necessarily So*, David Murray, Joel Schwartz and S. Robert Lichter point out "the tension between being a scholar (aiming to understand the world) and being an activist (aiming to make it 'a better place')." They quote climatologist Stephen H. Schneider, who explains that even scientists sometimes editorialize their otherwise objective findings in an attempt to advocate their own personal agendas:

> On the one hand, as scientists we are ethically bound to the scientific method, in effect promising to tell the truth, the whole truth and nothing but — which means that we must include all the doubts, the caveats, the ifs, ands, and buts. On the other hand, we are not just scientists but human beings as well. And like most people we'd like to see the world a better place, which in this context translates into our working to reduce the risk of potentially disastrous climatic change. To do that we need to get some broad-based support, to capture the public's imagination. That, or course, means getting loads of media coverage. So we have to offer up scary scenarios, make simplified, dramatic statements, and make little mention of any doubts we might have.[45]

Journalists such as Schleifstein say that the best safeguard against biased scientific sources is choosing to cite only peer-reviewed scientific studies. Peer review is considered a gold standard in judging the value of a study's findings because a scientist's claims are more likely to be valid if they've passed muster with competent scientific peers. In practice, though, peer reviewers may also have their own substantial biases, which can lead to an inclination to praise research findings that support their own beliefs and to reject research that does not.[46]

• THE EVIDENCE •

While it is clear that bias is present in environmental coverage, it seems more likely to result from institutional practices and external factors than from journalists' personal agendas. The environment beat may present a particularly compelling temptation for reporters to slip into partiality, but most mainstream journalists operate in good faith under the traditional professional principles of accuracy, fairness, and balance.

Nonetheless, bias appears to be a prevalent problem that creeps into environmental coverage in many insidious ways. The bias toward negative news seems to be not only an inevitable part of environmental coverage, but an inherent bias present in all news. Biased sources, particularly when they happen to be respected scientists or reputable agencies, present a complex challenge for journalists, especially those who lack the training and scientific education to question those sources and verify their claims. Subconscious bias will likely be present, in some degree, for all journalists who care about the environment. However, if journalists are trained to heighten their awareness of their own potential bias, it should be possible to curb it.

The question of objectivity vs. advocacy remains a relevant and functional debate, particularly because continual discussion will keep both sides in check. In the context of past social movements, such as civil rights and the war on drugs, proponents of advocacy make a strong argument that the media have a unique responsibility to educate the public and instigate change. However, it is beneficial that the objectivity camp exists to create a sense of balance within the profession itself.

• RESOLUTION •

Regardless of their stance on that issue, journalists should learn about the many types of bias that can appear, not only in their own work but in the sources they use. Kenneth Green, chief scientist of the Reason Public Policy Institute, a public policy think tank, lists a number of different types of bias that can creep into "ostensibly unbiased environmental publications, whether landmark government report or environmental textbooks." Journalists, he proposes, should become aware of the following types of bias that might otherwise go undetected in sources or even their own work.

• **Certainty Bias:** Over- or under-representation of the true state of certainty regarding a given claim, as determined from the weight of available evidence;

• **Selectivity Bias:** Selective use of data or timeframe, or inclusion of available policy options or ramifications, to support a point that would not be supportable using the full spectrum of available data;

• **Order Bias:** Using the order in which claims are presented to emphasize their positivity or negativity;

• **Qualifier Bias:** Selective use of qualifiers ("may be," "might be," "definitely," etc.) to push the reader in one direction or another;

• **Imagery Bias:** Selective use of imagery to influence the readers' emotional associations with the data;

• **Perspective Bias:** Selecting perspectives (timeframes, arbitrary geographic areas, etc.) for interpreting or presenting information that make something seem different than it would be in larger or longer perspectives [Framing?];

• **Unjustified Conclusions:** Conclusions drawn improperly from available data, or drawn from non-existent data;

• **Static Perspective:** Presenting certain situations as static when they are dynamic, or vice versa;

• **False Cause:** Attributing an effect to a certain cause without substantiation;

• **Personal Attack:** Assigning labels to people to discredit their point of view, i.e., "climate skeptics," "pro-industry groups," "radical environmentalists," etc.;

• **Appeal to the Masses:** The invocation of large numbers of people to lend authority to a concept the validity of which is not determined by consensus (i.e., "the majority of scientists think that..."; and

• **Appeal to Authority:** The citing of a high-profile expert (whether in the same field, or another field) as the validation of a concept, rather than the citation of the underlying evidence for that concept.[47]

In addition to scrutinizing their sources for bias, journalists should sensitize themselves to the many subtle ways in which bias can creep into their work: in their reporting, as a result of personal proclivities; in the editing of their stories, when editors may delete key facts or qualifiers; or in the presentation of their work in graphical form. Two researchers who performed a content analysis of industry and mainstream media to search for sources of bias in agricultural news found bias in many subtle forms, as discussed in Kathryn Whitaker and James E. Dyer's article "Identifying Sources of Bias in Agricultural News Reporting." Sources of bias included story length and placement, variety and number of sources, art, and the range of reporters assigned to cover the story.[48]

Editors love drama, and often snip out qualifying words such as "may" or "might," which scientists use to hedge their conclusions. Procedural and methodological components of scientific research — which often determine the conclusions, and always shape them decisively — tend to be downplayed if not altogether ignored in news accounts that concentrate on a study's substantive conclusions."[49]

Jim Detjen, director of the Knight Center for Environmental Journalism at Michigan State University and the founding president of the Society of Environmental Journalists, believes an approach called "sustainable journalism" could possibly appease both the staunch supporters of objectivity as well as those who believe in advocacy. His approach is discussed in the article "A New Kind of Environment Reporting is Needed." Characteristics of this approach include: a push for open-records and FOIA laws that would provide more access to environmental information by citizens and news gatherers; expanded coverage of international environmental issues with an emphasis on the interdependence of environmental, social and economic issues; new global institutions that would enforce greater environmental accountability among multinational corporations; and increased coverage of promising solutions — not just problems.[50]

Roy Peter Clark of the Poynter Institute envisions a curriculum that would teach editors and reporters how to systematically prevent bias. He would like to see reporters examine their own background and past experiences to search for potential sources of bias and then report those findings to an editor who could then be on the lookout. Education and attention, he believes, are the best ways to inoculate against bias.

• POINTS OF VIEW •

Alexander, Charles. "Missing the 'Big Story' in Environment Coverage." *Nieman Reports* 56:4 (2002): 45–47. Environmental journalists are not over-reporting environmental problems, as many charge, but under-reporting them.

Anderson, Alison. *Media, Culture and the Environment.* New Brunswick, N.J.: Rutgers University Press, 1997. An over-reliance on biased sources, such as the environmental activist group Greenpeace, can lead to bias in environmental coverage.

Bailey, Ronald. *Eco-Scam: The False Prophets of Ecological Apocalypse.* New York: St. Martin's Press, 1993. The "natural process of highlighting bad news" encourages journalists to cross the line of objectivity to become environmental advocates.

Blum, Deborah. "Investigating Science: Lots of Time Is Required to Cultivate Sources and Verify their Claims." *Nieman Reports*, Special Issue (2004): 14. Environmental journalists must raise their standards of investigation by taking the time to verify scientific sources' claims.

Charles, John A. "Shading the Truth Green: An Inside Report on Bias from the Society of Environmental Journalists Conference." Brainstorm NW (January 2004), http://www.brainstormnw.com/archive/jan04_feature.html. Pessimism seems to be the default mode for many environmental journalists, who contribute to an erroneously bleak public perception of the environment by ignoring information that suggests otherwise.

Decorla-Souza, Kevin. "Newsweek Editor Admits Green Media Bias." Briefing posted on the Accuracy in Media Website, dated June 27, 2001. http://www.aim.org/publica tions/briefings/2001/27jun2001.html The media give increased attention to the alarmist claims of environmental groups, particularly on the issue of global warming, while ignoring the claims of skeptical scientists who refute the environmentalists' claims.

Green, Kenneth. "Weighing the Words: Getting the Bias out of Environmental Communications." Policy update No. 12, published by the Reason Public Policy Institute, October 26, 2001. www.rppi.org. Several types of insidious bias can creep into "ostensibly unbiased environmental publications, whether landmark government reports or environmental textbooks."

Jackson, Rosalind. "Source Use in Environmental Coverage of San Francisco Bay Area Newspapers." Berkeley: University of California at Berkeley, 2003. http://ist-socrates.berkeley.edu/~es196/projects/2003final/introduction.htm. Certain sources, particularly governmental and business sources, are cited more frequently in environmental coverage, resulting in bias.

Keegan, Mike. "Green Bias in the News: You are Getting All the News That's Fit to Print — It's Just Not All You Need to Know." *Rural Water Magazine*, 2003. Prevalent source bias skews media coverage of environmental issues toward the views of environmental activist groups with alarmist messages.

Lomborg, Bjorn. *The Skeptical Environmentalist: Measuring the State of the World.* Cambridge, New York: Cambridge University Press, 2001. The state of the environment is actually not as bad as coverage in the media suggests.

"Matching the Scenery: Journalism's Duty to the American West." Report published in 2003 by the Wallace Stegner Initiative of the Institutes for Journalism and Natural Resources. www.ijnr.org/wsi/report2003.html. While many environmental journalists think their peers are "too green," others say that environment reporters should sometimes be advocates for the environment.

Murray, David, Joel Schwartz, and S. Robert Lichter. *It Ain't Necessarily So: How the Media Make and Unmake the Scientific Picture of Reality.* Lanham, Md.: Rowan & Littlefield, 2001. Most environmental coverage tends to paint the state of the environment as an imminent crisis — a bias toward dooms — when science suggests quite a different reality.

Rogers, Paul. "Complexity in Environment Reporting Is Critical to Public Decision-Making." *Nieman Reports* 56:4 (2002): 32–34. There is a bias toward negative environmental news over good news.

Shabecoff, Philip. "The Environment Beat's Rocky Terrain." *Nieman Reports* 56:4 (2002):.34–36. There has been a bias against environmental stories within news organizations — often promoted by editors themselves — because the macro-issues associated with environmental problems do not lend themselves to news values that emphasize new events, new angles, and distinct developments.

NOTES

1. Rachel Coen, "Rare, Not Well-Done: U.S. Coverage of Climate Change Talks," http://www.fair.org/extra/0103/climate-change.html.

2. Joel Schwartz, "What Americans 'Know' about Air Pollution Is False," http://www.heartland.org/Article.cfm?artId=19130.

3. Unpublished personal interview with Mark Schleifstein, reporter for the *New Orleans Times-Picayune*, March 5, 2004, by phone.

4. Bud Ward, "Environment Journalists Don't Get Much Respect," *Nieman Reports* Special Issue (2004): 58–59.

5. "Matching the Scenery: Journalism's Duty to the American West." Report published in 2003

by the Wallace Stegner Initiative of the Institutes for Journalism and Natural Resources. www.ijnr.org/wsi/report2003.html.

6. Quoted in Paul Rogers, "Complexity in Environmental Reporting Is Critical to Public Decision-Making," *Nieman Reports* 56 (2002): 50.

7. Bjorn Lomborg, *The Skeptical Environmentalist: Measuring the Real State of the World* (Cambridge: Cambridge University Press, 2001), xxi.

8. David Murray, Joel Schwartz, and S. Robert Lichter, *It Ain't Necessarily So: How Media Make and Unmake the Scientific Picture of Reality* (Lantham, Md.: Rowman & Littlefield, 2001), 9.

9. R.M. Entman, "Framing: Toward Clarification of a Fractured Paradigm," *Journal of Communication* 43 (1993): 51–58.

10. Anders Hansen, "The Media and the Social Construction of the Environment," *Media, Culture and Society* 13 (1991): 443–444.

11. Holly Stocking and Jennifer Pease Leonard, "The Greening of the Press," *Columbia Journalism Review* 29 (1990): 37–44.

12. Hansen, "The Media and Social...," 449, 443–458.

13. Michael T. Maher, "How and Why Journalists Avoid the Population — Environment Connection," *Population and Environment* 18 (1977): 3.

14. G.G. Strodthoff, R.P. Hawkins, and A.C. Shoenfeld, "Media Roles in a Social Movement," *Journal of Communication* 35 (1985): 100–118.

15. Alison Anderson, "Source Strategies and the Communication of Environmental Affairs," *Media, Culture and Society* 13 (1991): 459–476.

16. Everette E, Dennis, "In Context: Environmentalism in the System of News," in Lamay and Dennis, *Media and the Environment,* 60.

17. Eric Alterman III, What *Liberal Media?: The Truth About Bias and the News* (New York: Basic Books, 2003).

18. Michael Parenti, *Inventing Reality: The Politics of News Media* (Boston, N.Y.: Bedford/St. Martin's Press, 1993), 221.

19. Charles Alexander, "Missing the 'Big Story' in Environment Coverage," *Nieman Reports* 56 (2002): 63.

20. Cited in "Matching the Scenery...."

21. David Croteau, "Examining the 'Liberal Media' Claim: Journalists' Views on Politics, Economic Policy and Media Coverage," Fairness and Accuracy in Reporting report, www.fair.org/reports/journalist-survey.html.

22. Brent L. Bozell and Brent H. Baker, eds., *And That's the Way It Isn't: A Reference Guide to Media Bias* (Alexandria, Va.: Media Research Center, 1990), 23.

23. James Bruggers, "The Beat Is a Tougher One Today," *Nieman Reports* Special Issue (2004): 54–55.

24. Unpublished personal interview with Lynn Cunningham, assistant to the editor of the *New Orleans Times-Picayune.*

25. Robert Lee Hotz, "The Difficulty of Finding Impartial Sources in Science," *Nieman Reports* Special Issue (2004): 7.

26. Murray et al., *It Ain't Necessarily So...,* 35.

27. Hotz, "The Difficulty...," 7.

28. Bozell and Baker, *And That's the Way It Isn't,* 95–96.

29. Schleifstein interview.

30. Ward, "Environment Journalists Don't Get Much Respect," 59.

31. Quoted in Lou Prato, *Covering the Environment Beat: An Overview for Radio and TV Journalists* (Washington, D.C.: The Media Institute, 1991), 25–26.

32. Unpublished personal interview with Dr. Roy Peter Clark, vice president and senior scholar at the Poynter Institute.

33. Prato, *Covering the Environment Beat,* 24.

34. Ronald Bailey, *Eco-Scam: The False Prophets of Ecological Apocalypse* (New York: St. Martin's Press, 1993), 168

35. Jim Detjen, "The Traditionalist's Tools (And a Fistful of New Ones)," in Lamay and Dennis, *Media and the Environment,* 93.

36. Everette E. Dennis, "In Context: Environmentalism in the System of News," in Lamay and Dennis, *Media and the Environment,* 60.

37. "Matching the Scenery...," 57.

38. Detjen, "The Traditionalist's Tools...," 93.

39. Craig L. LaMay, "Heat and Light: The Advocacy-Objectivity Debate," in *Media and the Environment,* 105.

40. Detjen, "The Traditionalist's Tools...," 94.

41. Kevin Decorla-Souza, "Newsweek Editor Admits Green Media Bias," Briefing posted on the Accuracy in Media website, dated June 27, 2001. http://www.aim.org/publications/briefings/2001/27jun2001.html.

42. Robert S. Lichter, Stanley Rothman, and Linda S. Lichter, *The Media Elite: America's New Powerbrokers* (Bethesda, Md.: Adler & Adler, 1986), 59–60.

43. Rosalind Jackson, "Source Use in Environmental Coverage of San Francisco Bay Area Newspapers," University of California at Berkeley report (2003), http://ist-socrates.berkeley.edu/~es196/projects/2003final/introduction.htm.

44. Geoffrey D. Gooch, "Environmental Concern and the Swedish Press: A Case Study of the Effects of Newspaper Reporting, Personal Experience and Social Interaction on the Public's Perception of Environmental Risks," *European Journal of Communication* 11 (1996): 107–127.

45. Murray et al., *It Ain't Necessarily So...,* 117.

46. Ibid., 149.

47. Kenneth Green, "Weighing the Words: Getting the Bias out of Environmental Communications," Policy Update 12, Reason Public Policy Institute, October 26, 2001. www.rppi.org.

48. Kathryn Whitaker and James E. Dyer, "Identifying Sources of Bias in Agricultural News Reporting," *Journal of Agricultural Education* 41 (2000): 132.

49. Murray et al., *It Ain't Necessarily So...,* 117.

50. Jim Detjen, "A New Kind of Environment Reporting Is Needed," *Nieman Reports* 56 (2002): 38–40.

11

Regional Bias

Randall S. Sumpter

"If this bias continues to go unnoticed, West Coast [sports] teams and players will continue to suffer from underexposure and we, as fans, will have a distorted national picture. You're free to believe whatever you'd like, but if you don't see an East Coast media bias, you must be looking in the wrong direction."— Phineas Lambert, thebackpagesports.com[1]

"This is classic left wing news thinking where they were trying to manufacture news. They thought those 'evil' conservatives and Southerners would take a swipe at a [M]uslim and they would then plaster it all over the news and say 'see, look at these evil racists.'... The great hypocrisy is that I encounter more racism here in left wing Los Angeles from liberals than anything at a [southern] NASCAR event."— Email comment to www.blogsforbush.com[2]

Most journalists and scholars and pundits who study the media — mainstream and otherwise — agree that the daily stream of news and entertainment incorporates some form of regional bias. They disagree, however, about what form the bias takes and whether or not its inclusion is deliberate.

For some, regional bias is a byproduct of the physical distribution of elite media and the routines that reporters, editors, broadcasters, and others follow to do their jobs. In this case, regional bias means states and cities at the core of the media system receive more coverage than those on the periphery. Stories devoted to the least covered geographic areas also may fit only some of the categories for news, not all. In this case, infrequently covered regions become twenty-first century "Afghanistanisms" (a term that editor Jenkin Lloyd Jones coined in 1948), receiving little media attention because they are considered faraway places where important matters seldom happen. Stories about them often are limited to bizarre accounts or disasters.

Other scholars and critics believe regional bias is a derivative of journalists' backgrounds. Journalists, they believe, unintentionally select stories that resonate with their

own life histories — geographic, economic, educational, and otherwise. Cultural geogra-
phers such as Howard Stein and Gary Thompson say that other places are outside the
"psycho-geography" of journalists, who find it difficult to identify with cultures and locations where they have not lived or worked.[3] This means groups unlike those found in the
journalist's background or workplace are seldom covered. Instead, as the sociologist Herbert Gans pointed out, writers and producers formulate their stories to please superiors,
acquaintances, and family members — people whom they are like or wish to emulate.[4]

A third group, composed mostly of media professionals and critics, say regional bias
is a symptom of the breakdown in traditional standards for reporting news and reflects a
new emphasis by the media, particularly broadcast and new media, on entertainment and
opinion. This emphasis, they believe, has blurred the difference for readers, viewers, and
listeners among legitimate news, opinion, and entertainment. Some believe this "slanting" of news and entertainment is deliberate and represents a media economic strategy
to cash in on the country's so-called "culture war." Whether deliberate or not, this regional
bias paradigm usually splits the nation into a "red" (conservative or Republican) heartland and "blue" (liberal or Democratic) coasts. John Tierney, writing shortly after the
2004 general election, said some perceive this division to be "like the ancient distinction
throughout the world between liberal cosmopolites and traditional farmers. The inlanders have always doubted the morals of merchants in port cities. And the urbanites have
always considered the inlanders backward."[5]

Media Core and Periphery

The unequal flow of news and entertainment from a media system's core to its periphery can cause regional bias in both domestic and international coverage. Researchers have
found this situation internationally, where industrialized societies such as the United States
constitute a core that controls the means for producing and distributing messages and
developing economies represent the periphery.[6] Others have found the same unequal flow
between the U.S. East and West coasts and some regions within the interior of the nation.

Considerable research also has studied subjects and what story types will be covered
from the peripheral regions. In an analysis of foreign news published in the *Los Angeles
Times* during the late 1990s, for example, Christopher Beaudoin and Esther Thorson concluded that the newspaper assigned different types of stories (feature versus hard news),
story topics, and "values" to different global regions.[7] In general, they found that developing countries were the subjects of hard news stories dealing with conflict while stories
about developed countries often incorporated more aesthetic themes.

Earlier work by William C. Adams, on network nightly news programs dealing with
major, global natural disasters, argues for another approach to this phenomenon. Three
factors, Adams reasoned, explained the amount of coverage these disasters received: dis-
tance from New York City, the number of American tourists the area hosted, and the
severity of the disaster scaled from loss of life. Considering those factors, Adams assigned
crude values to the lives of global residents. "Overall, the globe is prioritized," he claimed,
"so that the death of one Western European equaled three Eastern Europeans equaled
nine Latin Americans equaled 11 Middle Easterners equaled 12 Asians," he wrote.[8]

Zixue Tai speculated that these sorts of relationships may not be limited just to media outlets in developed countries. In a study of the top world events as ranked by eleven media in eight different countries, he found that no matter what country a medium represented, it showed a preference for stories from other regions that shared cultural, geographical, and psychological proximity. "Except for a few elite nations," he concluded, "news in all media about small Third World nations tends to focus on limited genres of events — natural disasters, coups and conflicts, and involvement of elite nations."[9] In addition, Hillel Nossek's recent content analysis of stories about political violence argued that the closer journalists perceive their cultural, geographical, and psychological ties to be with an event, the "looser" their application of professional standards becomes.[10]

Within the United States, most investigators consider the "core" of the media system to be powerful news and entertainment companies that maintain their headquarters on the East and West coasts. These companies, according to this line of reasoning, influence the judgments by peripheral media that want to mimic the content decisions of their elite competitors. Warren Breed has called this top-down flow in content decisions the arterial effect, but it's more like a vacuum, which pulls decisions by smaller organizations closer and closer to the elite media's orthodoxy.[11]

A cluster of studies examining these and other media relationships within the United States generally define geographic bias as news coverage that is disproportionate in volume to a region's actual population. These disproportionately represented regions appear to shift with time, and the investigators do not agree about why the imbalances form or shift.

Joseph R. Dominick, who analyzed national network news, was among the first to document empirically these suspected imbalances between regional populations and news coverage.[12] Studying a sample of network newscasts from 1973 to 1975, he found about 21 percent of airtime was devoted to the Pacific region states of California, Oregon, Washington, Alaska, and Hawaii. Those states, however, accounted for 13 percent of the nation's population. The Northeast — comprised of New York, Pennsylvania, New Jersey, Maryland, and Delaware — also received a disproportionate amount of airtime. The most underrepresented region was the Midwest — Ohio, Michigan, Wisconsin, Minnesota, Iowa, Illinois, Missouri, and Indiana. Those states, with 25 percent of the population, received 18.5 percent of the networks' attention. A more fine-grained analysis found that Washington, D.C., California, and New York accounted for almost two-thirds of national newscasts. Washington, D.C., stories alone consumed 50 percent of the airtime. Indirectly, the District of Columbia also accounted for many stories produced by regional media that localized national stories by reporting readers' reactions to federal legislation. Dominick called this ability for one or two states to command more attention than the other states the "eclipse effect." This same "eclipse effect" meant that some states in sparsely covered regions received no coverage. In his study, for instance, no airtime was devoted to Oklahoma. He attributed the preoccupation with Washington, D.C., to a "federal bias" on the part of the networks.

A later study of nightly news broadcasts aired between 1985 and 1987 found new regions in the South and West received disproportionate airtime. The investigator, Doris Graber, speculated that the imbalance might reflect different economic conditions or growing populations. She also found the same "eclipse effect" that Dominick had discovered. California and New York, for instance, received almost as much coverage as the thirty least covered states. When the infrequently covered states did receive media attention, the stories were about disasters, crime, and trivial events. Graber, however, rejected the argument that networks avoided significant state news because viewers were not interested. She pointed out that the networks also broadcast foreign news, another category that reputedly ranked low in viewer interest. She argued instead that there were basically two types of news — high- and low-priority — and that the selection criteria for each differed. High-priority news represented the types of stories that journalists selected previously and audiences had found interesting. News in this category was timely, proximate, exciting, and about prominent people who often are the subjects of media stories. State news, even if important, fell into the low-priority category. "Normally, it [state news] has been covered almost exclusively as an entertainment or convenience item," Graber reasoned. "This explains the narrow focus on a few locations and the flashlight character of coverage — a brief spotlight here, a brief spotlight there, with little effort to report important events systematically."[13] Once set, patterns of news coverage that apply to high- and low-priority items are difficult to change, she argued.

Dominick's and Graber's findings were extended by a research group headed by D. Charles Whitney, which analyzed network nightly news broadcasts between 1982 and 1984. Unlike the earlier studies, these investigators looked for a disproportionate distribution of both stories and sources. Once more the Pacific Coast and Northeast were found to be over-covered, and once more the "eclipse" and "flashlight" effects were documented. Whitney and his co-investigators, however, argued that particular states within a region were not responsible for the disproportionate air time. They concluded that cities caused the "eclipse effect." The investigators concluded that "news, in other words, is made by and in cities, and states which do not have large cities (and news crews or easy airport access to them) or which stand in the shadow of states with large cities are not on the network evening news."[14]

This conclusion, that media convenience and economic issues are responsible for the regional bias in the news, matches more closely to Edward Epstein's pioneering analysis of broadcast news.[15] Phyllis Kaniss' later ethnography of print and broadcast news found similar economic dynamics at work. Print editors and writers work downtown and their readers live in various suburbs, Kaniss observed. This tends to splinter local identity, which threatens the commercial well being of metropolitan newspapers that must offer large audiences to advertisers. Readers also seek a communal bond, Kaniss argued, that transcends the individual suburb. As a result, metropolitan newspapers develop "city myopia" and focus "on the affairs of the central city, because the city is the only source of symbolism strong enough to bind the regional audience."[16] She found that the stories journalists generate under these conditions rely heavily on city government sources and generally are uncritical pieces on downtown development projects like convention centers and sports arenas.

Source distribution also was disproportionate in the Whitney study. Seventy-five percent of the sources used in stories were either current or former officials from governments or institutions, and the remaining 25 percent were identified as victims of crime and economic hard times or as participants in criminal endeavors or bizarre activities. Although these researchers did not draw the connection at the time, their results indicate that source bias in broadcast stories may accompany regional bias.

As Dan Berkowitz and Douglas Beach and others have argued, sources are instrumental in determining what will be news either because they develop attractive story ideas for journalists or withhold information.[17] In the day-to-day newsgathering routine, ethnographers like Gaye Tuchman and Mark Fishman have found, reporters seek stories through established "new nets" or "beat rounds" that connect them to sources affiliated with businesses, government agencies, and others who help defray the cost and effort of gathering and preparing stories.[18] Sources who prove to be dependable will be picked more often by reporters, while less productive sources will be eliminated. The survivors may inject bias into media content because they are "right-thinking people" who create story types and content that benefit a particular commercial or political ideology, block news that might embarrass those benefiting from the status quo, and displace sources such as ordinary citizens or political and ethnic minorities, argue liberal/radical cultural critics such as Todd Gitlin, Edward Herman, Noam Chomsky, and C. Wright Mills.[19] These processes can make story sourcing very homogeneous, both geographically and demographically.

News "Monocultures"

Others argue that the media write frequently about some regions and ignore others not because of an imbalance of resources between a core and periphery, but because of an unconscious bias for the familiar or because of their socialization to a particular group. Eli Avraham and earlier researchers have observed that a journalist's personal background will determine whether these stories are favorable or unfavorable. Those places that have what Avraham calls "close social-ideological" proximity with media decision-makers will receive "wide and positive" coverage.[20]

Researchers David H. Weaver and G. Cleveland Wilhoit found that America's more influential journalists tend to cluster around the centers of financial and political power in the Northeast.[21] Besides covering high-profile assignments like the White House, these journalists receive better pay than their peers, hold degrees from private universities or graduate degrees, and work for the elite news organizations that serve as reference points for other journalists. A substantial minority of print journalists, about 46 percent in 1996, did not hold college degrees or held degrees in something other than journalism. This means that many practicing journalists did not learn the rules and techniques of their profession beginning with college. Instead, they learned them through "socialization" in the workplace.

News organizations, in effect, represent closed societies or what *U.S. News & World Report* writer John Leo calls "monocultures" that unconsciously bias the news toward certain places and toward political and cultural ideals associated with those places.[22] Interestingly enough, media critics have argued at different times in recent history that these news monocultures have produced, on the one hand, news and entertainment biased in favor of "coastal state liberalism" or, on the other hand, in favor of "Middle America conservatism." For instance, conservative media critic Bernard Goldberg argued in his book *Bias* that elites in big-time journalism "are hopelessly out of touch with everyday Americans. Their friends are liberals, just as they are. They share the same values. Almost all of them think the same way on the big social issues of our time: abortion, gun control, feminism, gay rights, the environment, school prayer. After a while they start to believe that all civilized people think the same way they and their friends do."[23]

Liberal critic Thomas Frank argues that explanations like Goldberg's are not believable because the corporations that own the media are managed, for the most part, by conservatives.[24] Journalists, Frank claims, are directed by business pressures that they do not control or that they are unaware of.

When journalists do write or produce the rare story about areas and peoples that are unfamiliar, they use techniques, critics charge, that amplify stereotypes about these lesser known regions and audiences. Gans believed journalists had an affinity for Progressive Era values idealized as coming from "Middle America" or the "heartland." He identified these values as ethnocentrism, altruistic democracy, responsible capitalism, small-town parochialism, individualism, moderation, and social order.[25] Even today, Frank argued, the Midwest and Plains states are venerated as "the repository of national virtue, a place of plain speaking and straight shooting."[26] In slightly updated language, he enumerated those regional virtues as humility, reverence, courtesy, kindness, cheerfulness, and loyalty. These preconceptions can tempt broadcast journalists to use certain story types or "models" when they try to inject geographic balance into stories to maintain a national audience. Epstein explained that one such model used by the networks followed the "nostalgia" format, which "focuses on a traditional value threatened or replaced by a modern value."[27] Stories following this format are popular with rural viewers.

While a story formula exploiting conflicting and stereotypical values might satisfy journalists, entertainment media, critics say, have worked with other sorts of stereotypes. For example, Stein and Thompson noted that Oklahoma politicians found the negative portrayal of their state in the *Grapes of Wrath* to be so odious that they deliberately bolstered the University of Oklahoma's football program to counter the negative publicity.[28] John Otto found fictional accounts dating from the early nineteenth century earned Arkansas an unfavorable national reputation as being populated by hillbillies.[29] This portrayal as a backwater region hindered the state's ability to attract industry or tourists well into the twentieth century.

Paul Farhi of the *Washington Post* has made related observations about current television entertainment programming, which New York and Los Angeles "monocultures" have controlled for half a century. In the past thirty years, he wrote, network television has slowly eliminated depictions of regions "we've come to think of as 'red' [Republican]: southern, Midwestern, mountainous, rural, exurban. Over the same period, TV shows have become 'bluer'— populated by people and stories set in locations identical to those that voted Democratic...."[30] The television westerns of the 1950s took place on the sparsely settled frontier of the nation where government influence was minimal and rugged individualism was valued, according to Farhi. Today's sitcoms and television dramas happen in New York, Chicago, Boston, or Los Angeles. The encoded values are somewhat different than those from the 1950s. For instance, stories located in New York, Boston, Seattle, and Washington, D.C., signal urban sophistication, Farhi wrote.

Sports journalists often ponder the notorious East coast bias, which spurs from the concentration of news outlets in eastern areas, such as New York. This bias allegedly leads the media to emphasize East coast sports teams instead of athletes across the country. Chuck Culpepper of *Newsday*, arguing that East coast bias is a myth, though, pointed out in his article "Go west, young man" that all but one of the first thirty Heisman trophies were presented to college football players in the Eastern or Central time zones.[31]

Media and the "Culture War"

The final explanatory model assumes that regional media bias reflects a business strategy or other conscious decision-making process to exploit the so-called "culture war." The "opinion journalism" that represents a key component of this strategy, critics argue, consumes the time and space previously devoted to traditional reporting, erodes standards for separating news from commentary, and confuses readers, listeners, and viewers about the difference. Paralleling this trend is the growth of the media's own critique of themselves, which also consumes time, space, and resources. Russell Frank of Pennsylvania State University speculated that the media's self-critique is an attempt to placate readers, viewers, and listeners who are dissatisfied with intrusive reporting. "It may be that reporters who are ashamed to be part of the pack call attention to media intrusion to try to forge a bond with readers who are ashamed to be part of the audience," he wrote.[32] In both cases, critics say opinion is cheaper to produce than news and draws larger audiences. Journalists and their critics rather than media researchers are more likely to advance this third explanation for the growth of bias or the perception of its growth.

Mainstream media traditionally have tried to strike the appearance of a geographic balance in stories that they present to readers, viewers, and listeners in the hopes of attracting the largest possible audience. Epstein found that network producers and news executives tried to select stories proportionally from different geographic regions; although, in practice, the distribution really was among New York, Washington, Chicago, and Los Angeles — the locations where network resources had been deployed and from which stories could be covered economically.[33] A dozen years later, Whitney found that the networks had tripled the amount of airtime devoted to stories that could be identified with no single domestic location. He speculated that this "news from nowhere" strategy was an attempt by executives to redefine news and appeal to an audience with diverse demographics.[34] The change halved the flow of network news from Washington, D.C. Ethnographies of newsrooms also have found the same effort to impart geographic balance to the front page of newspapers.

Although not as successful in striking a geographic balance, a somewhat similar shift driven by economics occurred in entertainment programming, Farhi argued.[35] In the case of entertainment, advertisers valued younger viewers, but television westerns appealed to older, more rural viewers and were eliminated. Like their news counterparts, entertainment producers, according to some observers, also generate programming from "anonymous" locations that appeal to wide audiences. Janna Bushman and James Davis studied one of these "anonymous" sites, the Bonneville Salt Flats. They found that filmmakers could use different techniques to portray the flats as a beach, a desert, or a mountain lake. "They [filmmakers]can change the seasons and make summer turn into winter, or the reverse," Bushman and Davis wrote. "They can create different worlds."[36] The authors also noted that gains in computer technology may eliminate the need for filming anything on location because any location can be constructed as a "virtual" reality.

New cable channels and the new on-line media, however, do not necessarily use geographic balance to attract large audiences. Instead, William Powers concluded that these news outlets sort audiences by "ethnicity, language, religion, profession, socioeconomic status, sexual orientation, and numerous other factors."[37] The other factors include the "red state, blue state" geographic dichotomy so popular with broadcasters and print journalists who reported the 2000 and 2004 general elections.

• THE EVIDENCE •

Which model best explains the presence and type of regional bias in the media?

From a research perspective, the three explanations are not based on equivalent evidence. Although the scholarly investigations of the "core and periphery" and "monocultures" models are systematic, they seldom use the same conceptualization of the term "bias." The first explanation basically is a quantitative argument; the second, a qualitative assessment rooted in ethnography. The final model often is based on anecdotal evidence drawn from several different types of sources. It does not always represent a "scientifically" disciplined approach to the problem, and it also represents a macro-discussion of bias, not a focused discussion of regional bias.

Separate quantitative studies by Dominick, Graber, and the Whitney group represent the strongest explanation for the occurrence and frequency of geographic bias. Their studies replicate each other, and they adequately explain most observations. Their work with the U.S. media also triangulates well with studies of international media. In that respect, those three investigations represent a sound explanation for the imbalance in media messages about and from different regions. This model can be understood as essentially a "news values" explanation for regional bias — that is, the media select and publish or broadcast stories that are proximate either geographically or emotionally to their readers and viewers. Mainstream media also are conscious of the need to cobble together the largest possible audience by either giving the impression of or actually trying to strike a regional balance in their stories.

The "monocultures" explanation argues that regional bias in the news reflects the professional socialization of journalists as well as their backgrounds. Journalists are not necessarily conscious of these influences, and they are susceptible to similar, unconscious decisions made by the elite national media. The problem with this explanation, however, is the lack of a convincing demonstration that journalists are mostly unconscious of these influences. Along with some other researchers, I have argued that print editors actively work to avoid these effects.[38] Finally, if we accept this explanation, little short of sending journalists to the equivalent of "re-education camps" will neutralize regional bias in the media.

The final model is of interest not because it represents a systematic study of the regional bias problem, but because it highlights a secondary question being asked by society: Whose values should the media reflect? Should they be the news organization's economic values? Should they be the audience's values? Or should they be the journalist's professional values, whether learned in a classroom or in a newsroom?

• RESOLUTION •

How can the media eliminate regional bias if the evidence best supports a "core and periphery" explanation for its existence? And should the media be asked to address this problem in a capitalistic democracy that routinely lets the marketplace sort out imbalances? Any solution must address two problems: the agenda-building influence of elite, core media on regional and local news and entertainment outlets; and the elite media's penchant for selecting news from the "heartland" that matches so-called "Progressive Era" stereotypes or that produces narratives about bizarre or catastrophic events. Media at either extreme of the "core and periphery" system seem reluctant to spend the money necessary to expand their newsgathering nets enough to snare other types of stories or to sift out disproportionately represented accounts. Instead, they have opted for "opinion" journalism and stories from "anonymous" locations. Meanwhile, entertainment producers seem to respond to a longer cycle, beginning first with stories situated in the heartland, then moving to coastal locations, and now arguably incorporating an "anonymous" strategy of their own with reality programs that skip from location to location each week, take place in exotic locales, or occur in studios at undefined sites.

In a capitalistic economy, entertainment producers are free to respond to marketplace conditions, but in a democracy, the news media are obliged to balance what the reader, viewer, or listener wants with what he or she needs to function as a citizen. If the proliferation of web-based, citizen-mediated news outlets cannot convince the traditional media to rebalance their news products, nothing can.

• POINTS OF VIEW •

Goldberg, Bernard. *Bias: A CBS Insider Exposes How the Media Distort the News.* Washington, D.C.: Regnery Publishing Inc., 2002. Goldberg supplies numerous examples of how broadcast producers and correspondents unconsciously inject class and Northeast metropolitan bias into their work.

Kaniss, Phyllis C. *Making Local News.* Chicago and London: University of Chicago Press, 1991. With suburbanization of American cities, editors and writers work downtown, but their readers, who seek a unifying bond, live outside the city proper. To keep their audience from splintering, the media generate uncritical stories about urban "symbols" like the construction of professional sports arenas that will unite their readers, viewers, and listeners.

Otto, John S. "Down in Arkansas: A State in the Popular Media." *Journal of Cultural Geography* 8 (Fall/Winter 1987): 1–13. A "bad press" dating from the early 1800s earned Arkansas an unfavorable national reputation as being populated by hillbillies. The reputation made it difficult for the state to attract visitors and capital for many years.

Powers, William. "The Massless Media." *Atlantic Monthly*, January/February 2005, 122–126. The new media, which cater to different partisanships, may unite rather than divide the country because they are not part of the established political order like the mainstream media.

Stein, Howard F., and Gary L. Thompson. "A Sense of Oklahomaness." *Journal of Cultural Geography* 11 (Spring/Summer 1991): 63–91. The basis of group identity is psychogeography or a "pool" of self-images shared by individuals living in the same region. In the case of Oklahoma, some of these self-images have been developed at the cultural core of the nation and then adopted by residents of the state.

Whitney, D. Charles, Marilyn Fritzler, Steven Jones, Sharon Mazzarella, and Lana Rakow. "Geographic and Source Biases in Network Television News, 1982–1984." *Journal of Broadcasting & Electronic Media* 33 (Spring 1989): 159–174. News crew location in major cities biases both the number of stories in newscasts devoted to specific regions as well as the types of sources used to tell the stories.

NOTES

1. Phineas Lambert, "Point: There Is a Media Bias Against the West Coast," http://thebackpage-sports.com/bp/sport_site/article_view.cfm?aid=313.

2. www.blogsforbush.com/mt/archives/006865.html.

3. Howard F. Stein and Gary L. Thompson, "A Sense of Oklahomaness," *Journal of Cultural Geography* 11 (Spring/Summer 1991): 63–91.

4. Herbert J. Gans, *Deciding What's News: A Study of CBS Evening News, NBC Nightly News, Newsweek and Time* (New York: Random House, 1979; Vintage Books, 1980).

5. John Tierney, "The Real Divide: Waterside Voters Versus Inlanders," *New York Times*, 7 November 2004, sec. 4, p. 5.

6. Zixue Tai, "Media of the World and World of the Media: A Cross-National Study of the Rankings of the 'Top 10 World Events' from 1988 to 1998," *Gazette* 62 (2000): 331–353.

7. Christopher Beaudoin and Esther Thorson, "Value Representations in Foreign News," *Gazette* 63 (2001): 481–503.

8. William C. Adams, "Whose Lives Count?: TV Coverage of Natural Disasters," *Journal of Communication* 36 (Spring 1986): 122.

9. Tai, "Media of the World," 351.

10. Hillel Nossek, "Our News and Their News: The Role of National Identity in the Coverage of Foreign News," *Journalism* 5 (2004): 343.

11. Warren Breed, "Newspaper 'Opinion Leaders' and Processes of Standardization," *Journalism Quarterly* 32 (1955): 277–284, 328.

12. Joseph Dominick, "Geographic Bias in National TV News," *Journal of Communication* 27 (Autumn 1977): 94–99.

13. Doris A. Graber, "Flashlight Coverage: State News on National Broadcasts," *American Politics Quarterly* 17 (July 1989): 288–289.

14. D. Charles Whitney, Marilyn Fritzler, Steven Jones, Sharon Mazzarella, and Lana Rakow, "Geographic and Source Biases in Network Television News, 1982–1984," *Journal of Broadcasting & Electronic Media* 33 (Spring 1989): 170.

15. Edward J. Epstein, *News from Nowhere: Television and the News* (New York: Vintage Books, 1974).

16. Phyllis Kaniss, *Making Local News* (Chicago and London: University of Chicago Press), 221.

17. Dan Berkowitz and Douglas Beach, "News Sources and News Context: The Effect of Routine News, Conflict and Proximity," *Journalism Quarterly* 70 (1993): 4–12.

18. Gaye Tuchman, *Making News: A Study in the Construction of Reality* (New York: Free Press, 1978; Free Press Paperback, 1980); Mark Fishman, *Manufacturing the News* (Austin: University of Texas Press, 1980).

19. Todd Gitlin, *The Whole World Is Watching: Mass Media in the Making and Unmaking of the New Left* (Berkeley and Los Angeles: University of California Press, 1980); Edward S. Herman and Noam Chomsky, *Manufacturing Consent: The Political Economy of the Mass Media* (New York: Pantheon Books, 1988); C. Wright Mills, *The Power Elite* (London: Oxford University Press, 1956).

20. Eli Avraham, "Cities and Their News Media Image," *Cities* 27 (2000): 363–370.

21. David H. Weaver and G. Cleveland Wilhoit, "Journalists — Who Are They Really," *Media Studies Journal* 6 (1992):63–79.

22. John Leo, "The Media in Trouble," *U.S. News & World Report*, 30 May 2005, 55.

23. Bernard Goldberg, *Bias: A CBS Insider Exposes How the Media Distort the News* (Washington, D.C.: Regnery Publishing Inc., 2002), 24.

24. Thomas Frank, *What's the Matter with Kansas? How Conservatives Won the Heart of America* (New York: Metropolitan Books, 2004), 129.

25. Gans, *Deciding What's News*, 42.

26. Frank, *What's the Matter*, 16.

27. Epstein, *News from Nowhere*, 174.

28. Stein and Thompson, "The Sense of Oklahomaness," 74.

29. John S. Otto, "Down in Arkansas: A State in the Popular Media," *Journal of Cultural Geography* 8 (Fall/Winter 1987): 1–13.

30. Paul Farhi, "Network TV, Ensconced in a Blue Period; Election Results May Signal Rebuff of Shows' Locales," *Washington Post*, 28 November 2004, N1.

31. Chuck Culpepper, "Go West, Young Man," *Newsday*, 11 December 2005, 31.

32. Russell Frank, "'These Crowded Circumstances': When Pack Journalists Bash Pack Journalists," *Journalism* 4 (2003): 453.

33. Epstein, *News from Nowhere*, 108.

34. Whitney et al., "Geographic and Source Biases," 172.

35. Farhi, "Network TV," N1.

36. Janna K. Bushman and James A. Davis, "Crafting a Sense of Place: Media's Use of the Bonneville Salt Flats," *Journal of Cultural Geography* 17 (Fall/Winter 1997): 91–92.

37. William Powers, "The Massless Media," *Atlantic Monthly* (January/February 2005), 122.

38. Randall S. Sumpter, "Daily Newspaper Editors' Audience Construction Routines: A Case Study," *Critical Studies in Media Communication* 17 (September 2000): 334–346.

12

The Military

Christina Jesson

"[Journalists don't criticize] ... when the cruelties are inflicted by the U.S. military—as if dropping bombs on civilians from thousands of feet in the air is a civilized way to terrorize and kill. When journalists maintain a flagrant double standard in their language—allowing themselves appropriate moral outrage when Americans suffer but tiptoeing around what is suffered by victims of the U.S. military—the media window on the world is tinted a dark red-white-and-blue, and the overall result is more flackery than journalism."—Norman Solomon, www.normansolomon.com [1]

"So why is it the media have been much less interested in the ... humanitarian work carried out every day by our troops in Iraq for the past year and a half? ... American humanitarian efforts in Iraq have been Herculean, yet have been barely touched on by the establishment media, which prefers instead to focus on rare foibles by individual soldiers, death tolls and perceived policy failures.... What the [liberal] media are trying to do, in essence, is define for us what is and is not an appropriate use of American military force.... The media are reluctant to report on these [humanitarian] efforts [in Iraq] knowing that doing so would likely increase support for the ongoing war there."—Scott Hogenson, CNSNews.com [2]

The claim that the U.S. media are biased against the U.S. military has been a point of contention between the two institutions. In the chapter "Military and Media Relations" in *Contemporary Media Issues*, first edition, author Hugh C. Cate says that the Civil War began a mutual distrust between the media and military.[3] During the last 250 years and through various military efforts, the media maintain that they have striven to report fairly and truthfully on the military in wartime and peacetime. They also championed the First Amendment rights of freedom of speech and freedom of the press. Contenders counter the media's argument one of three ways: first, the media are supportive of the military until it is not convenient for the media; second, the media are conservative or liberally biased, one way or the other, depending on who is talking; and third, the media are genuinely anti-military.

The power struggle between the media and the military, in addition to the apparent partisan media that have emerged in the past few decades, have led to claims of media bias for and against the military and allegations that the military withholds information from the press. The following appeared on the *Chicago Tribune*'s editorial page on September 30, 2001, "There is a tension between the Pentagon's need for secrecy and the press' job to serve Americans who want honest information about the war" in Iraq. When the *Chicago Tribune* was criticized for its coverage of Union setbacks during the Civil War in the 1860s, the newspaper's editorial page revealed, "We hold it to be a duty to denounce all who stand in the way of the triumph of the good cause, and it matters little to us whether those who impede it are of our own faith and party or belong avowedly to the enemy."[4]

The war in Iraq is the first war of the Internet era, and many Americans receive their news through the Internet and cable television networks. Josh White, in an article in the *Washington Post* in 2005, "Confidence in Military News Wanes," quoted retired Maj. Gen. David L. Grange as saying: "The mass media gets negative points from the people because they think that the big media is taking a position and shaping stories to fit their agenda. The military gets negative points because they come across sometimes as being deceptive or using [operational security] as an excuse."[5] In the same article Cori Dauber, an associate professor of communication studies at the University of North Carolina at Chapel Hill, said, "One of the most important findings here is how interested the public is and that both the military and the media underestimate how many national security topics the public cares about."

There are three major opinions about media bias and the military. They are the following:

1. The media support the military in peacetime and at the beginning of any effort, but then become biased against the military as an effort or war progresses.

2. The media are biased along political party lines.

3. The media are biased against the military regardless of the situation.

Media Mood Swings

The bias argument

For years, especially since the Vietnam War, journalists have claimed that the media struggles to report about the military for various reasons. One reason is the limited access to service members and military situations. Another problem is that they claim to receive partial news from military leaders. At the beginning of the Vietnam War, the media showed a bias toward the military and America's involvement in the war through bolstering articles and positive reports. After the Tet Offensive of 1968, according to the military, the media became increasingly critical and presented shocking images to the American people that, in turn, led the public to denounce the entire war and showed the media's bias against the military and the Vietnam War. Military members blamed the media for their lack of home-front support and continue to do so today.[6]

In *Newsmen and National Defense*, published in 1991, Bernard E. Trainor said the military still blames the media for loss of public support for the Vietnam War. Today the hostility manifests itself in complaints that the press will not keep a secret, that it is biased against the military and that it endangers the lives of military members. "The myth of the media as an unpatriotic, left-wing, anti-military establishment is thus perpetuated."[7]

Howard Kurtz, in his article "Media vs. the Military" published in the *Washington Post* on May 23, 2005, interviewed several news authorities about the reasoning behind the media "deliberately slandering the military." *National Review* Editor Rich Lowry said there is a "media culture, set during Vietnam," aimed at "exposing wrongdoing and failures of the U.S. military. Instead of tending to give the military the benefit of the doubt, there's a tendency to believe the worst." Because of the media's apparent bias against the military during the Vietnam War, efforts were made to help the two groups cooperate. Torie Clarke, the Pentagon's top spokeswoman at the beginning of the current Iraq war, said, "There is a greater appreciation and respect for what the military does than 10 or 15 years ago."[8]

An article by Rachel Smolkin titled "Media Mood Swings" that appeared in the June 2003 edition of the *American Journalism Review* addressed the theory that the media support military efforts until they have a "mood swing." Smolkin says that before the war in Iraq began, upbeat media reports of "shock and awe" flooded television, radio, and newspaper outlets. One week into the war the media reports were replaced by dreary pronouncements about insufficient forces and overextended supply lines. "We have seen mood swings in the media from highs to lows to highs and back again, sometimes in a single 24-hour period," said Defense Secretary Donald H. Rumsfeld on March 28, 2003. Some critics of the coverage suggested that reporters would benefit from calming medications and quality time on a therapist's couch. Jonathan Riskind, Washington bureau chief of the *Columbus Dispatch*, chided his colleagues, "We in the media need to continue asking tough questions and tracking this war as closely as possible. But let's resist the temptation to jump to grand conclusions, optimistic or pessimistic, every hour."[9]

The counter-argument

Defenders of the media argue that many journalists simply record successes and setbacks as they occur. ABC News Vice President Jeffrey W. Schneider said, "What was clear is there were ups and downs in the story. The media were reflecting the way the military and the administration and the country were feeling." Early media amazement with available technology and embedded reporters' access to troops also contributed to initial excitement about military operations at the beginning of the Iraq war.[10]

Smolkin also says that more widespread attention to alternatives in both print and broadcast could have tempered perceptions of media mood swings regarding the Iraq war. Embedded reporters provided authoritative, absorbing accounts and vital information but could not gauge the entire battlefield. Neither could active-duty Army officers in Iraq or Kuwait or retired generals on television, whose newsworthy concerns dominated coverage in late March 2003.

The concept that the media are pro-war and pro-military at the beginning of every effort, but become less enamored with situations involving the military is purported to be either because the effort takes longer than originally planned or because the media become bored with the news.

Michael Scherer's article "Framing the Flag," published in the March/April 2002 issue of the *Columbia Journalism Review*, examines the shift of the media's optimism regarding the military after the U.S. bombing of Kabul, Afghanistan. Scherer said that one month after the first U.S. bombing of Kabul, Fox News correspondent Brit Hume, on his nightly broadcast, said that Peter Jennings and his team at ABC News devoted far more time to the coverage of civilian casualties in Afghanistan than either of their broadcast network competitors. Citing a report, Hume said that ABC spent fifteen minutes and forty-four seconds covering these casualties during the previous several weeks, nearly twice the time spent at NBC and about four times as much as CBS. The implication was clear: War coverage on ABC, free of patriotic announcements, was quite possibly drifting from the national interest.[11]

The Media Research Center, the author of the report cited by Hume, took on a "new and vital mission" in the months after the terrorist attacks on Washington, D.C., and New York, according to its founder, L. Brent Bozell III. "We are training our guns on any media outlet or any reporter interfering with America's war on terrorism or trying to undermine the authority of President Bush," he wrote in a fundraising letter.[12]

Anthony Arnove, editor of the book *Iraq Under Siege,* wrote in an article titled "Pro-War Propaganda Machine" for a Socialist Workers Website, that no matter what President George W. Bush says about Iraq's "threat" to the United States, the corporate media won't ask him the hard questions. Bush and his administration know that they can count on the "patriotism" of the press. And Bush, Arnove argued, won't have to issue any order or appoint any news censors. That's because the press in the U.S. censors itself.[13]

In May 2002, CBS news anchor Dan Rather acknowledged the same. "What we are talking about here — whether one wants to acknowledge it or not, or call it by its proper name or not — is a form of self-censorship," he declared. "It starts with a feeling of patriotism within oneself. It carries through with a certain knowledge that the country as a whole ... felt and continues to feel this surge of patriotism within themselves. And one finds oneself saying 'I know the right question, but you know what? This is not exactly the right time to ask it.'"[14]

Partisan Biases

The bias argument

Arnove says that the media support the Iraq war overall, despite restrictions that the government places on the ability to report freely — and despite the administration's open manipulation of information. The Iraq war will be sanitized. During the U.S. bombardment of Afghanistan, Walter Isaacson, chief executive of CNN, told his staff that it was "perverse to focus too much on the casualties and hardship in Afghanistan." During the 1991 Gulf War, the media buried images of slaughter carried out against retreating soldiers and civilians on the "Highway of Death" at the end of the war.

Arnove says that the media get in line with the government on fundamental matters not because of any conspiracy or backroom deals, but because the media themselves are huge corporations that share the same economic and political interests with the tiny elite who runs the U.S. government. In some cases, they are the same people.

Dan Rather's work is sometimes pointed out as an example of liberal bias in the media. Arnove said he finds it hard to understand why because of what Rather has said about the war on terrorism. "George Bush is the president," Arnove quoted Rather as saying, "he makes the decisions, and, you know, as just one American, if he wants me to line up, just tell me where. Whatever arguments one may or may not have had with George Bush the younger before September 11th, he is our commander in chief, he's the man now. And we need unity, we need steadiness. I'm not preaching about it. We all know this. I would willingly die for my country at a moment's notice and on the command of my president."[15]

Brenton Kenkel wrote an article for the *Kentucky Kernel* in March 2006 stating, "Foreign policy reporting suffers from an information problem: The only way to have any clue what's going on during a war is to ask the government, which has no real incentive to tell the truth. The other option is to report from the ground and risk getting killed."[16]

Kenkel added that the financial expense and the risk of trying to report fairly during a war means that much of foreign-policy coverage will have a pro-administration bent. For example, Gulf War coverage favored George H.W. Bush; Bosnia and Kosovo coverage favored Bill Clinton; Iraq war coverage (especially during "shock and awe" and the rest of the pre-occupation period) favored George W. Bush. "Media bias isn't a simple left-right issue, and by talking about it as such, we're hindering progress toward actually improving journalism in this country," Kenkel said.

In his *U.S. News & World Report* article "The Media in Trouble" in May 2005, John Leo said: "The culture of the newsroom is a factor, too. In all my years in journalism, I don't think I have met more than one or two reporters who have ever served in the military or who have even had a friend in the armed forces. Most media hiring today is from universities where a military career is regarded as bizarre and almost any exercise of American power is considered wrongheaded or evil."[17]

In the article "Don't Blame the Media for Mismanaged Perceptions" published in the June 2004 issue of the *U.S. Naval Institute Proceedings,* the author Pascale Siegel says that President George W. Bush's administration has complained of biased media coverage against the military and the war in Iraq. According to Bush's military leaders and officials, the media focus too much on deadly attacks against the U.S. and coalition forces and not enough on the progress and reconstruction of Iraq.

Negative media coverage comes from discrepancy between optimistic official power assessments and the harsh realities. To bolster support for the war, the administration downplayed the immense problems that might arise after initial victory on the battlefield. Because of this negative fallout regarding the war in Iraq, officials have launched a campaign to turn media coverage toward reconstruction progress.[18]

Peter Beinart, in his article "Media Bias" published in the April 14, 2003, issue of the *New Republic,* says that the bashing of media coverage of the Iraq war is a diversionary tactic that isn't fooling anyone. Fox News' Brit Hume said in April 2003 that the media's war coverage is superficial. "It's all totally inappropriate," Hume said. "You want to find out how it's going in some aggregate, overall sense. And I think that the coverage cheats people of that, and it dwells on the minute at the expense of the large and the direction of things."

Beinart says that the other charge is that the media are providing too much of an "overall, aggregate sense" of the war's progress, and that the media's overall sense is that the war is a disaster. The *National Review*'s David Frum wrote, "To read the media commentary, you'd think that the Pentagon's less than perfect clairvoyance represents some terrible failure rather than the normal 'friction' of war."[19]

The counter-argument

Beinart says that the media are simply the messengers, and attacking them has become a way for political hawks to avoid confronting two far more formidable foes: the uniformed military and the prewar expectations set by the hawks themselves. Instead, hawks have trained their fire on journalists, whose motives are easier to impugn.

The article "The Military versus the Media" published in the *Chicago Tribune* on September 30, 2001, claimed that on the whole, information serves the military's purpose. The military needs the support of the American public to wage war; and the public is likely to grow disillusioned if it suspects that bad news about the military effort is not being divulged. However, the groups' respective goals often find themselves at odds. There is a tension between the Pentagon's need for secrecy and the press' job to serve Americans who want honest information about the war.[20]

The article claimed that media access changed after Vietnam. The Reagan administration declined to take the press on the invasion of Grenada in 1983. George H.W. Bush's administration tried to restrict media access during the Panama operation in 1989 and set up a pool reporting system in the 1991 Gulf War. In exchange for access to Gulf War bases, the media had to submit to Pentagon controls and censorship. The author of the article concluded, "The press has an obligation to protect the security of the nation's military. The Pentagon has an obligation not to obstruct the reporting of the war effort to a free and democratic society."

Perceptions of media bias may also be contributed to the different way that American media cover military campaigns compared with other news mediums. "The View from Abroad" by George A. Krimsky published in the January/February 2002 issue of the *American Journalism Review* states that there is a difference in the way the Iraq war is covered by U.S. journalists and how the war is covered by foreign journalists. Krimsky says that the main difference between the two seems to be the emphasis, spin, and play of news that American editors regard as secondary. When the American press bannered the start of the bombing campaign of Afghanistan on October 7, 2001, it usually gave also-ran status to the simultaneous food drops, while many foreign media gave equal play to the "bread and bomb" campaign.

There's also America's patriotism. While journalists in the United States debate whether they should wear flags on their lapels, or balance every report about civilian casualties in Afghanistan by reminding the public that thousands died on September 11, it should come as no surprise that the foreign media couldn't care less. The Arab media were indignant about U.S. allegations that the Saudi and Egyptian governments were lukewarm in the anti-terrorist effort. "The American media campaign against Saudi Arabia is clear evidence that the American community is arrogant, backward and lacks any knowledge about other countries," wrote a commentator in Kuwait's *Al-Qabas* newspaper. Another Kuwaiti newspaper said, "America wants to hear nothing but obedience."[21]

Those keeping a regular eye on foreign coverage agree that an underlying subtext creeps into even breaking news reports. David Anable, a British-born journalist who heads the International Center for Journalists in Washington, D.C., claims an addiction to the BBC's nightly broadcasts but voices a frustration. "Most of the younger reporters seem unable to resist this wonderful chance to be prophets, ending their pieces with forecasts of doom," Anable said. "The old good rule was that you played it straight, no matter what." Krimsky notes that one of the worst-kept secrets in journalism is that the foreign press corps in the United States, no matter how critical it might be of America and its policies, "doesn't go to the bathroom without first checking *The New York Times* and CNN." The *Wall Street Journal, Washington Post,* MSNBC, and a few others also are on the "must-check" list.[22]

Biased. Period.

The bias argument

A third school of thought is that the media are biased against the military, period. In 2005, ABC's Terry Moran, in an interview with radio host Hugh Hewitt, argued: "There is, Hugh, I agree with you, a deep anti-military bias in the media. One that begins from the premise that the military must be lying, and that American projection of power around the world must be wrong. I think that that is a hangover from Vietnam, and I think it's very dangerous. That's different than the media doing its job of challenging the exercise of power without fear or favor."[23]

According to Cate's "Military and the Media," the technological innovations and the emphasis on speed of reporting pervaded the atmosphere of combat coverage among the media during the Civil War. However, the military placed the priority on security. This is where the mutual distrust between the two sides began and it has evolved through various wars and conflicts, Cate said. During the Gulf War there were many instances where the media accused the military of changing stories for public relations reasons, rather than security ones.[24]

Since that war, reporters have been allowed to "embed" with the troops. Especially during the current war in Iraq, embedded journalists say they have proven effective at getting out a more accurate message than journalists reporting from a bureau with no firsthand knowledge or experience with actual occurrences.

A survey of embedded journalists conducted by Shahira Fahmy and Thomas J. Johnson and published in the *Journalism & Mass Communications Quarterly* in the summer of 2005 showed that, overall, most embedded journalists had a positive view of their work during the Iraq war. Of the 159 journalists who completed the online survey, most agreed that their reports provided a narrow slice of the conflict, but they said that embedding provided access to the battlefield and a better understanding of what was happening on the ground. About three-fourths said they believed that their stories were accurate, trustworthy, and fair.

The survey measured factors that influenced perceptions of performance. For example, embedded journalists who supported the war said the rules of coverage allowed more freedom than earlier conflicts, while critics said the rules were designed to ensure that only the official perspective was reported. The more objective embedded reporters tried to be, the more they said embed reporting was successful.[25]

The military's stance is that no matter how hard a journalist tries to be objective and fair, the reporter can never cover the military accurately because they don't understand military operations. According to Cate, the military believes that media representatives, as a whole, lack the necessary military experience to accurately portray events to the public. A correspondent not well versed in the tactics, techniques, and procedures of the services cannot accurately relay truthful information without bias or misunderstanding of the overall concept. In the military's view, negative coverage is the result of inadequate understanding.

The media reject these notions, saying that military experience is not necessary to report the news in a fair and accurate manner. The media say they are proud of their traditional role as outside observers, and they believe that this kind of coverage is simply the best, most objective way to communicate the truth. If a report is negative, then the situation was negative.

The second facet of this issue deals with the emphasis that the military places on operational security. To the military, the media represent a chronic security risk. There is the belief that a journalist with little or no experience may inadvertently release information that jeopardizes human life.[26]

In an October 2004 Naval Institute report titled "Who's Responsible for Losing the Media War in Iraq?" reservist and embedded reporter James Lacey argued that the military is to blame for losing the media war in Iraq. It's not because the media are biased against the military. "The reason the military is losing the war in the media," he declared, "is because it has almost totally failed to engage and where it has engaged, it has been with a mind-boggling degree of ineptitude. It is a strange circumstance indeed when virtually every senior officer agrees that the media can make or break national policy, but no more than a handful can name the top military journalist for the *Washington Post, The New York Times,* or *The Wall Street Journal.*"[27]

Lacey added that despite the successes of the embedding process and the tens of millions of dollars spent on public affairs infrastructure, relations between the media and the military continue to be strained. Military officers constantly lament that most of the successes in Iraq and Afghanistan went unnoticed, while every little setback or problem seemingly received national attention. Many believe national policy is set by the media's intent on painting every U.S. military commitment as an unwinnable quagmire. The media will always get a story out; it is the military's responsibility to make sure that story is informed and correct, Lacey said. It is useless for officers to scream in frustration that the media got a story wrong, particularly if they did nothing to help journalists get it right. "Anyone who thinks a journalist is ethically bound to go back and fix wrong information or impressions is fooling himself. Even current military stories are competing for space against J-Lo's latest wedding," Lacey said.

The April 2003 incident of the looting and theft of the Iraqi National Museum was an example of how stories can be misconstrued or exaggerated when reporters cannot get anyone to give official information. In Andrew Lawler's "Lifting the Fog of the Bias War" published in the November/December 2003 edition of the *Columbia Journalism Review*, Lawler said that radio and newspaper reports grimly told the world that 170,000 objects in that repository of Mesopotamian history had vanished. Many of these first reports were full of basic factual holes. The impact of stories written at the beginning of the war was heightened by dramatic quotes from outraged academics in the United States, comparing the disaster to the burning of the Library of Alexandria or the Mongol sack of Baghdad.

Amid such conditions, no one expects the proverbial first draft of history to be accurate. The *Chicago Tribune*'s Bill Glauber said, "I basically just tried to write what I saw." In the aftermath, reporters need to use their analytical talent and investigative drive to bang out a more accurate and nuanced second draft, Lacey said.[28]

The counter-argument

In August 1998, Reed Irvine and Cliff Kincaid wrote an article for Accuracy in Media titled "Dan Rather Should Apologize." In it Rather is quoted as saying that "there is not now and never has been any anti-military bias in the media." He said in his column that the real bias is "decidedly pro-military.... This includes Vietnam. It's a myth that most American journalists in Vietnam didn't like the military."

Irvine and Kincaid said that either Dan Rather has a poor memory or he is deliberately trying to rewrite history. Their example is Peter Arnett, who covered Vietnam for The Associated Press for eight years. He won a Pulitzer Prize for five stories he wrote in 1965. Four out of the five reflected his strong anti-military bias. His reporting played an important role in converting the stunning defeat the Viet Cong suffered in the 1968 Tet Offensive into a psychological victory.

Rather displayed his own anti–U.S. military bias in a newscast on March 30, 1987. Rather's report said that a Soviet publication had charged that an American military laboratory had developed the virus that caused the AIDS epidemic. He did not accompany this charge against the U.S. military with a comment from the Pentagon or the State Department.[29]

Norman Solomon's article "Blaming the Media for Bad War News" points out that President George W. Bush and his administration are not doing much to help the media information about what good things might be taking place in Iraq. At a town hall meeting with President Bush in March 2006 in Wheeling, W.V., a woman introduced herself and said that her husband was an Army officer in Iraq where "his job while serving was as a broadcast journalist" and "he has returned from a 13-month tour in Tikrit," she said. "He has brought back several DVDs full of wonderful footage of reconstruction, of medical things going on. And I ask you from the bottom of my heart for a solution to this, because it seems that our major media networks don't want to portray good news." President Bush's recommendation was "Just got to keep talking.... I would suggest you reach out to some of the groups that are supporting the troops ... and that's one way to deal with an issue without suppressing a free press. We will never do that in America."[30]

Bernard Trainor said a factor that influences the two groups' interrelationship is the fact the military is hostile toward the journalists, while the journalist is indifferent toward the military. "To the journalist, the military is just another huge bureaucracy to report on, no different from Exxon or Congress." Whereas businessmen and politicians try to enlist journalists for their own purposes, the military man tries to avoid them, and when he cannot, he faces the prospect defensively with a mixture of fear, dread and contempt.[31]

In a 2005 report by the McCormick Tribune Foundation, the *Washington Post's* Pentagon correspondent, Bradley Graham, concluded: "I think there's also still an issue in handling bad news. Overall, my greatest concern about the military-media relationship now is the claim we've started hearing again about how our reporting, particularly about the war, is so negative. To some degree this is a perennial complaint about the press, but coming now with such intensity by some senior people ... and I think the argument can be made that the press should be, not necessarily more negative, but more skeptical. The press has been very critical of itself for its pre-war reporting. I don't think that it now ought to be concerned about not highlighting things that are not working well in Iraq or elsewhere."[32]

• THE EVIDENCE •

Each of the three arguments presented is well-reasoned and is depicted in the media in some way everyday. Regardless of which opinion a reader or viewer has regarding media coverage of the U.S. military, each of those views will most likely be reinforced in some way or another every time a television program is viewed or a newspaper read. As humans, we take knowledge given to us and process it according to our own biases and beliefs. The way people feel about coverage of the military is no exception.

The first viewpoint, that the media have mood swings and support the military or denounce the military according to how they feel, is a good argument that many people accept. After the Tet Offensive in 1968 the media became disenchanted with the Vietnam War and the military leaders who believed in the mission. The media began airing and printing stories that depicted the horror of the war and were perceived by the military as not supporting the troops or the war after that point. It is understandable how the military could feel betrayed by the media, since the media are the military's direct link to the public. The military felt that once the support from the American people was gone, the reasons for fighting weren't clear anymore.

The same can be seen happening with the war in Iraq. At the beginning of the war and during the first days of the campaign, media outlets stationed reporters in Baghdad, Iraq, and Afghanistan in preparation for the "shock and awe" campaign. The round-the-clock coverage seemed to show that the media were biased in favor of the American military. TV stations and newspapers ran stories of vigils for the troops and troop departure ceremonies filled with emotion as families said good-bye. Consumers couldn't turn a channel or a page without seeing a picture of an American flag.

As the war churned on, the media transitioned from almost unanimous supportive coverage to reporting on the daily breaking news such as car bombs, death, and how unhappy the American people were about how long the war was taking.

The counter-argument to this viewpoint is justified. Journalists said that the reason the media's coverage fluctuates so radically is because of the information needs of the American people and because events occur quickly. Reporters must adapt to those changes and learn to give readers and viewers what they want and need. Also, technological advancements such as the Internet and 24-hour news networks added to the initial excitement depicted by journalists and felt by American citizens at the beginning of the Iraq war. After September 11, 2001, Americans felt so much patriotism that when the government announced that the military was going to Afghanistan to retaliate, the surge of American pride was evident everywhere, everyday. This may have led to the media's overwhelming support of the military at the beginning of the Iraq war. As with all things, the media and the public tire of most subjects, and a large portion of the public grew weary of the wary.

The second argument, that the media are biased along party lines, is well founded, especially in recent years with certain TV stations and newspapers priding themselves on the fact that they are the media outlet for "X" type of person (i.e. Democrat, Republican, conservative, liberal, black, white, etc.). For example, many people believe that since the terrorist attacks of September 11, Fox News has been the champion of the Bush administration and all things Republican/conservative. It is evident that party-line politics extend past legislative officials. Some viewers perceive Fox News as pro-military and supportive of the war in Iraq. CNN, on the other hand, prides itself on being the "world's network" and claims to give balanced coverage of the military, while critics claim that it and other outlets, such as the *New York Times*, are clearly critical of military actions.

Brenton Kenkel said that media bias isn't a simple "left-right issue" and that journalists must move past party-line biases if journalism in America is to improve. Journalism is, theoretically, supposed to be based on fairness and accuracy, not on partisanship or journalists' peculiar perspectives. Members of the public depend on the media to be fair and balanced so that they can form their own opinions about issues. However, because people's own biases and political affiliations play a part in how they perceive bias, it is hard to prove that media outlets are biased along party lines.

The evidence does a good job of showing that there are party-line biases on some level, but it is not quantitatively measured and may be based mostly on personal opinions. To get an accurate picture of how biased the American people think the media are regarding military issues, a larger study than has been done would have to be conducted.

The third school of thought, that the media are truly biased against the military, has questionable support. The arguments are not strong enough to be convincing. Its proponents don't present strong enough evidence to be convincing. However, it is possible that the media may have moved slightly in that direction. It seems clear from historical studies that the media have grown generally less supportive of the military since World War II.

• RESOLUTION •

If the media have grown less supportive of the military, and if the trend continues, the potential exists for considerable impact. The media have the power to influence. The American public clearly gets much of its information about the military through the media, and it is clear that the media have some influence on people's thinking. If the media should take an anti-military stance and the people begin to support that viewpoint, voters could replace congressmen, money could be reallocated, and the military could lose funding and support.

The power struggle between the media and the military, and their persistent distrust for each other, may not ever be completely erased, but they do need to learn to cooperate with and respect each other to ensure that the American people receive the fair and balanced news that they deserve. The military and the media, two independent organizations that are forced to coexist, must learn to work together in an effective way that will provide pertinent news about the military to the public, as well as retain the military's priorities on safety and security for service members. The military needs to foster the idea that the media can be an effective means of relaying information to the public, and the media need to make sure that information is processed and relayed fairly and accurately. Nothing should be sensationalized for the sake of ratings or awards.

Because the American people have access to news twenty-four hours a day, the media should be more aware of the stance they take regarding the military at all times. It is confusing to viewers and readers if before a military campaign the media are pro-military and pro-war, and then later do nothing but report how badly the war is going and how horribly the troops are holding up. Journalists need to learn all sides of an issue and give the public the full story from the start, not just when the media are tired of trying to bolster the military and move on to something else.

A military officer at a McCormick Tribune Foundation conference described the disconnect between his experience in Iraq and what he saw in the media. He said that until he came back and read the newspapers, he hadn't realized the war in Iraq was going so badly. But he added that the optimism he was hearing from the Pentagon also was not realistic. The result, he said, is that he doesn't trust the media because they seem biased against the military and he doesn't trust the civilian leadership because it isn't telling the complete truth.[33]

The American public should feel that regardless of their individual viewpoints, the media will present all sides of an issue thoroughly so that viewers and readers can form their own opinion. More efforts should be made to embed journalists with the military in peacetime so that when presented with a combat situation, the journalists and military members will have a mutual trust and respect for one another.

• POINTS OF VIEW •

Arnove, Anthony. "Pro-War Propaganda Machine." Socialist Worker Online, 21 March 2006, www.socialistworker.org/2003-1/445/445_06_Media.shtml. Corporate media are biased toward the military.

Beinart, Peter. "Media Bias." New Republic, 14 April 2003, 6. Media reporting seems biased because hawks sold the Iraq war as a rosy, short-lived intervention.

Cate, Hugh C. "Military and Media Relations." Contemporary Media Issues, eds. Wm. David Sloan and Emily Erickson. Northport, Ala.: Vision Press, 1998. This evenhanded treatment of the military-media issue was one of the earliest proposals suggesting embedded reporters as a means of assuring a good working relationship between the two.

Kurtz, Howard. "Media vs. the Military." Washington Post, 23 May 2005. Conservatives believe the news media are deliberately slandering the military.

"Military Versus the Media," *Chicago Tribune,* 30 September 2001. Media are not biased but are often misled or misinformed by the military.

Scherer, Michael. "Framing the Flag," *Columbia Journalism Review*, March/April 2002. U.S. news media were biased toward the military when the bombing of Kabul, Afghanistan, began.

Siegel, Pascale. "Don't Blame the Media for Mismanaged Perceptions." *U.S. Naval Institute Proceedings* 130:6 (June 2004), 30. The media aren't biased; they're just reporting on the Bush administration's mismanaged pre-war perceptions.

Smolkin, Rachel. "Media Mood Swings." *American Journalism Review,* June 2003. Media's mood swings during the first week of the Iraq war led to distorted public perceptions of the military campaign.

White, Josh. "Confidence in Military News Wanes." *Washington Post*, 24 August 2005. A poll of Americans shows that the media are perceived as biased because people think they are taking a position to fit agendas.

NOTES

1. Norman Solomon "Media Tall Tales for the Next War," http://www.normansolomon.com/.

2. Scott Hogenson, "Coverage of Military Tsunami Response Betrays Media Bias." http://www.cnsnews.com/ViewCommentary.asp?Page=%5CCommentary%5Carchive%5C200501%5CCOM200 50107a.html.

3. Hugh C. Cate, "Military and Media Relations," *Contemporary Media Issues,* eds. Wm. David Sloan and Emily Erickson (Northport, Ala.: Vision Press, 1998), 106.

4. "The Military Versus the Media," *Chicago Tribune,* 30 September 2001. http://la.indymedia.org/news/2001/09/11043.php.

5. Josh White, "Confidence in Military News Wanes." *Washington Post,* 24 August 2005, www.washingtonpost.com/wp-dyn/content/article/2005/08/23/AR2005082301290_pf.html.

6. Cate, "Military and Media Relations...," 108.

7. Bernard E. Trainor, "The Military and the Media: A Troubled Embrace," in *Newsmen and National Defense,* ed. Lloyd J. Matthews (Washington, D.C.: Brassey's, 1991), 122.

8. Howard Kurtz, "Media vs. the Military," *Washington Post,* 23 May 2005, www.washington post.com/wp-dyn/content/blog/2005/03/23/BL2005040701385_pf.html.

9. Rachel Smolkin, "Media Mood Swings," *American Journalism Review* (June 2003), www.ajr.org/article_printable.asp?id=3040.

10. Ibid.

11. Michael Scherer, "Framing the Flag," *Columbia Journalism Review*, March/April 2002, www.cjr.org/issues/2002/2/flag-scherer.asp?

12. Quoted by Anthony Arnove, "Pro-War Propaganda Machine," Socialist Worker Online, 21 March 2006, www.socialistworker.org/2003-1/445/445_06_Media.shtml. The original quotation is not available, and Arnove's Socialist anti-war website is the most readily available source for citing it.

13. Arnove, ibid.

14. Quoted in ibid.

15. Ibid.

16. Brenton Kenkel, "Media Bias is a Two-Sided Phenomenon," *Kentucky Kernel,* 30 March 2006, www.kykernel.com/home/index.cfm?event=display.

17. John Leo, "The Media in Trouble," *U.S. News & World Report* 138:20, p. 55.

18. Pascale Siegel, "Don't Blame the Media for Mismanaged Perceptions," *U.S. Naval Institute Proceedings* 130:6 (June 2004): 30.

19. Peter Beinart, "Media Bias," *The New Republic,* 14 April 2003.

20. "The Military Versus the Media," *Chicago Tribune*. 30 September 2001.

21. George A. Krimsky, "The View from Abroad," *American Journalism Review* (January/February 2002), www.ajr.org/article.

22. Ibid.

23. Kurtz, "Media vs. the Military."

24. Cate, "Military and Media Relations"..., 109.

25. Shahira Fahmy and Thomas J. Johnson, "How We Performed: Embedded Journalists and Perceptions Toward Covering the Iraq War," *Journalism and Mass Communication Quarterly* 82 (2005): 302–303.

26. Cate, "Military and Media Relations...," 112–113.

27. James Lacey, "Who's Responsible for Losing the Media War in Iraq?," The Naval Institute, October 2004, www.military.com/Content/MoreContent1?file=NI_1004_Media-P1.

28. Andrew Lawler, "Lifting the Fog of the Bias War," *Columbia Journalism Review* (November/December 2003), www.cjr.org/issues/2003/6/voice-lawler.asp?

29. Reed Irvine and Cliff Kincaid, "Dan Rather Should Apologize," Accuracy in Media report, 10 August 1998, www.aim.org/media_monitor/A3538_0_2_0_C/sendpage/sendpage/index.php.

30. Norman Solomon, "Blaming the Media for Bad War News," Truthout.org, 23 March 2006, www.truthout.org/docs_2006/032306B.html.

31. Trainor, "Newsmen and National Defense...," 124.

32. Quoted in *The Military-Media Relationship 2005* (Chicago: McCormick Tribune Foundation, 2005), 21–22. An executive summary of the report is available at http://www.mccormick tribune.org/journalism/milmedia05_execsum.pdf.

33. *The Military-Media Relationship 2005*, ibid., 79.

13

Television News

Jenn Burleson Mackay

"Since its 1996 launch, Fox has become a central hub of the conservative move-ment's well-oiled media machine. Together with the GOP organization and its satellite think tanks and advocacy groups, this network of fiercely partisan outlets ... forms a highly effective right-wing echo chamber where GOP-friendly news stories can be promoted, repeated and amplified. Fox knows how to play this game better than anyone."—Seth Akerman, Fairness and Accuracy in Reporting[1]

"Could it be gross incompetence? It's theoretically possible. But it seems perhaps the reason for gross incompetence was incredible bias.... [I]t seems CBS definitely had an agenda, which for CBS was more important than the facts. Every publi-cation, every network has its biases. The question is, do you let those override the facts, or do you go through the normal practice of checking and verification that even [journalism students] in school are told to do?"—Marvin Olasky, University of Texas professor[2]

The scenes were bloody and horrific, but people were addicted to the images of the Vietnam War. Viewers couldn't get the pictures out of their minds. So they kept going back for more. Then, CBS news anchor Walter Cronkite stepped in front of a camera and issued an unapologetic proclamation. "We have been too often disappointed," he declared, "by the optimism of the American leaders, both in Vietnam and Washington, to have faith any longer in the silver linings they find in the darkest clouds. But it is increas-ingly clear to this reporter that the only rational way out then will be to negotiate, not as victors, but as an honorable people who lived up to their pledge to defend democracy, and did the best they could."

His words clearly echoed an opinionated passion during that broadcast. Cronkite was speaking with his own heart and mind, rather than with objectivity. Scholars and politicians could spend weeks arguing whether he was out of line during that February 1968 broadcast, but most anyone would agree the noted anchorman gave viewers a taste of biased television news.

Television has changed since that broadcast. Today's viewers can surf hundreds of channels to listen for commentary from pundits who openly announce that they lean to the left or the right. Reporters from various newspapers and television stations appear on these politically charged shows to give their personal insight into events.

Audiences have also lost some of the trust that they once had in the news media. A little more than thirty years ago a Gallup Poll found that 68 percent of Americans trusted the media. The Gallup Poll's annual survey found in 2005 that about half of Americans have faith that the news media report accurately and fairly. That number is slightly up from the previous year's poll, but the decrease is still alarming.[3]

To further complicate matters, network news has met competition from 24-hour cable news. People can spend a few hours watching CNN and complain about its liberal tendencies or turn to Fox News and criticize its conservative stance. With so many options for news, no matter what your political ideals are, it is easy to find a reason to argue that some TV news is biased.

The allegations of bias might have started decades ago with Cronkite's criticism of the Vietnam War or some other journalist's impassioned story, but the number of news options has thrown America into the heyday of a partisan TV news controversy. The various perceptions on TV news bias range from those crying for an end to liberal bias to those harping that America's conservative broadcasters must be stopped.

"Nattering Nabobs of Negativism"

Vice President Spiro Agnew once referred to journalists as those "nattering nabobs of negativism." His comments go to the heart of the perspective that television has a liberal bias. Proponents argue that TV journalists intentionally support Democrats or liberal agendas, and they claim that the overwhelming majority of TV news outlets are liberal. For years people have noted that the majority of journalists vote Democrat, and therefore the news must be biased to support those political views. Those criticism recently became even more potent when Dan Rather's credibility was put on the line.

The CBS anchorman assisted with a *60 Minutes* report, which focused on George W. Bush's military record during the 2004 presidential election campaign. Much of the story emphasized documents that the news staff collected while preparing the story. The documents indicated that Bush received preferential treatment while he served in the Texas Air National Guard. Shortly after the broadcast, a flurry of reports began suggesting that the documents were forgeries and that CBS staff members had not done enough to ensure their accuracy. Rather defended the story twice on air. Nonetheless, journalists at some of the other major networks, including ABC and NBC, questioned the accuracy of the documents. After it was determined that they were forgeries and that the CBS staff had rushed the story onto the air, critics of CBS quickly reacted to the news, citing it as the ultimate proof of liberal television bias. Rather eventually retired, and other staff members were fired or asked to resign.

Some critics cheered that CBS was caught red-handed. *National Review*'s Jonah Golderberg wrote, "For his entire career Dan Rather has insisted on saying a palpably untrue thing in the most dismissive and condescending tone possible: that he is not remotely liberal. And yet there is simply no conceivable way this debacle could have transpired without liberal or anti–Republican-bias."[4] Others also cited the National Guard report as fundamental proof that the media have an agenda. Eric Fettmann of the *New York Post* called the incident "journalism's Watergate." He said Rather stood by the initial airing of the story in a way that resembled Richard Nixon's "stonewalling."[5]

This certainly was not the first time that critics had called Rather a zealous liberal. He had challenged former President Nixon to talk about Watergate during a news conference in 1974. In 1998, he had a face off with then Vice President George Bush regarding the Iran-Contra affair. Then in 2001 he appeared at a Democratic fundraiser that his daughter co-sponsored. Those long-remembered events made him an easy target after the Bush story fell apart.

Other news shows have also been accused of liberal behavior. ABC's news magazine *Nightline* with Ted Koppel raised a number of eyebrows in 2005 when the show read off the name of every American soldier killed during the Iraq war. To make the show even more potent, the staff also aired a photograph of each solider. The show was twenty minutes longer than usual and featured more than 500 soldiers. Critics quickly condemned the network, calling the segment a partisan attack aimed at destroying support for the war. Those on the other side of the debate hailed the show as a tribute to lives lost in war.

Bernard Goldberg's book *Bias: A CBS Insider Exposes How the Media Distort the News* took on other issues that lead to liberal bias, including the ratings war.[6] Goldberg argued that news broadcasters spend so much time worrying about winning ratings that they let important stories slip by. They have to make sure that they keep their audience in order to keep their advertising revenue. That means that the important but perhaps boring stories take a backseat to sleezier, eye-popping tales of sex and crime.

In addition, Goldberg said that the love of ratings forces television to consider the impact a story might have if it offends viewers. He compares the media to a politician up for re-election. The media are regularly up for that re-election. If they offend viewers with stories, their ratings might plummet. Goldberg sites this ratings fear as one of the reasons that important stories about conservative issues are left off the air.

Another part of the problem is that journalists frame stories around their own perspective, according to Goldberg. Among other things, he argues that liberals view the world as more racist and more anti-gay than it is. Those fundamental beliefs seep into their stories. He sees the bias as an unintentional yet undeniable phenomenon.

That assessment is similar to an argument from the Media Research Center, which accuses CBS, NBC, ABC, and CNN of having a liberal bias. The center says, for example, that its research shows that between 1997 and 1999 the news networks showed nine anti-gun segments for every one segment that supported guns. The MRC cited ABC news as being the most one-sided, particularly the shows *World News Tonight* and *Good Morning America*.[7]

Critics found a more blatant form of bias in network news when George Stephanopoulos, a former Clinton aide, found his way into network news. When the initial announcement was delivered that he would act as an analyst and a correspondent, criticism abounded. *Los Angeles Times* syndicated columnist Cal Thomas said it was a sign of the "deplorable state of today's broadcast journalism." He argued that the appointment would give the public more reason to question the fairness of TV news, especially since President Clinton was still in office.[8]

PBS has also stirred criticisms that it has a liberal bias. PBS chairman Kenneth Y. Tomlinson hired a consultant to track the political preferences of guests on *Now with Bill Moyers*. The report found that the majority of guests on the show were "anti–Bush." Tomlinson acknowledged that he was concerned that PBS was overly liberal.[9]

Scholarly research has also indicated the existence of a liberal bias. Dennis T. Lowry and Jon A. Schidler found signs of liberal TV news in their study, published in *Journalism & Mass Communication Quarterly*, of sound bites during the 1992 and 1996 presidential campaigns. They collected sound bites that aired on ABC, CBS, CNN, and NBC. Their task was to determine what sound bites journalists were choosing to use in their news stories. They then evaluated whether each sound bite said something positive about a candidate or something negative. They found that more negative comments were aired about Republican candidates than about Democrat ones.[10]

A bumper sticker during the 1992 presidential campaign succinctly voiced the argument of those who claim that television has a liberal bias: "Annoy the media, Re-elect Bush." Those who believe in the liberal media hypothesis remain convinced that, even if there is not an intentional left-wing conspiracy, there is certainly an overwhelming echo in the media that supports a liberal lifestyle. From blatant political support, to ratings fears and the subconscious framing of stories from a leftist point of view, many Americans are convinced that TV news is utterly, liberally biased.

Corporate America's Media Puppetry

While the majority of criticism of TV news bias claims that it is liberal, there are also critics who are convinced that it has an unyielding conservative slant that comes from television's corporate ownership. Proponents of this argument say the media are under complete control of giant conglomerates, which have the power to control the news.

Rupert Murdoch stands at the forefront of the hypothesis that TV news has a conservative bias. The chairman of the News Corporation has a reputation for personal involvement in his media outlets' editorial stances. His company owns the *New York Post*, *The Times* of London, and the ever-popular Fox News Channel.

According to David Kirkpatrick of the *New York Times*, media outlets owned by New Corporation closely aligned their editorial policies to match Murdoch's during the war with Iraq. The powerful executive freely voiced his opinion to support the war during interviews. In addition, from the early days of the war, Fox aired a waving American flag. Anchors referred to the American and British troops as "liberators." Murdoch regularly sits in on news meetings when he is in New York. Fox News Senior Vice President John Moody said that during major news events Murdoch sometimes attends the morning meetings two or three times a week. He asks questions and makes comments during the meetings.[11]

Fox News calls itself the "fair and balanced" news option, but critics argue that it strives to attract conservative viewers, particularly those who tend to listen to conservative talk radio. Critics claim that evidence shows that it has a strong conservative viewer base. Case in point: the 2000 Republication National Convention. The station's audience increased significantly as the convention aired. The audience decreased when the Democratic Convention aired.[12]

Additional evidence of the station's conservative base came, critics say, in 2004 when it declined airing a commercial from the liberal publication *The Nation*. The 60-second ad, which would have aired during the Republican convention, criticized Murdoch, stating that "nobody owns *The Nation*. Not Time Warner, not Murdoch. So there's no corporate slant, no White House spin. Just the straight dope." CNN, which is owned by Time Warner, aired the commercial as did NBC, Universal's MSNBC, and Bravo. A Fox News representative said the commercial was denied because the station did not appreciate the implication that it presented biased coverage.[13]

Some critics extend the allegations of conservative TV bias beyond Fox News. Robert McChesney and John Bellamy Foster, writing in *Monthly Review: An Independent Socialist Magazine*, argued that claims of liberal bias are actually an attempt by conservatives to control the media. They argue that politicians and other staunch conservatives benefit from the continuous debate over the "left-wing" media. TV journalists water down their coverage and analysis, McChesney and Foster claim, because they do not want to appear biased.[14]

Political pundits, with their quick wit and feisty discussions, have also attracted the attention of those who believe there is a conservative bias in TV news. Eric Alterman, in *What Liberal Media? The Truth About Bias and the News*, argued that with the exception of ABC's George Stephanopoulos and Bill Moyer, who previously hosted a public affairs show on PBS, all political pundits come at issues from a conservative perspective. Conservative pundits, he argued, are more likely to back the positions of the Republican party while liberal pundits are more likely to try to cover issues from a neutral perspective. The result is that the conservatives use the pundits to push their agenda while the liberals take a less-focused approach.[15]

In another book, *Sound and Fury: The Making of the Punditocracy*, Alterman argued that pundits are the only people in the nation who are in a position to put political information into perspective. Journalists tend to be barred by objectivity from discussing the contextual information that might help their audience to understand issues, but pundits are free to speak their minds. They are watched by politicians and wield a power over them. All pundits also have a tendency to focus on the same issues at the same time. The topics they do not talk about remain out of sight and out of mind. For example, during the 1990s Gulf War, pundits remained focused on the battle, and issues such as unemployment and foreign policy outside of the Gulf were neglected. Because conservative pundits dominate TV shows, Alterman argued, television analysis has a heavy conservative bias.[16]

There are still other factors that can create conservative bias in TV news, according to some critics. Martin A. Lee and Norman Solomon argue in *Unreliable Sources: A Guide to Detecting Bias in News Media* that the financial needs of the media bias content. For example, it is not unusual for a local station to air a ready-made commercial, which is designed to look like legitimate news. These video news releases are actually advertisements that are designed to look deceptively like news.[17]

In addition, Lee and Solomon argue, the conglomerated nature of the news industry can bias TV news. They cite the influence that General Electric has had over NBC. Network executives argued that its owner has no influence over news content, but in 1989 a reference to GE was eliminated from a report that discussed poor quality products. The report looked at a federal investigation of bolts that GE and other companies use to make airplanes. With very few corporations owning all of the media outlets, Lee and Solomon lament, people really have limited ways to access information via TV news. Rival networks often report the same stories in the same order in a single newscast. Newscasters can be uncomfortable covering stories that are directly connected to their parent company. Lee and Soloman cite as an example the lack of interest that NBC staff members showed for investigating potential environmental abuse by GE, even after New York State officially banned bass fishing because GE had polluted the Hudson River.

Rumor Mongering and Mythical Distortions

There is yet another argument floating in the TV news debate. It claims that partisan bias is a myth. In his book *Tilt? The Search for Media Bias*, David Niven considers the various arguments of media bias and concludes that they greatly exaggerate reality. From presidents to mayors, Niven argues, Democrats and Republicans get the same treatment from the media. One of the reasons that people may think that there is a bias is because of the differences between the politicians. There is no reason to assume, Niven argues, that two different people with different skills deserve the exact same media coverage.[18]

In addition, Niven says, rumors can cause people to have the perception that there is a media bias. As examples, he refers to coverage of the terrorist attack on the World Trade Center in 2001. Shortly after September 11, radio talk show host Rush Limbaugh began ridiculing ABC News anchor Peter Jennings. "Little Peter couldn't understand why George Bush didn't address the nation sooner than he did, and even made snide comments like, 'Well, some presidents are just better at it than others," Niven quotes Limbaugh as saying. It turned out that Jennings had never made the comments, but he received hundreds of angry phone calls from an alienated public. Eventually, the conservative Media Research Center issued a public announcement stating that he did not make the comments.

As another example Niven considers CNN's treatment after the terrorist attacks. CNN was accused of not using the word "terrorist" or "terrorism" to describe the events. Michael Kinsley ridiculed the station in the *Washington Post* as did syndicated columnist Thomas Sowell, who compared CNN's behavior to giving Adolf Hitler fair media play during World War II. In reality, CNN did call the attackers terrorists from the morning of September 11. Niven acknowledges that other forms of bias may exist in the news, such as negativity, race, and gender, but he argues that the debate for liberal or conservative leanings is unfounded.

• THE EVIDENCE •

On the question of whether there is a liberal bias in TV news, we must conclude that, at some point, there most likely is some. There is enough evidence to establish the existence of some degree of liberal bias. The incidents surrounding *60 Minutes'* report on George W. Bush's military record, for example, certainly indicate some biased decisions.

Is there a conservative bias in TV news? Probably. There is enough evidence to make that argument, too. While Fox News calls itself fair, having at the helm a vocal conservative like Rupert Murdoch, who admittedly enjoys affecting the editorial content of his news holdings, provides some evidence.

Herbert Gans argued in *Deciding What's News: A Study of CBS Evening News, NBC Nightly News, Newsweek, and Time* that it is impossible for the news to be totally unbiased, but it is difficult to determine how biased TV news is. The problem is that there is no set standard that acts as a bias measuring stick. Any standard would have to be based on some biased ideas, such as societal ideals.[19]

Perhaps there is a mixture of both types of bias. The opportunity for bias also exists in the push for high ratings, the need for advertising dollars, and the seemingly repetitive discussions of pundits. There does not seem to be any strong evidence indicating that TV outlets work together to push a sweeping form of bias into the news. It would be dangerous for all of the mainstream media to conspire to institute some form of extreme political bias. It might very well be a financial risk that could alienate advertisers as well as viewers. Networks would be foolish to enter into a partnership that could potentially destroy them.

• RESOLUTION •

If the bias does seep into newscasts, perhaps it comes in a case-by-case basis. It is possible that a reporter could unconsciously select sound bites or quotes for a story, which frame it so that it supports a particular stance. Many TV reporters, however, are conscientious enough to know that if they have strong feelings about a particular topic, then they should step back from covering it. If a story is accidentally biased by the way the reporter frames the sound bites, it may be just as likely that it happened as the reporter put together a story on an issue that he or she did not have an extremely strong opinion about. Perhaps deadline pressure could lead him to put the story together quickly without considering all of the implications of the words he chooses.

On the other hand, a TV reporter sometimes does write about an issue that he has strong feelings about. That does not necessarily cause him to write it in a biased manner. I can recount my own experiences as a green reporter writing a newspaper story related to an abortion clinic bombing. It was an issue that I had a very strong opinion about, but it was an important story and multiple reporters were working on it. I was not in a position to step back and ask someone else to cover the issue. A few days after I wrote the story, I noticed that it seemed a bit biased. The bias, however, did not reflect my own personal opinions about the issue. On the contrary, it seems that I had overcompensated for my own biased views and written a story that seemingly supported the opposing side. Other journalists probably have had similar experiences.

Or perhaps what happened to me that day is what happens to many readers on a regular basis. Perhaps when I re-read that story, I saw it as biased simply because it did not totally agree with my own opinions. Maybe that's exactly what happens to most viewers when they watch the news. If they see a story that does not emphasize their own opinions, their instinct is to consider that story unfair and biased. Perhaps news bias is in the eyes of the beholder.

We may have reached a point when Americans do not really want our news to be objective and fair. We may not want to admit it, but perhaps most viewers really want to see news that supports their own opinions. Perhaps that is the real reason behind the successes of CNN and Fox News. Maybe neither station is truly unbiased, but both are simply catering to the special interests of their viewers. We may be ushering in a new age of the partisan press.

• POINTS OF VIEW •

Ackerman, Seth. "The Most Biased Name in News." Fairness and Accuracy in Reporting. July/August 2001. http://www.fair.org/index.php?page=1067. Fox News Channel has an "extraordinary right-wing tilt" while claiming to be "fair and balanced." Republicans have embraced it.

Card, Orson Scott. "High Bias." WSJ.com Opinion Journal of the *Wall Street Journal*. July 12, 2004. http://www.opinionjournal.com/extra/?id=110005312. "'Mainstream'" reporters aren't just liberal — they're fanatical.... Fox News Channel has left both CNN and MSNBC in the dust. There's no guarantee that this is permanent, of course. But it certainly has the left in a panic. They hated it that American conservatism had any voice at all."

Cohen, Jeff, and Norman Solomon. *Adventures in Medialand: Behind the News, Beyond the Pundits.* Monroe, Me.: Common Courage Press, 1993. Corporate influence results in bias in TV news.

"Does TV Have a Liberal Bias?" http://www.cybercollege.com/bias.htm. Although the majority of the public thinks TV news is liberal, it is really conservative, particularly Fox.

Gans, Herbert J. *Deciding What's News: A Study of CBS Evening News, NBC Nightly News, Newsweek, and Time.* Evanston, Ill: Northwestern University Press, 2004. It is impossible for the media to be totally unbiased. The media should try to include as many perspectives as possible.

Goldberg, Bernard. *Bias: A CBS Insider Exposes How the Media Distort the News.* Washington, D.C.: Regnery, 2002. Former CBS journalist Bernard Goldberg focuses primarily on Dan Rather as he concludes that there is a liberal bias in the news, with CBS being particularly bad.

Groseclose, Tim, and Jeff Milyo. "A Measure of Media Bias." September 2003. http://www.polisci.ucla.edu/faculty/groseclose/Media.Bias.8.htm. This study comparing the news media's stances on political issues with the stances of members of the U.S. Congress concludes that Fox News is the most centrist of all the major news media.

Keely, Joseph Charles. *The Left-Leaning Antenna: Political Bias in Television.* New Rochelle, N.Y.: Arlington House, 1971. Although the text is dated, Keely argues that liberal political bias dominates television network news.

Media Research Center. "Media Bias Basics." http://secure.mediaresearch.org/news/MediaBiasBasics.html. "Conservatives believe the mass media, predominantly TV news programs, slant reports in favor of the liberal position on issues. Most Americans agree."

Stossel, John. *Give Me a Break: How I Exposed Hucksters, Cheats, and Scam Artists and Became the Scourge of the Liberal Media.* New York: HarperCollins, 2004. ABC journalist John Stossel talks about his career and the liberal bias in the media.

NOTES

1. Seth Ackerman, "The Most Biased Name in News Fox News Channel's extraordinary right-wing tilt," http://www.fair.org/index.php?page=1067

2. Quoted in Jody Brown and Chad Groening, "'RatherGate': Was It Incompetence — or Was It Bias?" http://headlines.agapepress.org/archive/9/232004f.asp

3. Joseph Carroll, "Trust in the News Media Rebounds Somewhat This Year," Gallup Poll News Service, 17 September 2005.

4. Jonah Goldberg, "Oh Happy Day," *National Review*, 11 October 2004.

5. Eric Fettman, "Eye on CBS's Mess: It Is Watergate," *New York Post*, 22 September 2004.

6. Bernard Goldberg, *Bias: A CBS Insider Exposes How the Media Distort the News* (Washington, D.C.: Regnery, 2002).

7. "New Two-Year MRC Study Finds Network News Blatantly Spins Gun Control Debate," 5 January 2000. http://www.mediaresearch.org/mainsearch/search.html.

8. Cal Thomas, "Dysfunctional Broadcast News," *New Orleans Times-Picayune*, 27 August 1999.

9. Stephen Labaton, Lome Manly, and Elizabeth Jensen, "Chairman Exerts Pressure on PBS, Alleging Biases," *New York Times*, 2 May 2005.

10. Dennis T. Lowry and Jon A. Shidler, "The Sound Bites, the Biters, and the Bitten: A Two-Campaign Test of the Anti-Incumbent Bias Hypothesis in Network TV News," *Journalism and Mass Communication Quarterly* 75 (Winter 1998): 719–729.

11. David D. Kirkpatrick, "Mr. Murdoch's War," *New York Times*, 7 April 2003.

12. Jon Lafayette, "Fox Casts Its Vote on Election Night," *Electronic Media* 19:41 (2000): 19–20.

13. David Carr, "The Left Asked to Speak to the Right, but a Gatekeeper Wouldn't Hear of It," *New York Times*, 30 August 2004.

14. Robert W. McChesney and John Bellamy Foster, "The 'Left-Wing' Media?" *Monthly Review: An Independent Socialist Magazine* 50:9 (February 1999): 32–42.

15. Eric Alterman, *What Liberal Media? The Truth About Bias and the News* (New York: Basic Books, 2003).

16. Eric Alterman, *Sound and Fury: The Making of the Punditocracy* (Ithaca, N.Y.: Cornell University Press, 1999).

17. Martin A. Lee and Norman Soloman, *Unreliable Sources: A Guide to Detecting Bias in News Media* (New York: Carol Publishing Group, 1990).

18. David Niven, *Tilt? The Search for Media Bias* (Westport, Conn.: Praeger Publishers, 2002).

19. Herbert J. Gans, *Deciding What's News: A Study of CBS Evening News, NBC Nightly News, Newsweek, and Time* (Evanston, Ill: Northwestern University Press, 2004).

14

Photojournalism

Patrick Beeson

"[W]hat possesses these photographers to do this [show President George W. Bush in a favorable light]? Is it merely money, or is it some other sort of freakish devotion? Or is it freakish devotion to money, because they know the Washington Times is going to snap up every picture of Bush with a subtle halo and beaming Latino schoolchildren?"— Ian Williams, www.xtcian.com[1]

"In the United States, journalism is one of the last bastions of freedom that thrives today. Guaranteed by our forefathers, and protected by the Constitution, the freedom of speech and expression is one of the most contested rights granted to us. Our job [as photojournalists] is to make sure that the truth is told.... Photographers who work in the journalistic field ... are upholding a level of public trust that cannot be violated."— Rob Miracle, Photojournalism Seminar Website[2]

In September 2000, Tuvia Grossman, a 20-year-old Jewish student from Chicago, Ill., and two of his friends were traveling through the Arab neighborhood of Wadi al Joz in Jerusalem when they were unwittingly propelled into the international media spotlight. Grossman and his friends, who had accidentally passed through a renewed outbreak of violence between Israeli policemen and Palestinian militants, were yanked from their taxicab by an Arab Palestinian mob and severely beaten and stabbed. A photo taken by an Associated Press photographer of the harrowing scene showed Grossman, bloodied and battered as he crouched beneath an angered Israeli policeman brandishing a club. The striking image and accompanying caption, "An Israeli policeman and a Palestinian on Temple Mount," ran September 30, 2000, during the Jewish High Holidays. It ran on page one of the *Boston Globe* and page five of the *New York Times*, and in other prominent media outlets around the world.

A few days later, Dr. Aaron Grossman, Tuvia's father, sent a letter to the *New York Times*, revealing the true nature of the photo and condemning its false caption. After printing a retraction identifying Tuvia Grossman as "an American student in Israel" and stating that "Mr. Grossman was wounded" in "Jerusalem's Old City," the *Times* received a flurry of complaints decrying bias against Israel. The newspaper then reprinted the photo, with a more detailed caption, and a full article describing the incident. Vin Alabiso, Associated Press executive photo editor, told the *Boston Globe* the faulty headline was a "horrible mistake" that was due to a lack of communication between the photo agency that provided the shot and the Associated Press's Jerusalem bureau. Unfortunately for the *Times* and the *Globe*, the debate over anti–Israel bias in the media had been given new life spurned by the simple click of a camera's shutter.[3]

The incidents involving Tuvia Grossman and the conflict between Israel and Palestine have been the catalyst for many bias accusations stemming from newspaper photos and their captions. This particular example was described in detail by an article titled "The Photo that Started it All" (updated in 2002) on the Israeli-advocacy Website Honestreporting.com, and in a column titled "Error Cited as Proof of Anti-Israel Bias" (2000) by *The Quill*, a magazine published by the Society of Professional Journalists. The Honestreporting.com article described the mistakenly captioned photo as "a symbol in the struggle to ensure that Israel receives the fair media coverage that every nation deserves" and *The Quill* said the episode "sparked concerns of a broader media bias that too often depicts the Jewish state as a ruthless aggressor without checking the facts." Both publications bring to light the controversial debate over media bias and some people suggest that newspaper photographs are as vehicles of bias.

Accusations of photo bias in newspapers also have roots in other areas, namely those of bias toward or against the U.S. government and its foreign policies, and the use of violent images to bias emotional responses from the public. These two issues, in addition to the Israeli and Palestinian conflicts, are the most hotly debated biased photograph topics.

The debate over bias in photos has critics on both sides, though it is not an issue as widely discussed or prevalent as partisan bias in the media. Most of the accusations of photo bias have been levied by media watch groups such as Honestreporting.com, a pro–Israel site, and the Committee for Accuracy in Middle East Reporting (CAMERA), a non-partisan organization that, according to its Website www.camera.org, seeks "to simply educate journalists and photographers in the proper manner of reporting on the subject." Opponents of the idea that photo bias exists in the media contend that many instances of alleged bias are simply reporter or photographer error or bad editorial decisions that underestimate the public's reaction. Regardless of the bias debate, Martin A. Lee and Norman Solomon write in their book *Unreliable Sources* (1990), "When it's words against pictures, the pictures carry the day."[4]

Accusations of bias leveled at newspapers' use of certain photographs tend to be targeted at a sparse number of topics. The most significant of these concerns today is newspapers' use of photographs to display bias against Israel in the nation's conflicts with Palestine. People also argue that biased photos in newspapers can sway U.S. foreign policy by the "oversimplification" of complex issues and promote terrorists' actions by the glorification of violence.

Anti-Israel Bias in Photographs

Perhaps no other news subject generates more complaints about media objectivity than the Middle East in general and the Israel-Palestine conflict. The majority of the bias complaints suggest an anti–Israel reporting stance with photos drawing the brunt of the accusations. Many newspapers report the charges of bias, while not especially new, have increased since bloodletting caused by Israel's military incursions and Palestinians' suicide-bombings.

The Quill (2002) reported in an "In Brief" column titled "Newsrooms Feel Heat over Middle East Coverage" that the *San Francisco Chronicle* found a marked increase in the number of complaints from readers citing bias against Israel. The column adds that in April 2002 nearly 1,000 *Los Angeles Times* subscribers suspended home delivery for a day or more to protest what they call "inaccurate, pro–Palestinian reporting of the unrest in the Middle East." *Florida Times-Union* (Jacksonville) Reader Advocate and Web Editor for the Organization of News Ombudsmen Mike Clark said in *The Quill* column, "As a hard news subject, [Middle East coverage] is probably the No.1 issue that's consistently coming up across the country."

The Quill column also mentions actions taken by CAMERA, one of several media advocacy groups that monitor instances of bias in major newspapers. The group ran a full-page *New York Times* advertisement calling National Public Radio's coverage "false" and "skewed" against Israel. The advertisement urged NPR's financial backers to stop supporting the network.[5]

The CAMERA organization has produced many articles condemning the news and photo wire-agencies Reuters, Agence France-Presse and the Associated Press for distributing anti–Israel coverage. Reuters, in particular, has been the perpetrator of biased photos in its Middle East reporting, according to CAMERA. The news service is "the world's leading provider of news photography for today's global media universe," according to the organization's Website. Ricki Hollander, in a CAMERA article titled "Reuters photos the picture of bias" (2001), said "the news service displays a pattern of misrepresentations and double standards in many of the photos it distributes." Hollander said Reuters' photos tend to portray Palestinians as victims, and show few, if any, images of Israeli victims.

The CAMERA article examines Reuters' photos of two 2001 Palestinian terrorist bombings for evidence of the lack of balance from the news service. One example of Reuters' bias is a photo of a Palestinian terrorist car-bombing near Moshav Mei Ami in northern Israel, which killed one Israeli man and wounded nine others, including the terrorist. The first Reuters' caption that mentioned the bombing appeared under an "irrelevant" photo of a Palestinian woman walking at the Deir El Balah refugee camp in Gaza Strip. The CAMERA article states that this was the seventh photo of Palestinians that appeared that day with five photos treating Palestinians as victims. Reuters distributed only four photographs of the Mei Ami bombing in Israel, with vague captions failing to identify victims as Israeli, reading instead: "Bodies of injured men lie on the road after a car bomb exploded in the Israeli town of Mei Ami"; "Injured woman awaits medical attention after car bomb blast in Umm Al-Fahm"; and "An injured man is carried away after car bomb blast in northern Israel." The days following the attack, Reuters distributed ten pictures of Palestinian funerals and mourning, but none of victimized Israelis.[6]

Alex Safian, a columnist with the *Jerusalem Post*, has also accused Reuters of biased photographs. The article, "Reuters roots for the Palestinians" (2001), contrasts the death of a 10-month-old Israeli child, Shalhevet Pas, by a Palestinian sniper, with the death of

13-year-old Palestinian Mohammed Helles, who died of wounds resulting from Israeli gunfire. Safian contends that "the flood of photos from Reuters, which inundates newspapers with images of Palestinian victims accompanied by anti–Israel captions, slows to a dismissive trickle for Jewish victims like Shalhevet.... When the casualty is Palestinian, the agency's photographers literally spring into action."

The *Jerusalem Post* column examined a search of the Reuters news photo database in the first three days after Shalhevet's shooting and found only four photographs of the girl, none implicating Palestinians in the captions (the killer was only referred to as a "gunman"). Two images were not even of Shalhevet, but rather "Jewish settlers" protesting the girl's murder by painting her name in a Palestinian shop. Of the two images of the baby, one showed her alive in her parents' arms and the other portrayed the child lying dead in a hospital bed. By contrast, the nine photos sent out by Reuters after Palestinian Helles' death were consistently more emotionally charged. Five photos were of his funeral, four of later rallies protesting his death and one from the hospital as doctors worked to save his life. Eight of the photos' captions "unambiguously" attributed the shooting to Israeli soldiers. One photo's caption a few days after Helles death read: "Palestinians pray beside the body of slained [sic] 13-year-old Palestinian Mohammad Helles who died of wounds after being hit by Israeli gunfire earlier this week...." Safian concludes "Intensive coverage of Palestinian losses, and grudgingly, dismissive and minimal coverage of Israeli losses is the routine at Reuters. Even, or perhaps especially, when the Israeli victim is a 10-month-old baby."[7]

Some organizations that say newspapers are using photos to promote bias against Israel suggest opinions are being disguised as news. The pro–Israel media watch group Honestreporting.com says that though most biased editorializing takes place in an article's text (through excessive use of adjectives or adverbs), even photos are subject to the practice. In the article "What is Bias?" (2002) on Honestreporting.com, several examples of photo bias in Israel/Palestine images are discussed as evidence of editorializing by newspapers. In one example, a news photo from Reuters depicts Palestinian youths throwing stones. The article describes the photo as "poetically surreal" in that the Palestinian attackers are heroically silhouetted on a mountaintop, their stones floating "triumphantly through the majestic clouds." The article also explains that photos are distributed and run in newspapers without context for readers. "By failing to provide proper context and full background information, journalists can dramatically distort the true picture," according to the article. As an example of this argument, the article describes a BBC photo depicting two Palestinians, hands tied behind their backs, kneeling on the ground. An Israeli soldier stands over them, pointing a rifle at their heads. The photo's caption reads "Tension has been high around the Jewish settlements"; a rather "benign" description without context the article suggests. The BBC does not answer many questions that could theoretically be posed from the photo: "Who are the Arabs in this photo? Did they just murder Jews in cold blood? Or were they innocently buying bread at the local market? BBC does not say." Nor, the article says, is the Israeli soldier explained: "And why is the soldier pointing the gun? Is he guarding dangerous prisoners until reinforcements can arrive? Or is he about to blow off their heads at point-blank range?" After many complaints from Honestreporting.com and others like it, the article says, the BBC changed the photo's caption to read "Israeli soldiers arrest Palestinian drivers in the West Bank."[8]

Biased Photos and U.S. Government Policies

The editorializing suggested by the biased photographs of the Israel/Palestine conflict has also been applied to photos depicting combat operations and tragedy in Somalia. Critics suggest that simple bias has morphed into a lobbying effort. Jacqueline Sharkey, in her *American Journalism Review* article "When Pictures Drive Foreign Policy" (1993), explains how the influence of media images on U.S. foreign policy was palpable in the coverage of U.S. actions in Somalia. Front page images in local newspapers of dead and captured American soldiers caused many retaliatory phone calls by the public to members of Congress suggesting the U.S. end its presence in Somalia, despite then-President Clinton's peacekeeping intentions. The often gory photographs and the emotional reactions that resulted fueled a nationwide debate on the political and ethical implications of using such pictures in the media. Government officials suggested the photographs "oversimplified complex issues," and that "emotions raised by the pictures of the dead and captured U.S. soldiers might overwhelm other political and military factors ... regarding Somalia." The pictures, Sharkey said, can "distort public opinion and government priorities ... [and] also lack historical and cultural context that could give the public greater — and sorely needed — perspective. As images can become symbols of something more than the actual event, journalists should be careful not to distort any situation."

Another issue concerning the impact of images on the debate about policy in Somalia is that the photos published in newspapers present a distorted view of the situation. Most of the photographs lacked context for Somali casualties, showing instead mostly American deaths. Marvin Kalb, director of the Joan Shorenstein Barone Center on the Press, said in Sharkey's article that "Image in and of itself does not drive policy.... Image heightens existing factors." Critics of biased photographs suggest that this heightening of factors (such as emotions) that could lead the public in a direction other than what was perhaps intended by the original context of the incident being photographed.

The *American Journalism Review* article also suggests that newspaper photos depicting searing images of the Somali conflict led to an anti-government bias, leading the public to be less willing to accept the government's word that the country's involvement in the conflict was justified. Air Force Reserves Maj. James Callard, who teaches U.S. foreign policy at Fort Lewis College in Durango, Colo., says newspaper photos of the conflict have "given the public an opportunity to reevaluate the principles underlying U.S. foreign policy, including using military force to achieve political objectives." The photographs of dead and captured U.S. soldiers in Somalia, when run in place of more positive images, carry an air of anti-government bias that, Callard says, has "led people to ask not only how and where armed forces will be used overseas, but why." This effectively reduces the time that governments have for deliberation and negotiation before the public demands action, thus presenting serious problems for foreign policy.[9]

In the same way that newspaper photographs of war can dissuade or stymie positive public reaction to foreign policy, some people argue that biased images can promote government foreign policy. In an article for the liberal news magazine *The New Statesman*, "A Conflict of Views; Photography — Jenny Matthews on the Inevitable Censorship and Bias in Documenting War" (2003), Matthews argues photos stemming from embedded reporters in the recent war in Iraq are biased to present a positive view of U.S. foreign policy. The use of embedded photographers and reporters during this war, Matthews argues, translated into their movements being tightly controlled by the military. Her article examines the "Iraq Uncensored" exhibition of more than 150 photos from the Getty and Agence France Presse news agencies and reveals that because of the embedded requirements, "more than half of all the photos in this show are of soldiers or military hardware, usually American.... Only one photograph — of an anti-war march in Berlin — acknowledges the strong opposition to the war." Yet, Matthews says, newspapers published the often one-sided photographs without concern for potential bias issues.[10]

This point of view is also argued by Deni Elliot, director of the Practical Ethics Center at the University of Montana, and Paul Martin Lester, professor of communications at California State University at Fullerton, in their monthly *News Photographer* magazine column "Ethics Matters" (2003). They contend that "government is increasingly sophisticated in shaping news coverage." They use the examples of photographs of American military forces, along with several hundred embedded journalists, conducting a war in Iraq; and President George W. Bush, wearing a pilot's jumpsuit, hopping out of a jet on the deck of an aircraft carrier to announce the end of major military action in Iraq. Elliot and Lester argue that Americans are constantly misled by photographers repeating governmental "manipulations" and "exaggerations and speculations" as fact. That could lead to questions of media bias in favor of government policy.[11]

Violent Photos as a Form of Bias

Violence has been an underlying theme in many arguments about biased photographs. Jessica Fishman and Carolyn Marvin, in their research for the Annenberg School at the University of Pennsylvania, published a study on photo bias and violence titled "Portrayals of Violence and Group Difference in Newspaper Photographs: Nationalism and Media" (2003) in the *Journal of Communication*. The authors analyzed group membership of violent agents and types of violence in front-page photographs during twenty-one years of the *New York Times*. They confirmed the hypothesis that "non-U.S. agents of violence are represented as more explicitly violent than U.S. agents, and that the latter are associated with disguised modes of violence more often than the former." Fishman and Marvin concentrated on photographs rather than news stories because "visual images are often thought to have powerful effects."

The study suggests, visually speaking, that U.S. residents are the "good guys" and foreigners are not. Social identity theorists, the authors argue, point out that group members compare their group with others on dimensions that cast a positive light on themselves. Theorists have also examined the "ideological tendency to create and reproduce photographic codes that mark cultural 'others' not only distinct, but often as bizarre, primitive, sexualized, dehumanized or otherwise lacking in moral quality." Fishman and Marvin ask "Is the observed pattern of violent images a deliberate choice by photo editors" in order to solve tendencies of bias on their behalf. The authors of this study agree with a statement by E. S. Herman and Noam Chomsky, writing from a leftist perspective in their book, *Manufacturing Consent: The Political Economy of the Mass Media* (1988), that "The operation of these filters occurs so naturally that media news people, frequently operating with complete integrity and goodwill, are able to convince themselves that they choose and interpret the news 'objectively' and on the basis of professional news values."[12]

Front-page images in the *New York Times*, Fishman and Marvin conclude, "effectively sanitize U.S. violence" and "delegitimize the violence of non–U.S. states, repeatedly rendering it in brutally explicit terms."[13]

Violent photos in newspapers are also believed to carry bias for seemingly unlikely groups such as terrorists. Bob Steele, in a column for Poynter Online, "Pearl Photo: Too Harmful" (2001), argues that the *Boston Phoenix*'s decision to publish pictures of the murder of *Wall Street Journal* reporter Daniel Pearl were the result of publisher Stephen Mindich's "emotional rage and ideological fervor." Steele mentions that some critics suggest that printing such photos such "plays in to the hands of terrorist," thus leading to possible bias. Steele doesn't believe there was any journalistic imperative to show the photos of Pearl's death to the public. He contends that it "may be cruel" to Pearl's family to print these photos, and that newspapers should strive to "avoid causing unnecessary harm." In this case, Steele believes "The harm far outweighs any benefit."[14]

Mistakes and Misinterpretation — but Not Bias

The majority of voices dissenting against the idea of photo bias are, perhaps unsurprisingly, either members of the media or academics in the field of communication. They contend that instances of bias in coverage of the Israeli/Palestinian conflict are the result of mistakes in captioning photos, editors' failure to listen to the public's concerns, or photos taken out of context by viewers. The question of photographic bias and its effect on government policy, these opponents suggest, is rather the media simply following the newsworthy content at the time. Violent photos are also not seen as a method of biasing public opinion, but rather as a way for readers to experience the full effect of a tragedy.

The September 2000 photo of Tuvia Grossman distributed by the Associated Press to newspapers around the world, and the resulting backlash by readers who believed it carried a staunch anti–Israel overtone are largely the result of the photo's erroneous caption, according to the liberal media watch group Fairness and Accuracy in Reporting (FAIR). FAIR writer Seth Ackerman, in an "EXTRA" column, "Those aren't Stones, they're Rocks" (2001), said the pressure American journalists feel about their coverage of Israel and Palestine should prevent most mistakes in articles and photos on the issue, but not all. When a mistake does occur, Ackerman said, many readers immediately accuse the publication of bias toward one side of the conflict. The mistakenly captioned photo involving Grossman is one example. The Associated Press photographer admitted the mistake, and all of the papers that ran the photo printed a retraction/correction. Yet pro–Israel media critics cried bias. The angry commentaries and letters by supporters of Israel brandished the mislabeled photograph as proof of their suspicions, Ackerman said. The *New York Times* published not only an immediate initial correction for the photo, but also a second a few days later. The paper then printed a 670-word news article that traced the source of the mistake to the Associated Press's Jerusalem office, and reprinted the original photo with an accurate caption.[15]

Dick Rogers, *San Francisco Chronicle* ombudsman, said that by judging a newspaper's visual coverage over a long period of time, bias becomes less apparent. He believes this is especially true in instances that involve the controversial Israel and Palestine conflict.

In his *Nieman Reports* article "Expanding the Lens on Coverage of the Middle East" (2002), Rogers tells of his newspaper's unscientific, but substantive photo bias study conducted to respond to readers' concerns of photographic bias in the coverage of Middle East issues.

For the study, the newspaper's copy editor, Heidi Swillinger, picked five readers who were not activists in Middle East affairs. They examined Middle East photo coverage during a three-month period, from December 2001 to March 2002. Each one looked at copies of the same seventy-nine photos and judged whether the photos were sympathetic toward Palestinians or toward Israel or neutral. Each photo package contained captions, the page and section in which the picture ran, photo credits, and publication dates. One member of the reader group, a retired nurse who described herself as "firmly pro–Zionist," said "after seeing the pictures I feel your coverage is actually fairly balanced." The group said "context means a lot" and noted that the "wording of the captions influenced [them] in determining if there was a bias." One group member said if he had seen the photos without captions, he would have found less bias. The result of the study revealed "almost equally distributed" findings: of the five readers, 130 votes were for pro–Palestinian, 139 for neutral and 126 for pro–Israel. Rogers said the study helped show photo editors at the newspaper the importance of selecting balanced photos and also that "If the *Chronicle* was trying to espouse a particular viewpoint through photo selections, it wasn't doing a very good job."[16]

This type of reader study dismissing the existence of deliberate photo bias in newspapers was also used by Debbie Kornmiller, a reader advocate for the *Arizona Daily Star*, in her *Nieman Reports* article "Images Lead to Varying Perceptions" (2002). She began her assessment of the paper's Middle East coverage by viewing more than 160 Associated Press photos of the Israeli and Palestinian conflict. She then grouped the photos into three categories that showed Israel and Palestine in a positive or neutral light about 40 percent of the time: Israel in a negative light 23 percent of the time and Palestinians 13 percent of the time. From this analysis, fifteen images were selected to use in interviews with eight readers in a two-hour roundtable discussion. Many of the readers in this conversation wanted photos showing "the human side of the conflict" and a more "balanced" coverage of the two sides. Following Kornmiller's study, the newspaper instituted trials of *Christian Science Monitor* and Reuters news services to broaden content possibilities; promised to publish photos that add human interest to the events; and "promised that every photo considered would be viewed by at least two sets of eyes and discussed before being run in the paper." Even after the paper's changes, Teri Hayt, assistant managing editor for photography at the newspaper, believes that "it doesn't matter what images run, someone will be offended.... I worry that we are being so sensitive to both sides that we are not covering the news story of the day."[17]

Many readers perceive the use of emotional images, such as those portraying the dead, as a way of taking sides on an issue. They believe that by portraying one side as killers in photographs, the newspaper is biased. Michael Larkin, in his *Nieman Reports* article "Deciding on an Emotion-Laden Photograph for Page One" (2002), examines how an image reflects "a crucial moment in a course of events." Larkin, the deputy managing editor/news operations at the *Boston Globe*, says photos of dead people are never run at his paper without prior discussion of the impact they are likely to have on readers, especially if that photo is to be placed on page one where it would be most likely to be seen by children. Larkin describes how a photograph of a dead infant (killed in an Israeli attack) being carried in a Gaza procession is "not only visually striking but also illustrates to our readers that something significant happened.... Our decision to publish this photograph in color on page one received little reader response" even with troubling political implications. A photograph such as this is important, Larkin argues, because it "represent[s] a crucial moment in a course of events." Even if the photo prompted a debate on whether it may be biased, Larkin believes it (and others like it) was necessary to run to accurately represent the deep emotions associated with the Middle East conflict.[18]

Photos Don't Shape Foreign Policy

Critics of photo bias accusations reject the notion that biased newspaper photos are used to change or modify government policy, especially when it relates to U.S. presidential elections. These critics suggest that by using a content analysis of election year newspaper photographs, it can be determined that newspaper photo bias has little or no effect in influencing the public.

Paul Waldman and James Devitt, in their research experiment "Newspaper Photographs and the 1996 Presidential Election: The Question of Bias" (1998) for *Journalism and Mass Communication Quarterly*, rejected the notion of "liberal bias in the press coverage of presidential campaigns," arguing instead for the presence of a "strategic bias benefiting the front-runner." The two authors of the study used a content analysis of photographs of Bill Clinton and Bob Dole appearing in the *New York Times*, *Washington Post*, *Los Angeles Times*, *Chicago Tribune*, and *USA Today* during the last two months of the 1996 presidential campaign. The basis for the experiment was derived from complaints issued during the final stages of the campaign by Republican candidate Bob Dole, who said the press, and particularly the *New York Times*, was treating him unfairly. He said reporters were giving him less coverage than Democratic candidate Bill Clinton and that it had a liberal slant. In short, the authors said, "individuals tend to see bias in any coverage that presents a picture of the political world at odds with their own" and that this unequal treatment is often confused with ideological bias (a different bias).[19]

Photographs play an important role in determining visual impressions of presidential candidates, Waldman and Devitt suggest. Readers of newspapers are potentially exposed to hundreds of photographs during a campaign lasting several months. Prior studies on past political campaigns and others focusing on treatment of facial expressions in photographs have indicated that pictorial representations "may have a substantial influence on opinions and attitudes toward candidates." The misinterpretation of bias, the study reveals, is the appearance of strategy coverage that focuses on tracking polls and evaluations of candidates' success and failures in amassing support; this coverage "by definition advantages front-runners." After examining the results of the study, Waldman and Devitt concluded that "based on the data and an impressionistic analysis of the photos is that with the exception of the *Tribune* (where photos of Clinton were often show in a positive light and photos of Dole in a neutral light), readers would scarcely be able to notice a difference between the candidates."

Violence Is Not Bias but Reality

Newspaper editors often face difficulties in determining which photos to run on the front page, especially if those photos contain violent or gory images that could be interpreted as biased. The potential for bias, many critics of bias accusations say, is vast since photos illustrate stories in a way words often cannot. Steve Outing, in a Poynter Online article, "Why Web News has Different Standards than Print, TV News" (2001), says the nature of events such as war or the terrorist attacks on the World Trade Centers are horrifying, but the public needs to be shown these images to understand the "true story." Outing also brings to light the different interpretation of photographs between the U.S. and other countries. He describes how a journalism professor informed him of a class conversation with students who are from the U.S. and elsewhere in the world. The professor said "Several of our international students expressed their confusion about why the U.S. media did not publish more graphic images," a more common practice in the foreign students' home countries. Those students "wondered why Americans were, in effect, being sheltered from the truth." To stymie the flow of graphic photos from being published in newspapers, Outing contends, not only prevents the revelation of truth, but also perhaps increases the potential for photographic bias.[20]

The viewpoint of sheltering a newspaper's public from potentially offensive photos is also espoused by Kenneth F. Irby in his Poynter Online article "Beyond Taste: Editing Truth" (2004). Irby explains how the recent train-bombings in Madrid, Spain that killed 190 people and injured 1,800 were captured by *El Pais* photographer Pablo Torres Guerrero in an eerie image that, to the lower left corner, reveals a visible human femur, but many newspapers edited it out to avoid disturbing readers. The photo, distributed around the world by Reuters, was picked up by newspapers, including many that choose to edit out the femur through a variety of methods. The idea of cropping the photo, "the photographic equivalent of paraphrasing or ellipsis within the photographic narrative of a picture," emphasizes material damage over the human toll, said Irby. By doing this, some of the media professionals interviewed for the article suggest, you can lessen the potential harm to audiences while still showing the effect of the terrorist attack. Irby says this might not always be the case. "It is the purpose of a free press to inform citizens and to maximize truth-telling through authentic reporting, while minimizing harm," but in doing so, Irby said, editors must take care to be unbiased in their display of reality and not negate its news value, something that can often be shown through violent or gruesome images.[21]

Dan Kennedy, a freelance journalist and former media critic for the *Boston Phoenix* agrees with this contention in his *Nieman Reports* article "The Daniel Pearl Video" (2002). He concluded "that the reason for publishing the photographs [of Daniel Pearl's death at the hands of terrorists]— to witness the evil with which we must contend— outweighed the reasons for not publishing." Being biased towards the terrorist organization that committed such acts, Kennedy says, should not be a real consideration. "Daniel Pearl didn't seek martyrdom, but martyrdom found him."[22]

Other Issues Explaining Photo Bias

Whereas most accusations of photo bias in newspapers are leveled towards political or international conflict coverage, there are underlying factors in photography that play a role in how bias might inadvertently become present. For instance, when taking a picture of crowds to show the level of support for a political movement or for a protest, the photographer must understand variables that, if ignored, could promote bias. Kelly McBride, in her Poynter Online article "Counting Crowds" (2003), says that everyone has a stake in crowd estimates, including the journalists reporting the numbers. Bigger numbers translate into critical mass while lower numbers are a way of detracting from the message. "Reporting [or photographing] bad numbers breeds distrust and charges of bias." McBride says that some newspapers refrain from reporting estimates of crowds or refuse to run photographs that could distort the accurate number of people gathered. Investing in a larger staff and better techniques for reporting crowds, McBride says, would "go far in generating credibility among a divided audience."[23]

The use of staged or doctored photos in newspapers could also be misleading to readers. Tony Case, in an article for *Editor and Publisher*, "Photo Illustration on Page One Story" (1996), examines how the nation-wide circulation newspaper *USA Today* created controversy by running a staged picture of a school girl snorting cocaine. The color photo was used to illustrate a front-page story about heightened drug use among teens. Though there was a small "photo illustration" caption below the image, many in the media felt it was unethical and "contributed to the media's growing credibility problem." The newspaper had been the subject of photo disputes in the past by running a misleading photo of a black gang wielding weapons. Ohio University School of Visual Communications Director Larry Nighswander said in Case's article that he believes news organizations "trip into an ethical quagmire" by staging pictures. Nighswander said many readers lack the ability to differentiate between an actual photo and a photo illustration, especially when that photo illustration is based on reality. "I think we need to be very prudent in using photographs to illustrate a subject so loaded it would draw immediate, emotional response.... [N]one of us can afford to lose our credibility one iota," Nighswander said.[24]

• THE EVIDENCE •

In mid–December 2001 Courtney Kealy, a photojournalist for Getty Images who is based in Beirut, was on assignment in Ain el-Helweh, the largest Palestinian refugee camp in Lebanon. It contained more than 70,000 Palestinians. She was sent to cover the Hamas (a Palestinian Islamic group) rally for its fourteenth anniversary and its context in the previous weekend's terrorist bombings in Israel that killed more than twenty-five people. As Kealy walked through the camp, she happened upon a small boy about three years old wearing a Hamas headband. A group of teenage boys wearing the Hamas white cloaks and hoods and suicide bomb belts gathered around the child, one teenager removing his belt to place on him. The group, with the child present, then pulled their hoods over their faces and were photographed by Kealy. This image was sold to Getty Images and published worldwide, including in an advertisement published by the American Jewish Committee on the opinion page of the Sunday *New York Times* with the headline "Some are born hating, and others are taught how to hate."

This sequence of events, described in Kealy's *Nieman Reports* article "Photographic Images Can Be Misunderstood" (2002), exemplifies the core aspect in the debate over photographs being biased. The use of a dramatic and emotional photograph of a small child being "inducted" into a group of alleged terrorists, especially if that group is but one side in a conflict containing passionate members on each, can be understood on many levels, or perhaps misunderstood on the same levels. The newspapers' public that believed in the Palestinian cause would interpret the photo far differently than the section of the public that was staunchly against Palestinian actions in the Middle East conflict. The fact that Kealy's image was sold to a pro–Israeli organization for use in an advertisement condemning Palestinians illustrates how controversial images can be potentially misunderstood when taken out of context.[25]

Photo captions, which are supposed to provide context for images in a newspaper, can be misconstrued themselves, or, such as in the case of Tuvia Grossman, be riddled with mistakes that lead to accusations of bias. The public's desire to have immediate access to news spanning the globe creates immense demands on newspapers to present images that explain, in more telling terms than the stories themselves, the reality of the situation. Conflicts such as the on-going Israeli and Palestinian conflict are often difficult to make clear through an entire article or series of articles, let alone a photo. The reality is often grisly violence that, as shown by evidence presented on both sides of this debate, is hard to set in a medium that will be viewed by an array of publics, some willing to accept less than others. The studies completed by researchers on the use of violence in newspaper photographs reveal a bias in themselves, but perhaps an acceptable level of violence to accurately portray the news. Placing a photograph of slain *Wall Street Journal* reporter Daniel Pearl's decapitated head within a newspaper (or almost any publication) will create controversy. The same is true with an image of a small Palestinian child sitting at the bottom of a stairwell that is splattered with his father's and uncle's blood.

• RESOLUTION •

The intense emotional impact images can have on readers seems to have some correlation with changes in the government's foreign policy. This being so, newspapers should stress the importance of providing images that balance, for example, harm to the country's troops in addition to that of other county's combatants. Photo balance in domestic events also remains essential to avoiding bias. Photojournalists and editors need to understood that liberals and conservatives constitute newspapers' publics and that showing, for example, a photo of the Republican candidate in a negative light followed by the Democratic candidate in a positive one will assure charges of bias. Though Waldman and Devitt's study of candidate newspaper photos during the 1996 presidential campaign revealed no real bias existed in the five newspapers examined, the potential for bias to exist is real and should be taken into account before running potentially offending photo.

The difficulty of trying to understand readers' perceptions of controversial images has been undertaken at many newspapers. Randy Rasmussen and Dick Rogers' use of reader focus groups and studies of their own newspapers' use of such images is testament to the level of self-governance that exists in the media. Reader studies that encompass information on potentially biased photos, especially on controversial political and international topics, should be performed on an annual basis not only in newspapers, but also for television networks, magazines, and news Websites. If the media are to eliminate their growing credibility problem, they must listen to reader's complaints, no matter how skewed they might be from the political views of editors. This interaction with readers, including immediate response to letters to the editor or attempts to point out incorrect information in captions, is the only solution to stemming what now appears to be the small trickle of genuinely biased photographs run in newspapers.

• POINTS OF VIEW •

Fishman, Jessica M., and Carolyn Marvin. "Portrayals of Violence and Group Difference in Newspaper Photographs: Nationalism and Media." *Journal of Communication* 53 (2003): 32. The authors analyzed group membership of violent agents and types of violence in front-page photographs from twenty-one years of the *New York Times* and concluded that non-U.S. agents are represented as more explicitly violent than U.S. agents, revealing how violence outside the U.S. is shown by photographs in a more brutal light.

Hollander, Ricki. "Reuters Photos the Picture of Bias." *Committee for Accuracy in Middle East Reporting in America*, 3 April 2001. http://www.camera.org/index.asp?x_con text=2&x_outlet=36&x_article=176. Reuters has frequently presented a biased picture of the Arab-Israeli conflict by displaying a pattern of misrepresentation and double standards in many of the photos it distributes.

Kealy, Courtney. "Photographic Images Can Be Misunderstood." *Nieman Reports* (Fall 2002): 64–66. The misuse of provocative photographs in newspapers could portray a certain bias for or against Israel or Palestine.

Kennedy, Dan. "The Daniel Pearl Video." *Nieman Reports* (Fall 2002): 80–81. The *Phoenix's* decision to link its Website to the terrorist propaganda video of *Wall Street Journal* reporter Daniel Pearl's execution and to publish two photos from the video on its editorial page was ethically sound and not biased.

Khouri, Rami G. "Do Words and Pictures from the Middle East Matter?" *Nieman Reports* (Fall 2002): 82–83. Khouri, a Jordanian-Palestinian syndicated political columnist, argues that photographs run in influential American newspapers do not necessarily constitute bias toward a particular side of the conflict.

Kornmiller, Debbie. "Images Lead to Varying Perceptions." *Nieman Reports* (Fall 2002): 74–76. *Arizona Daily Star* reader advocate Debbie Kornmiller developed a listening approach to analyzing her newspaper's pictorial Middle East coverage; and, based on readers' suggestions, the paper made changes to avoid accusations of bias.

Larkin, Michael. "Deciding on an Emotion-Laden Photograph for Page One." *Nieman Reports* (Fall 2002): 77. Larkin, deputy managing editor/news operations at the *Boston Globe*, explains how a particularly graphic photo of a dead child ended up on the paper's front page and led to its possible misconception as being biased toward Palestine.

Rasmussen, Randy L. "Arriving at Judgments in Selecting Photos." *Nieman Reports* (Fall 2002): 67–70. Rasmussen, assistant director of photography at the *Oregonian*, explores the ways in which reader reaction is factored into decisions made about which photographs to publish and where to place them in order to avoid the perception of bias in the Israel/Palestinian conflict.

Rogers, Dick. "Expanding the Lens on Coverage of the Middle East." *Nieman Reports* (Fall 2002): 71–73. See also Rogers, Dick. "Numbers Offer Guide to Better Coverage." *San Francisco Chronicle*, 25 February 2004, A-21. A newspaper discusses its own content analysis of photographs featured in each front page of the paper's various sections, concluding that, despite a misrepresentation of the diversity of the community, such a misrepresentation does not necessarily point toward a gender or racial bias.

Safian, Alex. "Eye on the Media: Reuters Roots for the Palestinians." *Committee for accuracy in Middle East reporting in America*, 29 May 2001, http://www.camera.org/index. asp?x_context=5&x_outlet=36&x_article=178, 15 March 2004. The article from the CAMERA organization, originally run in the *Jerusalem Post*, concludes that the Reuters wire agency promotes an anti–Israel bias in its lack of photographs and slanted captions of 10-year-old Shalhevet Pas' death by a Palestinian sniper.

Sternthal, Tamar. "Disassembling Demolitions." *Committee for accuracy in Middle East reporting in America*, 15 December 2003. http://www.camera.org/index.asp?x_con text=2&x_outlet=2&x_article=595. This article from the CAMERA organization examines several photographs from Reuters and the Associated Press and their captions (all showing children and destroyed apartment buildings), and contrasts them with what really happened. Either the children did not live in the buildings or the buildings were not destroyed by Israel.

Waldman, Paul, and James Devitt. "Newspaper Photographs and the 1996 Presidential Elections: The Question of Bias." *Journalism and Mass Communication Quarterly* 75 (1998): 302. Photographs taken during the 1996 presidential campaign of Bill Clinton and Bob Dole treated both candidates fairly, thus revealing no liberal bias.

NOTES

1. http://www.xtcian.com/arch/002295.php.

2. Rob Miracle, "What Is Photojournalism?" http://www.photo-seminars.com/PhotoJournal ism/pjle1.htm.

3. "Error Cited as Proof of Anti-Israel Bias," *The Quill* 88:10 (December 2000): 49.

4. Martin A. Lee and Norman Solomon, *Unreliable Sources: A Guide to Detecting Bias in News Media* (New York: Carol Publishing Group, 1990), 46–47.

5. "Newsrooms Feel Heat over Middle East Coverage," *The Quill* (June 2002): 57.

6. Ricki Hollander, "Reuters Photos the Picture of Bias," *Committee for accuracy in Middle East reporting in America*, 3 April 2001, http://www.camera.org/index.asp?x_context=2&x_outlet=36&x _article=176.

7. Alex Safian, "Eye on the Media: Reuters Roots for the Palestinians," *Committee for Accuracy in Middle East Reporting in America*, 29 May 2001, http://www.camera.org/index.asp?x_context=5&x_ outlet=36&x_article=178.

8. "What Is Bias," *Honestreporting.com*, 2002, http://honestreporting.com/a/What_is_Bias_p.asp.

9. Jacqueline Sharkey, "When Pictures Drive Foreign Policy," *American Journalism Review* 15 (1993): 14.

10. Jenny Matthews, "A Conflict of Views; Photography — Jenny Matthews on the Inevitable Censorship and Bias of Documenting War," *The New Statesman*, August 2003.

11. Deni Elliot and Paul Martin Lester, "Ethics Matters: The Outrage of Governmental Distortion," *News Photographer*, July 2003, http://commfaculty.fullerton.edu/lester/writings/government.html.

12. E.S. Herman and Noam Chomsky, *Manufacturing Consent: The Political Economy of the Mass Media* (New York: Pantheon Books, 1988).

13. Jessica M. Fishman and Carolyn Marvin, "Portrayals of Violence and Group Difference in Newspaper Photographs: Nationalism and Media," *Journal of Communication* 53 (2003): 32–42.

14. Bob Steele, "Pearl Photo Too Harmful," *Poynter Online*, 7 June 2001, http://www.poynter.org/column.asp?id=36&aid=839.

15. Seth Ackerman, "Those Aren't Stones, They're Rocks: The Pro–Israel Critique of Middle East Coverage," *Fairness and Accuracy in Reporting (FAIR) Online*, March/April 2001, http://www.fair.org/extra/0103/not-stones.html.

16. Dick Rogers, "Expanding the Lens on Coverage of the Middle East," *Nieman Reports* (Fall 2002): 71–73.

17. Debbie Kornmiller, "Images Lead to Varying Perceptions," *Nieman Reports* (Fall 2002): 74–76.

18. Michael Larkin, "Deciding on an Emotional-Laden Photograph for Page One," *Nieman Reports* (Fall 2002): 77.

19. Paul Waldman and James Devitt, "Newspaper Photographs and the 1996 Presidential Elections: The Question of Bias," *Journalism and Mass Communication Quarterly* 75 (1998): 302.

20. Steve Outing, "Why Web News Has Different Standards Than Print, TV news," *Poynter Online*, 20 September 2001, http://www.pynter.org/content/content_view.asp?id=6350.

21. Kenneth F. Irby, "Beyond Taste: Editing Truth," *Poynter Online*, 30 March 2004, http://www.poynter.org/content_print.asp?id=63131&custom=, 31 March 2004.

22. Dan Kennedy, "The Daniel Pearl Video," *Nieman Reports* (Fall 2002): 80–81.

23. Kelly McBride, "Counting Crowds," *Poynter Online*, 27 February 2003, http://www.poynter.org/column.asp?id=53&aid=22367, 1 March 2004.

24. Tony Case, "Photo Illustration on Page One Story," *Editor and Publisher* 35 (1996): 3.

25. Courtney Kealy, "Photographic Images Can Be Misunderstood," *Nieman Reports* (Fall 2002): 64–66.

15

Corporate Ownership

Katharine A. Birchall

"The mass media in the United States is extremely concentrated, and the messages that they send are too broadly uniform. Six global corporations control more than half of all mass media in our country: newspapers, magazines, books, radio and television. Our democracy is being swamped by the confluence of money, politics and concentrated media. We must reclaim our democracy from the accelerating grip of big-money politics and concentrated corporate media."— votenader.org[1]

"... [T]he pointless analysis of the conglomeration of the media ... never manages to show that corporate owners have conservative beliefs, let alone that these beliefs translate into a conservative message. The Bagdikian/McChesney approach does not establish either an ideological or a financial reason why corporate media would want to bias their coverage rightward.... [Critics] fail to recognize that there is a distinct separation between corporate ownership and the media personnel ... who are responsible for creating the content of the mass media."
— Anna Schwartz, The Dissident Website[2]

"Florida Milk Supply Riddled with
Artificial Hormone Linked to Cancer;
Reporters Say They Were Ordered
to Lie about It on Fox-TV."

So ran a Tampa newspaper headline. Steve Wilson and Jane Akre, a husband-and-wife investigative reporting team at WTVT, Fox's Tampa Bay affiliate, thought they had a dynamite story. The reporters found that despite promises to consumers not to sell a potentially harmful product, supermarkets in Florida were selling milk produced with rBGH, a synthetic growth hormone developed by Monsanto that boosts milk production. Scientists believe the rBGH-boosted milk contains heightened levels of IGF-1, a hormone associated with increased risk of cancer. However, on February 21, 1997, days before the first installment of the story was scheduled to air, Monsanto sent a letter to Roger Ailes, the head of Fox News, urging him not to run the story or there would be dire consequences.[3]

The story never aired, and Wilson and Akre sued Fox — because of Fox's efforts to alter their story to make it acceptable to Monsanto. They claimed WTVT and its corporate bosses preferred to cover up the important story, rather than broadcast it honestly and accurately. The lawsuit charged that Fox television, strongly pressured by BGH-maker Monsanto, violated the state's whistleblower act by firing the journalists for refusing to broadcast false reports. "Media managers who are not journalists," Wilson argued, "have little regard for the public trust and they actually order reporters to broadcast false information and slant the truth to curry the favor or avoid the wrath of special interests."[4]

There is an ongoing debate about media and business: Does fear of ownership lead to favor toward ownership? Are the terms "profits," "journalistic responsibility," "shareholder value," and "the public's right to know" compatible? In an article in *Newsweek,* reporter Jonathan Alter asked, "Remember that book *Men Are From Mars, Women Are From Venus?* Well, business is from Saturn, journalism is from Jupiter. As the media monopoly grows, the culture clash between the two is becoming a major source of discomfort.... Adopting the values of another species can be confusing." He noted, "In a tight job market, the tendency is to avoid getting yourself or your boss in trouble. So an adjective gets dropped, a story skipped, a punch pulled."[5] Is he right? Does corporate ownership cause reporters and editors to bias their stories in order to placate the interest of their owners?

In 1983, fifty corporations dominated most every mass medium in the United States. By the end of 1986, the number had decreased to twenty-nine; by 1987 it was down to twenty-six.[6] In 1996, Todd Gitlin, a leftist cultural critic from New York University, warned in the *Media Studies Journal* that a "conglomeration juggernaut" had infiltrated the media industry and deemed it unstoppable.[7] Four years later, six firms dominated all U.S. mass media. A 2003 decision by the Federal Communications Commission reduced the regulation of media ownership, enabling even fewer companies to own even more media outlets.[8] Critics of corporate ownership contend that these companies are profit-driven. That may compromise journalistic integrity because reporters operate under the assumption that they are essentially slaves to the interests of their parent company. Critics fear a lack of diverse views may also ensue as fewer companies own more media outlets.

Proponents of media conglomeratization, on the other hand, emphasize the undemocratic nature of government regulation and interference in business and believe that corporate owners can actually defend themselves better from advertising companies because they themselves generate more income and are not dependent on advertising revenue. This financial freedom implies that media owned by corporations exercise greater independence in their content because of their resources and monetary stability. They do not feel pressure to alter content or slant stories.

The debate is simple: Does corporate ownership of media enhance a democratic society that appreciates and respects the First Amendment, or do conglomerates hinder democratic ideology and manipulate an unassuming public?

Critics of Corporate Ownership

Five global-dimension firms dominate American media. These five conglomerates are Time Warner; The Walt Disney Company; Murdoch's News Corporation, based in

Australia; Viacom; and Bertelsmann, based in Germany.[9] As Ben Bagdikian notes in his book *The New Media Monopoly*: "Today, none of the dominant media companies bother with dominance merely in a single medium. Their strategy has been to have major holdings in all the media, from newspapers to movie studios. This gives each of the five corporations and their leaders more communications power than was exercised by any despot or dictatorship in history."[10] The primary goal and purpose of the profit-driven businesses is to increase their bottom line, critics argue. So they cater to their shareholders instead of their audience's needs. Joan Konner argues in her article, "The Last Nickel," in the *Columbia Journalism Review*, that journalism "has always existed in two different realities — the reality of the economic marketplace, and the reality of a special institution protected by law in order to serve the public interest."[11] In his article "Bad Work," from *The Nation*, liberal critic Eric Alterman argues that journalists find themselves in a profession where "much of the control ... has passed from professionals to corporate executives and stockholders, with most of the professional decisions made less on the basis of ideals than on profit."[12] His point hits the heart of the argument: journalism suffers because stories become biased to please the owner and increase profits.

Media reporter Norman Solomon claims in "When Corporate Media Cover 'Independent Media'" that big corporations "don't like us [independent journalists] very much. They want to tell the story their way. We believe that objectivity is, in fact, a myth — that everyone has a bias — and that corporations like major news corporations have a bias."[13] Another reporter, Tim Redmond, argues in "Tim White Takes the Fall," that "all big media chains these days see journalism first and foremost as a business, a way to make money. And when it comes to the bottom line, all ethical rules are off."[14] If the bottom line is the main concern, pressure to manipulate stories in the interest of business increases dramatically.

There are many shortcomings of corporate-controlled journalism for fair and unbiased reporting, according to critics. Robert W. McChesney, a journalism professor and opponent of corporate ownership, in his book *Rich Media, Poor Democracy* argues, "Many problems result from the enhanced corporate pressure to make journalism a source of huge profits; this leads to easy-to-cover trivial stories and an emphasis on the type of news that will have appeal to the upper and upper-middle classes."[15] In an article from *Journalism and Mass Communication Quarterly* titled "Effects of Public Ownership and Newspaper Competition on the Financial Performance of Newspaper Corporations," Professor Stephen Lacy notes that media scholars, such as McChesney, assume that "[p]ublicly traded companies necessarily are concerned with short-term profits and return to shareholders that are driven by stock analysts' reports.... The focus on profitability, some scholars argue, can result in decisions based on narrow financial goals, rather than news and public service considerations."[16] Consequently, news coverage is biased because stories are chosen from a financial perspective, not a journalistic one.

The problem ensues when reporters and newspapers do not have higher ideals than simply placating important shareholders and keeping them happy by altering content and choice of story. As one reporter quoted in an article by Neil Hickey titled "Money Lust" declared, "If a story needs a real investment of time and money, we don't do it anymore."[17] The basic implication of these priorities suggests that if news organizations specifically cover only stories that they deem financially beneficial, the public does not receive adequate coverage of all pertinent events. Consequently, their ability to evaluate important policies is completely negated by the fact that important information is withheld. Critics of corporate ownership argue that as fewer conglomerates own and hence are in charge of information distribution, reporters will feel more pressure from their owners to present stories that will benefit the corporation.

Additionally, as Bagdikian points out in *The New Media Monopoly,* "To meet the profit pressures, newspapers have been cutting reportorial costs by reducing staff size and news space.... As a result, many newspapers have lost some of their best journalists, and the public has lost daily access to their reporting."[18] This profit-driven mentality, the argument goes, has consequently compromised journalistic integrity and newsroom ability to seek out the truth and deliver all possible information to the public. As McChesney and John Nichols argue in *Our Democracy, Not Theirs: The Democratic Struggle Against Corporate Media*: "The problem with their media system is that it exists to serve their interests, not ours. Profit trumps civil society every time. No wonder civil society is in crisis. Consider the diminution of basic values of community, service, and charity that we see as media-driven hypercommercialism pervades every nook and cranny of our culture."[19] McChesney and Nichols ask the public to consider the dramatic levels of disengagement that results when journalists leave citizens uninformed.

In 1971 Bagdikian declared in his book *The Information Machines,* "The press has evolved as a private enterprise. This means that the press can survive only if it shows a profit, which influences its behavior and is a force shaping its future."[20] McChesney and Nichols argue: "The media delivers first and foremost for their stockholders — major media in the U.S. can be enormously profitable. To maintain that profitability, they serve the major corporate interests that bankroll so much of the media with fat advertising checks. To avoid regulation in the public interest, they serve a political class that returns the favor by giving media conglomerations free access to the public's airwaves while routinely removing barriers to the expansion of corporate control over communications."[21]

Bagdikian emphasizes another less obvious danger inherent in the idea of five megamedia companies that, unlike any imperial ruler in history, have multiple media channels that include television and satellite channels that can saturate entire societies with controlled sights and sounds. He claims that the leaders of the Big Five operate like a close-knit hierarchy. They are "American and foreign entrepreneurs whose corporate empires control every means by which the population learns of its society.... They find ways to cooperate so that all five can work together to expand their power."[22] Hence, they go through motions to actually lend each other money and swap properties when it is mutually advantageous. The blaringly obvious result of this type of practice is the growing potential of these companies and the power they will gain over journalists to present news beneficial to their businesses.

McChesney and Nichols agree with Bagdikian's argument wholeheartedly. They declare, "The oligopolistic structures they have created make a mockery of the traditional notion of a free press.... Decades ago, A.J. Liebling wryly observed: 'In America, freedom of the press is largely reserved for those who own one.' We would update his line only by removing the word 'largely.'" Consequently, they argue that as fewer companies monopolize the industry, fewer perspectives will be shared with the public. More importantly, the stories that are covered directly reflect the interests of these conglomerates because the power they yield intimidates journalists, causing them to slant their stories.

This change in story lines can be done by placing emphasis on certain aspects of the story, indicating to the audience members where they should direct their attention, or omitting stories altogether that would have negative consequences for the owner.

For example, ABC might omit a story about a defective ride at Disney World that resulted in the death of a child because Disney owns ABC and such a story would damage Disney's image. Or, reporters would feel obligated to tell the story, but instead of focusing on the mechanical error of the ride, which implicates Disney, they might deflect blame and contend that the child was not wearing the seatbelt properly. Or, ABC editors might report the story quickly and then cut to another longer story featuring a young cancer patient enjoying a trip to Disney World, compliments of Disney itself. The duration, content, word choice, and other characteristics of stories can affect how the audience receives and interprets the news. There are many subtle ways, critics argue, that reporters can manipulate the news in favor of their corporate owner.

Thus, the door has been opened for corporate cannibalism and the Darwinian, "survival of the fittest" process of mergers and acquisitions. Richard Cohen illustrates the argument in *Conglomerates and the Media.* "Since the 1980s," he writes, "we have observed small companies eaten by bigger companies and devoured by even more mammoth corporate interests. This has become the new food chain of capitalism." He argues that the concentration of power in the news business has devastating consequences for the critical importance of news in American society. This is because the "content of news has changed from what is important to what sells, which means it is no longer pure news at all. The utilitarian value of news has been decimated."[23]

McChesney and Nichols believe the media have experienced a disintegration that has eroded the intended function of news media: informing the public. How can the public, they ask, adequately criticize their government when they receive only a small portion of information from a small number of companies whose interests are purely financial and decisions are made based on advertising revenue? "The media system as it operates in the United States today," they argue, "fails to provide basic support for citizenship.... We are subjected today to not our media, but the media of a handful of enormous conglomerates that have secured monopoly control of vast stretches of the media landscape."[24] They reason that it is impossible for America to maintain a democratic position when the information the public receives is a direct result of profit-driven journalism, increasing the bottom line, and ultimate deference to parent corporation wishes.

Bagdikian claims, in *The New Media Monopoly,* that executives are motivated almost solely by making money for themselves. "Media conglomerates," he declares, "are under demands from Wall Street to show ever higher stock profits, and the pressure is welcomed by many media top executives, whose high compensation is buttressed or [increased] in the form of company shares or stock options." The result, he argues, is democratic disaster. "Control of public information by a handful of global firms weakens democracy by omission of news that might interfere with media's maximizing their own profits." He cites the seemingly endless accounts of dishonesty and criminal behavior at the top levels of some of the country's largest corporations as evidence that corporations sacrifice truth for profit. Names like Enron, Tyco, WorldCom, Arthur Andersen, Merrill Lynch, J.P. Morgan, and Citibank have been corrupted by committing fraud or theft. "Almost worse," he laments, "most of the major media were turning a blind eye to it all. Every metropolitan newspaper in the country has a daily special section specializing in business and corporate affairs ... but they devoted most of their space and energies to the celebration of top corporate executives as heroes...."[25]

In an article published in *The Nation*, "What's Wrong with This Picture?" Mark Crispin Miller examines the media cartel of today versus the landscape of the media in 1996. Back then the national television news appeared to be a tidy tetrarchy: two network news divisions owned by large appliance makers/weapon manufacturers (CBS by Westinghouse, NBC by General Electric,) and the other two bought by the nation's top purveyors of Big Fun (ABC by Disney, CNN by Time Warner). "Today the telejournalistic firmament," he argues, "includes the meteoric Fox News Channel, as well as twenty-six television stations owned outright by Rupert Murdoch's News Corporation (which holds majority ownership in a further seven). Meanwhile Time Warner has now merged with AOL, so as to own the cyberworks through which to market its floodtide of movies, ball games, TV shows, rock videos, cartoons, standup routines and (not least) bits from CNN, CNN Headline News, CNNfn (devised to counter GE's CNBC) and CNN/Sports Illustrated."[26] The CBS network, he adds, is now property of the voracious Viacom, the matchless cable occupier (UPN, MTV, MTV2, VH1, Nickelodeon, the Movie Channel, TNN, CMT, BET, 50 percent of Comedy Central, etc.), radio giant (Infinity Broadcasting, which owns 184 stations), movie titan (Paramount Pictures), and giant publisher (Simon & Schuster, Free Press, Scribner). It also lays claim to a share of the Web. The result is the sad loss of diversity of thought — the result not only of fewer voices in control, but more importantly, the amount of power and influence those voices have on their reporters and their willingness to skew content.

Richard M. Cohen argues in *Conglomerates and the Media* that one of the greatest declines in journalism integrity stems directly from the advent of television news. "Most of what we know about ourselves," he claims, "is dispensed on the tube. We live in a time when perception quickly becomes more powerful than truth. These days, television news is the source of most perceptions in the public mind.... [I]t has become an institution that fails America everyday."[27] He contends that the objectives of television journalism have changed from being propelled by responsibility to inform to act now as audience-driven companies trying to maximize profit and sell advertising revenues. He believes the loudest complaint of TV news should be that it doesn't serve the public interest. "Corporate ownership of the networks and local stations," he argues, "is destroying the integrity of news. The dumbing down, the demise of news is all about the hunger for advertising revenues and how that plays out in the newsroom. It's about the decline of news values. Altered objectives. The real crisis in TV news today is about corporate control and the emerging corporate culture."[28]

The so-called corruption in media policy-making culminated in the passage of the 1996 Telecommunications Act, which rewrote the regulatory regime for all of electronic communications. In *The Problem of the Media,* McChesney explains the premise behind the decision to lift regulations and ownership restrictions from commercial media that was intended to "allow competition in the marketplace to develop and reduce the government's role to that of protecting private property.... Corporate CEOs regarded the bill as their 'Magna Carta.'"[29]

The FCC is required to review its ownership rules every two years. In 2000 it let the 35 percent cap on media-ownership rules stand and was then sued by the network owners. A federal appeals court in 2002 agreed that the FCC had not provided a "single valid reason" that the 35 percent rule was in "the public interest" and told the FCC to reconsider its decision. The result was a new 45 percent rule, which Congressman David Obey (D-Wisc.) said is "a severe threat to democracy." FCC Commissioner Jonathan Adelstein wailed, "it [new media-ownership rules] will degrade civil discourse and the quality of our society's intellectual, cultural, and political life."[30] Congressman Sherrod Brown (D-Ohio) said the FCC decision will "throw sound public interest and market soundness principles out the window, allowing some of America's biggest companies to decide what you see, what you hear, and in part what you think.... It's a story of how three commissioners are working with corporate-owned media conglomerates to expand their control over what news the public receives." His argument proceeds simply and deliberately to its conclusion. "The FCC's vote to undermine ownership restrictions," he declared, "will mean that the acronym F-C-C will no longer stand for the Federal Communications Commission. It will stand for another F-C-C: Furthering Corporate Control."[31]

In his article "Ready, Set, Consolidate," Neil Hickey argued that the FCC's action is "part of a larger picture: a natural extension of the present administrations' policies on taxation, the budget, and the environment, which have supported the interests of the business community. Reed Hundt, a former FCC chairman, told Salon.com that the voice was less about principles of diversity, competition, and localism than an effort to strengthen a powerful alliance between the political right and Big Media."[32]

Corporate ownership and media conglomeration and concentration have many critics. They believe that the monopolistic holdings in America's media system are profit-driven, compromising the profession and practice of journalism. Big ownership makes reporters more vulnerable to outside forces and demands that they mold their stories in their parent company's interests.

Proponents of Corporate Ownership

The proponents of multi-billion dollar companies argue that running media organizations as for-profit businesses does not compromise the First Amendment and result in biased stories. They believe there are positive outcomes for media operations and their ability to practice objective, investigative journalism. As William B. Shew argues in his article "Are Media Mergers a Menace?" in the *American Enterprise Journal*, "Mergers do not substantially lessen media competition or diversity. It is difficult to believe that the recent spate of media mergers presents a threat to competition."[33]

Aside from posing no economic threat, Shew contends, it is not a likely possibility that media conglomerates constitute a social threat by reducing media diversity, which he freely admits is crucial to a democratic society. "Economic theory," he points out, "suggests that larger media organizations may have an incentive to offer more diverse content than would many tiny organizations, most of which might be drawn to targeting the popular middle of the market. Thus, some reduction in source diversity might actually lead to a gain in content diversity. More importantly, though, recent mergers are more likely to have an appreciable effect on the number of distinct media voices. Media owners remain too numerous, and the public's media consumption too fragmented, to worry that media diversity will be seriously compromised."

Shew argues that the main challenge to a vigorous and competitive media industry actually is found in public policy that restrains competition. Public policy artificially limits the number of media competitors and then restricts the behavior of competing firms. "Even more trouble," he declares, "given the critical role played by the media in a democratic society, is the movement afoot to expand government regulation of media content. It is these policy measures, far more than recent mergers, that pose a threat to media competition and diversity." In essence, Shew agrees with opponents of media mergers that upholding a democratic society should be America's greatest concern. However, he sees government regulation of business conglomerations as the main threat to democracy, not the mergers themselves.

Conrad C. Fink writes that the United States is premised on an economic system of capitalism and a philosophy of individual libertarianism. So there is nothing wrong with newspapers and other media companies making money. They need money to survive and provide an environment conducive to solid, investigative reporting.[34] As Clay Calvert points out in his chapter "Dual Responsibilities of the Corporate Newsroom" in the book *Contemporary Media Issues*, "Sound business judgment allows newspapers and television news magazines to survive. Defunct newspapers and broadcast properties serve neither the public nor shareholders. The argument goes a step further when defenders argue that long-term survival requires sacrificing short-term journalistic goals. Economic stability (and growth) may require changes and adjustments in news and editorial content. It may require, in some cases, letting business executives dictate news judgments."[35]

The FCC's decision to increase the number of U.S. households a broadcast TV owner may reach from 35 to 45 percent has outraged many critics. However, an editorial in the *Wall Street Journal*, "Beltway Media Meltdown," concludes that FCC Chairman Michael Powell should be praised for encouraging this healthy deregulation. The editorial contends: "It is our own view that the FCC would have done better to get rid of ownership caps altogether, given today's world of nonstop cable, Internet blogs, cell phones, satellite, radio, magazines, and newspapers." The editorial calls the "threat of Network Mind Control" overblown upon examining two network companies, Viacom and News Corp. They are both already violating the caps (at 40 percent and 38 percent, respectively), yet democracy lives. "Fox owns 37 of the 1,340 stations in the U.S., and the rules would allow it to buy maybe another five. Even Rupert Murdoch will need more than a few outlets in Topeka and Palm Springs to affect world domination."[36]

The too-big argument also neglects the many other ways Americans get their news. According to the *Wall Street Journal*, "Today, 86 percent of the country obtains TV primarily through cable and satellite. A 2002 Nielsen survey found that only 33.1 percent of Americans listed broadcast TV as their most- used source of news."[37] The argument of the editorial reasons that media mergers are not a threat to democracy because (1) America continues to flourish as a wealthy, competent, democratic nation (2) the caps in place will prevent one or two giants from dominating all media outlets, and (3) Americans rely on many sources for news.

Patrick Maines also writes in *Television Week* in an article titled "Defense of Ownership Rules" that the "FCC's media ownership rules, adopted by a 3–2 majority, taken together, represent a measured and patently non-ideological response to dramatically changed circumstances. More than this, the threat they represent to the First Amendment is precisely zero." He contends that, "[b]ecause all these new media outlets are supported at least in part by advertising, many broadcasters are at risk because there are too many outlets chasing too few ad dollars.... Absent the synergies and efficiencies that certain mergers may provide, many local TV stations, especially in smaller markets, face an incredibly bleak future."[38] He argues essentially, then, that mergers are, in fact, vital.

Keeping in line with this train of thought, the "Beltway Media Meltdown" article contends that because of deregulation and competition, the NRA and special interest groups have never had more outlets for their messages. Cable stations have become so successful that they are pulling valuable advertising dollars away from traditional broadcast networks. It is therefore ironic that the same people arguing to preserve free-to-air broadcast TV are the same ones in favor of ownership caps that will actually prevent them getting what they want. This is because local stations produce far more local content than is profitable and networks depend on local stations. There are new and expensive industry demands that broadcast companies must deal with. Thus, if they are allowed to own even a few more local entities, they will be better prepared to meet these demands, including the switch to digital TV. So, the article argues, "Far from stifling viewpoints, allowing media companies to expand lets them earn enough money to continue offering competing viewpoints."[39] This autonomy also protects journalists from outside influences and encourages investigative, unbiased reporting.

Some concern has been expressed not only about large corporations' threat to unbiased reporting, but also their threat to advertisers. Common sense would seem to suggest that more media consolidation means higher advertising rates, but that is not necessarily the case. In the article "FCC Move Isn't Bad News for Marketers," which appeared in *Brandweek,* Brian McHale notes that "[i]t is wrong to consider it a forgone conclusion that local media rates will rise if there is a greater concentration of media ownership in a given market.... The question is whether rates in highly consolidated markets are apt to rise more significantly than rates in markets with less consolidation. The answer is probably not."[40] He cites the fact that in Cincinnati, which has one of the most highly consolidated radio markets in the country because Clear Channel and Infinity dominate, the city has not seen radio rates rise more than they have in any other comparably-sized markets across the country. The city has also not experienced an increase in business stories that would benefit the parent corporations, which suggests that concentration of ownership is a neutral factor in objective reporting.

Consolidation might, indeed, offer potential benefits to marketers. "A stronger media owner," McHale argues, "would have a greater incentive to make the package as synergistic as possible. They'd be more inclined to think creatively and come up with proposals that show real imagination, as opposed to merely trying to peddle a commodity." The idea is that in consolidated markets, media agencies have more availability to brainstorm ideas with a media company that owns enough components to produce exciting discussion. Both sides work together to create new ideas and approaches. Both companies win, and the public receives the best possible product with the most up-to-date, unbiased information.

David Pearce Demers, a professor at Pennsylvania State University, has arguably done the most extensive amount of research concerning the effects of corporate structure on an objectively run newsroom. Every study he has conducted suggests that corporate ownership does not adversely affect quality news production. In fact, his studies have shown that larger newspapers are less profit-driven than smaller newspapers. So they are less likely to slant stories for a profit motive. This is precisely his contention in his article "Corporate Structure and Emphasis on Profits and Product Quality at U.S. Daily Newspapers," published in *Journalism Quarterly*. His data showed that "large newspapers emphasize profits less than do smaller newspapers, supporting John Kenneth Galbraith's argument that large organizations pursue a variety of goals, not just maximum profits." He defines "corporate newspapers" as organizations that are "characterized by a high division of labor, role specialization, hierarchy of authority, rationality in decision-making, and more formalized rules and procedures. In other words, corporate newspapers are complex bureaucracies. Ownership structure (chain versus independent) and newspaper circulation are two empirical measures of corporate structure."[41]

In order to fully understand Demers' argument and conclusion, one must first recognize that basic economic theory of business states that all businesses pursue one primary goal: make money. Profit maximization is the ultimate objective, regardless of who manages the firm. Even if business people are not consciously trying to maximize their profits, competition will drive them to do so. This theory assumes then that profit motive is no stronger for a corporate firm than one that is individually owned.[42] Although it is a widespread belief that chains and large news organizations care more about profits than independently owned papers, many scholars have argued the opposite. In *The New Industrial State,* Galbraith argues that — since large corporations are controlled not by the owners or stockholders who benefit directly from the profits, but by professional managers who obtain most of their income from a fixed salary — these people are actually more likely to place less emphasis on profit. Why, he asks, should those in control (the managers) try to maximize profits for others (the stockholders)? Why would reporters feel threatened by corporate influence to bias their stories when they have a fixed salary and the protection from their managers? This behavior would not be rational. He argues that the prevention of loss is more important, since low earnings or losses make a company vulnerable to outside influence and loss of autonomy. Galbraith believes that managers place greater emphasis on autonomy, organizational growth, planning, knowledge, and expertise, since these factors are recognized as the basis of power in the organization and are essential for long-term survival.[43] These are the very factors that drive good, investigative reporting.

Demers argues that a second reason corporations place less value on profit maximization is simply that they are more stable and secure. He says, "[L]arge organizations, which have greater access to human and capital resources and greater control over markets and prices, should be less vulnerable to changes in the marketplace."[44] Stability breeds good, unbiased reporting because stable newsrooms can support large staffs. Hence, reporters have time to devote to investigative reporting. One study Demers conducted asked top editors at daily newspapers to identify the importance their newspaper placed on profits and product quality as an organizational goal or value. "No difference between chain and independent newspapers," he concludes, "was found in terms of product quality, and some data actually show that larger newspapers place less emphasis on profits. This latter finding ... may be interpreted as supporting Galbraith's argument that large organizations pursue goals other than profit maximization."[45]

Demers continued his investigation and researched other reasons to support his notion, which challenges conventional wisdom, that corporate newspapers place less emphasis on profits and more on product quality. He believes that corporate newspapers are structurally organized to maximize profits. "[H]owever," he argues, "increasing role specialization, a characteristic of large-scale organizations, decreases emphasis on profits as a goal and increases emphasis on quality and goals other than profit."[46] This increase on quality inherently implies reporting unbiased stories and operating under professional journalistic standards. A study done by Olien, Tichenor, and Donohue titled "Relation Between Corporate Ownership and Editor Attitudes about Business," published in *Journalism Quarterly*, also used the role-specialization argument and found that editors of independently owned or locally headquartered weekly and semiweekly newspapers in Minnesota — when asked to list reasons for being satisfied or dissatisfied with their jobs — were more, not less, likely to mention profit.[47]

In "Corporate Newspaper Structure, Profits, and Organizational Goals," Demers contends that, "[a]t the corporate newspaper, role specialization means that journalists have greater freedom to focus their efforts on what they do best: gathering and reporting the news. This means that journalists at corporate newspapers would be expected to place greater emphasis on producing a quality product as well as such goals as winning reporting awards, acquiring the latest technology, or being innovative in news gathering." He believes that these are the goals that journalists most revere because they are the factors that will lead to a promotion, an increase in pay, a better job, or more prestige and power. "At the same time," he argues, "it would be expected that other managers and workers in the corporate news organization will place greater emphasis on maximizing the growth of the organization and conducting readership research. Maximizing the growth of the organization has direct benefits for professional managers, increasing their power and control."[48]

He reasons that corporations are less vulnerable to changes in the marketplace because they have greater access to human and capital resources and greater control over markets and prices. "Consequently," he declares, "they have less need to be concerned about the bottom line and can turn their attention to other matters. In contrast, survival is a major concern in small companies." In "Revisiting Corporate Newspaper Structure and Profit Making," he argues that corporate newspapers place greater emphasis on product quality because "they have a greater division of labor and role specialization that removes editors from concern about the bottom-line and increases emphasis with news production, are more financially stable and secure, which means they can pursue goals other than profit, and are managed less by the owners than by highly skilled and educated managers, who place a premium on professionalism (quality) and benefit less directly from profits than the owners...."[49] This attention to quality produces unbiased stories.

The FCC itself has defended its deregulatory policies. The Telecommunications Act of 1996, as mentioned earlier, brought sweeping changes to the media landscape and was "intended to lead to a better match between the regulatory law and the contemporary media marketplace."[50] Its stated purpose was "to promote competition and reduce regulation in order to secure lower prices and higher quality services for American telecommunication consumers and encourage the rapid deployment of new telecommunication technologies."[51] The presumption was that increased competition brought about by deregulation would, almost automatically, promote diversity and localism. The Commission placed diversity at the forefront in defining the framework for review. It recognized three types of diversity: "1) viewpoint: 'helping to ensue that the material presented by the media reflect a wide range of diverse and antagonistic opinions and interpretations,' 2) outlet: 'a variety of delivery services (e.g. broadcast stations, newspapers, cable, and DBS) that select and present a programming directly to the public,' and 3) source: 'promoting a variety of program or information producers and owners.'"[52]

Also, as Ann L. Plamondon says in her article "Proposed Changes in Media Ownership: A Study in Ventriloquism," "There are other ways of promoting 'diverse and antagonistic sources' that are not based upon limitations of ownership—a right of access to the media and the fairness doctrine." The fairness doctrine refers to the obligation of broadcasters to "discuss important, controversial public issues, and to present conflicting viewpoints with respect to the issues."[53] Hence, the production of unbiased and objective stories and a variety of views. The FCC has repeatedly stated that its ultimate concern is to promote diversity. Members believe diversity this will follow from decreased regulation. Corporate ownership, they argue, is simply not a threat to democracy because owners are committed to upholding democracy and respect the role that an informed public plays. It is their commitment to upholding democracy, this line of reasoning goes, that encourages the practice of unbiased reporting.

The proponents of corporate ownership thus conclude that predominantly corporate-owned media do not result in biased stories because they promote diversity, competition, and can practice investigative journalism through their financial stability.

• THE EVIDENCE •

Both sides in the argument—the critics and supporters of corporate ownership—make valid points. However, the argument of critics, although extensive and clearly the most vocal, fails to support its claim. The most notable problem is the lack of empirical evidence against corporate ownership. It rests more on narrative statements that address the issue with emotional claims of threats to democracy than on proving negative-biased effects of corporate ownership. The case is certainly strong for wanting to maintain journalism as it is rooted in the Constitution. The importance of journalists continuing to act as America's watchdog and the press' role as the Fourth Estate of government must not be undermined by corporate influence. But the evidence does not adequately show that corporate ownership has such an impact as the critics claim.

The evidence they do present has two major methodological problems. The first is that their arguments are based on non-probability samples or individual case studies, which means that the findings cannot be generalized to the broad population of newspapers and other media. Obviously, one unavoidable reason that researchers have relied so heavily on these types of samples is that it is difficult to collect data on profits. Much of that information is kept private by smaller papers, and the papers that do make it public tend to be large, publicly held newspapers, which are not representative of most newspapers in the country. The second problem is that many studies rely too much on relatively crude measures of organizational structure. They use chain ownership or organizational size as the independent variable, which is not an adequate indicator of structure. Until recently, measuring the change from the entrepreneurial to the corporate form of organization could be done fairly well by using chain ownership. However, now the diffusion of chain ownership is too widespread for it to be a good indicator of structural complexity.

Aside from the methodological problems, the most glaring issue is the weakness of the case that the critics make for the "potential problems" of corporate ownership. The works of McChesney and Bagdikian routinely resemble the narrative structure of a novel, only occasionally referring to empirical data. Additionally, the data they use was collected by other people. Neither one of the them actually conducted his own studies. The arguments also tend toward partisanship — that is, to attack Republicans, since they are the ones who typically adhere to conservative ideologies that frown upon government interference in business. Instead of examining the effects of government deregulation, opponents focus their social commentary on the "money hungry, hard-hearted, callous, faceless" figures who run these businesses. Such ideological motivation thus clouds their ability to over detached, incisive analysis. Ultimately, their works seem to be simple exercises in stubborn efforts to destroy the operation of big businesses and are not grounded in substantial evidence.

On the other hand, the empirical data presented to support the claim that corporate ownership does not result in biased reporting and actually promotes the practice of pursuing goals other than profit is extensive. David Demers' body of work consists of numerous studies that avoid previous methodological problems by the use of national probability surveys and a multiple indicator system for organizational structure. He varies the critical models used to assess his data, making his findings even more credible and reliable. Also, Galbraith makes a compelling point when he explains that professional managers at corporately owned businesses have a fixed salary, so that they are not biased by profit-driven motives. It is more reasonable to assume that independently owned newspapers are more influenced by monetary concerns because their income fluctuates and corresponds directly with their bottom line. The evidence advocating corporate ownership is stronger than that of the critics because it rests on statistical findings and analytically demonstrates that bias is minimal.

• RESOLUTION •

To reduce the likelihood that corporate ownership will eventually have adverse effects on unbiased reporting, owners and journalists must understand each other's position and function. There must be an internal acknowledgment that they need to remain separate to avoid conflicts of interest. Opening the lines of communication should edify both sides and decrease misunderstandings. They must resolve to operate independently of each other. A proverbial wall needs to be erected between owner and journalist so the owner does not compromise the journalist's ability to report the news objectively. In essence, they need to operate according to a code of ethics that embodies the First Amendment. The two sides also need to trust each other because mutual distrust leads to destruction in any organization. Owners need to trust that journalists are not out to attack the parent company or its interests. Owners must cooperate with journalists by assuring that they have the independence to practice investigative journalism. In turn, journalists need to trust that the owners are not out to harm the quality of the news. Journalists need to inform the public about how business interests influence their journalistic decisions. Corporate ownership should not corrupt the Fourth Estate with biased stories — and it will not, as long as both sides act professionally and continue to be aware of potential conflicts of interests.

• POINTS OF VIEW •

Bagdikian, Ben. *The Media Monopoly*, 7th ed. Boston: Beacon Press, 2004. Monopolization of mass media hurts democracy, and unbiased communication merits and needs an attack on concentrated ownership.

Barnouw, Eric, et al. *Conglomerates and the Media*. New York: New Press, 1997. As corporations essentially transform into private governments, diversity will decline and the quality of news will suffer.

Demers, David P. "Revisiting Corporate Newspaper Structure and Profit Making," *The Journal of Media Economics* 11:2 (1998). Corporate newspapers place more emphasis on product quality and other nonprofit goals than profit.

Galbraith, John Kenneth. *The New Industrial State*, New York: Mentor, 1978. Corporate organizations are controlled by professional managers who obtain their income from a fixed salary. So these papers are less likely to emphasis profit than independently owned papers.

Lee, Martin A., and Norman Soloman. *Unreliable Sources: A Guide to Detecting Bias in News Media*. New York: Carol Publishing, 1990. Corporate ownership biases the media and results in some stories not being covered.

McChesney, Robert W. *The Problem with the Media*. New York: The Monthly Review Press, 2004. Corporate domination of both the media system and the policy-making process that establishes and sustains it causes problems for a functioning democracy and a healthy culture.

NOTES

1. "Opposition to Media Bias and Media Concentration," http://www.votenader.org/issues/index. php?cid=8.

2. Anna Schwartz, "What Conservative Bias?" http://www.the-dissident.com/bias.shtml.

3. "We Paid $3 Billion for Those Stations. We'll Decide What the News Is," http://www.fair.org/extra/9806/foxbgh.html.

4. "Reporters Blow Whistle on News Station," http://foxbghsuit.com/bgh2.htm.

5. Jonathan Alter, "A Call for Chinese Walls," *Newsweek*, 14 August 1995, 31.

6. WIFP, "Corporate Mass Media," http://wifp.org/MassMedia.html.

7. Todd Gitlin, "Not So Fast," *Media Studies Journal* 10 (1996): 1–6.

8. WIFP, "Corporate Mass Media," http://www.wifp.org/MassMedia.html.

9. Ibid.

10. Benjamin Baddikian, *The New Media Monopoly*, 7th ed. (Boston: Beacon Press, 2004), 3.

11. Joan Konner, "The Last Nickel," *Columbia Journalism Review* (November/December 1995): 4.

12. Eric Alterman, "Bad Work," *The Nation*, 20 May 20002.

13. Norman Solomon, "When Corporate Media Cover 'Independent Media," http://www.fair.org/index.php?page=2076.

14. Tim Redmond, "Tim White Takes the Fall," sfgb.com, February 23, 2006.

15. Robert W. McChesney, *Rich Media, Poor Democracy* (New York: The New Press, 1999), xv.

16. Stephen Lacy, "Effects of Public Ownership and Newspaper Competition on the Financial Performance of Newspaper Corporations," *Journalism and Mass Communication Quarterly* 73 (1996):35.

17. Neil Hickey, "Money Lust," *Columbia Journalism Review* (July/August 1998), 28.

18. Bagdikian, *The New Media Monopoly*, 2004, 105–106.

19. Robert W. McChesney and John Nichols, *Our Media, Not Theirs: The Democratic Struggle Against Corporate Media* (New York: Seven Stories Press, 2002), 26.

20. Ben Bagdikian, *The Information Machines* (New York: Harper and Row Publishers, 1971), 115.

21. McChesney and Nichols, *Our Media, Not Theirs*, 2002, 26.

22. Bagdikian, *The New Media Monopoly*, 2004, 4.

23. Ibid.

24. McChesney and Nichols, *Our Media, Not Theirs*, 2002, 25.

25. Bagdikian, *The New Media Monopoly*, 2004, 105, 103.

26. Mark Crispin Miller, "What's Wrong with This Picture?," *The Nation,* January 2002.

27. Richard Cohen, "The Corporate Takeover of News: Blunting the Sword," in *Conglomerates and the Media,* Erik Barnouw, et al. (New York: The New Press) 1997, 32.

28. Barnouw, et al., *Conglomerates and the Media,* 1997, 33.

29. McChesney, *The Problem of the Media,* 2004, 51.

30. "Beltway Media Meltdown," *Wall Street Journal,* 25 July 2003, 14.

31. Sherrod Brown, "The FCC Must Not Limit Media Competition, Public's Access to Diverse News Sources," http://www.house.gov/sherrodbrown, February 27, 2006.

32. Neil Hickey, "Ready, Set, Consolidate," *Columbia Journalism Review* (July/August), 2003, 6.

33. William Shew, "Are Media Mergers a Menace?," *American Enterprise* (March/April) 1996, 48.

34 Conrad C. Fink, *Strategic Newspaper Management* (Boston: Allyn & Bacon, 1996), 8.

35. Clay Calvert, "Dual Responsibilities of the Corporate Newsroom," in *Contemporary Media Issues, 2nd ed.,* eds. Emily Erikson and Wm. David Sloan (Northport:, Ala.: Vision Press, 2004), 32.

36. "Beltway Media Meltdown," *Wall Street Journal,* 25 July 2003, 14.

37. Ibid.

38. Patrick Maines, "Defense of Ownership Rules," *Television Week,* June/July 2003, 15.

39. "Beltway Media Meltdown," *Wall Street Journal,* 25 July 2003, 14.

40. Brian McHale, "FCC Move Isn't Bad News for Marketers," *Brandweek,* 15 September 2003, 25.

41. David P. Demers, "Corporate Structure and Emphasis on Profits and Product Quality at U.S. Daily Newspapers," *Journalism Quarterly* 68 (1991): 15.

42. Ernest Gellhorn, *Anti-Trust Law and Economics* (St. Paul: West, 1986), 51–54.

43. John Kenneth Galbraith, *The New Industrial State* (New York: Mentor, 1978), 102–118.

44. David Pearce Demers, "Structural Pluralism and the Growth of Chain Ownership in the U.S. Newspaper Industry" (paper presented at the annual convention of the Association for Education in Journalism and Mass Communication, Minneapolis, Minnesota, August 1990), 5.

45. David P. Demers, "Corporate Structure and Emphasis on Profits and Product Quality at U.S. Daily Newspapers, *Journalism Quarterly* 68 (1991): 25.

46. David. P. Demers, "Corporate Newspaper Structure, Profits, and Organizational Goals," *The Journal of Media Economics* 9 (1996): 1.

47. C. N. Olien, P. J. Tichenor, and G. A. Donohue, "Relation Between Corporate Ownership and Editor Attitudes about Business," *Journalism Quarterly* 65 (1989): 265.

48. Demers, "Corporate Newspaper Structure, Profits, and Organizational Goals," 10.

49. David P. Demers, "Revisiting Corporate Newspaper Structure and Profit Making," *The Journal of Media Economics* 11 (1998): 20.

50. Ann L. Plamondon, "Proposed Changes in Media Ownership Rules: A Study in Ventriloquism," *Communications and the Law* 25(2003): 1.

51. Preamble, Pub. L. 104–104, 110 Stat. 56 (1996).

52. Telecommunications Act of 1996, supra note 2, 202 (h).

53. Ann L. Plamondon, "Proposed Changes in Media Ownership Rules: A Study in Ventriloquism," *Communications and the Law,* 25 (2003): 64.

16

Management and Labor

Karen Watts Perkins

"[W]orking as a union activist, I have too much experience with real media bias—the complete blackout of major events if they have to do with working people and union organizing. Just check out this story about the first Congressional hearing in 18 years dealing with the illegal violations of labor laws by corporate America, 24,000 documented acts of corporate lawbreaking in 1998 alone. Yet the media barely gave it a notice, much less a full-scale analysis."—www.nathannewman.org[1]

"As big and as important as Microsoft is, the coverage of the company is quite mediocre. This is particularly true in the mainstream press.... What's bad for Microsoft is that the bias against it is subtle—kind of like any sort of media bias, whether religious or political. As one critic once said regarding the supposed left-wing slant of the daily news media, 'It's not what they write, it's what they write ABOUT that matters.' Story selection."—John C. Dvorak, www.pcmag.com[2]

In 1997, the International Brotherhood of Teamsters, the union representing workers at United Parcel Service, went on strike. With the work stoppage, shipping services for most of the country came to a halt, which threatened the day-to-day operations of U.S. businesses and society as a whole. According to the media, the union movement was causing trouble.

In the past few years, corporate scandals have rocked the business world. The high-level management of large corporations, hungry with greed and self-satisfaction, overlook the potential effects on their employees. In terms of media coverage, corporate power was causing trouble.

As America's watchdog, the media are expected to cover the issues of labor and management because they are newsworthy and of interest to the general public. The question is, however, if the coverage is fair and accurate or biased and negative against a particular side.

The question of media bias in the coverage of management and labor is not a new issue. From the peak of labor unions and workers' rights in the first half of the twentieth century to the rise of big business in the last half, management and labor has been widely discussed. While the focus of the issue may have changed throughout history, its significance remains. As labor unions decrease in size, globalization increases, and the economy remains in peril, media professionals and critics will continue discussing management and labor issues.

The definitions of labor and management are starting points for the media coverage debate. Each side claims the media are unfair and negligent of their respective views. These assertions are very general and encompass several distinct issues. For example, what do journalists and media critics mean by the terms labor and management?

Do the pro-labor and pro-management advocates intend to imply the broad labels of labor and management, or do they mean to convey individual components of each term? Management can stand for the highest of executives or low-level managers. It can include a specific individual business or the corporate world in general. The term labor can take on varying definitions as well. Labor can stand for the work force employed by corporations or the labor unions that support them. It can also include strikes by labor unions or the workplace issues that affect most of America's workers.

Often, the terms labor and management are not clearly defined, which creates the ambiguity surrounding media bias in covering America's business. When the terms are defined, anti-labor claims usually imply the terms to mean labor unions specifically and the corporate businesses of their members. However, anti-business advocates — those reporting fair coverage — usually classify the terms by workers and workplace issues as they are compared with business and individual management. The vagueness about the terms from each side of the argument leads to inconsistencies when observing the issue of media coverage.

As many critics also conclude, labor and management can be euphemisms for a related, yet much more complicated issue: economic class separated along the lines of the powerful elites and the working class. Those groups claiming a strong bias against labor in the media are most known for making this argument of economic class. While this chapter does not cover the intricacies of economic class in relation to media bias, it is important to note the assumption does exist.

As with any issue of public significance, coverage of management and labor in the media creates arguments on two sides. Workers and labor leaders feel neglected and abused by the mainstream press, while business executives claim they are slighted and taken for granted.

Various studies find favor on both sides. Other research has shown bias exists against both management and labor, and the opinions of each group cause them to see the media as biased in favor of the opposing side.

Bias Against Management

Most arguments that maintain the media provide fair coverage of labor — or that accuse them of leaning negatively towards management — come from business leaders and media professionals. The two groups disagree, however, on why business is portrayed the way it is. There are three areas that make up the argument: labor receives fair treatment, business is portrayed negatively, and the labor press promotes biased coverage.

Pro-labor coverage

To start with, there is evidence that labor receives appropriate coverage in the news media. Accusations of media bias in favor of labor have been made since the 1920s when labor unions were at their peak. Proponents contend journalists do not seek out good stories involving business but jump on stories in which businesses come across negatively. Accordingly, labor or workers' issues receive better coverage.

Senior editor for the *Columbia Journalism Review*, Mike Hoyt, discussed labor-management coverage as the Teamsters union campaigned for a new president in his article titled "Labor History is Being Made in the Big Union, but its Coverage has an Alice in Wonderland Quality" (1996). He wrote as "mounting unemployment and stagnant wages emerge as hot topics on the national political scene, general problems that workers face, such as pay and benefits, begin to receive more prominence in the news media."[3] He credited the resurgence in organized labor as another source for better coverage of labor issues. In a more recent CyberAlert (2005) from the Media Research Center, the same assumption is made concerning better coverage of labor issues. In this report, *TODAY Show* host, Katie Couric, was accused of vigorously pursuing the problems of working Americans who lack employee benefits. What she failed to mention, the report pointed out, is any reference to the employer's side of the story, and how he or she might be affected if such programs were put in place.[4]

Several articles from the editorial pages of newspapers also support the notion that labor receives appropriate coverage in the mass media. In a December 2004 editorial in Denver's *Rocky Mountain News*, Chris Nevitt commended the publication's pro-labor perspective.[5] A pro-labor view is also found in the *St. Louis Post-Dispatch*. Benjamin Israel wrote about this concept in his article titled "Is the Post-Dispatch Only Pro-union for Its Readers?" (2003) for the *St. Louis Journalism Review*. In it, he discussed the relationship between the paper's editorial page and the St. Louis Newspaper Guild. Israel reported "the editorial page has supported the labor movement since the paper was founded."[6] He provided examples of this support through editorials such as "The Revival of Organized Labor"[7] following the 1997 UPS strike and "No OT for You"[8] opposing an overtime rules amendment by the Bush administration.

Although many media critics and labor advocates allege a pro-management bias in the corporate media, mainstream periodicals reveal news stories with more of a pro-labor stance. In a 2004 editorial in the *Daily News of Los Angeles*, Gary Galles lamented the paper's support of advertising promoting Wal-Mart as a "health-insurance miser." He wrote that "unmentioned in the media coverage is that the anti–Wal-Mart study cited in the ad campaign is so biased that its conclusions are indefensible."[9] Several other publications pit management against workers, with labor receiving a more positive take. *Fortune* magazine's May 2004 issue tackled the anti-union practices of Wal-Mart in an article titled "Up Against the Wal-Mart." Reporter Cora Daniels portrayed Wal-Mart's management as corrupt.[10] Another article from the Associated Press titled "United Locked in Standoff With Unions" (2002),covering a bankruptcy dispute at United Airlines, focused more on the worker's issues than the plight of the corporation.[11] Throughout the pages of newspapers, a pro-labor slant can be identified.

This stance also shows through the nation's airwaves. The use of radio programming by labor unions to promote their views is often recognized as a valuable venue for the voice of workers. In a *Wall Street Journal* article titled "Labor: Unions Are Making Some Noise on Their Own Radio Shows" (1995), reporter Raju Narisetti chronicled labor's utilization of the airwaves. In the article, several labor advocates described the context of labor programming.

Union member Timothy Heyden told the reporter that radio shows from the labor perspective "tell the truth to the American workers about what's going on." Also included was the host of "America's Work Force," Bob Becker, and his view on labor programming. He said his show, "doesn't apologize for having a point of view." The article showed that labor was making its mark on the airwaves, and sources used in the article all came from a labor perspective. Narisetti noted the pro-labor bias in his writing. He declared that the labor radio show's "stances are predictable." He continued to give his take on these productions, using the show as an example. He said of the show's content that "corporate managements and Republicans in general are seen as bad."[12] The pro-labor biases of these programs are evident, critics argue, and show that radio provides a voice for the labor movement in the mass media.

Some researchers have written on how labor has utilized the media and, in return, received fair coverage in the mainstream press. Newport University communications professor, Jim McCafferty, discussed his findings in a *Dispute Resolution Journal* article titled "Labor-Management Dispute Resolution and the Media" (2001). McCafferty used the 1999 dispute between the United Steelworkers of America and the Newport News Shipbuilding Company to analyze media coverage of labor-management disputes. He explained that both parties attempted to use the media in two ways: to send messages to each other and to sway public opinion. The union aggressively targeted the media. McCafferty wrote that the stories used in his research "at the outset of the strike, featured a number of articles and used several quotations that highlighted union strength."[13]

Business portrayed negatively

Another accusation by business and management of the media is that businesses/corporations receive unfair and negative coverage in the news. Business and the media are both vital institutions in American society. The difference between the two, as corporate leaders assert, is that business is subject to government regulation, while the First Amendment protects the media. According to many management executives, this disparity leads to biased and negative reporting in the news.

David Finn analyzed business and the press in a 1981 American Management Association Research Study titled "The Business-Media Relationship: Countering Misconceptions and Distrust." The survey of business executives found they believe business reporting is inaccurate, biased, and least favorable regarding plant accidents, hirings/layoffs, environmental issues, and labor negotiations.[14] Howard Simons and Joseph A. Califano, Jr. also addressed the business-media relationship in their book, *The Media and Business* (1979). Simons and Califano reported the biggest complaint of business reporting is the lack of coverage of good stories because media professionals concentrate on the bad. The authors used a quote by media critic Herbert Schmertz describing special criticism of the broadcast media. He says, "most business stories, save those involving national strikes, layoffs, shortages, or rising prices, fail to meet network entertainment requirements."[15]

More recent examples cite coverage of corporate scandals as evidence of bias against big business. Richard M. Scrushy, former CEO of HealthSouth who was accused of accounting fraud, continually posted new releases on his website denouncing his negative portrayal in the media.

One release titled "*Birmingham News* Continues Biased Publishing" (2004) addressed the "slanted, one-sided reporting and publishing." "The government dropped 31 of the fraud counts from the original indictment, adding 4 additional counts," attorney Jim Parkman said in the release, "yet the *News* slanted their story to focus on the four new counts, barely mentioning the 31 dropped."[16]

The labor press

In addition to the groups claiming an anti-business bias in the media, there are advocates for a labor press. This may be the strongest argument for the labor point of view.

While admitting the mainstream media have wronged the labor movement in the past, promoters of the labor press say that, in today's society, neglect of a group by the media should not be a concern. The proponents clearly assert that labor has a place within the national media when and if labor participants seek to utilize a labor press. Sara Douglas described the labor press in her book *Labor's New Voice: Unions and the Mass Media* (1986). In the book, she listed the first labor newspaper as published in 1828 and wrote "the primary purpose of labor publications was to provide labor leaders with outlets for their opinions ... rarely were two sides of any issue printed."[17]

As the strength of labor unions grew less prominent in society, the labor press faltered as well. However, today's labor press is regrouping, providing a voice strictly on the side of labor. A project directed by James Gregory and sponsored by the Harry Bridges Center for Labor Studies at the University of Washington reports more than 100 periodicals serve the labor movement today.[18] As the union movement gains momentum, labor journalism will also increase, providing a voice for the workers of America. Dave Elsila explained how the labor press strengthens and enlivens workers and unions in the book *The New Labor Press* (1992). His essay titled "Taking Readers Seriously: UAW *Solidarity*" draws on his experience as the editor of *Solidarity*, the magazine published by the United Auto Workers. *Solidarity* focuses on human-interest stories, such as a profile of a union blues musician, investigative reporting, such as looking into the deaths of members on the job, and submissions from union members.[19] In his description, Elsila mentioned reaching out to all union members, other unions, and other social movements. He does not mention a relationship with management.

Other essays in *The New Labor Press* describe various aspects of labor publications. One, written by Mike Konopacki and Gary Huck, discussed labor cartoons. The bias against management is shown through the sample illustrations. In one example, there is a series of cartoons. The first scene shows a worker at a machine with his boss standing over him telling him to work faster. Subsequent scenes follow depicting a conversation between the boss and another man:

MAN: "How much do you pay him [the worker]?"
BOSS: "$25.00 a day."
MAN: "Where do you get the money to pay him?"
BOSS: "I sell products."
MAN: "How many products does he make in one day?"
BOSS: "$100.00 worth."
MAN: "Then instead of you paying him ... he is paying you $75.00 a day to tell him to work faster."
BOSS: "Huh? But the machines belong to me."
MAN: "How did you get the machines?"
BOSS: "I sold products."
MAN: "And who made those products?"
BOSS: "Shut up! He might hear you."[20]

The labor press is a voice for workers and unions. Without references to management and with editorials strictly from one perspective, labor has its place in the mass media. While the labor press is not as strong or as large as the mainstream media, it cannot be overlooked as a vital expression of labor's views.

Bias Against Labor

Advocates for labor and worker's rights allege a strong pro-management bias in today's mainstream media. Critics of the increasingly corporate owned media, many of which are former labor beat reporters, claim bias against labor in the mass media as well. These proponents hold many complaints and allegations against the media for catering to the interests of management and corporations. Many critics draw on the history of labor coverage in the media and the current state of the economy for a basis of their arguments.

Economics journalist, Murray Seeger, highlighted the changes in labor coverage throughout history in a *Nieman Reports* article titled "The Old and Future Labor Beat" (1999/2000). He wrote "hardly anyone covers labor anymore" after describing the changes in labor reporting today as compared to the labor beat in the past.[21] Critic Geov Parrish used General Motors as an example as he discussed how power in the economy contributes to the lack of fair labor coverage in an article for the online magazine *Eat The State*. In the article "The Myth of the Conservative Media" (1998) he wrote that General Motors is more powerful than the United Auto Workers, therefore General Motors receives more favorable coverage during a strike than the workers.[22] History and economics help support a pro-management bias, which can be categorized in three areas: unfair media coverage, connection to corporate owned media, and lack of a labor beat.

The shift to bias

Looking back through history to the rise of the labor movement, it is relatively easy to discern a pro-labor stance in the national media. In the time of the muckraking press, journalists instinctively dug up the crimes of large corporations. The hazards of poor working conditions and the perils of the working class were consistently documented. However, times have changed, and these issues are virtually nonexistent in the media

today. Richard Kaplar, vice president of the Media Institute and monitor of current eco-
nomics journalism, described this change in a *Columbia Journalism Review* article titled
"Blinded by the Boom: What's Missing in the Coverage of the New Economy" (2000).
He said, "It's definitely different today, a completely different environment."[23]

Instead of daily reports on working conditions and highlights on trade unions and
workers' events, today's media present little or no coverage of the labor movement. And,
critics assert the coverage provided presents labor in a negative light. William J. Puette
wrote on the coverage of labor in the media in his book, *Through Jaundiced Eyes: How
the Media View Organized Labor* (1992). The book analyzed the portrayal of labor in
newspapers, editorial cartoons, television news, television drama, and movies. He documented the "pervasively unfavorable image of organized labor projected in the communications media." In the final chapters of the book, Puette looked at the media coverage
of two labor disputes. These case studies lend valuable information to the nature of media
bias against labor. They show how the placement of stories, types of sources, lack of
trained reporters, and tone of headlines can contribute to bias in reporting. For example,
during one of the disputes, a newspaper headline read, "FBI Probing Carpenters, Kapau
[the union leader] Says." Further down in the article, the actual statement by Kapau is
given. He said the FBI was "harassing" the union.[24] Puette noted how the twisting of
words presents a bias toward labor.

Christopher R. Martin paralleled the information in Puette's book in his own book,
Framed! Labor and the Corporate Media (2004). Martin reaffirmed that the "main issues
of analysis has been the frequency of coverage and the nature of portrayals." In his book,
he examined coverage of labor in a range of mediums finding in all of them infrequent
coverage of labor news with magazines and broadcast media being the worst offenders.
Martin cited a 1990 study by Jonathan Tasini, which analyzed more than 1,000 network
news broadcasts as proof of bias. The study found that out of 22,000 minutes of broadcasts, only 1 percent, or 265 minutes, went to labor.[25]

Martin, along with Puette, used Michael Parenti's generalizations regarding media
treatment of labor. Parenti developed seven descriptions of how the media create an anti-
labor bias in his book, *Inventing Reality: The Politics of the Mass Media* (1986). They are
the following:

1. Portrayal of labor struggles as senseless, avoidable contests created by unions' unwillingness to negotiate in good faith

2. Focus on company wage "offers" omitting or underplaying reference to takebacks and
   employee grievances, making the workers appear irrational, greedy, and self-destructive

3. No coverage given to management salaries, bonuses, or compensation, and how they
   are inconsistent with concessions demanded of the workers

4. Emphasis on the impact rather than the causes of strikes, laying the blame for the strike
   totally on the union

5. Failure to consider the harm caused to the workers' interests if they were to give up
   their strike

6. Unwillingness or inability to cover stories of union solidarity and mutual support

7. Portrayal of the government as neutral arbiter upholding the public interest when it is rather protecting corporate properties and bodyguarding strike-breakers.[26]

The concept that labor is covered infrequently and negatively is made clear by these generalizations. Philip Dine, a longtime labor reporter for the *St. Louis Post-Dispatch,* helped to clarify the significance of minimal coverage of labor in an interview with Ed Bishop for a *St. Louis Journalism Review* article titled "Dine Talks About Labor and the Press" (2002/2003). Dine provided this comparison "The marginal way labor is often covered would be tantamount to covering education by focusing on school shootings or teacher arrests." In other words, labor coverage that focuses on strikes and the sensational events that can result from them does not begin to provide insight to what really makes up the labor movement. What fails to be covered, Dine emphasized, is the "essence of what unions do"- represent workers, fight to keep jobs in America, and protect benefits and wages. It is this form of partiality by the press that creates many of the accusations of bias.[27]

To go along with the infrequent and negative coverage of labor in the press, Dine noted the style of language used in pieces concerning labor. The following are some examples: "We hear about management *offering* a contract or the union *demanding* a raise." This phrase could easily be presented as the union *offering* to work for certain conditions and management *demanding* something else." The mere placement of the words "offering" and "demanding" denote a negative image of labor. Because journalists use more wording along the lines of the former, labor unions come across as the party that instigates disagreements. Dine also referenced the use of the phrase "labor boss" to describe union officials. This makes them appear overbearing when, in fact, they are elected officers. This simple matter of phrasing, according to critics, promotes a subtle bias in news stories covering labor and management.

Lack of a labor beat

One common complaint by pro-labor groups is that labor news is often relegated to the business or financial sections of newspapers. As time has passed and roles have shifted in the economy, the existence of a labor beat has diminished, and labor reporters have become nonexistent. Seeger discussed this in his *Nieman Reports* article. "There was a time when the labor beat held front rank," he wrote. "It produced great human-interest stories on a broad front of social, economic, and political issues." Now, he says, workplace issues revolve around brokers, engineers, and managers who are similar to reporters in their education and social background.[28]

Corporate-owned media

The main reason suggested for the pro-management bias in the media is that most media organizations are corporately owned. Consequently, the editorials of media outlets will most likely reflect the nature of their owners. Because of this relationship, the mainstream media are often accused by critics of forgoing their roles as America's watchdogs. Kari Lyderson addressed this issue in her article "War on Workers" (2002) published by Chicago Media Watch. She wrote "many people feel corporations and the government sometimes play a direct role in shaping media coverage of labor issues to fit their agendas."[29] As media consolidation increases with non-media corporations controlling more media outlets, the anti-labor bias becomes apparent.

Many critics have used this situation as a basis for their conclusions of media bias. Media critic Jo-Ann Mort did so in a *Dissent* article titled "How the Media 'Cover' Labor" (1992). She concluded that media corporate owners don't find it in their best interest to cover the concerns of working people.[30] Tiberius Gracchus, a writer for Purple Ocean.org, an affiliate of Service Employees International Union, also discussed corporate ownership in a January 2005 posting. "They [corporate media] have a financial interest in not covering labor issues," he wrote, "Or, in the rare times that they do cover labor, it will be to make it look as though labor is inconveniencing consumers with their disruptive strikes."[31] For corporate media to take any other stance would mean a loss of advertising and revenue.

The influence of ownership on the media is seen largely in choices of source selection. Labor leaders and media critics blame the unbalanced use of sources as a corporate influence on media outlets. Ina Howard, U.S. Research Director for Media Tenor International, offered proof of unbalanced source selection in an article "Power Sources: On Party, Gender, Race and Class, TV News Looks to the Most Powerful Groups" (2002) published in *EXTRA!* She found, in a study concentrating on nightly news programs broadcast in 2001, that labor representatives accounted for less than 0.2 percent of sources, thirty-five times less than management representatives.[32] In addition, William Hoynes, a Vassar College sociologist, found similar results concerning source selection in his recent study of public television. His study on PBS stations found that three-quarters of the sources in economic stories are from corporate representatives while those from the labor perspective received less than 3 percent of the on-air time.[33] Taking source selection a step further, those claiming an anti-labor bias in the media can cite a 1998 FAIR survey of journalists. David Croteau presented this survey in an article "Examining the 'Liberal Media' Claim: Journalists' Views on Politics, Economic Policy, and Media Coverage." Croteau found, in terms of the sources journalists contact most often, labor representatives accounted for 30 percent. On the other hand, business executives were approached 63 percent of the time.[34] The issue of source selection creates a viable argument for those who claim a pro-management slant in the media.

William Hoynes, who conducted that the PBS study, concluded the business class dominates coverage of economics, which includes business, management, and labor.[35] Goozner's *CJR* article looked into the change in economic coverage as it relates to how worker's issues are covered. The growth of a "new economy" is discussed, and Seth Ackerman with FAIR said, "journalists are overly proud of stories they do on issues like the problems of low-wage workers." Instead, Ackerman concluded they "gravitate to the big story, which is ... the booming economy."[36] By default, the plight of workers is overlooked.

Neither Side Is Right or Wrong

Advocates on each side of the labor-management debate strongly believe the mainstream press is biased against their side At certain points in media coverage, the accusations of bias by both sides may hold true. There are several factors that can influence media coverage of management and labor, such as the media's objectives, the different connotations of labor, and the critics' own biases. Various studies have proven the validity of these arguments, demonstrating that bias does exist in media coverage of management and labor — against both sides. At what time each form of bias develops depends on the context of the situation. Some researchers argue that no bias may exist at all due to the slanted opinions of those individuals deeply involved with the issue.

First, the media may have overarching objectives that they are trying to achieve through the coverage of a labor-management dispute. Deepa Kumar, a communications doctoral candidate at the University of Pittsburgh, documented media coverage of the 1997 United Parcel Service strike in an article titled "Mass Media, Class, and Democracy: The Struggle over Newspaper Representation of the UPS Strike" (2001).[37] She found that the media exemplified bias toward both labor and management at different times during the dispute, depending on how the media wished to be viewed. The study looked at coverage from *USA Today*, the *Washington Post*, and the *New York Times*. She concluded that their strike coverage "spanning about 191 articles, went through three distinct phases." The first and third phases show a pro-management bias, while the middle phase leans pro-labor.

In the first phase, Kupar explained the strike became newsworthy because "it disrupted the normal functioning of capitalism." Thus, the newspapers focused on the inconvenience to businesses and consumers rather than what caused the strike. Kupar found that the *New York Times* made the best attempt at balanced coverage, but "in the broader scheme this was neutralized by the overall tone taken towards the strike." Source selection was also noted for the pro-corporate stance during this phase. Union representatives were used approximately nine times compared with approximately seventy-three times for UPS and other businesses.

In phase two, Kupar documented a shift in coverage due to the influence of public opinion and class solidarity. She wrote of coverage in the *Washington Post*, "[T]he overall tone in both sections [news and financial] was now more favorable to the workers." Also during this phase, more emphasis was given to the general problems in the economy that greatly affected workers. Source selection was evened out with the *Washington Post* and the *New York Times* cutting business sources by at least half and increasing the number of labor sources. Kupar noted that although *USA Today* held to its pro-management stance, articles about workers did appear.

When a settlement in favor of the union was made in the dispute, media coverage lost its pro-labor slant. Kupar found the newspapers would not acknowledge a union victory, opting instead for the opinion that "no one ever comes out of a strike unscathed." Kupar concluded that media coverage by the three papers "follows the standard patterns of representing labor and yet deviates from them," which illustrated that both a pro-management and pro-labor bias exist in the mainstream media.

Secondly, it is difficult to separate the issue of bias in media coverage of management and labor as strictly pro-labor or pro-management. As discussed earlier, the term labor does not have a singular definition in regards to this issue. Depending on the context, two different ideas make up the argument of biased media coverage of labor. Each idea supports the opposing arguments of both management and labor, helping to give validity to each side's case.

When labor stands for workers and the problems they face in the workplace, the claim of an anti-business bias proves true. That the media provide fair coverage, and, at times, better coverage of labor in this situation is evident. Several works discussing the topic of labor and management in the media touch on this concept. Even those critics who are adamant that the press holds definite biases against labor acknowledge this fact. For instance, AlterNet.org columnist Norman Solomon admitted in his column that workers are given appropriate coverage. He wrote "news accounts may portray workers as admirable." In this same column, we also find the opposing argument. Solomon goes on to say it is only when workers come together in an organized way that the media become critical and unfair against labor. He provided a quote by David Bacon, longtime labor journalist and associate editor for Pacific News Service. Bacon said, "there's a bias in the media which reflects a discomfort with workers organizing."[38] Additionally, Lyderson offered supporting information in her Chicago Media Watch article. In the article, she quoted Eric Smith with the University of Illinois at Chicago Labor Education program, who studied ten years of labor coverage at the *Chicago Tribune*. "From reporters there is sympathy for workers," he said, "but not for the unions."[39] In other words, when the term labor implies unions or workers in a group, the arguments of those who claim an anti-labor bias in the media are most valid.

The basic generalizations that can be concluded from the different concepts of labor win support for both sides of the management-labor debate. On one end, workers and workplace issues are treated sympathetically, therefore resulting in an unfavorable image of the management team that creates the problems. Conversely, labor unions are given negative media coverage because they are seen as the root of economic problems, thus providing a positive view of management. Through these two distinctions, it is easy to see how clearly defining the term "labor" can help to classify the labor and management issue in relation to media coverage.

Finally, a critic's own bias can be interjected into his/her opinion on media coverage of labor and management, thus canceling out the argument that any bias exists. Cindy T. Christen, Prathana Kannaovakun, and Albert C. Gunther applied the theory of hostile media perception to the coverage of management and labor in their *Political Communication* study "Hostile Media Perceptions: Partisan Assessments of Press and Public During the 1997 United Parcel Service Strike" (2002). They found that "partisan groups perceived neutral news coverage as biased against their own positions and in favor of the opposing side."[40] They concluded this to be a result of the vested interest that participants, union workers and UPS representatives, have in the issue. In summary, even when media coverage of disputes between labor and management is actually neutral in tone, those deeply involved in the issue fail see past their own biases. Their resulting assessments result in a perceived bias in the media against their respective side.

• The Evidence •

The advocates for both management and labor make justifiable arguments concerning media bias. The management side asserts that the media do, at times, inaccurately portray the role of business and also accuses the media of being more proactive toward stories involving corporate deviance. Conversely, the labor side argues that because of corporate ownership and advertising influence, the media rarely cover labor or workers issues, and when they do the coverage is negative. Each side provides evidence to show the media are biased against labor or management.

However, when comparing the arguments, charges of a pro-management bias are supported by stronger empirical research. Advocates of this view provide study after study finding unbalanced coverage of labor. That these studies run from the early twentieth century to the present further helps the argument. By comparing today's coverage with that from sixty years ago, critics are able to provide solid evidence for how media coverage has changed. The change in media ownership and economic structure is also documented, along with the decline in organized labor. These are three reasons given for the diminished coverage of labor. The bias may come from the story placement, the wording of headlines, or reporters with limited training.

Those who argue that there is a bias against management provide less empirical evidence. Instead, the pro-labor argument can be found mainly in short newspaper editorials and articles. Those articles often focus on specific instances of bias, such as accusations that *TODAY Show* host Katie Couric pursued stories emphasizing workers' problems without considering the employer's point-of-view. The frequent coverage of corporate scandals and other negative business stories is also cited as an example of biased coverage.

Some researchers conclude that no bias exists, but rather that media consumers' own biases affect how they see the media.. People have a tendency to believe that the media are biased against issues that are important to them, regardless of how reporters cover stories. Despite these arguments, research confirms that the media often project a bias, whether it is against labor or management.

• RESOLUTION •

The labor-management debate on media bias offers an excellent opportunity for journalists. Since the American press holds the valued distinction as the nation's watchdog, journalists should stress and seek out objectivity and fairness in their coverage of management and labor. Both social groups are needed forces in our country's economic structure and, therefore, neither should be treated negatively nor be ignored. There are two areas that journalists can improve upon to help prevent biased and unbalanced reporting: a labor beat and education.

First, labor news needs to be taken out of the business section. Labor, while associated with business, is obviously a separate entity. As long as labor news gets placed with all other business issues, it will be difficult to give fair coverage. Also, if a labor reporter is designated as such, he/she should cover strictly unions and workplace issues. As Seeger noted, there are "many 'good workplace' stories awaiting broader discovery."[41] Source selection needs to evolve as well. Journalists should not let ignorance or indifference prevent them from seeking out a labor perspective simply because there is not one in their Rolodex. If a reporter consistently covers the labor beat, relationships can be formed that will allow a more recognizable labor voice in the media.

Second, lack of education or knowledge in a subject area is a complaint common to both labor and management. Critics of each side believe that much of unfair and inaccurate reporting comes not from outright bias, but because the journalist is not knowledgeable in the types of news he/she is covering. While the process of learning the ins and outs of each group would be different, journalists should strive to understand the topics they cover. Labor advocates suggest journalists understand the facts and history of the labor movement and look past the surface of labor disputes to discover *why* the dispute is occurring. Management and executives want journalists to be schooled in business terminology and policies. Both sides would prefer journalists to research the situation and be adequately prepared when talking to sources before undertaking a story that will affect the labor-management relationship.

"At its best, the press is a servant and guardian of institutions; at its worst it is a means by which a few exploit social disorganization to their own ends," wrote Walter Lippmann in his book *Public Opinion* (1960).[42] This quote can apply to the accusations made by both sides of the labor-management debate. The media have a responsibility to cover, promote, and investigate both labor and management. As the economy and the business sector continue to evolve, journalists have greater opportunities for objective, consistent coverage of such critical issues.

• POINTS OF VIEW •

Bishop, Ed. "Dine Talks About Labor and the Press." *St. Louis Journalism Review* 32 (2002): 26–27. A *St. Louis Dispatch* journalist believes labor is covered infrequently and that language used is derogatory.

Douglas, Sara U. *Labor's New Voice: Unions and the Mass Media.* New Jersey: Ablex: 1986. The ownership of mass media outlets affects the coverage of labor. However, when labor groups plan and utilize the opportunities of the media, while at the same time making themselves accessible, media will cover and even support the labor movement.

Finn, David. "The Business-Media Relationship: Countering Misconceptions and Distrust." American Management Association Research Study, 1981. An AMA survey found executives believed business reporting to be inaccurate, biased, and least favorable in regard to hirings/layoffs, labor negotiations, and environmental issues.

Kumar, Deepa. "Mass Media, Class, and Democracy: The Struggle Over Newspaper Representation of the UPS Strike." *Critical Studies in Media Communication* 18 (2001): 285–302. Newspaper coverage of the 1997 UPS strike went through three stages showing both pro-labor and pro-management bias.

Martin, Christopher R. *Framed! Labor and the Corporate Media.* Ithaca, N.Y.: Cornell University Press, 2004. The news media, while avoiding the appearance of bias, frame labor stories from a consumer perspective. This approach, like advertising, comes off as critical toward labor and supportive of the business behind it.

Mort, Jo-Ann. "How the Media 'Cover' Labor." *Dissent* 39 (1992): 81–85. Most corporate media owners find it in their best interest not to cover the concerns of working people.

Pizzigati, Sam, and Fred J. Solowey, eds. *The New Labor Press: Journalism for a Changing Union Movement.* Ithaca, N.Y.: ILR Press, 1992. In response to misleading and declining labor coverage in favor of the business elite by the mainstream media, the creation of a more effective labor press is addressed with a national labor paper as the definitive goal.

Puette, William J. *Through Jaundiced Eyes: How the Media View Organized Labor.* Ithaca, N.Y.: ILR Press, 1992. Over the years, media coverage of labor has been uniformly negative, which is related in part to the media's ideological bias.

Rubin, Bernard. *Big Business and the Mass Media.* Toronto: Lexington Books, 1977. Executives believe that journalists' coverage of business is biased in that it is often negative and inconsistent.

Simons, Howard, and Joseph A. Califano, Jr., eds. *The Media and Business.* New York: Vintage Books, 1979. As a private entity, the business community sees the press as inaccurate, unfair, negative, and biased, failing to cover the positive aspects of business.

NOTES

1. Nathan Newman, "Media Bias Against Labor," http://www.nathannewman.org/log/archives/000216.shtml.

2. John C. Dvorak, "Media Bias and Technology Reporting," PCMagazine.com, http://www.pcmag.com/article2/0,1759,1872175,00.asp.

3. Mike Hoyt, "Working the Teamsters," *Columbia Journalism Review*, July/August 1996, 44–49.

4. "Katie Couric Pushes Ted Kennedy's Latest Regulatory Intrusion," Media Research Center CyberAlert, mediaresearch.org/cyberalerts/2005/cyb20050222/asp#1.

5. Chris Nevitt, "Pro-Union Column a Breath of Fresh Air," *Rocky Mountain News* (Denver), 11 December 2004, 14C.

6. Benjamin Israel, "Is the Post-Dispatch Only Pro-union for Its Readers?" *St. Louis Journalism Review*, November 2003, 21–22.

7. *St. Louis Post-Dispatch*, 4 September 1997.

8. *St. Louis Post-Dispatch*, 9 September 2003.

9. Gary M. Galles, "Wal-Mart Study Shows Clear Bias," *The Daily News of Los Angeles*, 29 October 2004, N21.

10. Cora Daniels, "Up Against the Wal-Mart," *Fortune*, May 2004, 112.

11. Associated Press, "United Locked in Standoff with Unions," MSNBC Business report accessed online 22 February 2005 at http://msnbc.msn.com/id/6790483/.

12. Raju Narisetti, "Labor: Unions Are Making Some Noise on Their Own Radio Shows," *Wall Street Journal*, 22 June 1995, B1.

13. Jim McCafferty, "Labor-Management Dispute Resolution and the Media," *Dispute Resolution Journal*, August/October 2001, 41–47.

14. David Finn, "The Business-Media Relationship: Countering Misconceptions and Distrust," *American Management Association Research Study*, 1981, 48.

15. Howard Simons and Joseph A. Califano, Jr., *The Media and Business* (New York: Vintage Books, 1979).

16. "Birmingham News Continues Biased Publishing," Richard M. Scrushy press release, 1 October 2004, http://www.richardmscrushy.com/newsarticle.aspx?newsID=50.

17. Sara Douglas, *Labor's New Voice: Unions and the Mass Media* (Westport, Conn.: Ablex Publishing, 1986), 18.

18. James Gregory, "The Labor Press Project," Harry Bridges Center for Labor Studies web project, University of Washington, http://faculty.washington.edu/gregoryj/laborpress/.

19. David Elsila, "Taking Readers Seriously: UAW Solidarity," in *The New Labor Press*, eds. Sam Pizzigati and Fred J. Solowey (Ithaca, N.Y.: ILR Press, 1992), 61.

20. Mike Konopacki and Gary Huck, "Labor Cartoons: Drawing on Worker Culture," in *The New Labor Press*, ibid., 126.

21. Murray Seeger, "The Old and Future Labor Beat," *Nieman Reports*, Winter 1999/Spring 2000, 66–70.

22. Geov Parrish, "The Myth of the Conservative Media," *Eat the State*, July 1998, http://eatthestate.org/02–44/Myth Conservative Media.htm.

23. Merrill Goozner, "Blinded by the Boom: What's Missing in the Coverage in the Coverage of the New Economy," *Columbia Journalism Review*, November/December 2000, 23–27.

24. William J. Puette, *Through Jaundiced Eyes: How the Media View Organized Labor* (Ithaca, N.Y.: ILR Press, 1992), 3.

25. Christopher R. Martin, *Framed! Labor and the Corporate Media* (Ithaca and London: Cornell University Press, 2004), 13.

26. Michael Parenti, *Inventing Reality: The Politics of the Mass Media* (New York: St. Martin's Press, 1986),

27. Ed Bishop, "Dine Talks About Labor and the Press," *St. Louis Journalism Review*, December 2002/January 2003, 26–27.

28. Seeger, "Old and Future Labor Beat."

29. Kari Lyderson, "War of Workers," Chicago Media Watch report, www.chicagomediawatch.org/02_1_work.shtml.

30. Jo-Ann Mort, "How the Media 'Cover' Labor," *Dissent* 39 (1992): 81.

31. Tiberius Gracchus, "Corporate Media Coverage of Labor," Purple Ocean.org posting 5 January 2005, www.purpleocean.org/node/view/2402.

32. Ina Howard, "Power Sources: On party, gender, race, and class, TV news looks to the most powerful group," *EXTRA!*, May/June 2002, www.fair.org/extra/0205/power_sources.html.

33. Norman Soloman, "Mass Media — Hatred of American Labor?" AlterNet column, 26 April 2000, www.alternet.org/columnists/story/1161.

34. David Croteau, "Examining the 'Liberal Media' Claim: Journalists' Views on Politics, Economic Policy, and Media Coverage," Fairness and Accuracy in Reporting report, www.fair.org/reports/journalist-survey.html.

35. Solomon, "Hatred of American Labor," 3.

36. Goozner, "Blinded by the Boom," 24.

37. Deepa Kumar, "Mass Media, Class, and Democracy: The Struggle over Newspaper Representation of the UPS Strike," *Critical Studies in Media Communication* 18 (2001).

38. Solomon, "Hatred of American Labor," 1.

39. Lyderson, "War on Workers," 3.

40. Cindy T. Christen, Prathana Kannaovakun, and Albert C. Gunther, "Hostile Media Perceptions: Partisan Assessments of Press and Public During the 1997 United Parcel Service Strike," *Political Communication* 19 (2002): 423.

41. Seeger, "Old and Future Labor Beat."

42. Walter Lippman, *Public Opinion* (New York: Macmillan, 1960), 363–364.

17

Health and Medicine
Carmen S. Brown

"Sloppy reporting, distorted editorial sensationalism, and conflicts of interest by researchers are unnecessarily alarming the public and threatening to destroy our trust in complementary health care.... Just what do the latest studies tell us? To find their real message, we need to look beyond the headlines, the skewed media spin, and the superficial analyses that pad these 'news' stories."— Lyle MacWilliam, Life Extension Magazine, www.lef.org[1]

"[A Newsweek reporter's] reluctance to tell both sides of this story is indicative of the wider media's handling of the issue. RFM NEWS reviewed press coverage of the possible connection between abortion and breast cancer during the last year. The results paint what some say is a troubling picture of the media's refusal to address an issue that may have an impact on the lives of millions of women. Critics of the press point to ... [the] reporting to illustrate their claims of media bias."— RFM News, www.abortionbreastcancer.com[2]

Jeanette Joyce had an abortion. She also had breast cancer. These facts might not be of substance to some people, unless they've been watching the news.

LifeNews.com, an independent newsletter for the pro-life community, issued its report, "CBS News Accused of Biased Reporting on Abortion-Breast Cancer Link," on December 2, 2004. Editor Steven Ertelt discussed how CBS interviewed Joyce for a story about medical reports that link abortion and breast cancer. The network used only two lines of the 20-minute interview. "We approached this invitation from CBS with hope that someone truly wanted to give the other side equal time," Joyce said. "How disappointing when the actual story revolved around 'how some states are trying to keep women from getting one [an abortion].'" Joyce is a medical educator and mammography technologist, but CBS only identified her as a breast cancer survivor. CBS also decided not to air an interview with Karen Malec, president of the Coalition on Abortion/Breast Cancer.[3]

In his "Shattuck Lecture — Medicine and the Media" in the *New England Journal of Medicine* (1998), ABC News medical editor Timothy Johnson discussed the role of the media in providing people health care information. He cited a National Health Council poll that found that 75 percent of respondents said they paid a moderate to high amount of attention to health and medical issues in the media. Fifty-eight percent of respondents claimed to have either changed a specific behavior or taken a specific medication after reading or watching a health news story.[4] However, occurrences such as the CBS report have become bases for media criticism. In "Medical Scientists and Health News Reporting: A Case of Miscommunication," in the *Annals of Internal Medicine* (1997), physicians Miriam Schuchman and Michael Wilkes listed bias as one of the four main problems of today's health news reporting. This bias often coincides with the other three problems, which are sensationalism, lack of follow-up on stories and not covering certain health stories.[5]

Common bias criticisms of health and medicine coverage are that the media cover specific treatments and medications for certain illnesses more favorably than others or that they tone down negative information about particular products because they have alliances with companies and research foundations from which they receive advertising revenue. Some critics state that the medical community produces biased information, which creates the illusion of media bias. But what is the evidence behind these statements? Are the media truly biased with regard to medical reporting, or do other confounding factors exist?

Accusations of Bias

Cigarettes and alcohol

One prominent accusation of media bias centers around the coverage of smoking by mainstream newspapers and magazines. Stephen Klaidman's book, *Health in the Headlines*, states a correlation between the amount of cigarette advertising and the amount of health coverage on the effects of smoking. Newspapers, which only receive a percentage or two of advertising revenue from tobacco companies, always cover the dangers of smoking much more than magazines, who receive about 15 percent of their advertising from tobacco companies. *Reader's Digest* and *Good Housekeeping* cover the dangers of smoking to the greatest extent, and accordingly, they do not accept cigarette advertising.[6] In Elizabeth Whelan's article, "When Newsweek and Time Filtered Cigarette Copy," in the November 1, 1984, edition of the *Wall Street Journal*, a spokesman for the Tobacco Institute and some editors vehemently denied that they avoided negative stories on cigarettes because they received anywhere from 5 to 40 percent of their revenue from cigarette ads. Their response came a few years after R.C. Smith's article in the *Columbia Journalism Review*, "The Magazines' Smoking Habit," which found that no comprehensive article over a period of seven years discussed the dangers of smoking. Whelan, founder and president of the American Council on Science and Health, also mentioned a 16-page special health and fitness section of that was published in *Newsweek* on November 7, 1983. The section, which was submitted by the American Medical Association, did not cover the negative effects of smoking, but *Newsweek* carried around ten full-page cigarette ads. *Newsweek* denied pressuring the AMA to avoid discussion of cigarettes, and the AMA said it did not intend for the section to be the answer to all health problems.

Terence Poltrack, former editor of *Media Industry Newsletter* (now editor of *Press Time*), said it was not unusual to notify advertisers before publishing a negative article on their products, although *Newsweek* denied this practice. On October 8, 1984, *Time Magazine* carried a similar section that the American Academy of Family Physicians submitted. In this case, the Academy claimed that its original contribution contained many negative statements about smoking, but *Time* asked them to approve an edited version that deleted most of this information. Even though the Academy left a few statements in the article, *Time* omitted most of the anti-smoking references and claimed it had the Academy's approval.[7] Ralph C. Heussner and Marla Salmon's book, *Warning! The Media May Be Harmful to Your Health! A Consumer's Guide to Medical News and Advertising* (1988) quoted an editorial in the *New Yorker* on this issue: "The publishers want the money and feel they need the money — and , indeed, for some publications the annual revenues from cigarette advertising do make the difference between profit and loss."[8]

A similar trend has taken place with media reports on alcohol. In an article in the *British Medical Journal* (2001), "Alcohol: The Media Are in Denial," Colin Brewer, medical director of the Stapleford Centre, a private drug treatment center in Great Britain, claimed that although the media normally like to appeal to the hypochondriac mentality by discussing the dangers of certain foods and medications, they do not take the same approach to the health dangers of alcohol. The media usually portray alcohol in a positive light in lifestyle and cooking sections and by covering new discoveries on the positive effects alcohol can have on the body. Newspapers often delete the mention of alcohol from stories on domestic violence, crime and alcohol-related deaths, such as cardiac arrest. Brewer attributed this trend to two factors: journalism tends to be one of the "heavy drinking" professions, and newspapers do not want to print negative information on alcohol because, just like the tobacco industry, they receive advertising revenue from alcohol ads.

This philosophy has manifested itself in "alcohol is good for you" stories. For example, a *Daily Mail* article released a report from the *Journal of Epidemiology and Community Health* that whisky has phenolic antioxidants that protect the body from free radicals that can harm healthy blood cells. However, the newspaper article did not mention that alcohol can still cause damage to cells. Brewer also noted the irony in the myriad of headlines on the dangers of the drug ecstasy, which has killed far fewer people than people who have suffered an alcohol-related death. Articles also criticize elected officials for smoking marijuana, Brewer wrote, but they suppress coverage of famous people who have died from medical conditions related to excessive drinking. Brewer acknowledged that positive health benefits can result from "very modest" alcohol consumption, but few newspaper articles point out the harm that "only slightly immoderate drinking" can cause.[9]

Mainstream vs. alternative medicine

Evidence of bias, however, is sometimes less apparent, according to critics. In a *PR Newswire* report (2003), "Stroke Report Proves Media, Medical Bias Against Chiropractic," the World Chiropractic Alliance claimed that the news media teamed up with the medical industry to degrade the reputation of chiropractic medicine. A study published in the journal *Neurology*, which included interviews with fifty-one stroke victims, discussed the condition of vertebral artery dissection, in which chiropractic treatment might have lead to strokes in patients. This condition is extremely rare, and the *Neurology* report showed a temporal relationship, not a direct link, between chiropractic care and strokes. However, the CCA claimed that media reports scared the public into believing that chiropractic care causes strokes. The PR Newswire report stated that money is probably the main motivation behind the media's willingness to partner with the medical industry, as drug companies spend more than $3 billion a year in media advertising. "When you depend on the medical and drug trades for much of your income, it's easy to fall into the trap of being their lackeys and using their propaganda without asking hard questions," said Terry Rondberg, president of the WCA.[10]

A similar potential bias regards breast cancer coverage. In Janice Tanne's "Mixed Messages on Breast Cancer: Green Light on Mammography, Amber on Tamoxifen" in the *British Medical Journal* (2002), a content analysis of U.S. television and newspaper reports showed that media coverage has praised mammographies but demurred the use of the drug tamoxifen, which a National Cancer Institute Study found decreased the rate of breast cancer. The previous year, a National Institutes of Health panel said that evidence did not support screening as a dependable method of breast cancer prevention. The study found that stories lauding mammography always quoted medical experts and politicians, but stories on tamoxifen tended to quote patients and investigators involved in the trial, producing the admonition that women should approach treatment with this drug with caution. Tanne, a medical reporter, stated that this discrepancy in coverage could be the media's preference in covering established medical practice rather than a new treatment.[11]

Medical reporter Anne Karpf addresses this issue of bias in her 1988 book, *Doctoring the Media: The Reporting of Health and Medicine.* She states that by minimalizing other approaches to the causes and treatments of illness, the media significantly narrow public debate about health and medicine. The medical world, Karpf claims, wants the media to reproduce the values and ideology of mainstream medicine. She states that the media should let go of the notion that mainstream medicine is the only frame through which to provide news accounts.[12]

Media bias and medical ethics

Since the Terri Schiavo case, media bias in regard to medicine has gained more attention. In another LifeNews.com report, "Media Bias in Terri Schiavo Case at Extreme Levels in AP, Reuters Reports" on March 21, 2005, editor Steven Ertelt discussed the biased efforts among media outlets to shape public opinion that favored "starving" the vegetative woman to death. The Schiavo case received much media attention when her husband decided that he wanted to take the feeding tube out of his wife, who was in a vegetative state for several years. Ertelt mentioned an AP article that, with the exception of a couple of comments from a Vatican newspaper, contained no quotes from world or religious leaders who opposed starving Schiavo. Ertelt also mentioned a Reuters release appearing in hundreds of newspapers and on news Websites stating that Schiavo "will almost certainly never recover from her unconscious condition" and added that "neurologists agree." This report contained a 10-year-old report on persistent vegetative cases and the testimonies from two doctors who had never seen Schiavo before she was in a vegetative state.

Ertelt wrote that the Reuters news story did not include the affidavits of dozens of doctors who supported her parents' wish to perform more tests on her. The article also did not mention doctors who did not believe that she was in a vegetative state, which included Dr. William Hammesfahr, a Nobel Prize nominated neurologist who examined her and thought that methods were still possible to help her.[13] A Media Research Center report "Slanting the News Against Terri Schiavo" by Rich Noyes found that CBS, ABC, and NBC evening news broadcasts produced an overwhelming number of news reports that indicated support for Schiavo's husband, Michael, to fulfill his wife's alleged desire to die in a permanent vegetative state. A physician who examined Schiavo told NBC "She's as unconscious as someone who is dead." However, one neurologist on CNN said she is "completely aware and conscious and responsive ... like a child with cerebral palsy." The report ended with the question of whether the media were "stacking the deck" against the Schiavo family.[14]

Some media bias accusations revolve around controversial moral issues such as stem-cell research. LifeNews.com posted a commentary, "Media Bias on Adult Stem Cell Research Continues," by Wesley Smith, a pro-life activist and author. Smith cited several incidents in which researchers successfully treated Parkinson's Disease and multiple sclerosis patients with adult stem cells, but he asserted that the media have not given these experiments the same amount of coverage that they have given the small advances with embryonic stem cells that researchers conducted on animals. Headlines touting the advances of adult stem cells were few and far between. The biggest Parkinson's success story that involved adult stem cells was an inside story in the *Washington Post*, but Smith claimed that the *New York Times* did not run the story at all. In one experiment with adult stem cells, diabetic mice were able to produce the appropriate level of insulin. Another group of diabetic mice that received treatment with embryonic stem cells only reached a 3 percent insulin production rate, but they all died. Smith claimed the media ignored the adult cell experiments while the embryo experiments received wide coverage.[15]

Nothing and its over-representation

Experts have also criticized the media for bias against null medical research reports and for giving a disproportionate amount of coverage to certain medications and illnesses. A timely example is that of the association between hormone replacement therapy and breast cancer. In "Media Coverage of Women's Health Issues: Is There a Bias in the Reporting of an Association Between Hormone Replacement Therapy and Breast Cancer?" in the *Journal of Women's Health and Gender-Based Medicine* (2001), Maura Whiteman and colleagues conducted a content analysis of more than 300 media reports on breast cancer and thirty-two scientific journals. Of the scientific journals, twenty concluded that a link between hormone replacement therapy and breast cancer existed, while the other twelve produced null conclusions. Of the 300 media reports, 203 cited a scientific publication. Eighty-two percent of the 203 citations quoted a scientific journal with a positive conclusion, which indicates an over-representation of number of scientific articles that showed positive findings. Whiteman and colleagues also illustrated the discrepancy by showing that out of fifteen research studies, positive and null findings were almost equal, but out of the 115 media reports of these studies, 90 percent quoted studies that found a link between hormone replacement therapy and breast cancer. The authors concluded that the media favor studies that indicate a link between hormone replacement therapy and breast cancer. They also noted that they found a similar bias in reporting a link between alcohol consumption and breast cancer.[16]

In Ray Moynihan's "Making Medical Journalism Healthier" in *The Lancet* (2003), a content analysis of newspaper coverage in the year 2000 of five new drugs that had received widespread media coverage found that only 32 percent of the articles mentioned negative side effects, and newspapers covered benefits five times more than risks associated with each drug. Thirty-two percent of the stories mentioned how much the drug cost, and only 26 percent that cited a scientific study mentioned who funded the study. One of the drugs, celecoxib, was causing "major financial burdens" for public and private health insurance companies, and accordingly, only 13 percent of stories covered the cost of the drug. In a similar study of U.S. television and newspaper articles over a five-year period, only 47 percent of stories mentioned negative side effects, 30 percent mentioned cost, and 39 percent revealed the funding source.[17]

In another study in Tania Bubela and Timothy Caulfield's article "Do the Print Media "Hype" Genetic Research? A Comparison of Newspaper Stories and Peer-Reviewed Research Papers," in the *Canadian Medical Association Journal* (2004), most newspapers correctly reflect the information they take from scientific journals. However, they exaggerate the benefits of certain treatments and medications and play down the risks.

The authors examined 627 newspaper articles in Canada, the United States, England, and Australia that cited 111 articles in twenty-four medical journals, which appeared before and after the cloning of Dolly the sheep in 1997 and the mapping of the human genome in 1999. About 11 percent of the newspaper articles had "moderate to highly exaggerated claims." Sixty-three percent had no claims at all, while 26 percent slightly exaggerated the information in the trade journals. Fifteen percent of the newspaper articles mentioned costs and risks of certain medications, while 97 percent of the newspaper articles covered the possible benefits of the treatments. The articles that contained the moderately to highly exaggerated claims were those that discussed genetic orientation for homosexuality, alcoholism, mental illness, and obesity, but a search on the Pub Med Website showed that "behavioral genetics" accounted for less than 1 percent of the total hits on this site. According to the authors, this indicates that media — or at least newspapers — devote an unequal amount of coverage to this subject. The research suggests that media do not always carry the primary responsibility in hyping news about genetic research. Rather, Bubela and Caulfield called them "complicit collaborators" in this process.[18]

Breast cancer falls into the over-representation category as well. In the article "When News, Actuality Don't Jibe," in the June 10, 2001, edition of the *Washington Times*, Elizabeth Whelan discusses how news distorts reality by giving breast cancer 200 percent more coverage than prostate cancer, although prostate cancer affects close to the same number of men as breast cancer affects women. Whelan notes how media reports often state that "one in eight" women will get the disease because it serves the interest of advocacy groups, whereas a more subtle statistic like "a 46-year-old woman has a 1 in 6 chance of developing breast cancer by the time she turns 50" does not fit the "bad news sells" mentality of the media.[19]

Are Journalists to Blame?

How do media professionals respond to the contention that some of their health reporting is biased or pro-industry? Vikki Entwistle showed evidence of responsible journalistic practices of health and medical stories in her article, "Reporting Research in

Medical Journals and Newspapers" in the *British Medical Journal* (1995). The journalists she interviewed claimed to go through major trade journals and read the abstracts and conclusions to determine whether the studies would make good news stories. Journalists claimed to be aware of manipulation by commercial interests and said that they preferred to find stories on their own — even if they received press releases from the trade journals. Entwistle analyzed ninety articles in Friday newspapers that came from fifty-seven *BMJ* or *Lancet* journal articles over an 18-week period. The content of 81 percent of the newspaper articles had appeared in a journal press release.

The reporters said they would write their stories from the full journal article, but deadlines kept them from getting additional information. They also said they did not feel obligated to get every side of the story if their information came from peer-reviewed journals, and they did not seek counterclaims unless the journal article claimed that a product was harmful. The reporters said that people with opposing viewpoints might not have read the journal article and might have their own biases, which might kill the newspaper story. They said they wanted to quote trusted leaders in the field and they often look for medical research press offices to provide them with experts, which in turn influence their reporting.[20]

In Andrea Hoffner's doctoral dissertation, "Agenda-Building, Source Selection and Health News at Local Television Stations: The First Nationwide Survey of Local Television Health Reporters" (2002), more than half of the TV health reporters admitted to selecting stories that a public relations agent had presented to them. Sixty percent of the reporters said that they often have to ask a health expert to explicate information, and the same percentage said that these same "sources" influence what they decide to report. Hoffner referred to this practice as "passive news discovery," in which promotional practices from PR firms and other corporations give reporters what they need to know and help set the public agenda to a larger extent than the media. While just 13 percent of the survey participants said that station sponsors were highly influential in story decisions, Hoffner suggested that it "sends up a red flag" that some bias exists for sponsored coverage in TV health news.[21]

Journalists also face the problem of competition. In *Warning: The Media May Be Harmful to Your Health! A Consumer's Guide to Medical News and Advertising,* (1988), Ralph Heussner and Marla Salmon wrote that competition forces reporters to publish preliminary results in order to get the story out first. A survey of twenty-seven medical reporters showed that the main cause of distortion in science reporting was the "competitive force" that "creates a tension between the incentive for reporters to hype a story and a counter desire to maintain credibility," according to Jay Winsten, director of the Office of Health Policy Information at the Harvard School of Public Health. Therefore, reporters feel like they have to make these stories attention-getting. However, at the same time, newspapers expect reporters with no training or background to translate medical stories. Also, the philosophy of journalism, as opposed to science, is that any research finding is newsworthy, especially because it fits the news value of timeliness. Advances such as the awarding of a grant, an animal experiment, or FDA approval, are important to journalists. Many reporters feel that the First Amendment entitles them and even encourages them to let people know about any new findings, no matter how small.[22]

Heussner and Salmon made the assertion that much biased reporting is not the media's fault because physicians often develop their own flawed conclusions about their research and sometimes present their findings to the media before their peers have reviewed it. The same assertion goes for drug manufacturers who want publicity. A veteran reporter attested to this fact. "Being a medical reporter today is much easier than when I started twenty years ago," he said. "Whereas getting doctors to talk to you back then was like pulling teeth, today my desk is covered by news releases, phone messages from PR people and even letters from doctors and researchers who want me to write stories about their work. They want the free publicity." The problem is that many of these public relations efforts stretch the truth or do not include crucial information, such as side effects of certain treatments.[23]

An *AScribe Newswire* report, "Documents Show Tobacco Industry's Attempt to Influence Journalists' Reporting on Secondhand Smoke" (2004), discussed the issue of cigarette coverage in the media. Mayo Clinic researchers reviewed some internal tobacco company documents that showed that these companies have attempted to influence reporters when covering the effects of secondhand smoke. The tobacco industry tried to defer attention from Environmental Protection Agency efforts by getting journalists to write news articles that twisted the statistics and supported the tobacco industry's agenda. The study also showed that these companies are financing a journalism school in the United States.[24]

In the article "The Hot Air on Passive Smoking" in the *British Medical Journal* (1998), University of Sydney public health professor Simon Chapman discussed an incident in which newspapers reported that secondhand smoke does not cause cancer. This surge of reports had come from what Chapman, who holds a doctorate in the semiotics of cigarette advertising, called the "spin doctors" at British American Tobacco. The media feeding frenzy began with a report in the *Sunday Telegraph* that the World Health Organization's International Agency for Research on Cancer had found that cancer-causing secondhand smoke was a myth. The *Sunday Times* then picked it up, which spiraled into media reports in the United States and a few other countries. Chapman noted that the tobacco industry had paid its own scientific researchers to confirm what the BAT wanted to be true, and then industry lawyers edited the information.[25]

A similar occurrence took place when *Mother Jones* published an article about smoking, and a tobacco company that advertised in the magazine immediately withdrew $18,000 worth of advertising. When a second article about smoking appeared, the other two companies also withdrew their advertising.[26] In their report on breast cancer, Whiteman and colleagues stated that such selective reporting might be the result of more assertive public relations efforts among the journals that publish the positive scientific conclusions.[27]

Freelance journalist Bob Burton described this issue in his article "Selling Drugs — With a Little Help From a Journalist," in the *British Medical Journal* (2001). Chandler Chicco Agency, a pharmaceutical and biotech public relations firm, placed an ad looking for a freelance journalist to go to a diabetes conference sponsored by the European Association for the Study of Diabetes. The ad indicated that the reporter would cover industry-sponsored scientific meetings and would produce articles in two to four publications in medical trade journals. CCA would cover all travel and out of pocket expenses. Drug companies embrace the practice of pharmaceutical marketing because they have equated their financial success with quality media coverage. A British trade magazine, *Pharmaceutical Marketing*, has declared that the most effective yet least expensive marketing is editorial, because consumers believe what they see or read in the media to a much greater extent than they believe paid advertisements.

CCA founder Bob Chandler said the language in his ad was misleading. Companies who engage in this practice of hiring journalists to attend health conferences do not control what reporters write, he said, and his firm expects reporters to write what is credible and legitimate. However, Boyce Rensberger, director of the Knight Science fellow program at Massachusetts Institute of Technology, said that these payoffs can cause problems for readers because they are unaware of such alliances, and it creates a conflict of interest for reporters, whose credo is fairness and accuracy.[28]

According to Jo Ellen Stryker's article, "Reporting Medical Information: Effects of Press Releases and Newsworthiness on Medical Journal Articles' Visibility in the News Media," in *Preventive Medicine* (2002), the medical community has its own biases of which even many reporters are not aware. Medical journals issue press releases that have the news values that journalists look for and what politicians and funding centers look for.[29]

Schuchman and Wilkes (1995) argue that medical researchers have biases in the information they produce because it helps to get research funding and gives them publicity for their work. Organizations hold press conferences that tout preliminary rather than conclusive research, and they invite reporters without giving them explanations of the scientific concepts they present. They do not mention scientists who might have a counterclaim. Because drug companies, hospitals, and research centers compete with other research institutions just as newspapers compete with each other, reporters receive an overload of press releases and kits that are often misleading.[30]

Moynihan (2003) attributed biased reporting to the vulnerability of journalists to the "avalanche of company-sponsored promotion that descends daily on any newsroom," which includes paid trips to scientific conferences and visits by experts whom the company pays. Many reporters also agree to cover stories outside the newsroom for which the drug companies pay them or offer them an all-expenses-paid trip, and some receive medical journalism awards that the drug companies sponsor.[31]

This increasing alliance of science with the corporate world sometimes has the opposite effect, leaving scientists reticent in their communication with media, which leads audiences to believe the media are keeping quiet because they have vested interests.[32]

According to an article in the *British Medical Journal*, "Unhealthy Spin" by Bob Burton and Andy Rowell (2003), many journalists do not understand the scientific process and also might not understand the art of public relations. They often do not ask about funding sources or conflicts of interests.[33] Perhaps no group of people understands this statement better than the journalists who have worked inside the public relations industry. Melissa Sweet, a freelance journalist who specializes in health reporting, wrote about her own experience in "Promoting Healthier Journalism" in *Media International Australia* (2003). After years of substandard pay as a journalist, she wanted to try a new career in a public relations consulting firm. Her job was to increase public awareness about particular health conditions in order to increase demand for particular drugs. "It made me realize just how gullible I had been as a journalist, and how effectively the media can be used to promote vested interests. Rarely were we asked awkward questions about who our client was, or why the {press} release was being issued," Sweet wrote.[34] According to Burton and Rowell, understanding the influence of public relations could counteract against "spin doctoring."

And what about consumers? What role do they play in these controversies? According to Heussner and Salmon, they fit into the bias equation by jumping to conclusions and exercising poor judgment, just as reporters do. To the layperson, a small step in research can be very meaningful, especially if the research relates to them on a more personal level. Even if a report contains all of the necessary qualifiers to make it objective, audiences "hear what they want to hear and believe what they want to believe."[35] Klaidman states in his book that attentiveness and skepticism should be traits of consumers as much as they should be traits of journalists.[36]

• THE EVIDENCE •

Evidence indicates that media bias in health and medicine exists, but critics have conflicting opinions about where the bias originates and who is more responsible for it. In some cases, the responsibility appears to lie with the trade journals and research foundations that have vested interests with pharmaceutical companies. At other times, the media, which accept the information from these sources and then present it to the public as fact, are the target. The commentary on this issue in the journalism literature is lacking in comparison to the abundance of stories in the medical literature. Even the articles by professional health journalists most often appear in medical journals, which may indicate that this area of media bias concerns the medical community more than journalists.

The sources in this synopsis, most of whom are either physicians, medical journalists, or another type of health care expert, are highly credible, and their statements are difficult to dismiss. The educational background and training of medical reporters and other health experts have given them awareness about the issue that journalists in general do not seem to have. Other journalists might be aware of it, but because it is not their area of expertise, they do not feel inclined to provide commentary on it.

The evidence indicates that most reporters believe they are not biased in reporting health and medical stories, although they might appear biased. However, commentary from reporters is sparse. More surveys and interviews are necessary to find out more about journalists' perceptions of their own reporting. Hoffner's survey (2002) offered some insight, but it focused specifically on TV health reporters, who constitute a small percentage of the overall press. Also, the survey consisted of self-reports, some of which might not be valid because people sometimes respond according to what they believe the interviewer wants to hear.[37] Few journalists specialize in health reporting, and therefore this survey might not reflect the opinions of many untrained reporters who cover medical stories.

• RESOLUTION •

Specialists in health and medical reporting offer several suggestions for dealing with bias. In his article in the *New England Journal of Medicine* (1998), Johnson discussed the pressures on journalists. They need to have more knowledge on the scientific process, including how to detect strengths and weaknesses of scientific reports, association, and correlation. He also suggested passing an examination to prove their abilities to report medical information.[38] In his editorial, "Credibility in Science and the Press" in the journal *Science* (1991), Daniel Koshland discussed the need for accountability on behalf of both the medical community and journalists. Newspapers should reveal the name of the journal from which they obtained the information and the name of the organization to which the quoted scientists or physicians belong. "A press that equates a peer-reviewed experiment with a public relations document should expect the public to equate *Time* with the *National Enquirer*," Koshland wrote.[39]

Schuchman and Wilkes (1997) recommend that reporters reveal at the end of their stories any possible financial benefit the source could incur by the release of the information so that readers can determine the credibility of the story.[40] Writing from personal experience, Sweet (2003) argued that journalists should have at least basic knowledge about research methods. When writing a story on a new type of drug or treatment for a health condition, reporters must be able to discuss the story in context and not just repeat the experts' statements.[41] These steps are necessary because, according to Tom Wilkie's article, "Sources in Science: Who Can We Trust?" in *The Lancet* (1996), the media have failed to acknowledge that science itself is changing. Commercial drug companies are taking the place of states in research funding, trying to turn what used to be public information into private intellectual property.[42]

Just as journalists discuss other types of stories with their colleagues, health and medical stories should not be any different. Reporters should not be afraid to ask questions of their colleagues and editors. They should also not be afraid to ask their sources questions, such as, "Who funded this research?" or "Do you know an expert who might have a counterclaim to what you're saying?" Journalists should always ask to see documentation of research studies and experiments, rather than take what the "experts" say at face value.

However, the deadline-oriented world of journalism does not always make these precautions realistic. Heussner and Salmon suggest that reporters might have to sacrifice the value of timeliness and wait for the truth to come out.[43] However, the whole truth sometimes takes a long time to reveal itself. Nonetheless, reporters should make an effort to include as much qualifying information in a story as possible in the time that they have.

Education should be the most important preventive measure. College students pursuing a career in journalism should have the opportunity to take at least one course that addresses ways to avoid biased reporting on health and medical issues. Schools such as the University of Minnesota, University of Tennessee, and University of North Carolina have master's programs specializing in science and medical journalism. Journalism instructors at all universities should incorporate assignments that involve health and medicine into their reporting classes.

Although the media might have credible excuses for biased statements in their reporting, they are responsible for any perception of bias and for changing it. As Sweet wrote, change will have to come from the media industry through better education and training of reporters because the values of journalism should instigate better reporting, not the values of pharmaceutical or public relations industries.[44]

• POINTS OF VIEW •

Brehm, Sara. "Media Misleads Us on Stem-Cell Research Issue; Conjection: Scientists Have Yet to Determine That Embryonic Cells Are Superior to Adult Cells." *Los Angeles Telegraph-Herald,* 14 August 2001, A-4. The Statistical Assessment Service, which reports instances of media bias in scientific and health research, found wide media coverage had been devoted to mouse embryonic stem cells as a possible cure for diabetes, but no reporters mentioned that the mice that received the embryonic stem cells still died from diabetes. The media play down the fact that no humans have ever had therapeutic success from embryonic stem cells.

Case, Tony. "No Dearth of Health Care Coverage." *Editor & Publisher* 127 (1994): 14–17. Health care and public relations are starting to blend as part of the growth of health care public relations. Health reporters often have trouble deciphering what is real news and what is public relations.

Connor, Steve. "Hidden Cost of a Free Lunch from a Drug Company." *The Independent,* 30 May 2003, 2. The *British Medical Journal* found evidence of bias in favor of research studies funded by drug industries, which has lowered the credibility of the medical press.

Heussner, Jr., Ralph C., and Marla E. Salmon. *Warning: The Media May Be Harmful to Your Health! A Consumer's Guide to Medical News and Advertising.* Kansas City, Mo.: Andrews and McMeel, 1988. Because the popular press is a business with constraints in both time and space, reporters often use press releases, patient testimony, and preliminary research findings to produce medical news stories. Consumers must become more perceptive to these biased reporting techniques.

Kemp, Sid. "The Case for Reporting on Medical Alternatives." *Nieman Reports 47* (1993): 40–44. The media have a tendency to cover mainstream medicine in a favorable light, although alternative medicine has been growing significantly in popularity.

Kopel, Dave. "Devil's in Details About Uninsured; Biased Coverage by Newspapers Often Revealed in Facts That Went Unreported." *Rocky Mountain News,* 15 March 2003, 24B. Newspaper coverage on the need for health insurance slants the issue not by changing facts but by omitting others, leading people to believe there are far more uninsured people and that lack of health insurance is the primary cause for most health problems.

Moss, Lyndsay. "Media Health Reporting 'Fails to Reflect Real Dangers.'" *The Press Association Limited,* 16 September 2003. The media show bias toward stories about health scares such as mad cow disease. They need to break the "bad news sells" mentality and report on broader issues such as smoking and mental health.

Moynihan, Ray, and Melissa Sweet. "Medicine, the Media and Monetary Interests: The Need for Transparency and Professionalism." *Medical Journal of Australia 173* (2000): 631–634. Coverage of medical issues is becoming more sponsorship-oriented. As a result, stricter guidelines regarding medical research in the United States are necessary if the media are going to give fair and balanced reporting of health and medical issues.

Powers, Angela. "Newspaper Coverage of the Breast Implant Controversy." *Women & Health* 30 (1999): 83–98. A content analysis of coverage related to the silicone breast implant controversy from 1992 to 1996 revealed that Dow Corning's public relations campaign led to more positive coverage for implant manufacturers and less attention toward the women affected. This raises questions about the validity of journalistic coverage of health issues that involve major corporations.

Rosenthal, Elizabeth. "Doctors Discover PR/Doctors Debate the Ethics of Promoting Their Practices." *San Francisco Chronicle,* 2 January 1992, C3. Many biased newspaper and magazine articles are due to an explosion of public relations efforts by today's physicians, but doctors believe their "medical marketing" is ethical.

Seymour, Rhea. "Bad Reporting Harmful to Health: Study." *Chatelaine* (April 2002): 80. Consumers must decipher the difference between a hyped medical story and one written by credible, experienced health reporters.

Spurgeon, David. "Media Hype? It's Not As Bad As It Seems." *British Medical Journal* 328 (2004): 1140. Newspapers have been the target of unnecessary criticism when it comes to coverage of health issues.

Wahl, Otto F. "Stop the Presses: Journalistic Treatment of Mental Illness." in Lester D. Friedman, ed. *Cultural Sutures: Medicine and Media.* Durham, N.C.: Duke University Press, 2004. The media portray people with mental illness as violent by giving preference to news stories about mentally ill people who commit acts of violence.

Whiteman, Maura K., Yadong Cui; Jodi Anne Flaws, Patricia Langenberg, and Trudy L. Bush. "Media Coverage of Women's Health Issues: Is There a Bias in the Reporting of an Association between Hormone Replacement Therapy and Breast Cancer?" *Journal of Women's Health & Gender-Based Medicine 10* (2001): 571–578. Although 62 percent of medical journals concluded a positive correlation between hormone replacement therapy and breast cancer, most media reports cited these studies but did not mention the null reports. This indicates a media bias against null scientific reports.

NOTES

1. Lyle MacWilliam, "Media Bias, Conflicts of Interest Distort Study Findings on Supplements," *LifeExtension* online magazine, http://www.lef.org/magazine/mag2006/jun2006_cover_media_01.htm.

2. "Mainstream Media Does Its Best to Downplay the Possible Abortion/Breast Cancer Link," Coalition on Abortion/Breast Cancer, http://www.abortionbreastcancer.com/media_coverage/index.htm.

3. Steven Ertelt, "CBS News Accused of Biased Reporting on Abortion-Breast Cancer Link," LifeNews.com report, 2 December 2004. LifeNews.com, www.lifenews.com.

4. Timothy Johnson, "Shattuck Lecture — Medicine and the Media," *The New England Journal of Medicine* 339 (1998): 87.

5. Miriam Schuchman and Michael S. Wilkes, "Medical Scientists and Health News Reporting: A Case of Miscommunication," *Annals of Internal Medicine* 126 (1997): 976.

6. Stephen Klaidman, *Health in the Headlines: The Stories Behind the Stories* (New York: Oxford University Press, 1991), 202.

7. Elizabeth Whelan, "When Newsweek and Time Filtered Cigarette Copy," *Wall Street Journal,* 1 November 1984, 1–3.

8. Ralph C. Heussner, Jr., and Marla E. Salmon. *Warning! The Media May Be Harmful to Your Health! A Consumer's Guide to Medical News and Advertising* (Kansas City, Mo.: Andrews and McMeel, 1988), 156.

9. Colin Brewer, "Alcohol: The Media Are in Denial," *British Medical Journal* 323 (2001): 580–582.

10. PR Newswire, "Stroke Report Proves Media, Medical Bias Against Chiropractic, Says World

Chiropractic Alliance," *PR Newswire*, 16 May 2003, 1. Lexis Nexis news report, www.web.lexis-nexis.com.

11. Janice Hopkins Tanne, "Mixed Messages on Breast Cancer: Green Light on Mammography, Amber on Tamoxifen," *British Medical Journal* 324 (2002), 1530.

12. Anne Karpf, *Doctoring the Media: The Reporting of Health and Medicine* (New York: Routledge, 1988), 2, 8.

13. Steven Ertelt, "Media Bias in Terri Schiavo Case at Extreme Levels in AP, Reuters Reports," LifeNews.com report, 21 March 2005. LifeNews.com , www.lifenews.com.

14. Rich Noyes, "Slanting the News Against Terri Schiavo," Media Research Center Media Reality Check Report. 22 March 2005. Media Research Center Media Reality Check, www.mediaresearch.org.

15. Wesley J. Smith, "Media Bias on Adult Stem Cell Research Continues," Lifeissues.net, 2. Reprinted from *National Review* (2002).Lifeissues.net report, www.lifeissues.net.

16. Maura K. Whiteman, Yadong Cui, Jodi A. Flaws, Patricia Langenberg, and Trudy L. Bush, "Media Coverage of Women's Health Issues: Is There a Bias in the Reporting of an Association Between Hormone Replacement Therapy and Breast Cancer?" *Journal of Women's Health and Gender-Based Medicine* 10 (2001): 572–575.

17. Ray Moynihan, "Making Medical Journalism Healthier," *The Lancet* 361 (2003): 2097.

18. Tania Bubela and Timothy Caulfield, "Do the Print Media 'Hype' Genetic Research? A Comparison of Newspaper Stories and Peer-Reviewed Research Papers," *Canadian Medical Association Journal* 170 (2004): 1400, 1399, 1402, 1404.

19. Elizabeth Whelan, "When News, Actuality Don't Jibe," *Washington Times*, 10 June 2001, B7.

20. Vikki Entwistle, "Reporting Research in Medical Journals and Newspapers," *British Medical Journal* Online 310 (1995).

21. Andrea T. Hoffner, "Agenda-Building, Source Selection and Health News at Local Television Stations: The First Nationwide Survey of Local Television Health Reporters," Ph.D. Dissertation, University of South Carolina, 2002, vi, vii, 17. 92.

22. Ralph C. Heussner, Jr., and Marla E. Salmon. *Warning! The Media May Be Harmful to Your Health! A Consumer's Guide to Medical News and Advertising* (Kansas City, Mo.: Andrews and McMeel, 1988), x, xi, 7.

23. Ibid., xiii, 16, 25.

24. AScribe Newswire, "Documents Show Tobacco Industry's Attempts to Influence Journalists' Reporting on Secondhand Smoke," *AScribe Newswire*, 6 August 2004, 1. Lexis Nexis news report, www.web.lexis-nexis.com.

25. Simon Chapman, "The Hot Air on Passive Smoking," *British Medical Journal* 316 (1998): 945.

26. Heussner and Salmon, *Warning! The Media May Be Harmful to Your Health...*, 152.

27. Whiteman et al., "Media Coverage of Women's Health Issues...," 575.

28. Bob Burton, "Selling Drugs — With a Little Help from a Journalist," *British Medical Journal* 323 (2001).

29. Jo Ellen Stryker, "Reporting Medical Information: Effects of Press Releases and Newsworthiness on Medical Journal Articles' Visibility in the News Media," *Preventive Medicine* 35 (2002): 526.

30. Schuchman and Wilkes, "Medical Scientists and Health News Reporting...," 978, 977.

31. Moynihan, "Making Medical Journalism Healthier...," 2097, 2098.

32. Schuchman and Wilkes, "Medical Scientists and Health News Reporting...," 980.

33. Burton and Rowell, "Unhealthy Spin," *British Medical Journal* 326 (2003): 1207.

34. Melissa Sweet, "Promoting Healthier Journalism," *Media International Australia Incorporating Culture and Policy* 108 (2003): 8.

35. Heussner and Salmon, *Warning! The Media May Be Harmful to Your Health...*, xiii.

36. Klaidman, *Health in the Headlines...*, 238.

37. Hoffner, "Agenda-Building, Source Selection and Health News...," 95.

38. Johnson, "Shattuck Lecture — Medicine and the Media," 92.

39. Koshland, "Credibility in Science and the Press," *Science* 254 (1991): 629.

40. Schuchman and Wilkes, "Medical Scientists and Health News Reporting...."

41. Sweet, "Promoting Healthier Journalism...," 10.
42. Tom Wilkie, "Sources in Science: Who Can We Trust?," *The Lancet* 347 (1996): 1310.
43. Heussner and Salmon, *Warning! The Media May Be Harmful to Your Health...*, 77.
44. Sweet, "Promoting Healthier Journalism," 11.

About the Contributors

Tamara K. Baldwin is a professor of communication at Southeast Missouri State University. She teaches courses in history and philosophy of American mass media, communication law, and diversity in media. She received her Ph.D. in journalism from Southern Illinois University. In 2006 she became president-elect of the American Journalism Historians Association and serves on the board of directors of the Stars and Stripes Museum/Library and the Missouri Center for the Book.

Patrick Beeson is an online production editor for the *Roanoke* (Va.) *Times* and has won several awards for his work with its Website. He has an M.A. in journalism from the University of Alabama and a B.S. in public relations from Appalachian State University. He has been published in *Quill* magazine, the *Tuscaloosa* (Ala.) *News*, and *Equipment World* magazine.

Katharine A. Birchall received her B.A. from Dartmouth College and is pursuing an M.A. in journalism at the University of Alabama. She has worked in Franklin, Tenn., at Alday Communications, a public relations firm that represents the PGA of America, Nike golf, and other companies.

Carmen S. Brown has an M.A. in journalism from the University of Alabama. Her research areas include media coverage of social issues and journalistic practices in health reporting. She is working on a second graduate degree focusing on health communication, and she has worked in the communications/marketing division of ARAMARK Corporation.

Dave Cassady is a journalism professor at Pacific University in Oregon. He received his Ph.D. from the University of Iowa. Before going into teaching, he worked as a reporter, editor, and photographer for daily and weekly newspapers in Arizona and Washington. One of his research interests is the social impact of Internet discussions of social issues.

Kim Cross is a travel writer and editor for *Southern Living* magazine. A graduate of the University of Alabama's undergraduate and graduate programs in journalism, she has published articles in the *St. Petersburg Times*, the *New Orleans Times-Picayune, Business 2.0* magazine, and *Outside* magazine.

Bruce J. Evensen is a professor in the Department of Communication at DePaul University in Chicago. He received his Ph.D. in mass communication from the University of Wisconsin. Before going into teaching, he worked eleven years as a broadcast journalist and news director. He worked four years as a network bureau chief in Washington, D.C., and Jerusalem.

Christina Jesson is a managing editor at Randall-Reilly Publishing Company. She worked previously as a design editor for the *Tuscaloosa* (Ala.) *News*. She received a B.S. in journalism from the University of Florida and is pursuing an M.A. in journalism at the University of Alabama.

Ginger Miller Loggins received her M.A. in telecommunication and film and is working on her Ph.D. in mass communication at the University of Alabama. Before beginning graduate study, she worked six years in television news production. Her main research interests are stereotypes in television news and the history of television news.

Jenn Burleson Mackay is an advanced student in the doctoral program in mass communication at the University of Alabama and is assistant director of the Graduate Project on Media Bias. Her research focus is journalistic ethics. She received her B.A. in journalism from the University of North Carolina and her M.A. from the University of Alabama. Her professional journalism experience includes work as a television news videographer and writer and as a reporter for the *Hickory* (N.C.) *Daily Record, Asheville* (N.C.) *Citizen Times*, and *Roanoke* (Va.) *Times*.

Kay Best Murphy, a graduate student at the University of Alabama, worked nine years for daily newspapers in Arkansas and Louisiana and served two years as director of student publications at the University of Louisiana at Monroe. She has written freelance articles for the *Dallas Morning News* and *Mobile Press-Register*. She received her B.A. in journalism from the University of Arkansas at Fayetteville.

Karen Watts Perkins has an M.A. in journalism from the University of Alabama. She has written for *Dateline Alabama, City Magazine* in Tuscaloosa, and *Tuscaloosa Business Ink*. She recently completed an internship program in the Custom Publishing Department of Southern Progress Corporation in Birmingham, Ala.

Katie H. Porterfield, a freelance writer, received her B.A. in American studies from the University of the South and M.A. in journalism from the University of Alabama. She has worked as a correspondent for the Natural Resources News Service in Washington, D.C.; for the consulting firm Booz Allen Hamilton; and as a reporter at the *Tuscaloosa* (Ala.) *News*.

Henry M. Sessoms is professor emeritus of English at Southeast Missouri State University. From 1968 to 1993 he was chairman of the Department of English, Journalism, and

Philosophy. His primary teaching areas were medieval and eighteenth century English literature and English language and linguistics. He has a Ph.D. in English from Vanderbilt University.

Wm. David Sloan is a journalism professor at the University of Alabama. He is the author or editor of twenty-seven other books, including such works as *Contemporary Media Issues, The Media in America, Pulitzer Prize Editorials, The Significance of the Media in American History, Media and Religion in American History, The News Media: A Documentary History,* and *The Age of Mass Communication.* He is the founder of the American Journalism Historians Association and served as editor of its research journal, *American Journalism.* The AJHA recognizes him with its annual "Sloan Outstanding Faculty Research Paper" award. He has been recognized with several research awards for his work. In 1998 he received the AJHA's Kobre Award for lifetime achievement. He is the founder of the Southeast Journalism Conference, a student-oriented organization of journalism departments at sixty universities. He has served as national president of Kappa Tau Alpha, the mass communication honor society. On its ninetieth anniversary, KTA selected him as one of the five most important members in its history. He received the Ph.D. in mass communication and United States history from the University of Texas. Before going into teaching, he worked as an editor on four newspapers.

Michael Ray Smith is a journalism professor at Campbell University. He has also taught at schools in Pennsylvania and Virginia. Before going into teaching, he worked ten years as a reporter and editor for newspapers in Pennsylvania. He has also written for the *Atlanta Journal-Constitution, Baltimore Sun,* and *Philadelphia Inquirer.* He received his Ph.D. in communication from Regent University.

Stephen E. Stewart is weekend editor and Internet supervisor for the *Decatur* (Ala.) *Daily.* He formerly was editor and publisher of the *Monroe Journal* in Monroeville, Ala. He received his A.B.J. from the University of Georgia and is working on an M.A. in journalism at the University of Alabama.

Randall S. Sumpter is an associate professor of communication and coordinator of the Journalism Education Program at Texas A&M University. He received his Ph.D. from the University of Texas. Previously, he worked as a reporter and editor for fifteen years at daily newspapers, magazines, and trade newsletters. His research has been published in *Journalism & Mass Communication Quarterly, Critical Studies in Media Communication, Newspaper Research Journal,* and other journals and books.

Debra Reddin van Tuyll, who teaches communications at Augusta State University, is the author of *The Southern Press in the Civil War: America's Wars and the Press in Primary Documents* and co-editor of *The Civil War and the Press.* Her current research deals with antebellum publishing in North Carolina. She received her Ph.D. in mass communication from the University of South Carolina.

Hubert P. van Tuyll, professor of history at Augusta State University, is the author of three books: *Feeding the Bear: American Aid to the Soviet Union, 1941–1945; America's*

Strategic Future: A Blue Print for National Survival in the New Millennium; and *The Netherlands and World War I: Espionage, Diplomacy and Survival.* His current research deals with the economics of warfare. He received his J.D. degree from Duke University and his Ph.D. in history from Texas A&M University.

Index